GIBRALTAR
The KEYSTONE

GIBRALTAR
The KEYSTONE

JOHN D. STEWART

HOUGHTON MIFFLIN COMPANY
BOSTON
1967

*The title-page photograph
is used by permission of
Fox Photos, Ltd., London*

For my mother Eva
the first woman

ACKNOWLEDGEMENTS

During my ten years in Gibraltar I gathered the material for this book from a multitude of people of many races, creeds and ranks, and read everything that was published in the place and about it. I was a civil servant sufficiently senior to survey the scene, but not so senior as to have to hold myself aloof. 'Once you become a governor, a judge or a bishop,' they say in Spain, 'you never hear the truth again.' I was never so exalted, and I am convinced that I found the truth where I sought it.

I made myself a wide field on The Rock. As a journalist and critic on the *Gibraltar Chronicle* I became involved in theatrical circles there, and in painting, and even in the bullfight fraternity. I sat on many official committees, dealing with such matters as youth welfare, museums, libraries and the promotion of tourism. The last named was a fascinating exercise, for Gibraltar had been built for repulsion and I had to help to rebuild it for attraction. None of my committees was central or secret, so that I feel myself free, within the limits of discretion, to make use of what I learned in them.

As a member of the management committee of the Garrison Library I had the fullest access to its comprehensive collection of books, pamphlets and papers on Gibraltar, and this was a basic quarry for this book.

The other basic quarry, and perhaps the more valuable, I found in the walking-books encountered on The Rock throughout the most constructive decade of its history. In addition, I returned to the proximity of Gibraltar in 1964, and spent a year in nearby Spain, visiting The Rock often to study the development of its worsening situation, and assessing the reactions of its citizens.

It would be impossible for me to remember, or to list, all those who aided me in my inquiries. Many of them may not have known that they were doing so, and would not wish to be named. Out of the hundreds, perhaps thousands, of them, the first to come to mind is Esmond Ryan, long time resident and Secretary of the great Garrison

Library. His knowledge of the past thirty years of Gibraltar's history is intimate and inexhaustible. Mrs. Dorothy Ellicott's work on the social history of the place was useful to me, too, and for my chapter on Moorish Gibraltar I drew heavily on her knowledge and researches. John Searle, a social scientist who is now editor of the *Gibraltar Chronicle*, is the expert on the myth, folklore and value systems of the Gibraltarian people, and I have spent many hours discussing these subjects with him.

The social history of Gibraltar, unlike the naval and military, is poorly documented, and I learnt much of it from the old people who helped to make it. I can only offer them a general acknowledgement.

I should make the point that I was a professional officer in the Overseas Civil Service, rather than an administrative or political officer. This means that I never had, nor sought, access to secret information, either in Gibraltar or in subsequent service elsewhere. It also means that I was able to remain independent of official pressure and advice, and free to fulfil my duty of criticizing the conduct of government.

Acknowledgement is due to *The New Yorker* in which chapter 13 ROYAL DIVERSION was first published.

My editor, Osyth Leeston, has skilfully carved and wrought the book out of an amorphous mass of literary matter. Finally, I must acknowledge my greatest debt, to the only other person who laboured with me for seven years on this book, and who, finally, typed it in a roasting Andalusian June. My wife Joan contributed many ideas and criticized many others. Where the book appears percipient and benign, that is where she has made her influence felt; where it is less so, or downright wrong-headed, that is where I have set aside her advice and had my own way.

PREFACE

The name Gibraltar means many things to many men. It carries strong associations of history, of geography, and of high politics. It links Great Britain unhappily with Spain, and reopens the door on the long, unlovely retrospect of Anglo-Spanish relations. It may symbolize steadfastness to some and arrogance to others, the British bandit or the British policeman, according to the point of view. But the strongest of all The Rock's suggestions, in Britain as in Spain, is that concept which used to be called Military Glory, and which we have come to reassess as the slaughter of young men for causes vaguely understood and rapidly discredited and cast aside. Almost all that has been written on Gibraltar is in the field of military history, and if this book makes any special contribution it will be because I have little interest in that well-worn subject.

Gibraltar, for linguistic and educational reasons, has no indigenous literature, beyond a handful of pamphlets and verses. Its documentation has always been in the hands of temporary British residents there, the ex-patriate officers. They described and recorded wars and rumours of wars, and very little else. Military considerations were paramount, and it was officially proclaimed as late as 1952 that Gibraltar was a Fortress first and a Colony second. Until the end of World War II no one in authority seemed to notice the Gibraltarian people, and, in fact, it was only in very recent years that they achieved the recognition of a name.

But for two and a half centuries a unique community had been growing quietly within the walls, under the guns. With their own religion and language, manners and values, methods and aims, their Latin customs and culture, with no voice, no press, and no communication with the outside world, this strange mixture of races toiled and schemed and multiplied until the day came when they issued from below stairs to the reception rooms and demanded—'What about us?' Now, most ironically, after some thirteen military sieges, we shall find that the last siege of Gibraltar—the present one—will not be decided by the generals, the guns or the fortifications. The international tribunals of today are not interested in the thundering voice of artillery, but in the voices of men.

The Gibraltarian community faces harsh reality today, and cruel choice. So does the British Government which remains responsible for it. Both of them, as this book must prove, have sinned for centuries on The Rock, sins of commission and omission, against the Treaty of Utrecht which is our charter to be there, and against all the ethics, customs and usages of good international citizenship. Fastened like some grim tick on the soft belly of slothful Spain, Gibraltar has grown fat, exploiting, defying, injuring and humiliating her unwilling host. At the worst, there has been a most unholy alliance there, between the proud soldier and the shrewd merchant, a gun in one hand, a packet of contraband tobacco in the other.

So Spain sees Gibraltar, and the image is not unjustified. Up to 1950, when the Gibraltarians were first allowed to vote, Great Britain with her military governors and her untrained administrators must be held entirely responsible. But since 1950, and especially since 1954, the offences against Spain increased, and this might be held to absolve Britain from some blame. On the other hand, for denying them responsibility for so long, for leaving them to live on their wits, for protecting and even facilitating their offences, the main guilt lies with Britain. We have bred up in Gibraltar a people who, in their commercial affairs, carry underdeveloped consciences, and tend to say 'The world owes me a living'. They are prone to claim their rights incessantly—the right to reside, to be British, to be untaxed, employed, supported and protected at all times; rarely, if ever, do they consider their duties. Such are the defects of colonial peoples everywhere, intensified in Gibraltar, in my view, where responsibility was so long withheld.

Man by man, woman by woman, the Gibraltarians are a fine people —good human beings, such as one finds everywhere in the world. An inhospitable race is as rare as a navy with inglorious traditions. The Gibraltarians are as good as my own people, individually, but in their corporate entity they are difficult to love and impossible to defend. Yet they must be defended. I note that they are not included in current lists of Britain's problems, but let Gibraltar not be overlooked on account of its small size. This is a matter of principle. This shaky statelet or, at least, this community of people, must be, for years to come, upheld by Great Britain and by the United Nations. However cruelly the Gibraltarians are criticized, the fact remains that they practise and are entitled to a form of democracy, of that system of government to which all men of goodwill are committed.

Let there be no doubt that—under pressure of world opinions, if you will—Britain accorded these people the vote sixteen years ago, and has since extended the franchise until, in 1964, they became responsible for their own home affairs. Let there be no doubt that in Spain, the country which is claiming to take over the Gibraltarians and rule them, the vote was taken from the people twenty-six years ago, and they have never voted, nor held a meeting, nor voiced a complaint, nor read a free newspaper, since then. In judging between Britain and Spain in the matter of Gibraltar, as they have tried to do twice before and soon must succeed in doing, the nations of UNO will also be judging between democracy and direction.

For more than two years now Gibraltar has waited for the final verdict on her future—two years of growing poverty, anxiety and frustration. 'Neither the U.K. Press nor the U.K. Government seems to know exactly what the Gibraltar Government wants,' writes Mr. Hector Licudi in the local weekly *Vox*, adding 'If it's any consolation to them, neither does Gibraltar. Some kind of unspecified assistance and some kind of slap-down action which will make the Spaniards understand that what they're doing to us is not a nice thing at all.' The Spaniards, picketing and obstructing the only land gate to The Rock, know it only too well. The British Government knows it, too, but our case is scarcely strong enough to stand on reason and it is too late in history to back it, as heretofore, with force. The Gibraltarian is, at last, beginning to realize that he is on his own.

'It is not possible,' wrote Mr. Kingsley Martin, veteran editor of *The New Statesman*, 'as I know from long experience, to write individually and frankly about any country without making some mistakes and giving patriots cause for offence.'

I shall be sad if any of my comments offend my good friends in Gibraltar, and sadder if they fall into the error of presuming that to be critical is to be inimical. I have no reason to be inimical of a people among whom I spent the happiest decade of my life. It is simply that I must tell the truth as I see it. My first duty is to my readers, and not to the people, much less to the Government of Gibraltar. The latter has ample opportunities and funds to present its own case. As for the mistakes which Mr. Martin fears, no doubt I have made my full share of them. I do not claim this book to be a work of scholarship, and even the scholars are not immune from error. I have tried to be careful, however, to verify my facts, substantiate my opinions, and declare my guesses as such. This book is my personal appraisal of a place and its people, and I am the sole authority for it and, in my view, the full authority.

I have called Gibraltar 'the Keystone'. Five hundred years ago, in her will, the great Queen Isabella called it 'The Key to Spain'. Later ages, more conscious of navies and commerce, have called it 'The Key to the Mediterranean'. Its arms incorporate a key, and ceremonial keys lie before its Governor at formal banquets.

My wife Joan and I found there some other keys. We found a key to the problem of racial and religious intolerance which our own troubled colony, Northern Ireland, and some others are still seeking. We found a key to the community spirit, based on an innate sense of friendliness and mutual aid; however much one Gibraltarian hates another, there is a strange bond of love beyond the hatred. We found a key to the proper course of the history of our times, as we watched the inflexible disciplines of authority give away to democratic compromise. We found many keys to the minor mysteries of Nature. There are more, and more important, keys to be found on The Rock. That little community is, in effect, a control culture, a microcosm of the macrocosm of societies and nations. In Gibraltar, given enough of time and wisdom, a man might find the key to all human associations, to the proper organization of the whole human race. If only for this reason, the Gibraltarian community, like those of Andorra and Montenegro, should be cherished and preserved, should it be within the borders of Spain or even, as I am forced to fear, in some more hospitable land.

CONTENTS

	Acknowledgements	vii
	Preface	ix
1	To Gibraltar	1
2	Digging in	11
3	As it was in the beginning	19
4	Learning the Ropes	25
5	The End of the World	34
6	Food and Fishing	42
7	Rock Apes	48
8	Rock Bird	56
9	Rock Scorpions	64
10	Rock Tarik and Rock Arcos	76
11	Rooke's Rock?	88
12	Teething Troubles	96
13	Royal Diversion	107
14	Round the Rugged Rock	115
15	Contrabando	122
16	The True Trafalgar	142
17	Victoriana	152
18	Albert Memorial	166
19	A Little Learning	177
20	The Goodness and the Grace	192
21	Beyond the Pale	203
22	Gibraltar Adolescent	217

xiii

Contents

23   GIBRALTAR'S COMING OF AGE   227

24   OUT OF THE FRYING-PAN   246

25   INTO THE FIRE   256

26   CONTRABAND CONTINUED   265

27   QUESTION TIME   282

28   THE DEBATE CONTINUES   299

     BIBLIOGRAPHY   323

     INDEX   327

GIBRALTAR
The KEYSTONE

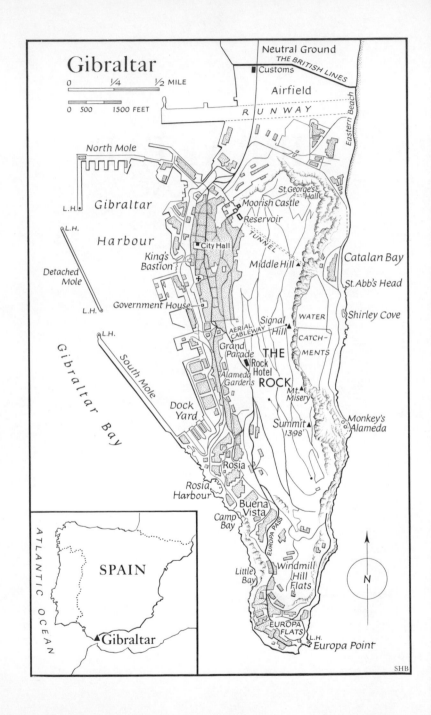

Gibraltar

0   ¼   ½ MILE

0   500   1500 FEET

Neutral Ground
THE BRITISH LINES
■ Customs
Airfield
R U N W A Y
Eastern Beach

North Mole

L.H.

Gibraltar

Harbour

L.H.

Detached
Mole

L.H.

King's
Bastion

City Hall

Government House

L.H.

South Mole

Gibraltar Bay

Dock
Yard

St George's
Hall
Moorish Castle
Reservoir
TUNNEL
Middle Hill ▲
Catalan Bay
St.Abb's Head
Shirley Cove

AERIAL
CABLEWAY
Signal
Hill ▲
WATER
CATCH-
MENTS

Grand
Parade
Alameda
Gardens
■ Rock
Hotel
THE
ROCK
Mt.
Misery ▲
Monkey's
Alameda
Summit ▲
1398'

Rosia

Rosia
Harbour

Camp
Bay
Buena
Vista
EUROPA PASS
Windmill
Hill
Flats
N

Little
Bay

EUROPA
FLATS
L.H.
Europa Point

ATLANTIC OCEAN

SPAIN

▲ Gibraltar

SHB

TO GIBRALTAR

Happy is the man who makes his first arrival at Gibraltar, as I did, from the west and in the evening. Across a dark sea, with a dark sky as backdrop, I saw the huge mass of The Rock all ablaze with deep golden light from the dying sun. The Levanter, that infamous east wind from the Mediterranean Sea, was blowing lightly, so that long and tattered trails of vapour, tethered to the highest peaks, streamed out westwards, over our heads, across Gibraltar Bay. Suddenly the setting sun caught these from below, lighting up their writhing bellies, filling them with flames, and casting a deep red glow over the scene.

For me, and for my small family, this was the end of the journey—or, in a way, the beginning. Here, on The Rock of Gibraltar, we were to stay and work and live and learn. I was on guard against early impressions, anxious to search for a surer assessment and to come to lasting terms with this strange and lovely place.

'Gibraltar!' exclaimed William Pitt to the crowded Commons, 'The most inestimable jewel in the British Crown!'

'Gibraltar!' exclaimed Don Ignacio Lopez de Ayala, the first and best historian of The Rock, 'Extraordinary events have given it a celebrity greater than that of any other part of Spain!'

These voices, from viewpoints diametrically opposed, spoke two hundred years ago. The celebrity they mention has increased a hundredfold since then, so that Gibraltar is a household word in most civilized countries. Gibraltar is famous and, to begin with, that was my one hard fact. But famous for what? Presumably for its history.

The Rock has been outcropping in history for twelve hundred years, since the day the first Moors landed on it. In ancient myth and legend it has been noted for three thousand years. Prehistorians might add many millennia more.

Gibraltar is a corner post at the cross-roads of two seas, two continents, two cultures and two climates. Great dominions, nations and creeds have collided there. It stands in a region of natural and human turmoil, at a vortex of currents, winds and tides, a whirlpool of the world.

All the business of the Old World ended here. The Phœnicians, Carthaginians, Romans, Visigoths, Moors and Jews came and went by this gate. So did Moloch and Baal, Mars and Thor, Zeus, Jehovah and Allah. St. Paul, they say, and St. James, passed in and stayed.

All the business of the New World began nearby, at the western entrance to The Straits of Gibraltar—at Palos of Columbus, Cádiz and Seville and San Lúcar of the *Conquistadores*, and Lagos of the Portuguese mariners. India, Africa and Indonesia, as well as all the Americas, were first linked to Europe at this place.

To Briton and Spaniard, down to this day, Gibraltar is a magic name. In the Briton it still evokes a glow of proprietorial pride and calls up the defiance and tenacity of his great century. Popular feeling in England saved Gibraltar from dynastic and diplomatic horse-trading on more than one occasion.

The common Englishman has learned to regret his country's colonial conquests, and his governments are making restitution to the dispossessed with all possible haste. But Gibraltar, he still feels, is in a category of its own. It is a prize of fair war, won and held against odds, and peopled—as I shall show—by proud volunteers.

The Spaniard sees it very differently. For him, it conjures up a whiff of nostalgia for greatness long past. It reminds him of Spain's decline and helplessness. It may cause him a faint flutter of aspiration for the future. But there is no real hatred for the British occupation of Gibraltar, except in official pronouncements. The vast majority of Spaniards today are *pancistas*—members of the Bread Party, who will swallow far greater insults than Gibraltar rather than hear another shot fired. I do not mean that they are cowardly, but they are great family people with no heart for trouble and war.

For the thousands of Spaniards who come here daily to work and earn good wages, Gibraltar may stand for modern progress, comfort and riches. Wistfully and wrily they call it *La Piedra Gorda*—The Fat Rock; greedily they carry off its goods and gadgets, its scrap and waste. It is their only glimpse of the world beyond Spain's jealous frontiers—the world of the Affluent Society which has passed them by.

Right up to the year 1942 Gibraltar was in the forefront of world events. Since then—since Eisenhower led the allied armies out of here to North Africa—the tide of history may have receded for good and left The Rock at last stranded and becalmed. Gibraltar would have been indefensible and useless in World War II, or even in World War I, had Spain been hostile to Britain. Every inch of it, dockyard, airfield, fortifications, magazines and town, is within sight and range of modern artillery, and commanded by mountains higher than The Rock itself. I have met soldiers who still adhered to the legend of the fortress's military importance and invincibility. They based their arguments on the possibility of local wars there, fought by traditional methods. Something might blow up in the Sahara or the Congo; Nasser's expansive notions might bring him to Morocco; some of the new African states might start to fight. But even as the experts talked, their Government was steadily withdrawing its troops from the place and trying to turn it into a holiday camp. I presumed that my informants had been, up to very recently, persistent cavalrymen.

* * * *

I had been invited to go and live in Gibraltar, and work there. I had been given a few days to decide on the proposition, and I had spent them making a hurried search of my home town, Belfast, for a picture of The Rock today. A few days may seem ample time to make a simple and realistic assessment of a tiny place like Gibraltar, but I found it too short. Very little has been written about the place—that is, very little that is useful and up to date.

As one of the world's smallest countries, the encyclopedias dismiss it briefly. Official publications give statistics and little else; they never paint a picture, although you can find some good reading between their lines if you know the tricks of officialdom. Not much is said or read of Gibraltar, in peaceful times, in the British press.

I found a few slim travel books on my subject, written by visiting journalists and retired officers of the armed forces. I suspected then, and know now, that they were mostly moonshine. Most of them were patriotic rhapsodies, written with more loyalty than logic, with climactic lists of familiar adjectives—strong, sound, solid, secure and unshaken.

I soon exhausted all these sources of information, and I had to fall back on interrogating everyone I met, or could find, who had been to Gibraltar. I combined this research with what I felt might be a last round of the literary and political bars of Belfast. The resuits were unscientific but graphic.

'It's a big, bare, idle mountain of a place,' a young soldier told me. 'And hot as hell!' To him, and others, I give the answer now, by hindsight. Son, you were there in midsummer and you came off your troopship in unsuitable uniform.

'Loathsome place! I was atrociously robbed and cheeked by a taxidriver there!' I sympathize with you, sir. I have irrevocably condemned the great city of Sydney on identical grounds.

'Absolutely idyllic place, old boy! I met my dear wife when I was soldiering in Gib.' How lucky for Gib, colonel, that the good lady has remained dear to you.

It depends on the man, of course, and on his mood and on the season. The eye finds—or fails to find—what it seeks. I was no further forward when my hour struck, and I had to make the decision.

The primeval woman, I suppose, longed to leave her safe and stuffy cave—to be taken out, as they say today. Her hunting and hunted man longed to get back to it and stay there. I left Ireland sadly, my wife in high delight, on a bleak day in March 1952.

'The poor Irishman,' said Ralph Waldo Emerson, watching one, 'a wheelbarrow is his country.'

We landed, sweating and bemused, by tender at the old Waterport. Here were swarthy porters quarrelling wildly in Spanish, smooth Customs officers addressing us in careful English, and a gentle young policeman, dressed in London style, waving us in with apologetic smiles.

'I think I've as much right to put my suitcase here as you have!' A nasty voice, that. I swung round to protest, and found her short, fat, old, tired and cross. She had landed with us, must have been in the tourist class.

'More, madam, more,' I said, pushing my case out of her chosen spot. We are a peaceful people in the main, fighting only when we get too rich or too poor.

There was plenty of room for all our luggage on the old Waterport Wharf. Here, in the lee of the Rock, the east wind was cut off and a gentle warmth surrounded us. The porters were still quarrelling in Spanish, and everyone must wait when that occurs. Spanish, even on the flat, takes about a third longer than English; over the hurdles of emotion it can be extended to infinity, and ended only by retreat or strong words. I had time to read, on the battered suitcase of my challenger:

> 'Mrs. Clytemnestra Latakia,
> Gibraltar.
> BRITISH AND PROUD OF IT.'

The policeman caught me reading this legend and staring sidelong at its owner. He smiled and put a finger to his temple, twisting his hand like a screwdriver. I must have looked blank at this, for he leaned over and whispered one word—'*Loca*.' I had enough Spanish to know that he had cast doubt on the lady's sanity, and I appreciated his wish to explain to a stranger that she and her rudeness were not typical of Gibraltar. Nor were they . . . what is? Ten years were to pass before I could attempt to answer that question.

'Mr. Stewart, no?' I turned to find a small dark man with a fine face, watchful eyes, and a free-smiling mouth now stiffened into formality.

'Yes, I am Stewart.'

'Ah, welcome!' A soft handclasp and a stronger smile. 'My name is Carvillo—Maurice Robertson Carvillo. I was sent to meet you. I hope you have had a very jolly good trip, eh?' The English was what we used to call '*babu*', as used by the book-educated Hindus. It is 'anglo-English', more English than the English themselves, and it is characterized by hard-won but stranded slang. The enunciation was clear and strong, however, and the accent was what the English call cultured.

'Fine, thank you,' I said. 'Very kind of you to meet us.' He was a very kind man, I could see, if a little unsure and injured, as is the heritage and condition of all colonial peoples. He was full of generous curiosity and glad to be the first Gibraltarian to set eyes on us. He was anxious to assess us and, if possible, give a good report of us to his colleagues in the civil service, which we were to join.

'Don't mention it!' he was saying now. 'A privilege!' Straight from the Spanish, I was thinking, intonation and all. '*Ni hablar . . . un privilegio. . . .*'

'My wife, Joan,' I said. 'Mr. Carvillo . . . my daughter, Eve. . . .'

We relax a little when we meet a woman. A Latin stiffens. It is not *his* woman, and he wishes to show you that he knows it. He is more afraid of women—the usherettes to eternal ruin—than he is of men, who can inflict only temporal damage. We are, perhaps, the opposite.

'How d'you do, Mrs. Stewart?' He spoke this phrase by ear, in purest Mayfair, but he did not extend his hand until she offered hers. I was glad she did not kiss his cheek as, being an Irishwoman at the end of a journey, she might well have done. 'And little Eve,' he said, bending to her and pinching her cheek. In her eight years Eve had not encountered this approach before, so she twisted away from him. We were to learn that the Gibraltarians pat and tweak every child they meet.

'Welcome to our old Rock,' said Maurice Carvillo, adding defensively, 'such as it is.'

'It looks magnificent to us,' we said together and with fervour.

'Oh, it's just a small place, and we are a small people. But we are loyal, very British. You will see. The Government have allocated to you a large quarter, quite high up the mountain. It has a stupendous view. We hope you will like it.'

Yes, Mauricio Robertson Carvillo, we liked it. After ten years we still liked it.

'These bally porters!' Carvillo exclaimed suddenly. Now, before our eyes, he turned on the porters and transformed himself. The neat, polite and precise 'Englishman' vanished; in his place a shrill and voluble Spaniard sprang to life. Streams of sound spurted from him, with sudden punctuations on high inflections and cruciform castings of the arms. His hands, eyes and teeth flashed in the lamplight. The porters turned truculently towards him, but he beat them down with words, with ardent protests and magniloquent appeals to manhood, justice and courtesy. They turned back to our cases, defending themselves as they worked with long rattles of words. When the baggage was loaded Carvillo turned back to me and winked.

'Good show, sir, what?'

'Jolly good show,' I said, using the expression for the first time in my life. And so Mauricio Carvillo and I began our joint studies in the Higher English.

Mr. Carvillo put us in a huge pre-war taxi, the biggest Packard ever made, and gave the driver the name of our hotel. We paused at the Dock gates to tell the apologetic police our names, proposed address, business, and duration of visit. Duration of visit? Months? Years? Indefinite, infinite? I settled for one year.

Next, the Customs, where the officers, straight-faced and careful, questioned us in neat English. Carvillo answered them in sprawling Spanish—'*Son contrabandistas nuevas, pero hasta ahora no han hecho nada,*'— They are new smugglers, but they haven't done anything yet. We sailed on, leaving them laughing. Colleague Carvillo is a character here, and I hope there are many like him.

'Here we have the Grand Casemates Gates,' he said, 'as you see written up over the arches. Nobody understands this name. Our Spanish friends, when they come to work for the first time, you see them trying to read it in Spanish—*Gran Casa mates gates*, or something like that. That means "big house for killing cats", or some such thing. Jolly good, eh?'

'Very good. They must think we are a cruel lot in here?'

'They know that the English call their bullfight cruel. Now they read that inscription and they say "Huh! The English are not so kind to animals for all their talk!" And then what happens?'

'What?'

'Then up comes our R.S.P.C.A. and tells them not to leave the donkey out in the sun!' He laughs with glee. We all laugh, even Eve. I recognize one of the keys of Gibraltar already—it is paradox.

'What do the Spaniards really think of us?' I asked him. I knew that I had to work with them.

'Oh, mad, quite mad,' said Carvillo. 'Mad English—but then, of course, they think all foreigners are mad not to be Spaniards. They still say *palabra inglesa*, meaning "my word of honour". They respect you for fair play. You should hear them appealing for fair play here, knowing they will get it. In Spain they might get a few good whacks with a stick for the same request. They respect you in Gibraltar, for keeping order and at the same time leaving people free to say what they wish. They have only had one or the other, but never both at once. They respect your generosity, too. The English officer is a good spender and a kind man. But in social matters—mad, they say, quite mad. This you may say of the Spaniards, too, when you see some of their customs. But you are not English, Mr. Stewart?'

'No. Irish.'

'Ah, *si*? And Mrs. Stewart?'

'More Irish than he is,' she said.

Mauricio Carvillo suddenly sings—

> 'My mother and father are Irish
> And I am Irish too!'

Joan is amazed. 'You know that song?'

'Aha!' said Carvillo, 'Here we know many Irish things! I was born near here in a street called Irish Town—how's that? And it is many years that we have an Irish bishop—God bless him—and priests, and nuns, and Christian Brothers. All we know, we learnt from them in the past—little as it may be,' he chuckles. 'You are Catholics, no?'

'No . . . I'm afraid not. . . .' The job is to offer polite regret without sounding so abject as to invite conversion.

'Well, jolly good luck to you, all the same!'

'Thank you, Mr. Carvillo.'

'Don't mention it! We like all religions here. Some of my best friends are Jews. But most of us are very ardent Catholics.' He grins a little and adds 'And we eat well enough here to be fond of our priests.'

While I was plumbing this profundity Joan switched the subject to shopping. We were in Main Street of Gibraltar now—main in every function of a street, diminishing and draining all its neighbours. We were bathed in the blaze from shop signs and windows, with our faces blenching and blushing with the passing neon lights.

'Ah, yes, we are a nation of chopkeepers. A chop is the dream of every Gibraltarian—a chop of his own. Plenty to shoose from, eh, Mrs. Stewart?' I soon learned that this interchange of *ch* and *sh* sounds was a characteristic of Gibraltar English. It has many other characteristics, all reflecting the difficulty of English to the Spanish tongue. But I will not labour the spelling out of dialect, a tedious and incomplete way of reporting it.

'Fantastic!' Joan was saying. 'And the crowds! Is it like this all day long?'

'No, no. This is the *paseo*—the evening promenade. It is a Spanish custom—a nice one, I think? Each town in Spain has an *alameda* for this walking up and down. You will see.'

The shops stay open late, and leave their lights on even when they close. The bars stay open until eleven o'clock, and a hundred varied clubs, great and small, do not close until the small hours. After eleven, the Law says, you may make a noise until you are asked to stop; after one in the morning you must stop your noise even if unasked.

Now tourists and sailors of all nations were swarming in Main

Street, mixing with the Gibraltarians—a cross section of humanity as rich and varied as the goods and gadgets in the shop windows.

Tribunals of broad women blocked the narrow roadway; *tertulias* of tired men gazed out cynically from the taverns; boys were meeting girls, usually in twos or threes. Every man, woman and child, said Carvillo, comes here at some time of the evening, to say 'good-bye' to his friends—that is *'adios'*, to bless his friends and, literally, to commend them to God's keeping. He wants to show, and they want to see, that he is well, and still with us. Hence the effusive greetings, the slaps on the back, the kisses and embraces on all sides. 'There's nothing British about this,' Joan said to me afterwards. I remembered reading that the greeting in Greenland is 'I am glad to be here', to which everyone replies in chorus 'We are glad to have you here!' Here is the herd instinct at its most benign.

'Nos veremos en la Calle Real,' is a usual farewell in Gibraltar. 'We'll meet in Main Street'—the exact equivalent of 'I'll be seeing you'. The proper reply to this is *'Si Dios quiere'*—'If God wills'.

Into this foaming millrace of mankind, at some places not more than twelve feet wide, our driver nosed his battleship of a car. He thrust on, slowly but remorselessly, drumming with his fist on a door panel, for hooting is forbidden within the city walls.

The crowds, conditioned to such intrusions, clove to let him pass and then closed at his tail. One person in four greeted him—

'Que hay, Obdulio!'
'Que dice el hombre?'
'Anda ya, puñeta!'
'Adios!'

No one scowled on him as a nuisance, nor did he protest to anyone, not even the slowest to clear his path.

'How friendly they all are!' said Joan.

'We have to be,' said Carvillo. 'Like the animals in Noah's Ark, there is no room for fighting.'

There is no room for anything in Main Street, Gibraltar, this golden mile of trade. The glaring lights signalled all the famous goods of Europe and the world beyond. They cried Scotch whisky, German cameras, Swiss watches, English tea, French brandy, Irish bacon, American pens, Italian cars and Japanese radios.

'You have everything here,' I told Carvillo. 'The free port?'

'Not so free as it was. But we have many fine goods. And some trash, too.' He jerked his head at an oriental bazaar, stuffed and festooned with garish tourist fodder. 'For the sailors,' he apologized.

'Quite a lot of Indian shops,' Joan said. 'Aren't they a bit far from home?'

Carvillo sighed. 'Yes. More and more each year.' He sighed again as we passed another one, and said quietly: 'Well, I've nothing against them. God bless them—so long as He blesses us first.'

We had shouldered through to our hotel. To a stiff-faced receptionist, surly shy; to a dark patio plastered with patterned tiles, a paddock of wickerwork chairs with all the aspidistras that Gracie Fields banished from England thirty years before; to a blessed bar. . . .

'For you, sir—a Guinness,' said Mauricio Carvillo, my first Gibraltarian. For that, and for many other things, I love him for life.

2

DIGGING IN

In 1952 you could meet the nineteenth century in the hotels and bars of Gibraltar, the furniture and décor long since discarded by England, tardily handed on to her colony. There was only one really first-class resort hotel, and it had the reputation—since improved—of high prices and low cuisine. The rest of the hotels were of the transit type, designed for travelling salesmen, with a maximum of grim little sleeping-cells and a minimum of bathrooms and of public space. In one such paleotechnic hostelry Joan and I spent our first strange days in Gibraltar. Its Victorian wallpapers, gloomy oleographs, plastic flowers, tarnished gilt, and ancient sanitation imposed a feeling of sadness, almost of nostalgia. We had travelled far, not only in distance, we felt, but in time as well.

Uneasily, among those dusty palms and aspidistras, we sensed the environment of our great-grandparents—those defiantly pompous people who pose and glare beside their tragic wives in yellowing daguerreotypes, those tyrants and tycoons of top nation days, now mouldering hideously in carved coffins under lush, lying epitaphs and hemispheres of waxen flowers. . . .

I did not know then that much of this atmosphere drifts inexorably into Gibraltar from the overpowering land of Spain which marches it and influences it in many subtle ways. There the horse-cab and oil-lamp, the chaperone and cuspidor, the masher and the mistress, are still in their heyday, and gilded furniture and crystal chandeliers are dashing innovations. Joan and I felt, as most visitors must have felt, that these nostalgic trappings, this oppressive Victoriana, were peculiarly Gibraltarian. You will still find strong traces of what I have described in the hotels of Gibraltar, but happily a new generation of hoteliers' sons, educated in England, has arrived and made much improvement, and most of the hotels have had, at least, their faces lifted.

Whenever we could, Joan and I took refuge in the streets. The Englishman's home is his castle because he has not much choice. There is nowhere to sit in the streets of England, nor even, after twilight, in the public gardens. The climate, very often, does not even permit him to walk abroad. Naturally, he stays indoors and creates a cocoon of comfort. That was the way we lived in Belfast.

These southern people, on the other hand, look outwards. The Spanish or Gibraltarian home is, typically, a small and crowded apartment up several flights of dark and dirty stairs. In it, one, two or even three old people share a few ill-lit rooms with the young family. Once he has eaten, changed his clothes, embraced his wife, kissed his children and his parents, there is nothing to keep the southern man at home. He hurries out, taking even his breakfast coffee at his local bar. He comes home late for his afternoon meal after an aperitive hour at his café. He sleeps for an hour, dresses, goes out again and stays out until late at night. His wife does not miss him, for she is out, too—at the market in the morning and in the afternoon sitting with other mothers, baby-minding in the sun.

The usual Spanish or Gibraltarian home has no sitting-room, living-room or lounge. The parlour of our working-class houses would be an intolerable waste of space. Easy-chairs, sofas, divans and such-like furniture are unknown. There are no book-shelves, because there are no books. Talking and drinking, as well as eating, are done on hard chairs round the dining-table, between a sideboard embellished with the best glasses and an inevitable display cabinet full of family treasures, photographs and souvenirs. The elaborate chandelier over this table and, in Spain, the rudimentary heating-stove beneath it proclaim it as the hasp and hub of the household and of the family. 'Hearth and home' makes no sense in the south of Spain, and very little in Gibraltar. One's home is one's town or village, and one's hearth is the sunshine.

Our northern towns are dormitories with cubicles, by comparison. When we congregate—in the churches it used to be, now in the cinema, say, impersonally, or at public meetings, formally—we are scarcely ever man to man. Only in our pubs can you find the truly gregarious and communal spirit surviving, and in England even the pubs are divided along class lines.

Along this Mediterranean coast, home is only a refuge and a retreat, The people live together in the open air—in the street, forum, *agora*. *plaza, piazza*, market-place. Down here, there is a far stronger feeling of community than we had ever known. In crowded and circumscribed Gibraltar, with its complicated inter-marriages, its identity of interests, its surviving sense of siege, one can see and feel an integrated society.

To live in a tiny town with all the organization and panoply of a state, with Viceroy, Premier, Parliament, Press and Pentagon, all in miniature, all within arm's reach, is an intensive course in civics. In such an environment, nothing can be hidden, for better or for worse. One's successes are seen and recognized; one's failures are immediately exposed. Social consciousness is at its strongest, with the result that there is a constant and firm pressure towards good social behaviour, towards courtesy and kindness. Gibraltar, with all its faults, is the friendliest and most tolerant of places. Straight from the cynical anonymity of a big city, we luxuriated in its happy personalism. We look back on it, like all its exiled sons and daughters, with true affection.

One step outside the grim portals of our hotel and the bright sunshine dispelled our gloom and filled us with warmth and optimism. This sun, which has made the Mediterranean shore a cradle for so many civilizations, what does it really mean to man? Warmth, of course, which permits free social intercourse and which, by minimizing the work of building and the burden of tilling allows more time for leisure and learning. But there is another quality, with less tangible results—the intensity of light.

Gibraltar is heavily tilted to the west and hangs over its bay, so that the afternoon light comes to it at double strength, directly from the sky and reflected from the water. Photographers doubt their exposure meters here, and stop down their lenses as never before. Architects scratch their heads at the tiny windows which can light large rooms. Sunglasses are the rule, rather than the exception.

The more light, the more colour. A grey stone in the sun here reminds you that grey is a mixture of colours. The light will find in it tints which we pay painters to find for us. Strong colours shriek in Gibraltar and even the drabbest deliver subtle, unexpected shades.

The southern people accept this gift of light, and live up to it. The women wear brighter clothes and hang bright curtains. Men paint their houses white or brilliant blue. Sober merchants buy vermilion motor-cars. Everyone rises to the occasion and pays his homage to the sun.

The people of Gibraltar take their sun for granted, and even decry it, at times, as a despoiler of feminine beauty and of infant health. They kept telling us not to trust it—it only felt hot, it was still cold. Do not change into cotton, until May, never bathe before June. The weather may deceive, the calendar never.

But we, straight from our dark north, embraced the sun and its culture without restraint or suspicion. Perhaps this late gift should always have been ours, I reflected, for the earliest Irish people are said to have come up from the Mediterranean, and the Celts fought their way right down through Portugal to the southern coast.

The sun alone, that unbuyable boon, kept us in Gibraltar through thin times, as it keeps the hungry peasants lingering still in Calabria and Andalusia. The sun, that is to say, and the community culture which it fosters. Over the years, many emigrant Gibraltarians have left opportunities of wealth behind them in Britain or America and returned to The Rock, to low wages, overcrowding and, in the past, second-class citizenship. There are many reasons for their return, but the strongest are the pulls of place and race, the mild and constant joy of living in community with one's own people, the rare ease of social relationships here, and the sun which forms and warms it all.

The street saunter, this pleasant purposeless promenade, is new to us. In Belfast, even in London, no one uses the streets for mere recreation, everyone hurries past, bent on his journey and his errand.

'That man spoke to me!' Joan said.

'What did he say?'

'Wappa—or something like that.'

'Just one word?' I asked her.

'Yes—wappa, I think it was.'

So it was, Carvillo told me, or to be correct, *guapa*, the Spanish word for pretty, or pretty-plus-sexy. She was to hear it many times more.

Carvillo explained the Andalusian custom of the *piropo*, the compliment murmured at the ear of a passing girl. It has invaded Gibraltar from Spain but, he said, is not so common here as there, and is, perhaps, in decline. In Spain it is a point of honour for a man to pretend to be excited by the passing females, even when his years have put him far past it. In the Calle Sierpes of Seville, where fat grandfathers sit in serried rows, girl-watching, you can hear them exclaiming—

'*Ay, que mostrador!*' What a counter she carries!

'*Que polvo tiene!*' How bedworthy!

'*Mira la mujer de bandera!*' Look at that fine fat one!

The women sweep past, eyes front, smiling to themselves when they have left the *piropista* safely astern. They never respond; it is all a harmless game. The only girls who answer strangers in the street, those of the Horizontal Profession, are hidden and busy at this *paseo* hour.

In Seville, that is; but here in Gibraltar, according to Mauricio Carvillo, it is all very prim and proper. No prostitutes at all.

'We are a very moral people, really,' he says. 'There is the Church, you see, and then, another thing—where could you go with a woman in a crowded little place like Gib? Eh?'

I started work from the hotel, while Joan busied herself getting our house furnished and ready, reconnoitring the local market, and arranging for our daughter's schooling.

I do not propose to say much about my work. My position was that of chief Civil Engineer to the Government and deputy Commissioner of Lands and Works. The profession of civil engineering is creative and challenging only for a tiny minority of its practitioners—the consultants. These are the self-employed professionals, men with some flair for the higher mathematics and applied science, and with the funds to back themselves. The vast majority of us, lacking flair or funds or both, are employed either by contractors or by public authorities of one kind and another. In either case, our usual duty is to design and construct the ordinary works of general utility. There are streets, sewers and water mains to be planned, specified and laid; we lay them with economy and in accordance with well-tried and standardized practice. Innovations in such matters are unnecessary and unwelcome. Such as they are, they come to us from the institutions employed in practical research, complete with full instructions for us to follow. My duty was to maintain good standards in all these workaday matters and to observe strict economy in them.

The roads, sewerage and the remarkable waterworks of The Rock were in the hands of the City Council, a body run and staffed by the Gibraltarians themselves. My mission was to help in the attack on that worldwide post-war curse, the housing problem.

Gibraltar's housing shortage was as bad as could be found anywhere. Before the Spanish Civil War some thousands of Gibraltarians used to live across the frontier in nearby Spain, enjoying more space and lower prices. At the outbreak of the Spanish Civil War, which began right there, in Algeciras and La Línea, these people took refuge in Gibraltar where, as British citizens, they had a right to protection and residence. In fact, the traditions of political asylum was such that they were sheltered here without much question of citizenship. To send a man back in those terrible times was to have his blood on one's hands.

Early in World War II the women, children and elderly men of Gibraltar were evacuated to Madeira, Casablanca, Jamaica, London and, finally, to Northern Ireland. They were reasonably well cared for wherever they went, but they suffered more than most people would by the disruption of family life and from a sense of exile. After four or five years away, the Government repatriated them hurriedly and *en masse*.

The face of The Rock, or such flat space as remained on it, broke out almost overnight in a rash of Nissen huts and temporary houses. Hotels and schools were taken over for use as hostels. Those who could do so moved in on their relatives. There was squalor and overcrowding in every corner. The Gibraltarians would live in any conditions to be reunited and back home.

The social shock of this sudden mass immigration must have been violent. This small town, stripped for siege and run for six years as an austere fortress, found itself flooded by its normal civilian population, plus the pre-war refugees from Spain, plus all their natural increase. But both space and funds were found, as they always are when they must be, and by the time I arrived there in 1952, six years after the repatriation, the worst of the emergency was past.

The remaining task was to replace the temporary housing with something better and permanent. It kept me busy for the next ten years, and it will be many more years before everyone in Gibraltar is decently housed. The demand for homes grows as you build them, as people grow up, marry and found families—a process which these Latin people are not inclined to delay.

We built apartment blocks, of ever increasing height, and converted old houses into flats. In the time I was there my Department rehoused some thousands of people, which is a large percentage of the total population.

Our own house, allocated to us by the Government, was, I blush to say, one of the grandest on The Rock. It had been built since the war, but on a scale fit for gracious living on the patterns of the past, when there was a great gap, both social and economic, between the imported official and most of the local people.

It was one of six mansions on sites hacked and blasted out of the steep hillside six hundred feet up the west face of The Rock. The approach road, a cul-de-sac, had a gradient of one in four. No loiterers ever approached us, the traffic was kept at arm's length, the noisy town was a mile away. We looked down on the treetops and the distant harbour and out across the sea to Algeciras and distant Tangier. Our balconies, too narrow for a deckchair, had been designed on the Spanish pattern, where their only use is for watching processions passing by. But there would be no processions up there—unless the Sherpas came under the banner 'Excelsior'.

Splendidly situated and built regardless of expense, our house stands as a fine example of failure for this simple reason—the plan was wrong. The grand exterior proved deceptive, for it contained a minimum of ill-conditioned rooms, with acres of space wasted on a pretentious entrance hall and landing, on three class-conscious lavatories, and a home laundry which would have served a cottage hospital. The biological use of the house had been overlooked or misunderstood, and it was born lagging behind the changing times. For me, that house is somewhat symbolic of Gibraltar—over-anxiously English, self-consciously colonial, resolutely un-Spanish, but consequently confused and finally ineffective.

We lived in a few rooms on the sunny side of the house. As a small family, and one without social pretensions, the waste and lack of space did not worry us. We lived a lot in the garden, too. We shall never live in a more beautiful place, and we are still grateful for the inspiration of that unforgotten view.

'What's a dressing-room for, anyway?' Joan asked me.

'I'm not sure,' I said. 'They used to have them in England—in big country houses. They're very useful on the stage—in bedroom farce, for instance.'

'That's only incidental. There must have been some proper use for them.'

'I suppose there was a time when a man had to leave the room while his wife undressed. Or, maybe, shove her out while he changed his trousers.'

'God save us! No wonder the Victorians were up to the neck in harlots and pornography!'

'Maybe they dodged in and out of the dressing-room for fun,' I said. 'You can see too much of a good thing.'

'*You* never seem to,' she said. 'I don't think you'll spend much time in there.'

'Will you? I mean, do you need it for anything?'

'Not that I can see.'

'Then it's mine,' I said. 'It's my study.'

Here it was, then, a long, narrow room with French windows at the western end leading to a high balcony. There I wrote some millions of words, writing sometimes all through the night when my day's work was done. There were plays for television and radio, stories for *The New Yorker*, *The Cornhill* and a dozen other magazines, endless daily journalism, and most of this book.

It was a room which commanded Gibraltar, Spain, Morocco and The Straits between, and all the ships that passed, and all the millions of birds following the sun. It commanded the sunsets, too, and the Pillars of Hercules, and the End of the World. If a man could not write in that room, he need not try to write anywhere else.

3

AS IT WAS IN THE BEGINNING

I must not get too soon entangled in twigs, blinded to trees, let alone the wood. I must stand back a little and take a broad view of The Rock and the basic facts of its existence.

Gibraltar is unique in many things—its position and prestige in history, its strange climate, its hand-mixed population, its ingenious water supply, and such minor matters as a mammal, a bird and a plant which occur nowhere else on the mainland of Europe. But as for the topography, there is nothing truly unique or rare about it.

It overawed our ancestors, and the first sight of it can astound a hardened traveller of today, yet it is not a phenomenon. It is, geographically speaking, a 'bill', which I take to be the exact opposite of a 'fiord'. The latter is a deep and narrow intrusion of the sea into the land; the former, a high and narrow intrusion of the land into the sea. I can think of no reason why the one should not be as common as the other.

Gibraltar's visual impact derives from its position on a bill-free coast. There are plenty of capes and headlands round about, but none so dramatically isolated from its surroundings.

There is another such rock at Ifach on the east coast of Spain, startlingly similar to ours. The Greeks applied their word *calpe* to Gibraltar, Ifach and several other Mediterranean bills. It means 'a vessel'—a ship, perhaps? High, narrow, prowed, and pointing seawards.

Our Mons Calpe, as the Greeks and Romans called Gibraltar, sweeps up from the sea to a jagged, saw-toothed ridge fourteen hundred feet high. No great height this, you may think, but The Rock achieves it in a mere half-mile on the western side and far less on the eastern. The west side, where most of us live, has a ruling slope of forty-five degrees—one in two. Like all slopes, when viewed from the bottom it looks even steeper. Happily for us, the lower reaches of it roll out in kindlier gradients.

Official hand-outs state that Gibraltar is three miles long by three-quarters of a mile wide and that, at two and a quarter

19

square miles of territory, it is the smallest of British possessions.

But even these figures are flattering. They omit to add that only about one-third of the total area is habitable—some three-quarters of a square mile—and that even this is difficult to develop, being narrow and tilted strips along the western shore. All the rest is the unconquerable Upper Rock, traversed only by hair-raising military roads, thicketted with thorn and scrub olive, haloed with vapour, haunted by apes and ravens. We look up at it in awe and admiration, we put guns on it, and radar masts and flags. But we cannot live there.

The basic fact of Gibraltar, the act of God, is geologically clear and striking. One can see at first glance how the mild little mountains of the nearby Sierra Carbonera disown The Rock, both in contour and colour. They are deeply red; Gibraltar is silver grey. They are rounded; Gibraltar is jagged and sharp. From its birth in the sea bed our Rock was separate and apart from the body of Spain. The low isthmus of sand which now unites them is, in geological terms, an innovation.

Gibraltar is formed of Jurassic limestone, twisted and tempered to a gritty hardness now, but once a soft deposit of dead organisms on the floor of The Straits. The earth's surface shrank, the Sierra Nevada and the Atlas of North Africa thrust towards each other and produced a titanic pincer movement in this narrow gap. For many miles inland the hard mountainsides still show their tortured writhings; the softer sea bed suffered more. The limestone heaved up out of the sea in concertina folds, and a cross-section through Gibraltar shows a perfect arc of an overfold in its curved western face. The precipices on the northern and eastern sides show where this fold faulted and cracked away.

Six successive sea levels as Europe froze, thawed out and froze again, have scarred the sides of The Rock with marine cliffs and caves, and surrounded it with narrow raised beaches and platforms of scree.

In one epoch, with the present sea bed high and dry for many miles around, a fierce east wind prevailed and piled sand a thousand feet high on that face of The Rock. Low down on the western side there is a deposit of fine red sand which may have blown there from the Sahara Desert. There is a little shale there, too, eroded off the western face where it once overlay the limestone. All the rest—all the heart rock— is strong and solid limestone, ideal rock for tunnels and for caves.

The sea caves, some of them stranded eight hundred feet above present sea-level, have been etched out by the rains of ages into vast caverns. The most famous of them is St. Michael's Cave, a great gothic cathedral of stalagmites and stalactites, with two connected systems at different levels, a fresh-water lake of icy black water, forty yards in length, and ramifications still uncharted. This has been a place of refuge since immemorial time and it reverted to its ancient use in World War II, when they built a small hospital inside it.

Ledesma Miranda, in his *Gibraltar, La Roca de Calpe*, advances the theory that the Scylla and Charybdis of the Odyssey were more likely to have been our Pillars of Hercules—Gibraltar and Mont Abyla— than those in the generally accepted Straits of Messina. Our Straits were more remote from Greece, therefore more mysterious; also, they are far more imposing in scale, a more fitting setting for dramatic events. And there are closer clues. Scylla is described as having her head in the clouds, a very common condition of Gibraltar. Also, the cave there 'looked out on the west', as does our cave of St. Michael. The Iliad's 'Styx in her glorious house, roofed over with long rocks, propped up to heaven all round with silver pillars', is a perfect description of our underground lake. Research into these claims continues. We may yet prove that Gibraltar holds the ancient gateway to Hell.

Be that as it may, our caves and caverns offered refuge from the wild beasts and wilder weather of prehistoric times, and brought the first men to Gibraltar—the Neanderthal men, unjustly so-called, who came here twenty thousand years ago.

The Gibraltar Man was a woman, a young female of the species, whose famous skull was found in a shallow cave on the North Face of The Rock, a few feet above present sea-level. The discovery occurred in 1848, that busy year, just before Darwin published his *Origin of Species*. The contemporary minute book of the Gibraltar Society states laconically: 'The Secretary reported the discovery of an old skull.' It reads as though he had been almost ashamed to waste the time of the Society—composed of British officers and their ladies—on such an unsavoury trifle. Perhaps he noticed some member fingering her smelling-salts. There was no discussion on the skull. They hurried on to the President's lecture on druidical remains elsewhere.

Eleven years later a similar skull and part skeleton was found at Neanderthal near Düsseldorf, and soon became the wonder of the scientific world. Our neglected little cranium was diffidently put forward as corroborative evidence, was accepted as such, and became a prized possession of the Royal College of Surgeons in London.

Neanderthal Man, in the causes of both science and chivalry, should be known as Gibraltar Woman. The case illustrates something of that professional thoroughness which seems to be a German characteristic, and also of that English cult of the polite and offhand amateur—a subject which must arise again in this book.

Why did the Gibraltar Woman die here alone, I wonder? Trapped in her little cave by the hungry wolves and hyenas which abounded in her time? Or, maybe, a refugee from Cro-Magnon Man, the master race of his epoch? If the latter, she was the first of an endless procession of fugitives to be sheltered by The Rock of Gibraltar. That procession reaches right down to present times. As I write this, Gibraltar is giving refuge to Jews fleeing from Morocco.

But it seems that we cannot claim descent from the Neanderthal people—not even here in Gibraltar. The whole race was driven to exile or exterminated by the handsome Cro-Magnon Man. Perhaps this was a tragedy. Our social behaviour reflects no great credit on our ancestors, whoever they were. Neanderthal Man, had he prevailed and survived, might not have bequeathed us any worse genes than we have. He was, by all appearances, a monkey-faced fellow, but he knew how to knap a fine flint and he buried his dead with loving care—and these were great achievements considering the size of his cranial capacity.

For twenty thousand years these simple, ugly people were the sole inhabitants of Europe, and there is, I think, some poetry in the fact that the only relics of them found outside Europe were discovered in the district of Galilee. There, we may be sure, they lived by patient and clumsy fishing in the Lake. Recent researches suggest that they may have interbred there with a race of Sapient Man and, if so, something of their ancient blood may have come down to us.

I cherish our Gibraltar Woman all the more because of her exiled brothers, driven all that distance—may I presume—by our clever and pitiless ancestors, and dying, as she died, in small caves beside the waters.

Twenty millennia passed and then the simple fisherman, James, answering the crook of a finger, 'left his father Zebedee in the ship with the hired servants', and returned, at last, to Spain. He landed, most probably, at old Carteia, the parent city, under the shadow of The

Rock. And from there he peacefully reconquered all of us, the violent descendants of the Cro-Magnon upstarts and usurpers.

This is too florid a conception, I know, to please the cool scientist. It is typical of the thoughts born in my mountain eyrie on The Rock towards the time of summer sunrise, as I watched the Pillars of Hercules materializing in the slow silver light. In that weird interlude, after eight silent hours of self-questioning, there seemed no limit to the mind's ranging. There I learnt the ecstasy of the hermit.

The northern ice cap of Europe spread and shrank in four long epochs. In none of these did it stretch as far south as Spain, let alone to Gibraltar, but the third extension, called the *Riss*, put most of England under ice. During that period Spain must have had a climate like that of Alaska today, and the sub-arctic animals, in retreat southwards, must have been crowded there.

As the *Riss* slowly receded and the climate of Spain grew milder, these animals found life easier, and so they throve and multiplied. The fourth and last advance of the ice, called *Wurm*, was not so extensive, so the conditions of Spain were never again as severe as they had been.

The recession of the *Wurm* ice, I imagine, left the Ice Age beasts in good heart and numbers, to live on through thousands of years of improving climate and vegetation. The time came, of course, when the climate had so changed that this sub-arctic fauna found itself outmoded, so to speak. It had to readapt or die. Woolly mammoths became elephants, or migrated northwards to die in Russian snowdrifts, or simply died where they were. But long before that time arrived our Neanderthal Man had appeared on the scene. There is evidence that he shared their last millennia—and his own—with the Ice Age animals. And it is now believed that he did not merely survive in misery and terror with all these fearsome beasts, but that he prevailed against them and preyed on them.

When a few human bones or teeth were found in cave earth, with the fangs of hyenas or sabre-toothed tigers predominating, it used to be concluded that the beasts which so outnumbered the man had dragged him there. Now we are told to believe the opposite. The man dragged the beasts there, year after year, and butchered them for meat, hide and bones. With the bones he made weapons to kill more beasts and, sad to say, other men.

The old joke of the caveman with a woman in one hand and a club in the other is even older, and certainly far truer, than one might expect. It may be seen, vividly drawn twenty thousand years ago, on cave walls about forty miles from Gibraltar, at Las Figuras in the province of Cádiz.

We know that Neanderthal Man, in his time, inhabited the land from Cape Town to Copenhagen, after the last glaciation. We may be sure that he did not spread from the north southwards, for all the north was frozen solid in all time before his epoch and, indeed, during most of it. He must have come from the south then—from Africa to Europe.

A quarter of a million years before Neanderthal Man an ape-man flourished—*Pithecanthropus Erectus*, a flat-headed, long-muzzled creature, far less like ourselves. *Pithecanthropus* has been found in many parts of Africa, including Algeria in the north and the Sahara Desert, but no evidence of him has been found in Europe. The time was not ripe for him there—he was warmer, no doubt, where he was, and since he went naked, that would be a factor of vital importance.

Neanderthal Man was the first European, and he was, originally African. So much is, I believe, widely acceptable now. Professor Riet Lowe, in a broadcast in 1955 (B.B.C.), said that the recent discoveries seemed to indicate that in coming to Africa, Europeans were returning to the home of their ancestors.

In 1936 the archaeologists unearthed the remains of two Neanderthal men near Tangier, only ten miles from the closest coast of Spain and in full view of it.

Now my own contribution, made with the greatest respect to the experts on this subject, but so obvious—or, at least, so likely—as to seem almost beyond dispute, is this:

Neanderthal Man, on his first sea voyage, crossed from Africa to Europe by the narrowest waters he could find, to the land which beckoned nearest. That is, he crossed these Straits below my window, and he left his traces—his very bones—here on this Rock.

This means, unless I have overlooked some strange factor, that the whole of western Europe was first manned by way of Gibraltar. If the cradle of our race was in Africa, then the gateway to its full manhood, and to all its subsequent achievements, lies here in Gibraltar Bay.

4

LEARNING THE ROPES

But I was in Gibraltar for months before I found time to begin studying it in depth and making speculations on its prehistory. There were far more urgent considerations. We had to learn how to live there.

Joan and I had a lot to learn—far more than most incoming officers. Everything was completely new to us. The Colonial Service itself, with its hierarchy, etiquette, regulations and traditions, was my chief anxiety. In other colonies you have only to deal with one such system; in Gibraltar, I found, there were five. Government, City Council, Navy, Army and Air Force, each had its own jealous dignitaries, powers, territories and rights, and before making any move you had to consider them all.

In early days there I received an irate and portentous minute from, I think, the Air Ministry Works Department, reporting that some person unknown had 'committed a nuisance' in a military installation taken over by the R.A.F. from the Army, which had leased the land, through my department, from Government. The City Council was involved too, this being a sanitary matter. The question was—whose duty was it to remove the nuisance? For further complication, the case was in a 'Secret' file, because the site of the crime was an old wartime gun post which had started its life in secret some twelve years before.

I dealt with this problem in the proper and traditional way, which is to hold the file, or send it around all those concerned for additional information, until the sun and rain have done their work and the nuisance has reunited with Mother Earth. But in the midst of such formidable protagonists as the Armed Forces of the British Crown I moved with some anxiety—for a while.

We had much to learn of the social scene, too. The rules and *mores* of the polite English society which surrounded us were new to us both. Joan had never lived in England, and I had done so but briefly. We had left a circle of Irish intellectuals, artists and politicians and found ourselves in the midst of formal Englishmen—senior officials, magistrates, colonels and clergy. It was a shattering transition.

Then there were the local people who, we were soon told, were full of strange ideas and very easily offended. There were also the Spaniards, whom we would both employ—my workmen, Joan's servants. We had better get an early understanding of their attitudes, in their strange position of ex-patriate workers. We would have to learn fast enough to keep one jump ahead of catastrophe. . . .

Even in such a peaceful colony as Gibraltar there were strong political tensions and, after these had been reduced by constitutional changes, even stronger social tensions remained untouched. To avoid envy and to reduce the inevitable criticism to a minimum, the imported civil servant had to lead an exemplary life—or, at least, appear to do so.

This is the essential difference, I found, between the Civil Service at home and its counterpart abroad. At home you do your work according to regulations, leave the office at five o'clock, and live your private life as you wish. Except that you may not publish 'a political manifesto' or stand for public election, you are not subject to any more restrictions than any other respectable employer might impose.

ˋIn the overseas service you are in the field, on foreign service. You have no business to be there, except through your appointment, which, in senior posts, is theoretically made by Her Majesty's Principal Secretary of State for the Colonies. You are in service or, at least, on call for twenty-four hours a day, for you are, like a soldier, on 'a tour of duty'. You are scarcely to be considered a citizen in the colony. You are a functionary, as the French put it, a faceless man. Your opinions do not count here, and your views are not to be heard except in the privacy of the office. Your sole duty is to 'advise the Governor', and your existence is supplementary to his.

On the other hand, if you are a Head of Department, as I was occasionally in Gibraltar and for two years in another colony, you are, in a sense a public man. In politically retarded colonies the Head of Department is the equivalent of a Minister, the ultimate authority in his field. The Governor, of course, can override him, even in his field, but Governors are not criticized in the local press. Heads of Department are, for the local politicians, or would-be politicians, thus criticize the Governor and the administration obliquely.

To criticize the Governor directly would be to risk calling down his wrath and his rusty but still unrevoked powers of arbitrary punishment. To criticize the administrators, His Excellency's top rank advisors, was held to incur the removal of one's name from the list of potential recipients of appointments and honours. The remaining targets of public criticism, the largest safe targets for the aspiring colonial demagogue, are the professional and technical Heads of Departments. Of these, those with the largest organizations, responsibilities and budgets, very naturally bore the brunt. They were the departments of Works, Medicine and Education.

In these late days of colonial development and emancipation, with the local politicians either already in the ascendancy or soon to be so, and with the eyes of the world watchful for any signs of colonial oppression, a persecuted colonial civil servant need expect no support at all from his Government. Civil servants are expendable and replaceable; the local politicians and their press must not be offended. One of my colleagues in Gibraltar was libellously and publicly accused of unfairly allocating the tenancy of an apartment; the Government had complete faith in him, but told him to take his own legal advice and pay for it out of his own pocket, with the result that he simply let the accusation pass and the reputation of the administration suffer. In short, the civil service was thrown to the wolves in developing colonies, in any conflict or dispute with the citizens. In many respects, I found, I had less effective rights than the humblest native labourer in the place. So much for the legend—the arrogant and privileged expatriate imposing his will on the terrified natives.

The Regulations are potentially fierce, but I found their application benign enough. The authorities never troubled me in any way, although I became a journalist, broadcaster and critic in Gibraltar and proclaimed my views—on everything except political issues—all over the place. I am glad to say, too, that none of my four Governors ever exacted his pound of flesh from me by forcing me to work twenty-four hours a day.

Reserving some criticisms of the Overseas Civil Service, ex-Colonial Service, I found it generally a kind and even thoughtful employer. It had a pleasant system for welcoming the new officer and his wife, for helping them to settle and making them feel at home, and steering them past the major pitfalls in which colonial life abounds. Joan and I were allotted a set of 'godparents' to show us the ropes, and our doubts and difficulties soon began to disappear. . . .

These good people offered us all their experience and knowledge of Gibraltar and the colonial complex, and all their many friends as well. They instructed us in the intricate observances of England's stratified society. They told us which visitors' books we must sign, which invitations to expect, accept and return, and the strange and arbitrary rituals of card-dropping. They told us whom to invite with whom, the table of equivalent ranks, which social mixtures to avoid, which clubs and pubs to patronize and which we must eschew.

The dominant social pattern, we found, was on the English upper middle class model, and of a rigidity hard to find, now, in England herself. There was no element of racialism in it; the rich Gibraltarians themselves—those who had been 'home', as they called it, to boarding school—admired the model and aspired to imitate it. They simply took it further back, to red plush, Landseer, aspidistras, and sideboards stacked with silverware.

Joan and I could see the limitations of this mode of thought and of life, but we saw no hope of reforming it, nor any reason to fly in its face. The *mores* and values of our English colleagues were completely alien to us, but they had produced a well-ordered and comfortable way of life, one with nothing offensive or malicious about it—except when, rarely and in self-defence, it turned to ostracism. We had joined the British Colonial Service, and this was the way it worked. For a while, and up to a point, Joan and I lived in old English style in Gibraltar, outwardly, at least. But we had our ears to the ground—or, say, The Rock—all the time, and we had one foot in Spain. We were exploring and assimilating cultures and values far different from the dominant norm. A time was to come when we would cut across all social frontiers, and live and do exactly as we pleased.

Joan's 'godmother' introduced her to the everlasting servant problem, the chief preoccupation of colonial wives, and gave her valuable advice on the recruitment of staff.

You will never find a Gibraltarian girl in domestic service, even though it is a major industry in the place. If he can help it, a father here will not let his daughters work at all. This is not a matter of snobbery but of Latin supervision of the females. A daughter, in their view, can cuckold a father—'put the horns on him'—just as well as a wife. In spite of strict Catholic upbringing and obviously decorous and pious behaviour, every Latin father lives in fear of his womenfolk's sex, an attitude rampant in England in Shakespeare's time and declining ever since. It remains a strong factor in the character of Gibraltarian society.

If, through economic circumstances, a Gibraltar girl must work, she will easily get a job in a shop or in some clerical capacity. She is sure to know English, more or less well. Domestic service was left to Spanish women, who either lived in with their employers, (with special permission), or commuted daily from La Línea and Algeciras.

The cohorts of cooks, maids, washerwomen and charwomen flocking into Gibraltar every morning and out again every night were part of the local scene. Naturally enough, they tended to be of a somewhat rough and raw type of woman. Very often they were the widows and orphans of men killed in the Civil War or after it, and deprived of education either by poverty or policy. Tough, raucous, cheerful and industrious, the *criadas* of Gibraltar were a colourful collection. They were in a constant state of war with the Spanish customs men, for they all augmented their wages by stuffing their underwear, and even their shoes, with tobacco and coffee and smuggling it into Spain. At five o'clock on a Friday, pay day, every quiet corner of the streets had two or three women with their skirts hoisted up, stowing the precious tobacco next to their skin, their habitual prudery conquered by the realities of economics. The Spanish customs had one hard-worked lady searcher to deal with them, but it would have taken two or three hundred to search them all. Their contribution to the community of Gibraltar, like that of their commuting menfolk, was twofold—their labour and their function as exporters. At this time they totalled, men and women, 13,000, or about half of the Gibraltarian population, and such was their impact that the whole economy of the place depended on them.

The English wives were always trading servant stories, for the Spanish women brought their drama and their lurid gossip into every home and their flamboyance delighted and amazed the reticent Englishwomen. Not untypical of their anecdotes of home life in the seamier streets of Spain was the true one about a man who came home early one night, caught his wife *flagrante delicto*, clubbed her, and sewed her up in the appropriate place with copper wire. Since this was a *crime passionelle* under maximum provocation, the police merely told him not to let it occur again. The lady, thenceforth known as *la mujer del alambre*—the wire woman—recovered and took some pride in having excited a more violent jealousy than had any of her neighbours. The effect of such tales, told to decent Englishwomen, whose peak calamity had been a flat tyre or a missed train, kept the coffee-tables a-twitter.

A high-ranking officer in Gibraltar had to entertain constantly, and a good cook was a very rare asset. Once found and schooled, well paid and cherished, top cooks are passed from Admiral to Admiral, Colonel to Colonel, as one incumbent follows another. As you would expect, they get to know the house, the market, the cuisine, and the very style itself, better and better—better, indeed, than the bewildered new *Señora* herself. Succeeding mistresses shrink in size until the cook towers over the household, does as she thinks fit, and brooks no impertinence from anyone.

Such a cook was the Brigadier's, called Inmaculada after the Immaculate Conception. She had worked up her pay and privileges through four Brigadier's wives, catching them either helpless upon arrival or sentimental just before they left. Not content with the highest cook's pay on The Rock, Inmaculada demanded the help of two batmen—young soldiers sent up from the regiment to polish the Brigadier's leather and so forth, but often pushed into more general duties.

The Brigadier would change these lads fairly frequently, since it was not fair to the man, or to the Army, to keep him on batman duties for too long. Besides, the modern soldier might write to his M.P. to say that his National Service had been wasted. . . .

One afternoon, soon after a batman had been relieved and replaced, Inmaculada strode up to Mrs. Brigadier and gave notice of leaving. With dinner parties pending, the lady was distressed at this. She brought Inmaculada, fiery, fortyish widow, into the lounge and sat her down and tried to reason with her. Did she want more money? More help? Anything!

The conference, with bad Spanish on one side and worse English on the other, must have been prolonged, but at last the cook made it clear that she didn't want more help, she wanted the help she was used to—the batman who had just been sent back to his regiment, the best young man she'd ever had.

The Brigadier's wife said she would ask her husband. But it would be no use, she knew. The Army had to come first—and the young man's future. He had been too long in the house already. The Brigadier was cross with her for keeping him; the replacement, a good quiet boy and a hard worker—

'Listen, *Señora*!' Inmaculada proclaimed. 'You are a woman, are you not?'

The Brigadier's wife said she hoped she was.

Then, being driven to it, and being of an age with the Brigadier's wife, and having that special independence in sexual matters which the Latin races grant to their widows, Inmaculada came clean. This new soldier was no use to her, she said, nor to any woman. The previous boy had come to her bed every afternoon during the siesta. The new lad didn't know what a woman was for! 'Take him out of my kitchen and bring me back my own boy—or I'll go!'

The Brigadier was difficult, and rightly so, but when his wife told him the whole story, and the choice between propriety and poor food, on the one hand, and a disorderly house with a fine table, on the other, he had to give way. 'Do the boy good, I suppose.' The amorous batman returned and Mrs. Brigadier retained her reputation for serving those fat *soufflés* which only a happy cook can make.

The Brigadier and his lady have gone long since, but Inmaculada still holds the house, and still passes the batmen through her hands. I study these young men when I see them loitering at the Tradesmen's Entrance, but their standard, scrubbed, saucy young faces give nothing away.

Joan, if she could not have both, would prefer happiness to efficiency in a servant. She hated a long face in the house, and sought someone young and gay. Her first choice for housemaid was a beautiful slut from the depths of the Spanish countryside. For the washing, which was done out of sight in our home laundry in the basement, she took on a stringy old character who complained all the time but got through the work. As anyone can see by stopping his car on a bridge and watching them at work in the river bed, there is no worker in Europe to touch a Spanish washerwoman.

The housemaid, we soon found out, knew nothing about a house, for the very good reason that she had never lived in one. She had been born and brought up in a stick-and-leaf hut on the banks of the Rio Guadarranque, a shelter built by a migrant labourer for a season and kept standing by easy repairs and *mañanismo*. It had no glass in the windows and the floor was of river gravel. The fire was on medieval lines, a stone hearth in the middle of the floor with a hole in the roof for the smoke to escape.

Our girl's parents, with unnumbered smaller children, still lived in that hut, as we discovered when we took her home for the week-end. It has never ceased to surprise me to see the girls of Spain, beautifully groomed and brightly dressed, with their lipstick, stiletto heels and golden jewellery, sallying from huts and tenements which would shock even Glasgow. These particular hut-dwellers were very happy and healthy people, I thought. The climate was on their side, of course.

Our girl worked with wild enthusiasm in our magnificent palace, with its tiled floors, bathrooms, pictures and fancy lampshades. She danced as she worked, breasts and hips a-jiggle, trailing shafts of flamenco and wafts of hay-sweet sweat and of the Rio Guadarranque. At her every error, she screeched with laughter, which meant that the sounds of mirth rarely died away. She was learning, however, and she was a joy to behold, but she was illiterate and very simple. She left us one day, without explanation, and never came back again. Later, I heard that she had gone with a man to Casablanca on a promise of riches. If there is a city in the world where lovely, wild young women were appreciated, that was it.

Joan, wiser now, replaced her with a strong, plain widow in her forties. Amalia, as I shall call her, was a butt of a woman, with a frank, ugly face set with beady black eyes, and a mouth full of long and battered teeth. Her normal voice was a shout, and she, too, shrieked with laughter at anything or nothing at all. She sang without inhibition, mostly *saetas*, those brief, passionate confessions which sound out from dark balconies when the Easter processions pass.

Amalia made it plain, Joan said, as soon as she entered our employment, that the house would be run for the convenience of the *caballero*—myself. Spain is a man's country since Moorish times —(and so, to a great extent, is Gibraltar)—and any male manifestation, however arrogant and selfish, is taken by the simpler women as an act of God. But further to the worship to be accorded to me for being born into the male sex, there was my noble, distinguished and influential position—that of Public Works Engineer. The Spanish assessment of such a post is, I was to find, amazingly high in the social scale, for reasons which I did not suspect. I was supposed to give jobs to all my friends and relatives, regardless of merit, and to make millions out of the public funds in kick-backs, off-sales and bribes. Needless to say, in British Gibraltar, I found no opportunity for doing either, but

I had great prestige with the simpler Spaniards in spite of my lack of enterprise.

Amalia had demanded and received much of our life story within her first week in the house. The direct Spanish approach did not alarm or annoy Joan, for she knew it from the remoter districts of Ireland. In fact, it is a universal peasant custom, this immediate frank exchange of biographies. It should never offend, for the questions and answers are so frank and free that it is obvious the information is not sought for harming or for hating, but rather to know and to love better—and sooner.

'How old are you?' Amalia would shoot at Joan. On being told, she might say: 'For God's sake! I thought you were far older than that!'

'Only one child?' she would ask. 'Any dead?'

'No—thank goodness!'

'But then—why haven't you more? Now you know the way, you can do the same again, can't you?'

'We do,' said Joan, 'but without result, so far.'

'Well, keep at it,' said Amalia, looking as though she might get down to detailed instructions.

Amalia stayed with us for six years, rattling, banging, singing, screeching round the house, banishing the spirit of melancholy with her vast voice and violent zest. She fought running battles with the succession of young girls who came to help her, with the gardener for being impervious to her charms, with the neighbours' maids for borrowing, or for being pretty, or superior. She grew to dominate the quiet precinct where we lived, and to some extent, ourselves as well. When we left we found her a post in an army house. She still sails down Main Street every evening, backslapping and kissing many whom she meets, on her way to bully Spain.

5

THE END OF THE WORLD

The public works engineer spends his days with his eyes dutifully fixed upon the ground. He probes the earth, inspects foundations, sees to the proper mixing of sand and stones. He tots up costs and calculates the safety factors. On the job his word is law, for he is qualified and endorsed, which means, in our society, that you may follow his advice with impunity even when it is wrong. Off the job, since he is a specialist and technician, he has no word at all. It is presumed that a man who knows one subject thoroughly could not possibly know anything else.

In the British system, as our public and business administration show, you must be unqualified for anything to be qualified for everything. In our colonies, as in our industry, as in our cricket, we play the amateur game—for as long as we can afford it, anyway.

But for such sad thoughts I had an unfailing antidote. With a study like mine a man could rise above all his daily drudgery. Up here, in this crow's nest on the rock face, Joan and I would sit for an hour before I began my night's work, and watch the sun spinning down into the sea.

We looked our across thickets of olive trees, a steep jumble of round-tiled roofs, and the tiny harbour of Rosia where Nelson's tired and tattered fleet carried in his corpse after the sad victory at Trafalgar. We looked across three miles of darkening sea to the rough coast of Spain, where Algeciras was becoming a chain of winking lights. Behind that was the Sierra de Luna—the Mountains of the Moon. The sun goes down behind these mountains, beyond The Straits, at the End of the World.

The ancients said that the sun plunged into the sea out there, and the sea boiled and blew out clouds of steam. Beyond that, all the waters of the world roared down into The Abyss, and perpetual mists marked their everlasting end. Between the twin Pillars of Hercules, Calpe and Abyla, the secret mists lay continuously, shrouding the forbidden mysteries of the gods. A man could sail through them only to his doom.

34

They did not say, but may have felt, that a narrowing passage between rising barricades, being the primeval form of animal trap, kindles deep fears in the human breast and a silent scream for retreat.

Here, we are in the Hesperia of the Greeks—'The Land of the Evening.' Just across from us, twenty miles away at Ceuta, (Septa of the Romans), the Hesperides lived, the seven daughters of Atlas. We can see them clearly, petrified now into seven little hills, with their father holding up the world behind them. Their task it was, and still is, to hang their golden apples in the evening sky.

*   *   *   *

The sunset is one of the chief features of life in Gibraltar—a bonus for living here. At this focus of mountain masses, the winds and clouds are in constant friction and collision, and their struggles accelerate as the temperature falls with the sun. From our grandstand, steeply tilted to the west, we watched the great sky battles across three hundred miles of south Iberian dustlands, which lends pigment to the pictures. The swirling clouds were the brushes, and every night they painted some new and wonderful fantasy.

It is no mere coincidence that citizens covet the west ends of their cities, and build their finest houses there. At the end of a day's work a man instinctively turns towards the declining sun, where light and warmth linger. So, for that matter, do the partridges, which are taken at night on the warmer western slopes. The city of Gibraltar is all west end.

Watching thousands of sunsets here. I have seen on three occasions the sun spin down into mid-ocean as a penny slides into a slot. I have also looked down, countless times, on the great hedge of mist in The Straits, lying low in the water, thick as wadding and nearly trimmed to fit, as though its sole purpose was to blind and muffle the waterway.

But both these phenomena, I notice, are to be seen in high summer, which is the very season when the Greeks would have ventured to the far end of their sea, with their little ships coasting in fair weather and long daylight on the steady wind from the east.

That wind would have brought them here fast and easily, but

at the same time, it would have faced them with fog at the end.
For this same east wind, laden with moisture from its long passage
over the warm summer sea, condenses when it meets the cooler
Atlantic breeze and casts its pall over The Straits.

Plato told them that the Pillars were not the end of the world, and
that they were living 'like frogs in a pond'. But what seasoned mariner,
who had been there and seen the difficulties for himself, would have
heeded an old Academic like that?

Nevertheless, had they come here in the mild midwinter, risking the
storms and hostile coasts and rowing against the west wind, they
would have found The Straits clear and sparkling in the sunshine. And
they would have seen the sun setting coolly and sedately enough and
painting a wide pathway out into the western ocean.

But, detained by traditions, superstitions and rumours, the great
Greeks never ventured out of their frog pond, and even the doughty
Romans, cursing in full armour, had to fight and footslog two thousand
miles overland to Britain.

We know that early man visited Gibraltar. But it is significant, I
think, that none of the numerous caves and caverns can show a dab
of painting, for there are fifty caves with prehistoric painting within
a day's run of The Rock. Many of these caves are far smaller and less
secure than ours.

It seems to me that early man did not wish to settle here. It was an
inhospitable place. Even the high rainfalls of the post-glacial period
would not necessarily solve Gibraltar's perennial water problem, for
the harder it rains the faster it runs off into the sea. There never was
a river, a lake, nor even a pond on the surface of Gibraltar, whatever
there may be hidden in its bowels.

A greater deterrent to settlement would have been the wind. The
Rock's spine runs due north-south, so that its flanks are exposed to the
full force of the dominant winds of both the south Atlantic and the
Mediterranean. Even in the mild and medium climate of our epoch
I designed new buildings here for a gust windspeed of one hundred
miles an hour, and they often suffer sixty. Lord knows the
speed of the howling gales of prehistoric times, when the frost
was shattering the top of The Rock and most of Spain was
ice and tundra. Gibraltar's caverns were not to be compared with
those close inland, which were more sheltered and safer, on

wooded slopes with water and game at hand. Besides, it is probable that, in those times, Gibraltar was an island a full mile offshore.

For many thousands of years The Rock of Gibraltar was of no practical import to the human race which swarms on it so thickly today. Its populations have always been artificial ones. Its natural use to mankind was as a seasonal fishing-pier, a place to be visited in necessity when the inland waters of the nearby Laguna de la Janda froze over and the wildfowl left the marshes.

Another primeval use for Gibraltar, and one which, like the fishing, continues to this day, was as a retreat and refuge from enemies. Here the outlaw or delinquent, or the victim marked for sacrifice, could flee and hide in the caves, and watch his backtrail from the commanding heights. Thousands must have done so, over all the years. The first of all, the Gibraltar Woman, died here alone.

I think of man venturing down in trepidation from the trees, contriving a brief mastery and safety in the forest and the plain, then finding that of all his enemies the worst, the most cunning and malicious, was his fellow-man, and so being forced to climb again to inaccessible and defensible refuges.

Ireland and other countries had their lake dwellings and, later, fortified farms. The south of Europe is strewn with impracticable hilltop villages, with nothing but safety and (for us) scenery to recommend them. Venice was built on stilts on sandbanks, and grew rich only because of its hard-won peace and security. The windswept Rock of Gibraltar, surrounded by the sea, is the most striking refuge of them all, for security and defence are its *raison d'être*. But for the mark of Cain, no one at all would live in such a place.

Ten miles to the westward of Gibraltar, where the broad river Guadarranque flows into the head of the bay, lies an ideal, natural site for a port and a city. Here the Phoenicians settled a fishing-village a thousand years before Christ, and called it Carteia after Melkarte, their god of the sea.

Carteia was sheltered from the prevalent east wind by The Rock itself, and also from the heavy seas from that direction. The Spanish headland, Punta Secreta, protected it from the west. North-west of it there were ranges of low hills. At its feet there was a fine estuary for the small ships of those times. There was unfailing and abundant water; there were salt marshes along the coast and a wide fertile valley stretching inland to endless woods of pine and oak. The moray eels skulked in the rocks there, the fat and foolish tunney passed offshore, and the murex whelk, which yielded royal purple, kept even the women and children profitably busy.

As time passed the primitive and gullible Iberians carried chunks of iron and copper down to the coast for trade. The Phoenicians were the first semitic people in these parts, which were later to be made and moulded by another semitic race. It is possible that they, with characteristic cunning, spread the terrible tales about the End of the World and the horrible fate of men who ventured there, at the same time sneaking round the western coast themselves, to Lisbon and, it used to be thought, to Cornwall. Wherever they went they traded purple cloth for tin, and tin was the uranium of the ancient world. Soft copper was not hard to find, but only with the addition of the much rarer tin could it be made into hard bronze, which gave mastery over materials and men.

Carteia, in its perfect site, throve so well that the Phoenicians—or Carthaginians, as they became—and the Romans who inherited their work and wisdom, founded a string of similar towns all along the north coast of The Straits.

Bits and pieces of these remain, so that you never know in this region what your foot falls upon. The names are remembered still— Barbecula, Portus Albus, Mellaria, Belon. They fell into ruins long ago and, like their great progenitor Carteia, they all lie buried in the blown sand.

Meanwhile, in 600 B.C. the Phoenician people of Carthage, as is the way of children and colonies, had come of age and defied their parent city, the tired and distant Tyre.

The people of the colony of Carthage, and of Carteia, refused to pay the ten per cent tribute to the mother country. They cut all ties and henceforth called themselves Carthaginians. But they kept many of the old customs, such as eating dogs, but never pigs, sacrificing children to the gods, killing all failing or ailing generals. They had not much culture, these colonial people. They were businessmen and proud of it. They had stolen their architecture from the Greeks, and most of their tools and utensils. They painted little or nothing, and wrote not a word. The only evidence they left of putting pen to pebble is contained in certain small, mean and detailed tariffs made out by professional priests. It is as though the sacred office in their towns was that of chartered accountant.

They were businessmen, first and last, exporting wine, panthers, spoons, drainpipes, anything, and dealing by barter only. They had four hundred years of rich trade, opening up Spain and West Africa to the ancient world, feeding on their agricultural slave state in Tunisia, and gathering goods for their own sake. But they grew greedier, as is the way of businessmen, and the day came when they overreached themselves.

In 220 B.C. the Carthaginians marched all over the south of Spain, disregarding the fact that it was now a Roman province. Cicero began to thunder in the Roman Senate: 'Carthage must be destroyed!'

The long and weary Punic wars ended by the Romans driving the Carthaginian armies out of Spain for ever—but no one knows how many of those who were conquered stayed and became absorbed in the new culture. The Carthaginian armies had to leave by the gates they had entered, eight centuries earlier, Cádiz and Carteia.

Too late, the old tycoons of fish sauce and purple dye raised their sad eyes to the great fortress they had never used, the Rock of Gibraltar which towered over their defenceless city of Carteia. They met a Roman navy in the bay and engaged in the first of many naval battles to be fought in the shadow of The Rock. On this occasion, it is written, the sea won. Perhaps the sea always wins.

The cunning Romans consolidated the fine city of Carteia by giving their legionaries a stake in it. Did they invent this technique of government, I wonder, along with so much else?

Rome declared Carteia a *Colonia Libertinorum*, which has been irreverently construed as 'a colony of libertines'. In effect, it meant that the soldiers of the garrison were free to trade, free to marry—or not to marry—the local girls, and, within certain fixed limits, free to govern themselves. There would be strings to all this, of course, and tribute to be paid, but it soon produced a city of rich and happy veterans at this favoured spot and, for the Empire, a firmly guarded and highly strategic strongpoint. Prosperity is the prime progenitor of loyalty, for 'Where your treasure is there will your heart be also.'

I can call those Roman veterans happy with full confidence. We know that the girls from the Cádiz region were held to be the most desirable in all Rome's wide dominions. In the evening of the Empire, when its taste was most sophisticated, the fame of the *gaditanas* was such, and their beauty, grace and gaiety, so highly prized, that they used to row them all the way, against the wind, from Cádiz to the Capital, a journey of—what? Three months, at least. Once in Rome these girls were given, we must presume, free ringside seats at the Decline and Fall—they may, indeed, have been a contributory cause of it.

Roman Carteia flourished for six hundred years. Since we know that she had four magistrates, which is twice as many as most provincial towns, we believe she may have had a quarter of a million citizens. Her vestiges stretch across miles of countryside. From my balcony I can see the stub of a pre-Roman defence tower, now deep in sand dunes, and above that, on a hill, lies a sketch of a Greek-style theatre. Recent excavations have traced docks far up the river, a complicated system of water supply, and some spacious villas.

In her heyday Roman Carteia had her own mint. Her coins, which are common enough in this district, carry on one side a woman appropriately fair, and on the other the great tunny fish which fed the town so freely. Blind in one eye they held him to be, for he swims right round the Mediterranean every year in an anti-clockwise circuit, with his good eye on the shore.

Whilst the windswept Rock of Gibraltar harboured only the Iberian guerrilla, the runaway slave, and the evader of Carteian and Roman income tax, our parent city of Carteia may well have welcomed the most significant man of the epoch.

'But now, having no more place in these parts, and having great desire to come unto you, whensoever I take my journey into Spain, I will come unto you.' Yes, it is the voice of St. Paul in an epistle to the Romans, and there is some evidence—tainted a little, like all hagiography, with holy wishfulness—that Paul kept his promise in A.D. 62 or 63.

If he did, it is most likely that he landed in Gibraltar Bay, where Carteia was the westward end of a long chain of Roman cities and settlements. And the first Christian bishop of Spain was St. Hiscus of Carteia.

The city went down with all the other glories of Rome. In A.D. 300, we think, an earthquake threw up a sand bar which ruined its harbour, its economy, and its population. In the year 412 the Vandals and Visigoths found it the weakest of the weak. They galloped down on it from the hills, mad with delight, we may be sure, for this was their journey's end. They sacked and burnt Carteia and left it ruined and empty.

The harbour silted up completely; the people scattered to safer places; the broken stones lay there until thirteen hundred years later, when the Spaniards who left Gibraltar to the British plundered Carteia for stones to build a new town at San Roque nearby. The coins with the fair maid on one side and the foolish tunny on the other are sold at the cross-roads by sharp-eyed little boys. Phoenicians, perhaps, surviving their conquerors? The heirs, maybe, to three thousand years of plunderers.

6

FOOD AND FISHING

Joan, with her servant problem solved, has been studying the markets of Gibraltar, and she has a lot to report about the local laws of supply and demand. The least I can do is listen to it, and I had better, she says, because we shall have to modify our diet.

She has found out that all imported foods cost much more here than they do in Britain or Ireland—freight and handling charges see to that. We may have almost anything we wish to eat—British, French, Spanish, Italian, Danish, Dutch, or even Chinese and Indian—but in general, as we know from previous travels, it is best to turn to the local food products. With food, as with drink, 'Ask what the boys in the backroom are having, and tell them I'm having the same.' It should be both fresher and cheaper that way. What are the local products then? What do the local people eat?

Not meat, Joan says. All meat is imported from overseas, and cold-stored until it is needed, which raises its cost and lowers its quality. Brought up on fresh Irish beef, we are more critical of meat than most people. What about fresh meat from Spain? Well, she has been told, you never quite know with Spain. There is always the chance of some error in the veterinary supervision there. At best, since they do not seem to know the techniques of either cutting it or hanging it, Spanish beef is a tough proposition.

We shall turn our attention to fish, Joan says, which will be good for my brain and her body. The fish market is small in extent but curiously rich in content. She has counted thirty different kinds of fish there this morning, from huge swordfish down to tiny sprats. There were four different members of the lobster family, too, and as many different shellfish, as well as squid and octopus.

No, she could hardly tell what the fish were, exactly, for the good reason that many of them do not occur in northern waters and have therefore no names in English. But there were fish which looked like cod—(groupers, we found out, or jewfish)—and there were small, unfamiliar soles, some sorts of hake and whiting, various spiney rockfish, a big mackerel—(*bonito*)—several kinds of sardines, large and small, and three or four species of sea bream, one of them bright red. There were red and grey mullet as well—the former she recognized as the highly prized *rouget* of France. Joan had also seen several 'Wonders of the Deep', as she called them, gruesome creatures, all head and no body, which I took to be some species of angler fish. A woman told her that they were full of brains and fine for making fish soup.

Joan suggested that we should work through this miraculous draught of fishes until we found our favourites. While she considered its practical possibilities, I speculated on an explanation for it.

The Straits of Gibraltar form a narrow highway for fish migration, which concentrates them for easy cropping. Also, the currents there carry a concentrated food supply. The resident and migrant fish populations are both very high.

There is a constant inward current from the Atlantic, running near the surface, and a corresponding outward current down in the depths, a result of higher evaporation and consequent higher density in the inland sea. The effect of this strange condition is that our fish can have it both ways. If they feed high in the water, they have here the Atlantic plankton and nekton funnelled in to them. Should they be bottom feeders, all the heavy refuse of the Western Mediterranean trundles past their snouts. Sea-anglers from Gibraltar, fishing the deep waters of The Straits for sport, measure their catch in hundredweights. Spanish boats from Algeciras and Estepona, fishing the surface for sardines, load themselves to the gunwale every night that weather allows.

Fishing is a popular pastime on The Rock which, as a great pier thrust out into deep water, seems to invite it. But the shorebound fishermen catch very little—as I learnt at high cost of time and temper. After months of misdirected effort, I was reliably informed that the countless depth charges used for harbour defence during the war had broken up the inshore feeding-grounds and littered the bottom with unpalatable scrap metal. After hearing this sensible piece of information I often wondered if the local addicts knew as much as I did, and if I ought to tell them. I decided against it. If they did know, it would not stop their fishing. The true angler is more hooked than any fish, and will carry on regardless of results. Some of those grave and earnest men who fish the Seine in Paris have not had a bite for half a century. You never know. . . .

A fishing-boat from Gibraltar could turn east or west, according to weather or technique, and take a haul of fish from either sea. Sad to say, there are no professional fishing-boats here now, for Gibraltar can provide better wages for less arduous work. There is only one dogged survivor of the craft, the poet-fisherman Alberto Pizzarello of Catalan Bay on the eastern face.

Gibraltar's fishing is done for her, while she makes her fortune in shopkeeping, by hardy Spaniards from Algeciras. They bring the Fat Rock the best of their catch and charge it their best prices. When the wind blows strongly from the east the Spaniards bring their heavy boats in under the lee of The Rock and sweep for sardines all through the night. They use big carbide-lamps to lure the fish to the nets and, either by tradition or for some practical purpose, they greet the rising net with a cacaphony of shouts and screams, alarming to newcomers but a friendly sound to me.

In the small hours, when everything else was dark and silent, I used to look down from my balcony on their scatter of bright lights far away below. I used to strain my ears to catch a word, to sift some meaning out of the fishermen's strange, urgent chorus, but all I ever made of it was a note of violence and a dash of ribaldry—neither far to seek in Spain. Could it be that their purpose was to scare the sharks away as the net surfaced? Maybe, but there are few sharks here. Perhaps the reason is too ancient to seek. Later, I was to troll for tunny in the Pacific in Polynesian canoes, and catch them to the tune of a certain strange and obligatory chant.

*   *   *   *

But Joan has got on with the job—hers the practice, mine the theory. She has studied the fruit and vegetable markets. We are to eat all the fine vegetables of southern Spain, and far ahead of their seasons as we know them. As for fruit, we may have strawberries in March, cherries in April, peaches in June, melons and grapes all through the summer, and oranges and lemons, with their green leaves attached, all the year round. We are to eat them when we see them, Joan says, for the Spaniards have no idea about spinning a crop out to make early or late prices. For two and a half months the melons will glut the stalls and overflow into piles in the street, at give-away prices. Before and after that short season there is not a melon to be had at any price. It's the same with all the fruits, she says. You gorge on the glut and then go without. In Spain it's always either a feast or a famine.

The potatoes, she says, are insipid by our Irish standards, so we shall eat less of them. More at home in this climate are the artichokes, pumpkins, aubergines and peppers, and this delights us because they were all in the luxury class in Ireland.

The bread is a disappointment. Joan has tried it all, and finds it standardized to a shiny, white, bubbly substance, as artificial as foamed cellulose. It seems that the bakers have got together. . . . The bread in nearby Spain is yellow and solid, but at least it tastes of bread. The Gibraltarians import it personally every time they get a chance, and *pan de Pelayo*, called after the best of the nearby bread villages, has come to be used as a general commendation.

We are not, however, to bring milk or cheese in from Spain. The young, curdy cheese causes an outbreak of Malta fever almost every year, and the milk is not trustworthy. We are to drink a good reconstituted milk or make do with condensed. Most Gibraltar babies are fed on British powdered milk and thrive perfectly well on it. There is not a cow on The Rock, she says. But excuse me, I have better information.

There is one cow on The Rock, well hidden away, which Joan has not discovered. It belongs to His Excellency the Governor, and it is an old and cherished privilege. Cattle, all kinds, are banned by law, for sound practical reasons—no grazing land, the water problem, the risk to health. But the Governor's cow is a relic of the days when that personage could do whatsoever he wished, law or no law. Latter-day governors, benign and well behaved, retain the cow and a few other old privileges for tradition's sake, and few people object to this.

But there was an old lady, I remember, who smuggled a kid in from Spain and took it to her house on the outskirts of the town, high up on the mountainside. She fed it until it was big enough to graze, and then tethered it out on the slopes—the only goat in Gibraltar.

Some jealous neighbour reported it to the police: 'Why should she have a goat when we're not allowed?'

The police told the old lady to take the goat back to Spain. The old lady defied them. They summoned her to court. There, in Spanish, she took a traditional British stand. She would get rid of her goat, she said, the day the Governor got rid of his cow. She drove it home by saying that the Governor could afford to buy milk, which was more than she could do. She knew her rights as British subject, she said, and added that if there was any more persecution Winston Churchill would hear of it.

This delighted the populace and embarrassed the bench and the Government. What would happen next? everyone was asking. Flogged to death in the public square? Skinned alive, and her pelt nailed to the Water Gate? Earlier Governors had taken such revenge. . . .

Nothing happened. The old lady was bound over to keep the peace. The goat, providentially, died. It ate Sodom Apples, they said, one of the very few plants which can kill a goat. No one suggested that His Excellency put them there, and I am not suggesting it now.

The home food of the Gibraltarians varies as widely as their income groups. No doubt the millionaires eat as they wish, but more interesting and typical is the diet of the working-class family, the majority of the population.

Dire primary poverty has been banished from The Rock, thanks to the pressures of local trade unions and to the development of a world climate of opinion. But the habit of strict domestic economy lingers. Well-to-do people will sit in the cold and even, in my experience, in the dark, to avoid an onerous bill at the end of the month—an inheritance of hard times, this. It may be more than a habit, because there is a strong element of secondary—self-imposed—poverty. Social emulation victimizes the people terribly—more strongly than in Britain or in the United States. The reason for this is that everyone knows everyone else, and that so much of life is social and public. To keep up with the Fulanos, with a car and a television set, the Gibraltar housewife must fight a constant battle at the market stall and kitchen stove.

She rations eggs, meat and butter, the dearest commodities, and turns to vegetables and fish. From the many varieties of fish she must choose the cheapest—not always the best value. She may buy a steak of swordfish, but more often she buys the ever-abundant squid, stuffs it with bread and sage, and boils it in sauce. She buys sardines and other small fry, chops them up, and fries them with onion and tomatoes. She may buy a sea bream and braise it with bay leaves, or a slab of hard, salt cod which calls for protracted boiling with all available spices and ends up as a food fit for heroes. She buys shellfish for her soups and *paella*, and small portions of chicken and rabbit.

Cuts of meat are too dear for most people—including us. The Gibraltarians fall back on the hot, hard, Spanish sausages, a little of which goes a very long way. They are connoisseurs of these sausages, in fact, and since they cannot make them—there are no pigs on The Rock—and cannot live without them, they are at the mercy of Spain for their supply.

There is a local delicacy called *callos* which is typical of all peasant dishes—cheap in ingredients, careful in preparation, piquant and plenteous. It is nothing more than chopped-up cows' tripe stewed and smothered in chickpeas and paprika sauce, tinctured with a delicate blend of herbs. In Gibraltar this is considered to be a gala dish and is served on festive occasions.

Almost everything is cooked in oil in Gibraltar, as in Spain. Good olive oil has been priced into the luxury class. The second grades, or the vegetable oils used instead, are inoffensive provided that they are not used too often, but they make no contribution to flavour. Since all cooking-oil is dear, the tendency is to use it too often. The typical smell of the residential streets of Gibraltar, as of neighbouring Spain, is a mixture of sour oil, boiling squid or codfish and burnt soap from the constant ironing process. It sounds distasteful, but it is an aroma which one learns to love.

The first cookery classes for Gibraltar girls started a few years ago. The few who were bold enough to cut the apron strings and learn at the alien stove may soon be challenging the immovable Latin matriarchs with their old iron *paella* pans, their Spanish sausages and slabs of sundried codfish. If there is a kitchen revolution it will be a happy day for Gibraltar and her now vital tourist trade.

7

ROCK APES

Carteia is quiet at last. The restless Visigoths have climbed The Rock, built a little temple on it to propitiate their god, to thank him at the end of their marathon of conquest, and then ridden off westwards towards the wide pastures of the Laguna de la Janda and Guadalquivir valley. The Rock is to have three more centuries of peace before it becomes the noisiest and most embattled place in the world. This interlude suggests a glance at its first—and, at this time, its only—inhabitants, the famous apes.

Our apes are famous because they are the only indigenous simians surviving in Europe. They are not anthropoid apes, but large monkeys of the species *macacus inuus*, whose lazy habits seem to have worn away their tails. There was a time of simpler zoology when a book was judged by its cover and the mere absence of a tail could qualify a monkey for promotion to the higher order.

The apes are the first goal of every visitor, for their fame has spread far and wide. Even the distant Finns come here to see them. In Britain, of course, they are a household word. Such is their news value that the people of Gibraltar, relegated by the newspapers to second place, regard the apes with a whimsical envy. 'I am going up the mountain on Sunday,' Maurice Carvillo said to me, 'to show my children to the blasted apes!'

Every effort has been made to show that the apes are a recent importation. The cave earth so far sifted has yielded no bones or teeth of simians, although there is ample evidence of bear, wolf, cat and hyena. Another suspicious circumstance is the presence of identical apes playing on Mont Abyla, just across The Straits. Perhaps there is a secret tunnel right across to Africa?

Dead apes are not often found on The Rock, and a pretty legend has arisen to the effect that they carry their dead comrades under the sea to lay them to rest in the old homeland. But I shall show how unburdened the apes are with brotherly love. Besides, dead apes, the victims of fratricide, are occasionally found; more often, the ravens find them first and scatter their bones over the hillside. Geology discounts the tunnel, for there is a great geological fault running through The Straits, and the Gibraltar limestone does not extend to Africa. Further, these apes abhor a tunnel or a cave, and cannot be driven into such a place—which is what one would expect of them.

Apes, like ourselves, are almost entirely dependent on their eyesight. Not a leaf falls but they see it before it hits the ground. Their sense of smell, on the other hand, must be relatively undeveloped. Like us, they have scanty olfactory apparatus. You can see them investigating small objects by lifting them right up to their nostrils. Naturally, then, they hate and fear darkness, for it makes them blind and helpless. Disturbed at night, if only by the calls of migrating birds, our apes set up a screaming chorus of fear. We have hopes and fears, they have fears only, to govern their behaviour. To enter a cave would be to put themselves into the claws of the predators which, immemorially, lurked in the inner darkness. So much for the tunnel theory.

Could the apes have drifted from Africa on chance tree trunks? Perhaps, but no one has ever seen such a thing happening anywhere—and there is a strong current in The Straits. Could they have been brought by the Romans, or the Moors? They could, but it is not on record.

The Visigoths were not chroniclers, so we do not know whether they found apes on Gibraltar or not. Also, they took little or no interest in Gibraltar. The Romans never mentioned apes, but then the Romans did not necessarily explore The Rock, which was right off-shore in their time and probably more awkward of access than it is today. They had no practical use for the place, and built little or nothing on it. The Moors, so far as I know, left no record of the apes. But, coming as they did from ape country, they may not have regarded them as worthy of mention. Their chronicles, so far as I know them, were highfalutin, never observant or intimate; apes may well have been beneath the notice of their aristocratic scribes.

The latest and, for me, the best theory is that of Mr. F. E. Zeuner, who essayed to prove (in the scientific journal *Oryx*) that the Gibraltar apes are ancient and true Europeans. Ten million years ago, he says, the ancient race of Macaques, to which our apes belong, roamed France, Holland and Germany. In the Great Interglacial, one hundred and fifty thousand years ago, they sported in the valley of the Thames. The next onset of ice would have driven the mainland apes southwards. It would have driven man southwards, too—man the hunter, later the tree-feller, herdsman, and cultivator, in all his stages of development a deadly enemy and rival to the apes, as he is in Africa to this day. Gibraltar would offer a last refuge to the apes at the end of their age-long retreat. Only in the extreme south of Europe does the treeline conquer the mountain tops—offering food and safety in one and the same place. Up there the apes could feed and breed and survive unenvied, remaining, by this last perilous foothold, our fellow-Europeans.

Mr. Zeuner is definite in blaming deforestation and cultivation for the southward retreat of the apes. The mean temperature of the Interglacial was not much lower than that of today, and apes have been proved hardy enough to live in northern countries. As food-collectors (unlike cultivators and carnivores), they needed extensive feeding-grounds. The feeding-grounds must be rich enough to provide an abundant and varied diet without the necessity of ranging too far and too fast. If the collection process uses up more energy than the intake provides, then the collector and his species must waste away.

Our apes, feeding patiently and painstakingly on the wooded slopes of Gibraltar, exhaust all possible sources of food in one spot before they move on to the next. This is the common sense—to them, the common instinct—of conservation of energy. I have spent hours watching this basic process of food collection.

A female ape with a baby at breast, and therefore all the more incentive for strict domestic economy, sits quietly at the foot of a pine tree, picking the bark off, flake by flake. She finds woodlice, and eats them one by one. When she has finished them, and without moving her seat, she begins to turn over the stones and to scratch in the pine needles in front of her. She disturbs ants, and snaps them up as they appear. Now, still without shifting, she nibbles some lichen on the bole of the tree, tastes some minute toadstools, nips the tops off nearby weeds, and finally dissects a pine cone and eats the seeds. Only then, after a last grudging survey of the spot, does she move to the next tree and begin again. This is true subsistence living, and calls for constant work throughout almost all daylight hours. If the population rises or the territory shrinks, the weakest will go to the wall and either starve or—more likely—migrate.

These were the inescapable economic facts which must have driven our ancestors from food-collecting to husbandry—the only alternative to death or migration. Husbandry would incur the need to defend territory, raising its value with the fixed assets of crops and fences and beasts. Hence the stick and stone developed into the bow and arrow and the sling.

The apes of Europe, man's minor rivals in the primeval food forests, could not meet the challenge. The more they bred and spread, the more food land they needed; meanwhile man, the enemy, bred and spread and claimed and cleared and defended the land. The apes began a long and slow retreat.

There was only one possible line of retreat—to the south. Where there is less frost, the fruits and insects are bigger and more numerous. The farther south, in our hemisphere and latitudes, the more calories per acre for the simple food-gatherer. Andalucia, of which Gibraltar forms the southern tip, is one of the best places in the world for easy living. For this reason half the gypsies of Europe are concentrated there, enough to dominate the culture and folklore of the whole vast region. In his *La Teoria de Andalucia* Ortega y Gasset says that the people do not believe in struggling to live, but rather in living by not struggling and, thanks to the blessed sun, they have got away with it for centuries. This is true food-collectors' country.

But it would not be as rich as the primeval jungle, so the apes continued to decline. At last, of all the great continent which they once roamed, from the Danube to the Tiber, Gibraltar was their only foothold. And here, in 1704, the conquering British found them.

The apes of Gibraltar are not oppressed by their racial tragedy nor by their position as the sole survivors of it. They have sad, hell-haunted faces, like all simians, but that is only skin-deep. They appear to take all life for granted, gratify themselves without gratitude, and react pitilessly and savagely to the first suspicion of opposition.

Captain J. Fitzgerald, M.B.E., R.A., relinquished his charge of the apes in 1947, and left a simple and outspoken chronicle of his four years of stewardship. He was a big enough man to love them even after he had learnt of the horrors of their lives. He describes how a young female called Pat was, for the good of the race, enclosed in a *mariage de convenance* with an old male who had once been called Adonis, but by this time was known as Scruffy. 'Next morning,' Fitzgerald writes, 'Scruffy had both arms torn from wrist to elbow, a wound in the centre of his back which exposed his spine for four and a half inches, and his testicles badly torn.' Such is the militant chastity of the she-ape—when it suits her. That bite on the spine seems to be the usual aim and not infrequent end of fights between the apes. Successfully administered, it paralyses the legs, and the vanquished dies in slow misery. Captain Fitzgerald and his successors have treated and saved many such victims.

The male apes mature at five years, weigh two or three stones, and are furnished with long fangs. Some of them live for twenty years, but most of them are not so lucky—or so strong. The circumstances of their lives are rawly Freudian, a sardonic comment on the pastoral idyll which a feeding pack presents. A fat and cruel king covers all the females in his pack, while the young bucks skirmish on the outskirts and wait for him to weaken himself down to murderable level. Meanwhile, according to Fitzgerald, even a female dog is not immune from their attentions.

Female apes are nubile at four, give birth once a year, go barren at nine, have short fangs, and never live to a great age. The implications of this statement are not endearing. What added strength for survival did primitive man gain by his establishment of matriarchy, one wonders . . . by cherishing, as his cave drawings and figurines prove, the fruitful, female principle?

On the other hand, how much impetus did matricide and fratricide add to the decline of the apes? How soon did man establish the family system and put those deadly instincts under control? An ape has no greater enemy than an ape. Fitzgerald describes how the idle males and barren crones, all frustrated and vicious, will surround a mother in labour, snatch her newborn apelet, and run about with it until it dies in their black hands from abuse or neglect. The poor mother, weakened by the birth and afraid to attack in case the baby suffers worse injury, follows the kidnappers in helpless distress. The infant is snatched from hand to hand, fought over and mauled. When it dies, they lose all interest, and toss it aside. The mother picks up the little corpse, cleans it, and carries it happily, day after day, sucking her own teats to drain off the surplus milk, and waiting for the baby to awaken. It takes human intervention to part her from it.

Dogs, horses and elephants are demonstrably grateful, and Androcles is said to have found some appreciation even in a hungry lion. But the apes are thankless to the point of perversity.

Captain Fitzgerald went to endless trouble to gain their confidence and friendship. He talked to them incessantly to familiarize them with his voice; he wore the same clothes on every visit to them; he studied all their wishes and ways, trying to please them, to keep the peace among them, to make them happy. His reward was endless suspicion and skirmish and half a dozen major attacks on his person, all of them unprovoked.

But he met attack in soldierly fashion, and advises his successors to do the same: 'Place your back against a wall so that the attack must come from in front. Keep your eye on the leader or the biggest male, and await the attack. Wait until one is within distance, and then kick *really hard*.' Then he adds in a kindly footnote: 'I have made it a practice after a skirmish with the apes to go back after thirty minutes and feed them. It is good for morale on both sides.'

Up to 1931 the Rock Apes were independent and unapproachable. The roads on the Upper Rock were then mere mule tracks, the fore-runners of the good motor roads up there today. The apes were shy, conditioned to extreme caution, I suppose, by the exigencies of sur-vival. They took refuge from the busy British on a shelf on the sheer eastern precipice. The place, still called 'The Monkeys' Alameda', is deserted now, save for ravens and peregrines, and all the apes are on the western slopes enjoying the sunshine.

It is a curious fact that the apes have declined in numbers with any decline of British fortunes in war. For instance, 1913 was a year of war clouds for us and of disaster for the Rock Apes. In 1910 there had been two hundred of them—far too many to consort in comfort in one feeding area. The leaders conferred, it seems, like Cain and Abel, and agreed to split up into two packs, each with its own territory. Familiar tragedy ensued—territorial disputes, rapine raids, fratricidal strife and, ultimately, genocide. The slaughter was almost complete and in 1913 there were only three female apes left on The Rock—which is to say, in all Europe—to carry on the race!

At this point the Colonial Government stepped in and granted a small fund for feeding the apes or, rather, for supplementing their natural food. The Royal Regiment of Artillery, traditional guardians of the Upper Rock, undertook to supervise them. The stock soon began to build up again through the incestuous union of mothers and sons. The policy of feeding had two aims. Firstly, by better and surer diet, to increase and improve the stock. Secondly—and more impor-tant—by allaying hunger and envy, and by giving each pack a fixed feeding base, they might be kept apart and peaceful. But, alas, the warlike tradition dies very hard! Old sores and old scores linger. The apes continued to compete and raid, and by 1924 there were only four survivors.

Why should murder suddenly stop at this date, as it did? Perhaps all the warriors had killed each other, like the cats of Kilkenny. Perhaps some obscure instinct called a halt at the point of racial annihilation. Or it may be that only a happy family remained. Whatever the reason, the four surviving apes reformed, bred happily and well, and in a few years had multiplied their numbers to twenty-seven.

But since all the breeding females save three must have been daughters of one father, and bred to him, it does not surprise me that the numbers were down to ten again in 1931. Nor is it strange that in that year and the year following the females all refused—or failed—to breed.

In the 1931 emergency Sir Alexander Godley, then Governor, took a hand. He had two young apes imported from Morocco, and—after a prudent pause to lessen the shock of invasion—five more. They were of the same species, *macacus inuus*, and they arrested the decline, but the apes still failed to multiply as expected.

There were many stillbirths at this time, which Captain Fitzgerald attributes to inbreeding, but which I suggest may have been the result of maladjustment of the two bloodstreams. There were infantile deaths due to hysteria in teething. There were pneumonia and fever, largely untreated in those days. But the greatest of all wastage in the ape packs was, as ever, by mayhem and murder. At the outbreak of World War II there were only eleven apes left to face the enemy, and by 1943 they were down to seven.

An old legend says that when the apes leave The Rock the British will follow, and the story had enough poetic probability to impress Sir Winston Churchill in the midst of his labours. When he heard, in 1943, that there were only seven apes remaining, he had seven more hurriedly imported from Africa. Sir Winston, one feels, has always been a pre-eminently lucky man, and these were certainly lucky apes. They turned the tide of war—theirs and ours.

There are two strong ape packs in Gibraltar today, one at Middle Hill and the other, more accessible and better known, at Queen's Gate. They are fed promptly and equitably at 9 a.m. and 4 p.m., each pack in its own place, so that each has a terrain and a routine, and supervision and control are made easy. They will eat almost any kind of fruit and vegetable to supplement their wild olives, locust beans, green figs and insects, but loquats make them vomit, strange to say, and given melons they will only eat the seeds. They ignore meat and fish, but the good Captain Fitzgerald, no doubt remembering many a bite, says darkly: '. . . if left hungry for long periods they might turn to meat, with dire results.'

The ape packs seem to have learned, at long last, to leave each other severely alone. Not long ago, their guardians courted trouble by forcibly exchanging two females, for reasons of eugenics. Each of them, in spite of pressure from her new lord, slipped back quietly to her own pack, and no reprisals followed. May we, who shared the sieges with them, begin to act as wisely.

Captain Fitzgerald gives a final warning which, I think, deserves wide publicity. Do not touch the apes, he says—and who should know better? Trust neither big nor little. They are all on one side—against you—in a split second, if they see fit. Do not even feed these apes, for it brings them too close to you, and it sets one against another. Also, it interrupts their natural behaviour, so that they lose any grace they had.

It is perfectly safe, and very rewarding, to stand still and watch the apes in their natural habitat, without a word or a movement to claim their attention. They will watch you for a few minutes, and then turn from you with disdain. Silently, the sentinels will post themselves, each in his appointed place, and squat there, quick eyes flickering under lowering brows. The mothers will sling their babies on their backs and amble off, searching the ground intimately for insects. The young males will resume their mock battles, sparring practice for their take-over bids. The king stalks through his harem, indifferently, baring his fangs in the direction of the skirmishing braves. . . .

Here before you is a tribe of food-collectors, absorbed in its ancient, patient struggle to survive, the last tiny handful of its kind on the whole continent of Europe. The sight used to strike some lost chord in my memory and hold me there, spellbound, while the evening light faded away and the Rock Apes straggled homewards, retreating before their oldest enemy, the night.

8

ROCK BIRD

Even more interesting than the apes, to my mind, is the indisputably natural phenomenon of Gibraltar's unique bird. The Barbary Partridge, scientifically *Alectoris Barbara*, is unique to this extent, that The Rock is its only breeding place and residence on the mainland of Europe. It breeds on the island of Sardinia, too, far out in the Mediterranean Sea, but that is only politically European and birds are not impressed by politics.

Like all the partridges, this is a beautiful bird. It is gallinaceous, which means that it is related to our domestic fowl. As you would expect from this relationship, it is gregarious, vegetarian, strong-legged, short-winged, proud, strong and noisy, and it prefers walking to flying. Cock partridges crow in a series of short barks, once heard never forgotten, and the hens answer with appropriately modest clucking. They nest on the ground, hatching up to a dozen chicks in full fluff, perfectly camouflaged and highly competent, ready-trained to lie still at a cluck of command. A hen partridge hurrying across a road with her brood strung out behind her is one of the prettiest sights a man can see.

Gibraltar's special partridge is the same size and shape as the species called Red-legged, which is commonly resident throughout Spain, France and the south of England, and which also breeds on The Rock. The difference lies in the configuration of the feathers. The Barbary Partridge is predominantly a delicate blue-beige; the Red-legged is tawny. The Barbary has blue cheeks trimmed by a necklace of bright reddish brown, polka-dotted in white; the Red-legged has creamy cheeks trimmed by a strong black band. There is no confusing the two birds, unless they are distant, and there is no denying the fact that they are separate species.

The question remains, why is Gibraltar so attractive to partridges that even this African species had made its home here? To answer it, I have had to make some study on the ground of the way of life, the vital economy of partridges.

Like all running birds, partridges are shy. Like all birds which nest on the ground, they seek solitude. The Upper Rock, where they breed and stay, is above the highest easy motor road. It is too steep to attract pedestrians, and it is unenvied by the apes which have better feeding lower down in the thickets of carob and wild olive. Up to recent years the heights of Gibraltar were scheduled as a military area, and out of bounds to all civilians unless they had a special pass to go there for a specific purpose. Restrictions have been raised, but few people go up there except at one or two noted viewpoints. The temperature of Gibraltar, especially in the summer season, does not invite strenuous climbing. Thus the birds have found their solitude.

They have some other advantages which they would not find in neighbouring Spain. There is little or no shooting—I mean shooting for sport—in Gibraltar. It is strictly limited by law, and the birds have full legal protection. The place is too small for successful poaching—people talk and the police get to know. The Gibraltar police, by the way, are on familiar and friendly terms with the whole population, which may account for the fact that the community is comparatively free from crime. As a further advantage for the partridges, there are no goats or sheep on The Rock; it is against the law to keep them there. In Spain, the swarming goats must ruin many a nest. But there must be, I considered, some positive attraction, as well as the negative ones of solitude and peace, to bring these birds so far from home.

I found a clue in the name 'Barbary'. Over there, across The Straits, on the Barbary Shore, the solitude is semi-desert, and in such country our bird abounds. Gibraltar has one thing in common with such country—an extreme shortage of water. On the face of it, The Rock has no water for birds for four or five months in a year, and those months cover the breeding season. The rain, should any chance to fall, runs off in a few minutes, down the steep hard surface, or into the eroded fissures and bed planes of the limestone, to caverns known and unknown, through the tortuous bowels of The Rock, and soon to the sea.

As for standing water, the puddles dry rapidly when the sun comes out, and every reservoir and tank is covered in, by law, because of mosquito control.

'What do the birds do for a drink?' I asked, soon after I arrived.

'The same as us,' they told me. 'They go to Spain!'

It is an old joke, because drink is untaxed and cheaper in Spain and many Gibraltarians go there in the evening in normal times to enjoy it. But it is no joke for the birds, I thought, and no joke for Gibraltar if they all deserted us. Perhaps we should be putting out water for them, as we do for the apes. . . . But do birds need much water? I think not. Only occasionally does one seen them take a few troublesome sips, throwing their heads back and gargling each one, like a tourist with his first vodka. They do not seem to have the mechanism for imbibing much, so I presume that thirst does not trouble them often. I can think of two reasons for this. One is that they do not sweat; their skin temperature is thermostatically controlled by their complicated coats of feathers and underlying down. The other reason is that they find sufficient moisture in their food. Nestlings never receive a drink until they leave the nest; seed-eating birds, such as finches, feed their helpless young on insects so that they swallow the juices with the meat. Partridges, as one can tell by their droppings, eat berries as well as seeds, enough berries, perhaps, to slake their thirst.

But even if the berries did not provide sufficient moisture, there are secret supplies of water on the Upper Rock of Gibraltar—even at the driest season of the year when the young birds are growing.

*   *   *   *

Now is the time to describe Gibraltar's strangest environmental factor, the phenomenon of the east wind there called the Levanter. Since it influences human life on The Rock, as well as making possible the life of the Barbary Partridge, it is well worth a little study.

The spine of Gibraltar runs due north–south. The eastern or Mediterranean face of the mountain is almost vertical; the western or Atlantic face slopes at forty-five degrees. The winds which strike the mountain in a typical year impinge as follows:

East wind —	150 days
West wind —	60 days
North-west wind —	70 days
South-west wind —	43 days
North wind —	1 day
South wind —	1 day

These figures, the average of ten years, tell a curious tale. It is not only that the prevailing wind is from the east, but that it is *due* east. There are, as a rule, only twenty-seven days in the year when the wind has any easting, besides the one hundred and fifty days, almost one day in two, when it is straight from the east, and striking The Rock at right angles.

This east wind can blow at any season, but it is most noticeable in the hot summer months, for it is then that it forces itself upon Gibraltar's attention. Since the town, with the vast majority of the population, is on the western face, nestling in the lee of the prevailing wind, you may wonder how it is troubled. The explanation is simple.

From June until September that east wind is blowing across a thousand miles of simmering sea and collecting humidity as it comes. The moisture content is, in the nature of things, heaviest at the lowest levels, just above the surface of the sea; it is, of course, invisible. Suddenly this strong wind strikes the steep eastern face of Gibraltar. Immediately, it soars up to fourteen hundred feet, to pass the obstacle. At that height, it cools rapidly and its moisture condenses into visible vapour—into dense white cloud, in fact. Trails of this vapour stream out from the high escarpment, westwards over the town, over the Bay, even over Algeciras, miles away, and the hills beyond. But the cloud ceiling is thickest where it starts, right over the western face of The Rock. It obscures the sun, raises the humidity to an uncomfortable degree, dims and dampens the town and the ardour and enterprise of everyone in it. It is, inevitably, hot weather—too hot—when this added plague arrives, and now it is hot and humid and without even the benefit of brightness.

Further, west Gibraltar is now windless. The wind is high overhead, and underneath it there is a perfect air pocket, still and stuffy. Flags at each end of The Rock now blow tiredly towards each other, and the sea is flattened as the wind rolls over us and down upon it with broad, battering fists. Ships move out, for this freak tail-draught could blow them inshore as readily as offshore. Fishing ceases. Men groan and grumble and sweat and carry on their work as best they can; but in times of Levanter, more even than usually, all errors are excused.

Meanwhile, on the western heights where the partridges live every bush is spangled with dewdrops, and the birds may drink their fill. No need now to sip and stretch and swallow; I have seen the happy birds standing under a bush, raising their pretty heads to selected drops, and letting them run straight down their throats. July and August are the months when the young birds are fast growing to maturity, and most in need of food and drink; and those are the months, the peak months, of the dreaded Levanter. I must here insert the old saw: 'It's an ill wind that blows nobody any good.'

When, partly by observation, partly by deduction, I had pieced together this strange set of circumstances, I reached for the atlas to scan Sardinia, the only other outpost of our partridge. I was glad to confirm that it too has a north–south spine, a steep flank presented to the damp east wind, a high escarpment to condense it, and dampen the western slopes where the partridges live in the same condition as they do on The Rock.

It is always the western slope, an old Spanish hunter told me. In Spain, where there are unlimited slopes to choose from, these birds always breed and sleep on the one which faces west. There he goes, with a little lamp, and lifts them with his hands, for they will not run in the dark, and takes them down to feed the village. No, it is not just to shelter from the wind, he says, but that the sun's warmth lingers there, the ground is warmer at sunset, and it stays warm through the night. A southern slope cools throughout the evening.

There is another reason, too. The day lasts longer on the western slope and for the birds this is of vital importance. Fledglings, faced with the great endurance tests of autumn migration, must grow fast to strength and maturity. To do so, they must feed constantly throughout all possible hours—and that means daylight hours. The longer those hours are, the better. It is for this reason that many birds fly north to breed, leaving lands richer in insects for those where there may be less food but a longer day. Do my partridges cross to the eastern face, then, to catch the morning light? They may do so, but I am not sure. Perhaps they do not need to, for the dawn at Gibraltar lights up the whole heavens suddenly, long before the sun rises; the death of the day is far more lingering.

Thus, I found, Gibraltar had invited this foreign bird and become its adopted country. Here this unthirsty partridge from the deserts of Morocco finds just enough moisture, while the dryness drives rival species away into Spain. Here it finds peace, and hatches its eggs and raises its brood undisturbed by man or beast. Here on this high, hot grandstand, facing the setting sun the Barbary Partridge pursues its private policy of peaceful colonization and struts its cloudy kingdom, crowing at the dawn.

'*El beso que Londres ha enviado a su colonia*,' said Blasco Ibañez, sitting on the waterfront of Algeciras, across the Bay, looking sourly across at The Rock of Gibraltar under its crown of clouds. 'The kiss which London has blown to her colony'—London of the fogs, a sad city to the Spanish way of thinking.

There is no doubt that this Levanter is the bane of the place, the only flaw in its otherwise perfect climate. In fact, the word flaw scarcely covers it, for Levanter conditions inflict themselves upon Gibraltar for at least a third of the year.

Ibañez had in mind, too, and in eye, that it seems to be a special curse. You have only to cross the isthmus to La Línea, the nearest point in Spain, to leave the grim cloud behind you and enjoy the dry, bright sunshine of Andalusia. The cloud rarely reaches Algeciras, three miles westward. Málaga and the towns of the Costa del Sol, to eastwards of Gibraltar, have a different and a better climate.

'But for this accursed Levanter,' they told me, 'we would live in paradise. But there is nothing to be done about it.'

Year after year it spoiled the summer for us. We could feel it when we wakened, before we opened our eyes. Researches on climatology and comfort, conducted at Singapore, established relationships between temperature, humidity and moving air, and showed that the last factor can save a man's health and strength, not to speak of his efficiency which is the first thing to forsake him. In Gibraltar our maximum heat coincided exactly and inevitably with our maximum humidity during the onslaught of the Levanter and, furthermore, afflicted us in the windless vacuum of the air pocket. Throughout a Levanter day—or week—work slackened, tempers frayed, appetites waned, children misbehaved, drunkards drank more, the violent revolted, friends fell out and enemies augmented their hatred. The effects on sexual relations, the basis of well-being in Latin communities at least, one could only guess.

Could anything be done about it, I pondered, now that we are making rain fall in Kenya? Could we, at any cost, control this hateful visitation, with all its hidden and insidious loss? At last, I think, I found a way.

You will have seen those small windmills whose sails turn a dynamo and produce a small output of electric power? A brilliant idea, it seems, power for nothing, the poor man's friend, removing one of the drawbacks of isolation, saving miles of expensive cable, enabling men to live where they wish. But the windcharger has its disadvantages. One of them is that the wind bloweth where it listeth, and may not blow at all. Another is that to use all the wind that blows, when it blows, you must store the output. You must buy and tend a large number of costly and troublesome wet batteries. Because of these things the windcharger has never come into extensive use, and is regarded, in places where electricity is otherwise out of the question, as a little better than nothing.

But say you had a place where the wind blew at a steady ten knots, or more, from a fixed direction, for one day out of two? And say you had an unobstructible ridge, fourteen hundred feet above sea-level, bare and useless and rent-free, where you could erect windchargers of such a size and as close together as you wished?

The basis of my scheme was to use the tremendous energy of the east wind sweeping over the spine of The Rock, by an unbroken line of large windchargers. I would link each charger, as directly as possible, to a simple resistance—a thermal radiator. The radiators, properly protected against the damp by convecting hoods, would lie in a line all along the ridge and just below it, on the western side.

When the Levanter blew the windmills would turn, the radiators would glow, the heat would rise, and the moisture would not condense into vapour. The stronger the wind blew, the faster would the sails turn, the greater the temperature of the radiators, and the stronger the upthrust of hot air. When the wind dropped the mills would fall idle, the heat would die, and the whole system would lie there in wait for the next onslaught. Simply, I would use the Levanter to destroy its own effects.

But the cloud might condense farther west, perhaps, and blow London's kiss to Algeciras? I think not, since it is the sudden cooling which forms the cloud. A more gradual cooling, with the hot sun above to temper the effects of the height, cannot have the same effect. As one can see on any Levanter day, the clouds rarely reach as far as Algeciras; as they attenuate the sun warms them up and the vapour disappears again. The critical point, the point of touch-off, is the ridge of The Rock, and to deal with it there, is to nip it in the bud.

My scheme required no fuel, no supervision, no maintenance, nothing but the initial cost. I would have started it cautiously, in case there is some force of nature of which none of us know. I would have installed a dozen or so of my machines along a length of the spine, and studied their effect in comparison to the untreated neighbouring areas. I have discussed it frequently with electrical engineers —which I do not claim to be—and not one of them has ever suggested a serious snag. There are calculations to be made, special plant to be designed and manufactured, estimates to be prepared, funds to be found. But public funds lead to taxes, and that last is the worst word a man can utter in Gibraltar. God's climate asked for my scheme, but the official and political climates did not. In the British Civil Service 'Nothing must ever be done for the first time'—especially anything creative or imaginative put forward by the boffin and the backroom boy.

Gibraltar still swelters under her Levanter, and probably will always do so. My provisional patent for Levanter Dispersal still lies dusty in my drawer.

9

ROCK SCORPIONS

'Rock scorpions', the soldiers called the denizens of Gibraltar, whether in contempt or in grudging admiration I cannot tell. The scorpion is tough and thrifty, and defends himself with courage until he dies. On the other hand, he is treacherous and venomous.

The expression is no longer used. The soldiers and civilians on The Rock are close friends and there is much social and sporting interplay and some intermarriage. Occasionally I hear my Gibraltarian friends resurrect the epithet and use it on each other, facetiously. They find no sting in it now.

First impressions of the Gibraltarians are very confusing. No fixed type emerges. For such a small population and area the apparent variation is amazingly wide. I say apparent because there is a strong common denominator to be found. This strange medley of people has a common background, with certain social trauma shared by all. No rich or powerful person was ever invited or admitted to become a citizen of this British fortress, nor, in its past perils and austerities, would such a person have wished to stay. Every citizen is, therefore, descended from the displaced and dispossessed who came to The Rock for shelter and sustenance. They came cap-in-hand, to serve the soldiers, and when they rose to more exalted tasks it took them generations to overcome the menial mentality and to win the respect of their proud English masters. Combatant soldiers nowhere admire or respect their civilian assistants, and the military mind was in the ascendancy in Gibraltar until very recent years. Gibraltarians are all, however different they appear, one and the same in their social anxiety, in their deep desire for respect, and in their quick pride and anger at the first sign of contempt.

A British serviceman, living out of barracks in Gibraltar, found that he and his wife were constantly disturbed and annoyed by the neighbourhood children. When some local journalist published something to the effect that all Gibraltarian children were angels, this honest soldier blew his top and burst into print. In a letter to the *Gibraltar Chronicle* he described his unhappy experience and accused the children of being inconsiderate, spoilt and cheeky.

It only requires a little common sense to see that there is truth in this. Children everywhere are more indulged than they used to be, and in Latin communities they can do no wrong. The soldier named no names, and his general observations and complaints would not have raised an eyebrow in England. That is why he, and the *Gibraltar Chronicle*, went wrong; in Gibraltar they almost caused race riots.

One after another the Gibraltarians weighed in to defend their race and culture. In letters hysterical with abuse, they told the soldier to go home—overlooking the fact that if all the soldiers went home there would be no more British Gibraltar. One of these letters of protest was signed 'C. O. Jones', one of the Spanish 'four-letter' words, and the editor fell for it. Another was published over the signature 'T. P. M. English', the letters standing for *tu puta madre*— 'your whore of an English mother'.

You criticize a Gibraltarian, however mildly, at your personal peril. This propensity was the first thing I met in Gibraltar, when Mrs. Latakia thought I might encroach on her luggage space. Every visitor to The Rock meets it at once, in shops, bars, restaurants, wherever he may go, he notes a certain surly watchfulness, a quick, unjustified defiance. It is the colonial complex. I recognized it at once because it lingers in Ireland after forty years of freedom and independence. I was brought up with it in Belfast.

The cultivated English, we found, tend to be highly exclusive, to the point of xenophobia. In Gibraltar, apart from the ordinary soldiery who can and will make friends with anyone anywhere, all the English were of the cultivated classes or, at least, claiming to be of them. As a result of this, the Gibraltarians, even at their highest level, found but uneasy acceptance in English society there, and many of them carried the smarts of previous slights, consciously or unconsciously administered by the ruling race. Some of them carried, not chips, but logs on their shoulders, and I have watched their smiles vanish at the sound of the upper-class English voice. Here is an example of the kind of contretemps which frequently occurred.

Lourdes, to give her the typical Gibraltar name, was a beautiful and well-educated Gibraltarian of prosperous middle-class background. She married an English officer on The Rock, and subsequently went with him to Kenya. During her years in Nairobi she found herself fully accepted and appreciated by the European, and even by the English settlers—much more so than she would have been among the English in Gibraltar.

When she went home on leave with her husband she gave her English friends her Gibraltar address, and told them she would be glad to see them there. Two refined old ladies from Nairobi duly arrived at The Rock and telephoned Lourdes. Her husband drove down to the docks and brought them home, to her parents' pleasant house, for tea.

During the visit, Lourdes had occasion to slap her knee, cautiously insert the thumb and forefinger of one hand under the flat of the other, extract something small, pinch it until it cracked, and throw it away.

'What was that, my dear?' one of the old ladies asked nervously.

'Just a flea,' Lourdes told her.

'Oh, my dear! Are there many in Gibraltar?'

'Well, in the hot weather there are quite a few about.'

'Goodness me! Er—I suppose they come from the native quarter?'

Lourdes looked her straight in the eye and said: 'This *is* the native quarter, and I am a native here.'

The old ladies did not prolong their visit.

With the language, the music, and even the style of Spain on all sides, the Latin appearance of the majority of the people, and their frequent Spanish names, the passing visitor jumps to the obvious conclusion. Gibraltar is peopled by Spaniards ruled by their British conquerors, and when they are set free the people will rejoin Spain! Nothing could be further from the truth.

The day after the British took The Rock in 1704 almost every Spaniard left it. Six thousand of them—men, women and children—walked out at their own request. They left one fine old priest, a legendary hero now, who refused to leave his church in the hands of heretics. They left a few pregnant women, invalids and old folk who could not be moved, for the destination of the exodus was uncertain. They left, too, a small colony of Genoese fishermen at Catalan Bay, on the uncoveted eastern coast. Perhaps—but we are not sure—a few Jews remained behind, uneasy under the Spaniards and glad to change their masters. All told, it seems, about a hundred citizens stayed on under British rule, and of these very few were Spanish.

Over the years, Britain built up a new population on the bare rock. The forebears of today's Gibraltarians were either invited here to serve the garrison and leave it free for defence or, as security and prosperity grew, came here of their own free will and sought and gained admission. Not a man was pressed to come here, and not a man was held here against his will. In fact, it is more likely that, to prevent overcrowding and obstruction, many were turned away. All the people of Gibraltar are voluntarily British—British volunteers. This is not to say, of course, that they are all ardent admirers of Great Britain in all her aspects. They are all for Gibraltar British, rather than British Gibraltar. It is not only that they put Gibraltar first, it is Gibraltar first and the rest nowhere. Should the British ever decide to withdraw from their expensive and embarrassing tenure of The Rock they may find that they have to deal with not, as they might expect, a hurt friend, but a voluble and bitter enemy.

The immigrants came from the ports of northern Italy, notably from Genoa, whose people had an early foothold here. Some came to escape from Napoleon's conscription, others to seek their fortunes. Some came from the Balearic Islands, notably Minorca, a British possession, and a poor place in pre-tourist times. Some Moors crossed The Straits again to Tarik's Rock, their first and last possession on the Spanish mainland. They came following their trade with the large garrison in its new 'free' port. Jews too, expelled by this same gate by the conquering Spaniards centuries before, moved back from Africa to make new commerce. Some Portuguese, old allies of the English, brought their skill and industry. Later, an influx from poor, crowded Malta was admitted, in the face of strong objections from the people already here. And there has always been a small, steady leavening of soldiers of the British Crown.

The soldiers—sailors, too—were often Irishmen, with little cause to return to their own tortured country. In Gibraltar they could marry their co-religionists, for the Roman Catholic Church has been predominant in Gibraltar throughout British—as throughout Spanish—rule. It still is, and the Anglicans, Jews and Presbyterians make up only a small minority.

*   *   *   *

Thus, from rock bottom in 1704, the population grew to two thousand in 1754. After another half-century, in 1804, it had surpassed the maximum of the Spanish period and stood at eight thousand. For a few succeeding years there was an influx of about a thousand people every year, many of them refugees from the press gangs and plunderers of Napoleon. Over the past century there has been a steady increase in population, only offset by occasional epidemics. At present there are about twenty thousand Gibraltarians on The Rock, and a few thousand more scattered in Great Britain and the Americas.

From my first hours in Gibraltar, I began to feel at home with the people. It has been said that the Irish always have poor relations, meaning that we have no 'side', no wish to impress on social grounds, at least. Our aristocracy was so long ago banished or ploughed under that it would be foolish to claim it or refer to it. We are all descended from kings, of course, and the present writer more so than most, but that is a general joke which hurts no one. Generally speaking, we have avoided the curse of class-consciousness, and its moribund result the stratified society, for our common heritage is hardship.

I met my new colleagues man to man, and I found that their social and psychological climate was exactly the same as my own—that of Northern Ireland. For Northern Ireland, whatever it may from time to time be called, is essentially a British Crown Colony like Gibraltar.

A conquered people in an occupied country will, naturally enough, feel strongly for its race, language and customs, and sooner or later express itself in nationalism and rebellion. There is no such feeling, no such possibility in Gibraltar. Gibraltarians have no race except that happy amalgamation of races welded under British rule there. They have no valued language, either, except English. They have no special pride in speaking Spanish, and scarcely any literature in that language. As for their customs, these are few and unchallenged, and they, too, grew in the shade of the British crown. Their religions, of course, unlike those of Ireland and India, will never now be attacked. They are the protégés and beneficiaries of Britain, throughout their history and to this day. Like Ulstermen, they are proudly and vociferously British.

At the same time, these planted people, like those of Ulster, have a continuing vague unease about their nationality and status. It manifests itself in three directions—unease towards the original homeland, so long ago deserted, towards the expropriated and exiled aboriginals wherever they may be, and towards their hosts, the rulers of the Colony.

After the passage of centuries—three in Ulster, two in Gibraltar—this unease is not acute, but it lingers deeply rooted, and forms the mainspring of our character and the key to understanding us. Professor Toynbee in his great *Study of History*, regards this Colonial Complex with its challenge and response as a prime factor in social motivation. Unknown and unrecognized by its inheritors, this complex is clearly seen by the observer, and the people of Gibraltar display it daily.

The Gibraltarian, we found, has one aim and ambition—to acquire the culture of his choice, of his present and his future, the culture of Britain. Be he Genoese or Jew, be his mother Maltese or Spanish, he might claim to be the heir to a culture far older than the English. But he has left that culture far behind, and he does not wish to be reminded of it.

Speak to him in Spanish and—unless he knows you very well—he will surely answer you in English. He may answer quite sharply, for he feels that you have taken him for a foreigner. Speak to him admiringly of Spain and he will affectionately deride it—even should it be the homeland of his wife and mother. Speak to him of England and he will refer to it as 'Home', even should he never have set foot in it. He eats Yorkshire pudding and Irish stew, he drinks beer and whisky; he plays endlessly at the English game of cricket, or fights a golf ball in and out of the prickly pear on the scorched hills of Spain. Sartorially, he is impeccably British, will buy nothing but British cloth and shoes, and used to go—three men out of four—in the dark double-breasted blazer and flannel trousers which form the off-duty uniform of the Royal Navy.

The womenfolk of Gibraltar, I am glad to say, have enough good sense and independence to avoid the flat-heeled, frizzy-haired tweedy-pearliness of the well-bred Englishwoman who abounds here in the form of the officer's wife. Gibraltarian women dress vividly and pile up their long, dark hair. In that, in their rich, cloying perfume, in their invariably Spanish speech, their religious attitudes, and several other aspects of their lives, the women of Gibraltar are so distinctly different from their anglicized menfolk that, on the face of it, they might seem almost to be two races, married yet subtly apart. But the dichotomy is not damaging, for the vast majority of Gibraltar marriages are happy ones.

At one end of the social structure of Gibraltar are the favoured or the lucky few, the sons and grandsons of men who made easy fortunes during the latter half of the past century. During that period Britain was the bully of the Mediterranean world, and the Royal Navy, her chief instrument, was largely based on Gibraltar. The coaling and supplying of those ships made The Rock a gold mine. Later, in World War I, more great fortunes were to be made with ease in similar fashion. Many a naval prize was towed to Gibraltar and sold for a song to the local merchants, in the absence of competition. This is not to imply that these gains were illegal, or even discreditable. 'Trade follows the Flag' was the British Empire's adage in those times, and the Gibraltar merchants, taking advantage of their unique position, took care to make it true.

Their descendants are the rich, urbane and sophisticated product of English public schools and universities. At first meeting, they are upper-class English people. On further acquaintance you will find them almost 'anglo-English', more self-consciously English than the English themselves.

At the other end of the scale there are people who are almost indistinguishable from the unfortunate working class of southern Spain—tough, lean, voluble, emotional people, who speak, think and eat Spanish. 'If there is any truth,' wrote George Orwell, 'it lies in the proles.' These are the people who embody and preserve the folklore and the true traditions of the Gibraltarians, for they are imitations of no one—they are themselves. Many of the poorer citizens used to live in Spain before the Civil War drove them back to The Rock. Many of them are actually half Spanish. They are as much products of Spain as the members of the upper class are products of England.

At the top they speak English—except to their wives and mothers —in what Cyril Ray described as a 'Cork Street accent'—Cork Street, Mayfair. At the bottom they speak a debased Andalusian Spanish, gobbling the letters as they go. The Spaniards call this lingo *Llanito*, and find it hard to follow, not so much because of its careless pronunciation but because it is heavily peppered with English words and phrases. These intrude into the Spanish grotesquely, for instance: '*Vamos tomarnos un* pint of beer'—since they do not serve litres, nor *cerveza* in Gibraltar. Even where there are Spanish words which cover the case, the Gibraltarian seems to prefer to use his English, or mongrel, term. He will say: '*He trabajado mucho* overtime *en el* dockyard,' although he knows that the equivalent Spanish for 'dockyard' is *arsenal*, and for 'overtime', *trasoras*. If they strike him as English, which is to say, as Gibraltar institutions, then he automatically gives them their English names.

Another factor in this strange jargon is pure ignorance. Never having read or studied Spanish, nor had anything except very simple conversation in it, the average man has to skip about from one language to the other to put his meaning across:

'*Quiero un* half-shaft *para mi* Ford Consul' is the kind of technical talk one hears daily. Since, outside cultivated circles, the Spaniards did not drink tea, the Gibraltarians have never known the Spanish for 'teapot'. They call it, simply, '*tipa*', a word which is, in this meaning, peculiarly Gibraltarian.

But quaintest of all, perhaps, is the *Llanito* title of a nursing sister. '*Enfermera*' is applied to the junior nurses, and the difference in rank is important. What is the Spanish, then, for sister? *Hermana*, we know, but that family relationship makes no sense here. They settled for *sista*, pronouncing it so that the second 's' is scarcely heard. To satisfy local prudery and notions of maleness, the health authority had to employ male nurses as well. That phrase is absurd, even in English, but what happens when a male nurse is promoted to senior orderly, or sister's rank? The Gibraltarians simply changed the gender of their *sista*, and called him *sisto*.

Little wonder that the bewildered Spaniards say of the Gibraltarian '*Ni habla ingles ni español tampoco!*' He speaks neither English nor Spanish. The *Llanito* language is a philological freak, a most ill-assorted marriage between two contrasting languages. But it is a strong ingredient in the cement which holds this heterogeneous community together and gives it its unique entity. Since that entity is now disputed by Spain, which contends that the Gibraltarians are a temporary and prefabricated population, the local *patois* seems to me to be of considerable significance.

Lt.-Colonel Cholmondely complains that a Gibraltarian woman has been rude to him. It seems that he made some remark about foreigners, and she chose to take it to herself.

'I am a good British object,' she said, wagging her finger in his face, 'as good as you!'

'The fact is,' says Cholmondely, 'that I didn't mean her, at all. But now that she's made her claim, I don't mind telling you that I've been round the world twice, and these are the most foreign people I've ever met anywhere!'

We could see what he meant. The foreigness of Africans or Japanese is expected and accepted. The Gibraltarians look and sound so like us that their off-beat English comes as a shock. The more they talk, the more they emphasize their un-English origin and background. And, the Spaniards tell me, they have the same effect in that language. The fact is that a Gibraltarian is a foreigner, and an obvious foreigner in England and in Spain. Only on his Rock is he truly at home, and that is why he will fight desperately to stay there.

I have mentioned the upper and lower classes of the community. But Gibraltar, being a commercial rather than an industrial place, is predominantly white-collar, and the average man there is a shop-keeper or a clerk. The middle-class is wide and numerous, which means that a majority of people are moderately well off and moderately well educated. But, unlike the British middle-class, not-able for its uniformity and conformity, the middle-class of Gibraltar is various and difficult to define. One can find in it the permutations and combinations of a dozen different races.

Am I right in saying a dozen? Let me list them, putting them down as they come to mind: English, Irish, Scots, Italians of several distinct states and strains such as Genoese and Sicilians, Catalans from the Balearic Islands which were once British, Maltese—an exotic mixture in themselves, Spaniards on the distaff side, Sephardic Jews, Indians of various races, Pakistanis, French. These are the races well established and interwoven into the fabric of Gibraltarian society. The thousands of visitors, more or less temporary, add further complications.

Such a community, confined, remember to a couple of square miles, must find a lingua franca if it is to co-operate at all, and the inevitable choice was English. All the schoolchildren in Gibraltar are taught in English, but not effectively. Recently the authorities have had to confess to sixty per cent failures in the British G.C.E. examination at ordinary level, and propose for the future to start the children on English at the age of five. There are special reasons for this difficulty. Spanish seems to be a far more direct, strong and simple language. Like all the Latin languages, it seems to have been designed for the Latin temperament. You speak English, they told me, lying back in a chair, for Spanish you sit forward on the edge of it. A Latin, with all the strong and dramatic emphasis which he finds it necessary to express, all the hyperbole, exaggeration and emphasis, must find himself curiously handicapped in English—especially in the limited English which is all that he is likely to possess. To begin with, he must talk with his hands in his pockets, to keep them from waving wanly in the air. English simply has not the force to call them out!

The Gibraltarian father, except in the case of a manual worker, carries on his daily business in English, and knows the value of it. He will try to learn more, if only to earn more. But the mother, be she Gibraltarian or, very often, Spanish, has little cause or opportunity to learn or practice our strange, perverse language. She meets few situations which call for it. In church, market, shop and club, everyone can meet her in Spanish. She need never meet English people unless her husband rises to some eminence in the community. Invariably, Spanish or its Gibraltarian dialect is the language of bed and board, and the language used with children. Before they come to school they are well launched and grounded in the mother tongue, so that they have to be taught English as a foreign language. And Spanish is a difficult language to displace, especially since the children lapse into it as soon as they leave the school gates.

In Gibraltar you will find Inmaculada Spink—product of ex-corporal Spink's marriage with a Spanish-Gibraltarian girl, Deigratias Witherspoon—of similar lineage, Patricio O'Hara—grandson of a left-over Irish soldier, without a word of English with which to bless themselves. On the other side of the street, Manolo Fulano, Belarachand Chulam, and Moses Savonarola, behind their respective counters, speak elegant English all day long. All the young speak some English, for there have been twenty years of compulsory education in it; few of the old know much of it, for no one used to care. And even here, I cannot make a rule, because some of the elderly spent the war years in England and others in the Canary Islands or West Indies. Intelligence and aspirations vary, too.

One thing was very clear to us, that we should make every effort to learn Spanish, fast and well. Accordingly we hired a tutor, entered for the examinations of the Royal Society of Arts in London, and proceeded to study and practice daily. We sat the examinations in due course—the first *importados* ever to do so—separated and invigilated by a Christian Brother and surrounded by giggling schoolboys. We passed well, and with that encouragement our Spanish snowballed. Soon we could think in Spanish, and now I have some difficulty in keeping the speech forms of that great language, and even the very words of it, out of my speech in English.

One result was that my local colleagues let me share their gossip and their jokes. In some departments of Government, Spanish was frowned on for sound reasons of policy. In the Works Department, where we were in constant touch with the Spanish-speaking building worker, it was in daily and general use.

Displacement and dispossession, then, lie at the roots of the Gibraltarian people. Their forerunners were refugees. They flocked to The Rock, to the Pax Britannica, from poverty and peril elsewhere. They came as sutlers and hawkers, labourers and camp followers. They became stall-holders, shopkeepers, dealers, moneylenders and, ultimately, wealthy merchants and shippers. For even the poorest of them, for those who could not succeed, there has been the safety and security of a rule of law and, in these enlightened times, more tangible benefits. It is not surprising, then, that they regard Gibraltar as God's Own Country.

These people love The Rock, their refuge and their strength, almost as they love their God. They will hear no ill of it. They will not leave it for a fortune. When, as sometimes happens, a local girl marries a soldier and goes off with him, be sure she will bring him back again as soon as he leaves the army. He returns at a disadvantage, for an Englishman may only take a job for which there are no Gibraltarian candidates. He narrows his scope and reduces his standard of living, but it cannot be helped—his Gibraltarian wife cannot be happy elsewhere! In this lotus land, the soldier finds consolations. . . .

When a Gibraltar family goes to Spain on Sunday, as most used to do, to stretch their legs and eat in the open air, they will return week after week to the same spot, usually a place well crowded with their compatriots. There, in all that wide, empty land, they will set up their picnic table with its legs in the same four holes that they occupied the week before—and every summer week, for years before. Then they tie up the childrens' swing to the selfsame tree whereon they themselves used to swing as children. Nor is this trait observable only in the simpler people. One of the leaders of the community, a man of considerable wealth and superior education, goes to a certain cinema every night regardless of its programme, after playing dominoes every afternoon in the same club and with the same people.

The Gibraltarian is first and foremost, British. He has many of the virtues of the British; he would like to have more. He is conservative, traditionalist, tolerant, generous, good-humoured. He has a strong sense of propriety and of personal dignity. Long conditioned in a tightly governed fortress, he respects authority and law, but he does not offer to any institution his automatic acceptance, much less his adulation. He will question and defy any decision or decree which clashes with his personal or family interests, and it will be no use telling him that it is for the public good. He will feel it his natural right to fight it.

His ultimate loyalty is personal and never institutional. He prefers personality, idiosyncratic and selfish as it may be, to the English ideal of conformity in character, of 'soundness', which means complete predictability.

James Joyce who, without ever seeing it, sketched Gibraltar in his *Ulysses* with brilliant truth and clarity, once listed the British beatitudes, among them 'beer, beef, business, bibles, bulldogs, battleships and bishops'. These remain, one and all, household gods in Gibraltar today. But there are many more, strongly and secretly cherished, and even more essential to the ethnic conscience of this rare alloy of humanity—the Gibraltarian.

Let us look into the melting-pot which made him, and the fires of the forge.

10

ROCK TARIK AND ROCK ARCOS

The Visigoths, a loosely knit people who might never have reached this southern shore but for the collapse of Roman centralization, conquered Carteia and ruined it and rode away, leaving Gibraltar Bay vacant, its arms outstretched to receive all invaders. It was their good fortune that it took three centuries for a power to arise to fill the Roman vacuum.

All through these centuries the Sahara sands had been encroaching on the neglected North African coastlands, which had been the granary of Rome. The Arab peoples there, Moor, Rif and reconverted Berber, became united by adversity, by force, and by a great new religion.

Here was a deadly pressure building up. Fierce herdsmen and horsemen bereft of pasture, a green and empty land in clear view ten miles away, and a Faith which demanded to be spread by the sword.

In the year A.D. 711 the freedman Tarik-ben-Zeyad invaded Spain for his Moorish masters. He landed, we believe, at deserted Carteia, where there was a broad beach and where the Roman moles, abandoned three hundred years before, might still have been usable. The clue lies in the arabic name for the river there—*Guadarranque*, the river of the mares. We know that Tarik brought five hundred horses with him. He had seven thousand foot soldiers as well, and he had to ferry his whole invasion force across The Straits in a shuttle service of four small boats. This proves the utter lack of opposition to his landing.

It proves, too, that the sensual and fatalistic potentates of Morocco did not care to risk too much on Tarik. But this freedman had his way to make in the world, and his actions prove that he was shrewd and tough and keen. He rode straight round the bay to The Rock and set his men to making it into a bridgehead and a fortified base, the Mulberry harbour of his D-Day. He was the first man to see what has been remarked so often since, and enshrined in the city arms of this place, that Gibraltar was the key to Spain.

76

And only when it was secure did Tarik sally out to meet the Visigoths, riding up reluctantly forty miles away. He met them on the plain of La Janda, a dried up lake inland from Tarifa, and he killed their king, Roderic, and scattered them forever. The Visigoths, by that time, had no defence in depth, little heart or purpose, and the Moors rolled up their opposition as fast as a horse could travel.

From the day of that battle onwards Mons Calpe has been Gibr-al-Tarik, Tarik's Rock. On that day, it became an artifact as well as a natural phenomenon. Islam entered Europe by Gibraltar, on a campaign four centuries long which travelled almost to the gates of Paris. And, as we shall see, Islam left Europe by the same door. Gibraltar was a Moslem stronghold for six hundred years, which is far longer than her two Christian régimes added together, yet the Moors left little to be seen. They never were great builders. Their famous works rest on Roman ruins and often incorporate Roman columns. They were great decorators, but that is a different matter.

They fortified and re-fortified The Rock, and fragments of their massive walls remain there. They built a mole, now land-locked but still surviving, two mosques whose remnants remain, a fine bath house copied from the Roman model, and the famous Moorish Castle commanding the only land entrance to the peninsula.

Up to recent times a wall of the Tower of Homage of this castle bore the legend:

'To the God of Peace, the Great Pacificator; to the Eternal God Who will be forever.' I find strange pathos in that cry, carved there a thousand years ago by cruel and relentless warriors.

There is no evidence that the Moors made a civil settlement on The Rock, or built much of a town here. Why should they? They had come to Spain to expand, so there was no point in cooping themselves in a rocky fortress. They had come for comfort—for running water, grain, grass and gardens. For women, too, perhaps. Gibraltar could offer none of these, and they soon found them all in abundance at Granada, Seville, Córdoba, Málaga and Jaen. Gibraltar was, for them, a fort and a port, a grim and practical place and—strange to say—a dangerous one. For as the wealth and power of the Moors in Spain increased it caused increasing envy in their homeland.

The fortress had to face both ways, as you can still see by the old walls at its southern end, fearing the foes behind it even more than those before. The treasons and treacheries of those times make tedious reading, with their see-saw action and their meaningless names, but I must quote one typical case—(from James's *History of the Herculean Straits* 1771)—to show the way the wind blew.

In the year A.D. 1001, Bali, Governor of Ceuta, crossed The Straits of Gibraltar with a private army, took Córdoba from his legal lords, but 'was strangled by his own eunuchs in the town of Jaen'. A sad fate, indeed, but a true poetic justice!

In A.D. 1177 the poet Abu-Abdullah ben Galib of Valencia wrote that Gibraltar had been harried by history as a camel caravan by its driver. What history? The Rock had had no history until Tarik landed, so he must have meant the past four hundred years of Moorish rule. Summing up the hectic, stab-in-the-back history of that epoch, the poet wrote:

'This mountain now deserves a safe repose, free from all fear and misfortune, even should (all) the other mountains of the earth shake to their foundations.'

Looking back with hindsight, one can only smile at the gentle poet's innocence. A thousand more fierce years lay ahead for Gibraltar, and still she seeks her safe repose.

*   *   *   *

The word 'Spain' means 'the distant place', the remote and hidden land. The Romans used to speak of 'all the Spains'. There are at least five Spains in Spain still, each with its own language and culture, and the strangest and most Spanish of them all is Andalucia, the hinterland and matrix of Gibraltar.

Down here they sing in arabic cadence, although they call it *flamenco*. Here, in nearby Tarifa, the women went veiled within living memory. Here, to this day, the women may be locked up, harem fashion, while a man goes out to his pleasure. Down here the great black bulls dominate the countryside and, to some extent still, the secret hearts of men. And the whole of life's business, as of nature and of course, is based on influence, contacts, baksheesh and bribes. Even the mules— the Moors brought them here from Africa twelve centuries ago—have zebra stripes on the insides of their legs. Can the leopard change his spots?

The professional and self-conscious Spaniards, if I may so describe those who first conceived the unity and claimed the title of this wide and diverse country, were the rulers of the northern realms, Castile and Aragon. For hundreds of years, gathering strength and momentum by piecemeal conquest, by marriage, alliance and amalgamation of men and munitions, they fought their way down this great peninsula, pushing southwards the fat and lazy Moor.

The Castilian and Aragonese reconquerors found here in Andalucia the Moors, Berbers and Jews, three distinct and different peoples, but fused somewhat in the melting-pot after seven centuries of living together. More Spanish, they may have been, than those who claimed and won the title.

The Moors had found scope to develop a civilization in Spain—a gimcrack one, it seems to me, judging by their unstable and florid engineering and their rhetorical and conventional poetry—but, still, a civilization.

They found scope, too, for the full flowering of the inherent weaknesses of their race and creed. They were fatalists, lacking in ambition. They were traditionalists, always looking backwards. They were sensualists, averse to arduous effort. Their polygamy, their subordination of many women to one man, backfired on them. The multifarious polygamy of their potentates left hosts of jealous sons, backed by even more jealous mothers, to bicker over their inheritance. So intertwined were secular and religious privilege in their system that they could neither share nor compromise. Arrogance, self-interest, intransigence and jealousy were qualities which a man owed to his manhood. Worst weakness of all, as extreme individualists, they were treacherous and disloyal. The worst enemy of a Moor was a Moor, and no man knew his enemies, nor his friends. The result was a society without love or tenderness, which is to say, without true wisdom.

The small Spanish armies had been welded by hardship and aspiration, as the Moors had been in the first flush of their nationhood, in the days of Tarik of Gibraltar. And the Spaniards had another weapon, one which had dulled, by this time, in the hands of the Moors—a fanatical religious faith, a sense of mission.

The Spanish reconquest of Spain was more than a Cause, it was a Holy Crusade, and a man could find eternal merit by dying for it. This was the momentum that carried it forward for three hundred

years, right down to The Straits and gates of Gibraltar, the Key to
Spain. And that momentum carried it far further, further than any
European had ever been before, to the West Indies and Mexico and
Chile and Peru, and the undreamt-of isles of the Pacific Ocean.

In the year A.D. 1238 these Spaniards took Córdoba, the religious
and intellectual centre of Islam in Europe, the Rome of their culture.
Forty years later they took Tarifa which commanded the narrowest
passage of The Straits, outflanked Granada, and cut off the supply
lines and escape routes of the Moors. For eighty years after that the
campaign swung to and fro, so that many a town and village down
here has its name suffixed '*de la frontera*'.

In the year 1309 Gibraltar suffered the first of its thirteen sieges,
with an archbishop of liberated Seville leading the attack on The
Rock. The Moorish garrison, a mere thousand men, were driven to
take cover in the fine fortifications by His Grace's well-blessed cata-
pults. Portuguese galleys aided the land attack. After a month of
siege, the Moors surrendered, and were banished to Morocco with
hand baggage only, a small portion of the accumulation of five
hundred and ninety-eight years of enrichment.

On that occassion, one sad old Moor told a king of Spain:

'I was born in Seville, where my people had been for many
generations. As a small child I had to flee that city when it was
captured by your great grandfather. We settled at Jerez, but had to
leave it when it was taken by your grandfather. From Tarifa I was
later driven by your father, and so I came at last to Gibraltar, the
last and strongest fortress in all Spain. But now I leave that, too. . . .'
All the long, slow attrition of the Reconquest is in his story. Ironically
enough, in their great days, the Moors had rolled up the whole
country in three years.

But that was only a beginning. In the next century and a half
Gibraltar changed hands eight times over. It was not until the year
1462 that a minor *hidalgo* called Don Alonso de Arcos took the
Fortress from the Moors for ever, in the name of Henry IV of
Castile. Arcos left no trace of himself, no records on The Rock. As
a mere working soldier, he held but short control of it. But I have
seen his strong, simple epitaph in the Cartuja of Seville, and that
says all that he could wish:

'*Aqui yace sepultado el honrado caballero*

don Alonso de Arcos
alcaide de Tarifa
que ganó a Gibraltar de los enimigos
*de nuestra Santa Fe.'**

The newly won Fortress was handed over to a major grandee, one perhaps better able to fortify and munition it—the Duke of Medina Sidonia. In sixteen years he improved it so much that the Catholic Kings gave it to him, creating him *Marques de Gibraltar*. When he died, in 1489, his son politely sought confirmation of his estates. Isabella reneged on Gibraltar, such was its fame by this time, and offered him many other titles if he would hand The Rock back to the Crown of Castile. The young duke refused to do so. Gibraltar had arrived, in the current phrase. The name Gibraltar had heroic overtones and had become a status symbol of national power.

A few years later, 1492—the year of Columbus—all the Jews of Spain were banished through Gibraltar. Conspicuously well placed and wealthy, the leaders in many walks of life under the Moors, they were unable to sign on the dotted line of Rome, so the Spaniards sent a million of them into exile in Africa.

The humble Moorish peasantry, long conditioned to submission, bowed their heads to the Church and stayed on and suffered. But it availed them nothing in the end. Two centuries later they too were thrown out of Spain by way of Gibraltar.

The first expulsion must have cost Spain much of her potential brain power. The second, in the south, at least, crippled her hands. For when the Moriscos, as they were called, were driven from their farms and irrigations the desert and the goat moved in and re-conquered, and they hold much of the land to this day.

Most ironic of all, the very year that the Jews were banished Columbus set sail from Palos, a hundred miles along the coast to westwards, on the first of his great voyages which were to make Spain the leader of the world. There is new evidence now that Columbus himself was a Jew. Certainly no one in the world, in those times, knew more of geography and navigation than the Jews of Genoa, his home port.

* 'Here lies buried the honoured knight don Alonso de Arcos, governor of Tarifa, who wrested Gibraltar from the enemies of our Holy Faith.'

In the year 1502 the Crown of Spain gently took Gibraltar back from the Duke of Medina Sidonia and gave it a grant of arms—a red castle with a golden key, described in heraldic terms:

'Party fesswise through the nombril point Argent and Gules, in chief a castle triple towered of the last, pendent therefrom by a chain a key wards downwards in base Or. Beneath the shield upon a scroll *"Montis Insignia Calpe"*.'

They added the inscription: 'It is the key of these Kingdoms, the guardian and defender of The Straits.' When the great Queen Isabella died in 1540 she left a will which one Spanish historian has called 'The Charter of Spanish Destiny'. In it she had written of Gibraltar:

'That they may always hold for The Crown and in Our Royal Patrimony the said City of Gibraltar, with all which appertains thereto, and may not give away nor alienate, nor consent to being given or alienated, any part thereof.'

In spite of this, in 1713 her descendant Philip V gave it away conditionally but effectively to the British Crown.

Spain only held Gibralter for a short time—two hundred and forty-two years—but she made good use of it. Not long after her conquest of The Rock, Granada fell, and Moorish rule came to an end. Immediately after that, thanks to the initiative of Columbus, the New World was colonized at amazing speed. The Spanish ports where the new wealth poured in were all at the western end of The Straits. It was Gibralter which secured them from the ancient enemy, the Moor and the Turk, now turned pirate and raiding and terrorizing the whole southern littoral of Europe.

Strange to say, there is some factual basis to the classic theory of the Abyss. The Mediterranean Basin is separated from the Atlantic by a sill at a depth of one hundred and fifty fathoms. The dense and deep-lying Mediterranean waters flow out fast over this, seeking the depths. The Atlantic water, of lower specific gravity, enters The Straits as a steady three-knot surface current. As a result of this, it needs a stiff breeze to take a sailing ship outwards. There was a time in 1855 when no ship could leave the Mediterranean for three months.

Whilst the inward trade—to Tyre, Greece and Rome—was all important, this current had beeh helpful, which is why Carteia throve so well, and the Romans had built other ports nearby. But once the outward traffic began, with the African west coast and, later, with the Indies, the inner ports were doomed to decline. The farther west a port was placed, the closer it was to the destination and, more important, the less current it had to run against, and less waiting for the eastward, outward wind.

Thus it was that Cádiz, Palos, and Seville, high up her wide river, grew in size and riches, all being clear of The Straits and with Gibraltar and Tarifa guarding their rear. Later, when sail gave way to steam and the current was conquered, and when the Suez Canal made the inward traffic as important, at least, as the outward, the competition between east and west ports became equal.

Then Spain lost her monopoly and finally her all in the New World. Cádiz declined, Palos silted up, San Lúcar lowered herself to oyster fishing, the ships outgrew Seville's muddy river. Gibraltar and Ceuta, British and Spanish rivals, arose and prospered, and their growth and rivalry in commercial matters still continues.

In spite of the grant of high-sounding titles by the Queen, it took the Spaniards ninety years to appreciate Gibraltar to the full. After the Reconquest the coastal populations on The Straits tended to retire to the inland hills. The Moors, in full view, might return at any time. No one wanted to live in Gibraltar, right on their doorstep, and so it was peopled largely by convicts, men whose sentences were suspended whilst they lived there.

All Spain's attention was on the miracle to westwards, the New World, with all its easy wealth and power. Gibraltar was left in the backyard, and a deadly dangerous backyard it was.

The Turks had taken Constantinople in the year 1500, so that the eastern sea was now entirely in their hands. Barbarossa, greatest of all the corsairs, terrorized Venice, Genoa, Naples and the Balearic ports from his safe base at Argel. Gibraltar, the key to Seville, Cádiz and the Indies trade, was his obvious ambition. The population of Gibraltar reached the edge of revolt, because the long-promised refortifications were still awaited, and the Governor, Don Alvaro de Bazan, resigned because he could get no support for his plan to strengthen the walls.

In 1540 Barbarossa came at last, with sixteen galleys, and did what he wished with the town and with its people. It was not until twelve years after that terrible event that the Spanish Emperor sent Juan Bautista Calvi, a Milanese engineer, to fortify The Rock in the

light of the latest knowledge. Calvi's South Port Gate, Charles V
Wall and other fragments may still be seen in Gibraltar.

From that time on, in a sense, the British fortified Gibraltar, for
as the sixteenth century advanced the Spaniards had more and more
cause to fear attack from them. In 1575 Fratino, another Italian
engineer, destroyed much of Calvi's work and rebuilt it to a new
design—there was built-in obsolescence in military matters even then.

The British threat to The Rock grew year by year. Drake sailed
into Cádiz and burned the Spanish ships; Raleigh and Essex returned there, took the whole city and held it for two weeks. Gibraltar
was only saved by her strength and smallness, and, maybe, by the
prevailing east wind which made her, at times, difficult to reach
from the west.

From 1585 onwards there was hot war between Spain and England, and three years later Drake scattered the Invincible Armada.
From then on The Straits were freely cruised by British ships, whose
captains must have cast their eyes often and enviously on The Rock,
longing for a foothold and a base there.

Cromwell wrote to one of his admirals: 'Six frigates there could
damage the Spaniards more than a whole fleet. . . .'

At last, in 1662, Britain got a foothold in The Straits. Charles II
received Tangier as part of the dowry of the Portuguese princess
Catherine de Braganza. But it was soon relinquished, in those
corrupt and muddled times, as being too expensive.

In the year 1687 the French were threatening Cádiz. Britain,
leader of the League of Augsburg whose aim was to keep the Bour-
bons off the Spanish throne, had switched her hostility to France.
There was not much pretence of principle in international affairs in
those times. Spain had declined to such an extent that she no longer
excited the full force of Britain's envy and rivalry; France, on the
other hand, was booming.

A convoy of four hundred merchant ships of the League, protected by five men-of-war under the command of an admiral called
Rooke, were attacked off Cape St. Vincent at the western entrance to The Straits. They took refuge in Spanish ports and in
the Bay of Gibraltar. The Spanish guns of The Fortress, to
protect their British friends, and at Rooke's request, crossed fire
with the French pursuers. Little did they know that but a

few years later they were to meet this naval gentleman again.

In 1702, in the interests of the Hapsburg Pretender to the Spanish throne, this Rooke assaulted Cádiz, where the bad behaviour of his men shocked all Europe.

He next appears in the spring of 1704 at Lisbon, at the headquarters of the Carlist cause, conferring with Charles, Archduke of Austria, Hapsburg Pretender to the Crown of Spain, and with the King of Portugal who supported his claim. Also present was that good soldier, the Prince of Hesse-Darmstadt, who proved himself against King James in Ireland, where he led the armies of William III.

Rooke's London orders did not refer to Gibraltar, unless they did so secretly. As territory it may have seemed a useless beach head in foot-slogging days, lying almost a hundred miles from any considerable Spanish city. Its naval value was not yet fully appreciated. During this epoch the tide of high strategy would seem to have left Rock Arcos stranded.

*   *   *   *

The Spaniards had fought for Gibraltar incessantly for a hundred and fifty years. In that period they fought no less than eight battles there, losing four of them and winning four. One dislikes such expressions as 'gave their lives', for in those times, as in our own, a pressed soldier had little choice of action, but there is no doubt that Spaniards of five generations had died, more or less bravely at The Rock. There is no reason why they should not look back on this with pride. I have yet to hear of an army which does not claim glorious traditions. . . .

They won the last battle, in 1462, thanks to Don Alonso of Arcos, the honoured cavalier; thanks to their fierce, prolonged insistence; thanks to the war weariness of the Moor; but they would have said, those Spaniards, all thanks to God.

If ever a place was well deserved and hard won, this was it. Gibraltar was a gain by God's will, in the face of all odds and vicissitudes. A glance at The Fortress is enough to show how difficult it was to attack, let alone to enter, with the weapons of those times. The defenders, high up and hidden by massive walls, commanding the narrow and only entrance, had a terrifying advantage, a complete superiority. The Spaniards must have felt that the walls of

Jericho had fallen for them. They rushed into the last stages of their Reconquest with renewed faith and courage.

The main development of Spanish Gibraltar was religious. Ledesma Miranda thinks that the new tenants were impressed by the awesome aloofness and grandeur of the place. I think it was much more obvious—the blessed end of a long religious war, the symbol of a holy victory.

Whatever the reason, they soon built a great church out of the Moorish mosque, now the Cathedral of St. Mary the Crowned. Also soon, they set up no less than twelve religious establishments of one kind and another, including the Franciscan Convent which was to become the residence and counting house of future British governors. When they lost Gibraltar in 1704 it had eighteen religious establishments. When one considers that the town was then one-quarter of its present small size, not much more than a village with its five thousand inhabitants, one may think of Spanish Gibraltar as a kind of Lourdes, a holy town first and foremost.

After a century of Spanish rule Gibraltar gradually became something more than a desolate fortress and a religious retreat. The Rock was a buttress of the Indies trade. The prevailing wind is from the east, so that a fleet at Gibraltar could—almost always—sweep down The Straits to protect ships or cities there. Even when the west wind blew, The Rock could prevent corsairs from entering The Straits at the eastern end.

The place became well fortified, munitioned and, at last, populated. Now that it was secure, with Spain the strongest power in the world, the merchants came to Gibraltar and traded there, and put some of their gains into bricks and mortar. The strong religious atmosphere would not deter them, for in Spain, as everywhere, big merchants and big churches are the best of friends.

Gibraltar was a prosperous trading port with more than five thousand inhabitants in the year 1704. She might have been greater, but for the fact that Spain had other ports—Cádiz, Seville, Tarifa— also well placed for strategy and with more convenient access from landwards, all sharing in the defence and trade of The Straits. The British, with no such choice, had to develop Gibraltar much faster, much more effectively.

There was, perhaps, one place too holy for the money changers.

At the extreme southern tip, the most beautiful place on The Rock, where one may look back at the great mountain or forward across the sea to Mont Abyla, the Hesperides and the mighty Atlas, there was a little chapel dedicated to Our Lady of Europa. It had twelve silver lamps, presented by the admirals of Spain, and it was a beacon and a blessing to the sailors of Christendom.

Not the first light-house in the world, and surely not the most effective, but one of the most necessary and, to my mind, one of the most benevolent.

But it would have taken much more than that kindly light to save holy Gibraltar from the ferocity of the British fleet.

ROOKE'S ROCK?

Admiral Sir George Rooke, as every British schoolboy knows, took The Rock of Gibraltar for the Crown of Great Britain. Very few schoolboys know that he took it for the Prince of Hesse-Darmstadt, as agent for one Charles, Archduke of Austria.

It is too easy for an Irishman, member of a race which has not and never had any extra-territorial ambitions—nor perhaps any other terrestrial ambitions—to criticize the acquisitions of the British Colonial Empire. The well-worn pleas of British apologists to the effect that there was never any policy or plan to conquer and acquire, and that the worldwide empire—the greatest of all time—was the result of a persistent series of absent-minded gestures, cause ribald laughter in Ireland, as elsewhere.

At the same time, case after case can be cited of independent Britons, in the days of slow communications, motivated by patriotism or mere commercialism, trespassing far beyond their orders and seizing lands and peoples in the name of an innocent and distant British Government. Such a case was Gibraltar.

Gibraltar—if we lay aside Ireland and the Channel Islands—is the colony nearest to the homeland. It is difficult, but important, to realize that in the days of its acquisition it was thirty or forty days out from London—far further out of touch than any place on the face of the globe today. Because of urgent events, and pressure from his immediate masters, Rooke had to attack it, and to attack it without asking London. It is a fact that he had no British orders to do so. Rooke, like Rhodes and Raffles and Pottinger after him, acted in his personal capacity. He was a tough, aggressive and acquisitive man—as an admiral, perhaps, has a right to be. His behaviour only represented Britain in so far as he was a classic English type, full of self-confidence and devoid of imagination. It is significant that his action, like those of other such demi-official marauders, was readily endorsed at Westminster.

Rooke set sail from Lisbon in command of a large combined fleet of British and Dutch. The Prince of Hesse, tagging along on his royal yacht, was the political and diplomatic head of the mission. He had been Governor of Catalonia in his day, an honour conferred on him for being wounded by the same ball as King William at the battle of the Boyne. He had reason to believe that Barcelona, the capital of that province, was disaffected with the new government at Madrid. Knowing that the Catalans were separatists, and always at loggerheads with Madrid, he placed a lot of store on this story. So should we, for the Catalans are still the same.

Hesse's plan was to land there, declare Charles III as rightful king, and start a revolution. Rooke, patting his pocket with its orders to engage the French fleet, went along willingly, for the headquarters of that fleet were at Toulon, not far from Barcelona.

But the Catalans came aboard and told Hesse that life was hard enough for them as things were, and that they would not risk making them harder. They begged him to go away.

Meanwhile Rooke had been off hunting on his own, had met the French ships and chased them, but got becalmed and dare not attack them close to their port. The French had galleys in Toulon, which could have hauled their ships up to the British fleet. The British, so far from base, had no such means of locomotion.

Sailing back from Barcelona down the east coast of Spain, both Rooke and Hesse were dejected and frustrated, and searching wildly for another opening. They anchored at the mouth of The Straits, across from Gibraltar, and sent to Lisbon for further instructions. They were told to do the obvious thing—take Cádiz.

Rooke, with unhappy and guilty memories of his abortive assault on Cádiz two years earlier, and with the knowledge that Cádiz would be ready for him next time, stalled on the order by asking for more soldiers.

On the 27th July he got word from Lisbon that he would get no more men from that source, and that the Navy 'must act from its own strength and initiative'. Officialese is a dangerous medium! It is not clear to me whether this reinforced the order to take Cádiz, or gave Rooke a free hand. It it was not clear to Rooke either, then he must have been glad of the ambiguity. He decided to take Gibraltar, and talked Hesse into agreement.

By an amazing coincidence, or by cunning and foresight, Rooke had furnished himself with a letter from Pretender Charles calling on the Governor to surrender The Rock to him. The famous letter was dated May 1704—that is, he got it before he even set sail on the Barcelona mission. No indication of absent-mindedness here! On the 1st August 1704, presenting 71 warships, 26,000 artillerymen, 9,000 infantry, and 4,000 pieces of cannon, Rooke sent in his letter to the Governor of Gibraltar, General Diego Salinas.

The Rock, neglected as so often before, had 80 trained soldiers, 470 half-trained peasants, 1,000 civilians more or less capable of bearing arms, and 20 working cannon. Salinas must have opened that letter with a shaking hand.

The dateline read: 'The King: to my city of Gibraltar.' The text set forth the Hapsburg claim to the Spanish throne and called upon Gibraltar to proclaim Charles as king, to admit the allies, and to ask Rooke for reinforcements in case of counter-attack from the mainland. The sting is in the tail of it: 'If you do otherwise, which I cannot believe of such faithful vassals to their legitimate and natural Lord, my distinguished allies will find it necessary to use against you all the hostilities of war, in spite of my astounded grief that those whom I love as sons should suffer, by their own wish, as though they were my greatest enemies. . . .'

The letter, which mentions Rooke by name, but does not mention his superior, Hesse, ends with the magic Spanish formula: '*YO EL REY*'.

Don Diego de Salinas replied so promptly that we may put aside any idea of a plebiscite. He said, on behalf of the frightened and bewildered people, that 'as faithful vassals of Philip V they would sacrifice their lives with that of their city'. We may suspect a trace of irony in the final line of his brave, foolish letter: 'And I hope that Our Lord will protect Your Excellency for as many years as He can.'

Rooke lined up his ships five hundred yards from the western face of the helpless fort, opened his bombardment at dawn on Sunday, 4th August, and in the next five hours fired some fifteen thousand cannon balls into the city, with all the angry cruelty of a man who had failed more than once to defeat worthier foes. In passing, this and subsequent terrible bombardments, explain why so little Spanish—let alone Moorish—Gibraltar stands today.

The invaders, led by the English majority, landed on the morning of 4th August, with very little opposition. They spent the day in street fighting, house to house, murdering and raping, it is written, and looting what was left of the houses and stores. It is clear, and confirmed by the subsequent behaviour of the Spanish residents, that the worst behaviour of the English was directed towards the eighteen religious institutions—all Roman Catholic, of course— which had grown up on The Rock. At the same time it should be said that English Protestantism had, at one time, suffered much from Spain, and there were two cases of Englishmen being burned at the stake in Seville by the Spanish Inquisition, an organization still active at this time. It is a fact, too, that some of these Englishmen, described by one of their own Captains as 'shacombe filthies, ragga-muffings and scrovies', had not set foot ashore for twelve months. Ned Ward (*The London Spy*) had referred to the British warship of the period as 'the great bridge of the ocean, conveying to all habit-able places Death, Pox and Drunkenness'. A very fair description of what, in the first instance, the Royal Navy conveyed to Gibraltar.

At midnight the last of the Spanish soldiers came out of the few remaining strongpoints. Salinas formally surrendered The Fortress and marched his tiny garrison out into Spain. The next day, after, one feels sure, a very bad night, the six thousand citizens left, said to be 'almost all'. One brave chronicler remained, Juan Romero de Figueroa, Vicar of the Church of St. Mary the Crowned. He wrote 'Oh my country, I shall not leave thee, and my ashes shall mix with thine,' and much more such melancholy poetry. He is the only articulate man linking the old order with the new, and amongst the rough and arrogant heroes and villains who have swaggered, fought and schemed over The Rock, he stands out as a noble and gentle figure.

Strange events, still largely unexplained, happened on the day of the surrender. The Prince of Hesse, as one would expect, hoisted the flag of his master—of the whole expedition's master—'Charles III, King of Spain'. British history tells that Rooke objected to this, had his way, hauled down the Spanish flag and hoisted the British.

One does not doubt, knowing that he had carried that letter in his pocket for three months, that he would have been apt and ready to do this. He would have felt that since British ships and soldiers had been mainly responsible for the victory, Britain had prior rights to the spoils.

On the other hand, there are facts which belie the story. The Prince kept the command of The Fortress to himself, but, not wishing nor expecting to be tied down in a minor appointment and an out-of-the-way place, he appointed as Governor the Count of Valdesoto. The count has been described by a Spanish historian as '*católico irlandes, mal visto por los ingleses*'—an Irish Catholic in bad odour with England. In other words, he was one of the 'wild geese', the refugees from England's protestant zeal in Ireland, who had taken service in Europe with a Catholic king. Only the engineered confusion of this dynastic war could have put him on the same side as Rooke!

One wonders why, if Rooke had pushed Hesse aside and hoisted his flag, he allowed him to appoint such a Governor. Further, the second Governor was the Spanish General Ramos. It is too much to believe that these two men fought off the counter-attack in the interests of Britain and under the British flag.

Rooke left The Rock—in a huff, perhaps, at Valdesoto's appointment—and went out to look for the French fleet, just a week after the surrender. It was a good thing he did so, for he met them at Málaga, a day's sail away and heading for Gibraltar. He fought them to a stalemate and then limped back gratefully to his new haven.

With the counter-attack beaten off, the French fleet held if not defeated, and Cádiz, with Gibraltar on one side and Lisbon on the other, rendered useless, the Archduke Charles deemed it safe to sally forth from his headquarters. The Anglo-Dutch fleet brought him to Gibraltar in July 1705, almost a year after its capture, and there—on what must still have been considered Spanish soil, in spite of Rooke's alleged flag-wagging, for otherwise there would have been no point in the journey—he was publicly proclaimed Charles III, King of Spain. The proclamation must have rung hollow, and echoed off the bare rock, for he stood on a piece of Spain with no Spaniards, and on land that, due to his own ambition, was rapidly slipping from Spain for ever. The imagination may toy for a moment with the ribald and *sotto voce* comments of the shacombe filthies of the British fleet as they watched these pretentious caperings.

A few months after this event the last Spanish governor of Gibraltar, General Ramos, quietly left the pages of history, and a Colonel Elliot took office as the first British Governor.

Exactly how this great change in policy, aim and outcome was brought about in so short a time is a puzzle for professionals. Probably the British began to realize that Charles had no hope of success in his claim. Some years later his father died, so that he became Emperor of Austria. Then Britain, judging that to be enough power for any continental and Catholic monarch, quietly dropped him. There was no question of offering him Gibraltar as a booby prize, for Queen Anne had quickly consolidated her dubious conquest.

But what kind of a conquest it was seems to remain unclear. 'The British captured Gibraltar', we are told and taught, 'in 1704.' There is no doubt that Admiral Rooke was the *de facto* instigator and leader of the attack, but *de jure* he was subordinated to the Prince of Hesse, who was the agent or plenipotentiary of the British-backed Pretender to the Spanish throne. There were Dutchmen, too, in the action, but Holland made no claim to The Rock; as loyal servants of the Hapsburg cause, they did their duty there and sailed away.

That Gibraltar was not to be considered a British prize is quite clear from the fact that the first two governors subsequent to the capture, appointed by Hesse in the name of 'Charles III', were Spaniards. Britain's true capture was made, not in 1704 at all, but at some later date when the first British Governor was installed. How was that arranged? By threat, negotiation, *coup d'etat*, *fait accompli*, bribery, blackmail, trickery, concealed purchase, or by mere default of stronger claimants? I do not know. But I do know that although the British played the main part in the capture, in alienating the place from Spain, they did not take Gibraltar by act of conquest in 1704.

Queen Anne, under pressure of circumstances there, soon declared Gibraltar a free port—free of import and export imposts and duties. The result of this was that alien people came to the alienated land. They were people of assorted origin but they had one thing in common, the prospect of gaining by the freedom of the port and the change of ownership. They gained, rebuilt, consolidated and stayed, to become, two and a half centuries later, a self-governing people styled The Gibraltarians. Thus the simple struggle to place this flag or that over an empty, rocky offshore fortress became the much more

complicated one of tenancy, rights and vested interests. The aliena-
tion of Gibraltar had been effected often before, but the complete
re-population gave it the quality of permanence. The roots of rock-
plants are characteristically deep and tenacious.

The displaced Spanish citizens walked sadly upland to their pil-
grimage shrine at San Roque, just out of the gunshot of those days,
and crowded and camped there with a full view of their rocky home,
to wait for the armies of Spain to win it back for them. When the
counter-attack failed, they began to build houses fit for a longer
period of waiting. They used the ruins of Carteia for their quarry,
and in time they built a sound little hilltop town. Later, the town
of San Roque was given the city arms of Gibraltar, the castle and
the key, and the legend underneath said: 'The most loyal etc. city
of San Roque, in which resides that of Gibraltar.'

On his first night on that bare hilltop the magistrate Don Barto-
lome Varela could not sleep. He spent it scratching on a stone with
his stiletto. He inscribed the profile of The Rock, surmounted it with
a cross, and wrote below it '*Aqui lloré a Gibraltar*'—Here I wept for
Gibraltar. And so we know that they felt it too, the strange, strong
grip that this place takes on those who find refuge here. To this day,
there is a sombreness in San Roque, and the British visitor meets a
grave and watchful courtesy, but nothing more.

And what of Rooke, a peerage, perhaps and a great grant of lands
and funds? So I should have expected, but it was not so. Rooke had
engaged the French twice without defeating them, so that he had
failed to fulfil his orders. On his own authority, he had attacked
Cádiz, and later Ceuta, without any lasting success. He had seized
a big, bare, undefended rock, but that was an action independent
of Whitehall too, and a conquest which might well have got into
the wrong hands! Rooke was given nothing, not even another
command, and he died a sad man in 1708.

My maternal grandmother was an English Rooke. I never heard
her mention the Admiral, nor claim kin with him, but she was from
his part of the country and she was very proud of her family and
its crest, which she carried on a gold signet ring. On a visit to her,
from Ireland, when I was a small boy, she showed me this crest
which carried a rook, most rapacious of the crow family, picking the

choice tips from a wheatsheaf. She explained that the rook was being thrifty—a good provider. With my more rural background, and that literal morality which we so soon outgrow, I piped up that rooks were robbers and that the wheatsheaf did not belong to this one. Grandmother calmly replied that it probably belonged to some bad man.

I was well satisfied with this answer at the time, and it was not until years later—years spent at a Scots-Irish school—that it gave me a flash of insight into the folklore of the English. It occurred to me that their folk hero, Robin Hood, who was, after all, an outlaw and a thief, could have been a tricky man to sell to youth during the period of Victorian commercial morality. The difficulty was overcome by pointing out that he robbed only the wicked and rich— those who deserved it and could well afford it. The casuistry lies in the obvious, yet overlooked fact that he had no alternative—the poor were not worth robbing.

However, with maturity and travel, and with eight years in Gibraltar, I lost my fierce Irish purism, and came to terms with the acquisitive ideal. When my son was born on The Rock I gave him Rooke as one of his Christian names, as much in tribute to the pragmatical admiral as to my casuistical grandmother.

12

TEETHING TROUBLES

As Rooke crept back to his new refuge at Gibraltar, after running out of his remaining ammunition in his foolhardy battering match with the French off Málaga, the counter-attack on The Rock began. It was led by Irish troops in the service of France, and amounted to about eight thousand men. Since Rooke had taken the marines with him, there were only about eight hundred soldiers in the Fortress. Since Admiral Byng, his subordinate officer, had taken all the bronze cannon off The Rock as his personal loot, the place was poorly armed. Byng had also taken all the wine captured there and most of the flour, so provisions were low as well.

Hesse had made a signal contribution to the mess by appointing Count Valdesoto as his deputy governor. Valdesoto, whose family name was Nugent, being an Irish Catholic, could not hold her Britannic Majesty's commission because of the disabling laws of the time. Hesse got round this by making him a major general in the Spanish Army of the Pretender, which seems to have been one of those Fred Karno outfits, with more generals than privates. The English Brigadier Fox, the senior officer who might have expected to be appointed deputy governor, took umbrage at once and asked to be sent home. In view of the impending danger, Hesse refused him leave. One may be sure that, outranked and pushed aside by these foreign and papist upstarts, Fox was a very weak link in the chain of command.

The attackers had waited outside Gibraltar until they mustered eight thousand men and an appropriate number of cannon. Then they opened fire, and deadly fire it must have been, for they killed one in three of the defenders inside three weeks. The dilapidation of the old Spanish walls must have aided them, and they had a fifth column in the form of some undiagnosed disease which raged inside The Fortress—a plague, perhaps, carried by rats and flies from the carnage of the Capture?

Gibraltar was saved from the sea, when the British Fleet easily landed two thousand men, munitions and provisions. A British squadron held command in The Bay, and the besiegers withdrew after seven months of fruitless assault.

This successful defence of Gibraltar, coming soon after the good news of its capture, fixed The Rock in the minds of the British people, and founded what is known as 'The Gibraltar Tradition'. Nursed by street ballads, pamphlets, later by music halls, and latest by the popular press, this tradition is alive and kicking to this day. 'Safe as The Rock of Gibraltar,' they say in England, and even farther afield. From the year 1704 onwards, Gibraltar has been to the good people of England a symbol of that fortitude and steadfastness upon which—rather than upon brilliance—they pride themselves.

The politicians of England were pressed by circumstances to be less sentimental, more realistic, than the people. They soon discovered—as they have discovered again, today—that Gibraltar was an embarrassing possession, with nothing at all to recommend it except in time of war. Expensive to man and munition, it produced nothing, except the illwill of Spain and France. Much later, it was to become an important, if questionable, outlet of British manufactured goods. Prior to that development it was not valued. On several occasions British governments attempted to horse-trade The Rock for more profitable advantages elsewhere. On each occasion, public opinion restrained them.

In 1718, a short fourteen years after its 'Glorious Capture', Lord Stanhope's government offered The Rock to Spain in return for the relinquishment of her claims in Italy. The Fleet Street pamphleteers exposed this proposal, and Stanhope hesitated to press it, until the redoubtable Admiral Byng destroyed another Spanish squadron and so made the bribe unnecessary. The Regent of France offered Stanhope an untold sum of money to bribe the Commons to accept the proposal. The Commons of that time were not, of course, democratically elected, but they had to face the public from time to time, and they liked to be as popular as self-interest permitted. They knew how public feeling ran on the subject of Gibraltar, and it must have run very high, indeed, for the Commons refused to be bribed.

The King of Spain was so disappointed and angry that he delayed signing Britain's annual permits for slave trading in his overseas dominions. This was considered by the English a highly unsporting gesture, and many a good cargo went bad in the holds of

John Bull's ships and had to be thrown overboard as shark fodder.

Such a blow in the pocket made the Government the more determined to placate Spain, and Stanhope gave a secret promise, in
1721, to manœuvre the cession of Gibraltar within a year. He died
soon after he made the promise, but his royal master, George I,
pursued the matter with Philip V of Spain, thus:

'Sir, My Brother,

. . . I do no longer balance to assure Your Majesty of my readiness
to satisfy you with regard to your demand touching the restitution
of Gibraltar, promising you to make use of the first favourable
opportunity to regulate this article with the consent of Parliament. . . .'

On the strength of that letter Britain's trading privileges in the
Spanish Indies were promptly confirmed. It occurs to me that Philip
did not see the catch in it, which lies in the words 'with the consent
of Parliament'. This was a factor, over which George I would have
had very little control, so that he could, at any future time, invalidate
his contract with a *non posse*. Philip, as a Holy Catholic and Absolute
Sovereign, sitting on a throne sanctified by Divine Right, might not
have understood the force of the proviso. George, either from pride
or duplicity, would not go out of his way to tell him. He had, in
fact, promised nothing, except to do his best; in return for this vague
assurance of goodwill Britain received documents which were worth
cash in hand.

After five years more of hanging about Philip lost his temper,
published the letter, and threatened to revoke his side of the bargain.
The all-powerful British merchants were faced with losses in the
Indies, so the Royal Navy was sent there to cut off Spain's gold
supply. Philip, who must have lived as hand-to-mouth as most good
Spaniards, had not enough money to start a major war. While he
cast about furiously for cash to implement his principles, the British
calmly strengthened Gibraltar.

In the year 1726 Spain—or, rather, Philip—attacked Gibraltar
with his Irish Brigade, led by 'Wild Geese'. Now twenty thousand
men—Irish, Flemings, Germans, and English and Scots Jacobites—
attacked Gibraltar in the name of Spain! They fired fourteen thousand cannon balls in four days, and then their guns melted—perhaps
they were not designed to fire under the Andalusian sun. There is

something truly Irish, I must admit, in such unwonted and ineffective enthusiasm, and the English, keeping their guns cool and their powder dry behind massive walls, must have had a good laugh.

They had made great improvements to the fortifications during their twenty-two year tenancy, for this terrific cannonade only killed twenty-six men within the Fortress.

Once again, Britannia ruled the waves, reinforcing and replenishing the beleaguered garrison as she wished. In effect, then, the garrison was not really beleaguered at all, and, after taking a year to find this out, the besiegers withdrew. The Gibraltar Tradition in England grew stronger.

*　　*　　*　　*

General George Augustus Eliott, First Baron Heathfield and Hero of Gibraltar, had fought the Spaniards in Cuba in 1762, and made a fortune out of Havana prize money. He was appointed Governor of Gibraltar when he was on the eve of retirement—almost sixty years of age. A dedicated, professional soldier, with a lifetime's experience in the Army, Eliott was an unusual man for his times and his profession. He was the younger son of a minor Scottish aristocrat and his father evidently believed in education. He was sent to Holland as a boy, and finished at the University of Leyden. That alone must have given him a head start on the English youth of the time—1735—but he proceeded to increase his lead by studying at a French military academy. They must have taught him that tradition was not everything, and that there was a practical and technical aspect of the military profession. From France he proceeded to Woolwich and took a course of instruction as a field engineer. Thus, and only thus, could a clever and determined young man without the funds to buy rank or promotion, advance himself in the British army. Lads like George Eliott, as they had learnt on their hide, could not be done without. Even he had to buy his way up, as soon as he could, and so he reached the rank of lieutenant-colonel in 1754, at the age of thirty-seven. He was austere, almost ascetic, a teetotaller and vegetarian, an early riser, and a health and exercise enthusiast. He was, in short, what the Army regards as a perennial nuisance, an eager beaver—but he was the right man in the right place. He took his new job seriously from the start.

It was a very serious job. Eliott found Gibraltar, in the face of the greatest threat in its history, with dilapidated defences, a weak garrison, and provisions below par. The Royal Navy had acquired a safe and central Mediterranean base in Port Mahon in the Balearic Islands in 1708, and the Lords of the Admiralty had long since lost interest in Gibraltar. There was only one man-o'-war, three frigates and a sloop in The Bay when The Great Siege began, although all experience had shown that the defence of The Rock depended on sea power.

Eliott had two years, as it transpired, to prepare for siege, but he could not have been sure of this. In spite of all his urgent and pleading letters to London, he had less than six thousand men on The Rock when the battle began.

Such was his thoroughness that Eliott had all the streets ploughed up to prevent ricochets, and all unnecessary high towers, including the church spires, were razed to the ground. No detail was beneath his attention; the issue was too important for him to delegate anything to his subordinate officers. The British officer of that time was typically a man who had bought a commission or a whole regiment, a kind of military sub-contractor, so that no question of ability— except ability to pay—was inherent in his office. More often than not he was a younger son, an embarrassment to his family, a man lacking ability to make his way in any other profession or trade. Later, during the siege, when Eliott had to consider minimum rations, he had to experiment on himself, and lived for eight days on four ounces of rice a day, to prove that it could be done. He took over, not a great fortress, but a do-it-yourself kit.

The civilian inhabitants of Gibraltar, Genoese, Jews and Moors, were offered free passages to Port Mahon and Genoa before the siege began. It is recorded that many went away, and this comes to mind when the modern Gibraltarians take pride in the sieges which their ancestors withstood. Some elected to stay on The Rock, and it turned out that they included men with heavy hoards hidden away and famine prices in view. Such allowed their cupidity to conquer their fears.

The greatest and last siege of Gibraltar began on the 11th July 1779 and continued unbroken for three years and seven months.

Sieges are, by their nature, deadlocks, static and uneventful tests of endurance. Even the best accounts of the Great Siege make dull reading. At the same time, I must respect it as an historical event of the first magnitude. Here were the three greatest nations in the world engaged on a very large scale, with all the other nations watching. It was all-out warfare, with one hundred and twenty thousand men involved, and all confined to an area of some three square miles.

There were about ten men outside The Fortress for every man inside it, yet the defenders never looked like losing, such was the strength of the place they held. Their only dangerous enemy was the matter of supply—of food and ammunition. During the siege they were relieved at least three times by the British Navy—roughly once a year. This time, the Royal Navy was not in full command of the seas, in this part of the world, for the very good reason that it was heavily engaged in the American War of Independence, and its aftermath and resulting threats to British colonies in the Americas. Had it been free of this commitment, there would have been no siege at Gibraltar. The word implies a place surrounded and closed. In this case, Gibraltar was nearly so, but Britain managed to raise the siege by occasional service at the back door. Many months of labour and vigilance, and many millions of money, could be placed to the besieger's loss every time a supply ship reached the garrison. After each relief, since starvation was the enemy's only effective weapon, the attack and siege began again from scratch, and the foregoing years and months were cancelled.

The attack with shot and shell was as ineffective as one would expect. In six weeks, in 1781, the attackers threw 56,000 shot and 20,000 shell into The Fortress. This deluge of scrap iron killed only seventy men. It destroyed hundreds of houses, of course, but these belonged to civilians and, in those circumstances, the military would not be unduly worried.

In the long history of The Great Siege I can find only two events of much interest. One of these was the daring and successful sortie into the enemy lines, when two thousand British walked out of the gates at night, spiked the enemy's guns and levelled his parapets, and walked back home. Eliott could never have hoped that such a limited action would persuade the besiegers to depart, or that the damage inflicted by his men would not be speedily repaired. It was within his capabilities to understand that the tedium of the situation, its sapping of his mens' morale, was a real enemy. If he planned this action to defeat boredom and lend encouragement, he succeeded brilliantly.

By 1782, the third year of the siege, the attackers were desperate. They must have felt, as well as the ceaseless drain on their pockets, the silent jeering of the neutral world. One Englishman was defying ten of theirs, and even sallying out to tweak their beards! Something must be done.

They staged a competition for the best means of subduing Gibraltar, and the Chevalier d'Arcon won it with his idea of mounting a flank attack by means of Floating Batteries. There were ten of them, made on the basis of cut-down ships, great and small, heavily decked and sheathed with timbers, roofed with rope nets and hides, fireproofed by an ingenious sprinkler system, and armed with from ten to twenty brass cannon of the heaviest gauge.

The combined fleets of France and Spain came into The Bay to support them, and in April 1782 the whole array of ships and contraptions lined up facing the west flank of The Rock and half a mile offshore and opened fire with five hundred guns. The British calmly answered this holocaust with ninety-six guns and a secret weapon invented by Lt.-General Boyd, Eliott's Irish deputy—red hot cannon balls.

The outcome was that every one of the fireproof Floating Batteries was soon burnt and sunk and fifteen hundred of their crewmen killed. The good Chevalier d'Arcon had overlooked the need for manœuvrability, and his heavy rafts proved sitting ducks for shore-mounted and heavily protected guns, targets greedily crowded with defenceless men. The rope and hide canopies were of good service to the British as tinder.

This farcical failure, witnessed from the crowded hilltops of Spain and noted by the whole civilized world, pointed towards the end of an era of military fooling and of amateur aristocratic commanders. A few weeks later, in October 1782, the Royal Navy relieved The Rock once more, and the Dukes, Marquesses, Counts and Chevaliers of France and Spain quietly gave up and went home. The leader of the long assault, the Duc de Crillon, was entertained by General Eliott when it was all over. He was shown the latest in British defences, galleries cut in the northern precipice with gun ports at intervals, and was heard to remark: 'These works are worthy of the

Romans.' This was taken as a compliment, and the visit ended with assurances of mutual goodwill.

Between these two events—The Sortie and The Floating Batteries —the journals of The Great Siege are made up of remarks about the weather, the occasional accident, the number of shots fired each day, and the occasional arrival of a deserter from the other side. There are also numerous references to the prices being demanded by the civilians for hoarded food, and to the savage punishments inflicted on those whose hoards were discovered.

The best chronicler of The Great Siege, potentially, was the artless, honest soldier, Sam Ansell of the 58th Regiment. He wrote for his own amusement, without policy or plan to publish, and had there been anything worth recording, he would have been the most likely man, in my view, to notice it. But even Sam, with his informal eye, saw little of real interest. He began his notes before The Siege started with the following bold ballad:

> With Martial Courage we our Foes defy,
> For George we live, and in his Cause we'll die,
> Nor fear we their attack upon this Place,
> For Eliott will the Foe courageous face.

This is interesting because it shows that Ansell, and presumably others, had faith in Eliott from the start, and perhaps affection for him. The output of a limited number of guns, as Nelson proved at Trafalgar, was in direct proportion to the men's esteem of their commander; the gunners can comply or excel. There is no doubt that under Eliott they excelled themselves.

But I find a wry pathos in Sam's sentiments in view of the fact that George had made every effort, and would do so again, to horse-trade The Rock for slaving permits over the poor man's head.

Four years later, Ansell ended his diary:

'This day has brought us joyful news . . . at about eleven at night all firing stopped on both sides.

'Everything wears a different aspect; our very foes jump upon their works and in strong vociferation send forth their congratulations!

'The thundering cannon that so often spread death around stand silent now.

'Almighty God be praised.'

Pick up thy musket, Sam. The Great Siege is over.

On a northern wall of Gibraltar, facing Spain, there is a plaque
with the following inscription:

'These walls suffered, on the 12th July, 1781, a Spanish bombardment estimated at about 150,000 balls and 60,000 thirteen-inch
shells. One hundred and twenty of the defenders were killed and
property in the town sustained eighty thousand pounds worth of
damage. The fortifications were almost undamaged.'

This is the short history of a long siege, and tells us all we need
to know. It tells us that the siege was fierce, the attack lavish to the
point of wild extravagance, the enemy aggressive to the point of
being insensate. About one ball in two thousand killed a man. There
had been a considerable advance in artillery since the siege of 1727—
those thirteen-inch shells—but an even greater advance in fortifications. As has been proved over and over again, (right up to the
Battle of Tarawa in World War II), no amount of bombardment
can dislodge or kill entrenched men nor win territorial battles.

In all my works in Gibraltar, and they covered the main part of
it from end to end, I never saw foundations excavated without
uncovering at least one old cannon ball, solid or hollow, large or
small, one of the 1,999 which went astray every time a man was
killed. These balls are too numerous in Gibraltar to be valuable or
even interesting, and there is no plant there to melt them down.
They lie about the place like pebbles on the seashore, quietly rusting
to rejoin their mother earth.

Again, the besiegers seem to have been anything but Spanish.
There were battalions of Irish, three of Walloons, two each from
Savoy and Naples, two from Flanders, one from France, and even
one from Switzerland. There were also—in case you can think of
anything more utterly useless for besieging a fortress—no less than
seventeen squadrons of cavalry, of which three were Dutch and one
was, of all things, Maltese!

The picture of Maltese cavalry charging The Fortress of Gibraltar
may seem to shift the scene from comedy to farce, but let us not,
in our hindsight, be too severe. British cavalry was still charging

artillery in the Crimea a century later, and, indeed, in 1916, fifty years after that again. Some say that but for General de Gaulle and a few more insistent and unpopular cranks, cavalry would have been charging the German *panzer* divisions in 1940.

But one serious question remains. What united all these peoples, some of them patently Protestant, under the banners of Spain? I have not been able to discover any national or political common denominator for them, and I can only assume that they were soldiers in the exact sense of that word—'hired men', there for guinea gold. Could it be for this reason that they were so ineffective, and—as the success of the British Sortie showed—downright inefficient and disinclined? That they lacked the sense of moral loyalty and the righteous indignation which drive men on beyond the bare demands of duty?

Or—worse—could it be that as steady wage-earners, safe in their siegeworks, with a rich countryside behind them, and pretty camp followers from Cádiz, and the sun shining, as it does there, for three hundred days a year, could it be that these good soldiers invented Go Slow and Work to Rule? *Si non é vero, é ben trovatto*—if it isn't so, it ought to be.

And even after all this, the British Government entertained a proposal from France offering Martinique and Guadalupe in exchange for returning Gibraltar to Spain. The obvious and deserved reply was 'Mind your own business', but the mercenary ministers went so far as to sound out Parliament on the offer. It shows how completely unrepresentative were the aristocratic ministers of Britain in those times, that they thought there was a chance of acceptance. Parliament was not so far out of touch with public opinion, and had sufficient strength to force the rejection of the impudent proposal.

When, a few years after The Great Siege, General Eliott was made Baron Heathfield of Gibraltar, the spotlight played on The Rock again, in the midst of popular acclaim. Even the hard-faced, hard-drinking men who governed Britain at that time, could hardly intend to sell the ground from under Lord Heathfield's feet. It looked as though, at last, the Crown had resigned itself to keeping the hard-won gift which Rooke and Eliott had forced upon it.

Tarik took Gibraltar, empty and undefended, in a matter of hours. The Spaniards took one hundred and fifty-nine years to oust the

Moors for good. Britain, considering the counter-attacks and their ultimate repulsion, spent eighty years in conquering and consolidating the conquest of Gibraltar. Now, at last, in 1784, it could be considered safely and securely British, and the Gibraltar Tradition reached its full flowering. Now it was clear that The Rock would not be sold or ceded, and even clearer that it could not be snatched by Spain—or even by Spain, France and all their mercenary allies added together. British interests there, a shrewd man could see, would scarcely be attacked, and if they were attacked, would be defended with the full might of British arms—arms growing stronger year by year. The ground was clear for settlement there, and for social and commercial development. The civil history of British Gibraltar had begun.

13

ROYAL DIVERSION

Now let us step aside and sally into Spain for a brief holiday. Our host today is one Fernando Cruz Guerrero, a Gibraltarian of opaque means of support, from whom my friend, Dr. James Johnson cut the tonsils. Dr. Johnson is an English doctor attached to the Colonial Hospital here. Fernando has the true hypochondria, and he is convinced that his tonsils—the only pair in which he had ever taken any interest—were unique in the annals of surgery. Hence, Dr. Johnson is the greatest surgeon of all time.

In anaesthesia Fernando talked of fighting cocks; Johnson mentioned this to him to cheer his convalescence; the invitation to go with him to a Spanish cockfight followed.

So here we are, Dr. Johnson and I, in the backyard of Cruz Guerrero, drinking sherry while he gets two cocks ready for battle. As soon as he has finished, we will be taking them to the cockpit, across the frontier into Spain. There is a law against it here in Gibraltar.

These cocks, Fernando says, are the best breed in the world—the English Game. He has one of them in his lap; the bird lies quietly while he files and measures its spurs over and over again, using a triangular glass file and, for measuring, the *escantillon*, or spur gauge, an ancient instrument made from a metal tube, with a slide in it like a spring balance.

It is true, as even Johnson and I know, that the English Game is famous. The gamecock was brought to England by the Romans, who got him, with other things, from the Greeks. No doubt they brought him to France and Spain as well. In France he rose to be a national emblem; in Spain he continues his public career as though the Romans were still there; but his finest development was in the more rigorous climate of England. Only there did he rise to royal favour and fight in Whitehall with great funds behind him. Only in England did the cockfight become known as the Royal Diversion.

'These cocks are fighting one to each other when they are the size of that wineglass,' explains Fernando, in his good off-beat English.

'When they have four months, I am having to raise myself at five in the morning if it makes rain.'

'Why's that?'

'Because the light comes at five o'clock, and one looks to the other. All are disfigured in the feathers with the wetness. They go by sight; they don't smell nothing never. One he is saying: "This fellow I do not know. Who the hell is he that is putting to me the hard face?" The other, his little brother, he is saying: "Who the hell is this stranger over there? Who let *him* in?" Then—poum!— they are off, killing one to each other until all remain killed but the last one.' Fernando wiped his brow and drank some sherry. Then he added: 'He dies.'

At five months each cock has to be put in a cage by himself, he tells us. Once he had ten of them in a row. One escaped during the night, and as soon as there was light enough to see, it ran up and down in front of the cages. The cages did not prevent those cocks from showing fight. They could not use their spurs, but with their English blood they did not hesitate. They stuck their necks out, and the free cock killed his nine brothers before Fernando came down to breakfast.

Now Fernando makes a final careful measurement of the spur. This cock is to fight at three pounds two ounces, with spurs of sixteen millimetres. There is up to an ounce of tolerance in the weight, but not a shade of tolerance in the length of the spurs.

They are the cock's own spurs. Spain is a poor country, and the cockfight is a poor man's sport. They cannot afford to throw a new cock into the pit every five minutes, Fernando says, to be slaughtered so quickly by steel. In England, yes—steel spurs two inches long. There, you have plenty. Plenty of cocks, plenty of steel. In Spain, a cock gets false spurs only if he has broken his own, and then they give him spurs from a dead cock, of natural length.

We are nearly ready. The cock has been clipped long before—the red, reptilian head, so that the enemy cannot hold him easily, the comb trimmed down to a stump, the breast and flanks plucked so that his wounds may be better seen and bathed. Now the bare bird is washed down with sherry—the alcohol will toughen his skin. Food? Not a bite for twenty-four hours back, but before that all he could eat, of the very best. As for training, he has had a run every day— half an hour's dancing, scratching and shadow sparring, alone in the little pen in front of his cage, and, once a week, a five-minute bout with another cock with gloves of chamois leather on the spurs. Thus he is made cunning for the duel and stiff in the thighs. We shall see why.

The cock that Fernando holds is called Tranquilo—the Quiet One—because he is so fierce. The other is Cuatro Minutos—Four Minutes—because he has twice killed a cock in that time. Yes, Fernando says, he would have called him Dr. Bannister had he thought of it.

With Tranquilo in one basket and Cuatro Minutos in another, we set out for the cockfight.

The cockpit is the first I have ever seen, yet it is familiar, for cockpits were standardized centuries ago and they have not changed since Hogarth made his prints. It is a twelve-foot circle with a matting floor and a white canvas wall two feet high. At one side, behind a little ringside shelf, sits the president. His face is dark and wizened, and he blinks behind thick spectacles. On his shelf he has the tools of office—a sponge in a glass of wine, a tin alarm clock, a sandglass to measure out the last, fatal minute, a spur gauge, and half a lemon. The assessor sits beside him—a sleek and glossy fellow with a tin tray to hold the stakes. All around, on four tiers of rough benches, sit The Fancy, about two hundred souls.

We are ushered to a back bench, high enough, we are told, to be clear of the blood spatters. Here Fernando presents us to a dapper man of middle age—an officer in the police, and a cock man of note, Fernando says, with a grand bird entered in the lists today. Now he must excuse himself; he has to present Tranquilo to the president. The commandant explains to us everything that is going on, and offers much polite admiration for England. No matter what may be said against our country, he says, she has made a great contribution to the noble sport we are about to witness.

Below us, the president, with Tranquilo docile in his hands, is consulting his list of weights and spurs. He announces that the rival to Tranquilo will be a cock called Bicicleta—Bicycle. In turn, the two cocks are put down, and prance around the ring to show their form. Bicicleta makes three rapid circuits to prove his name, and everyone laughs at this.

The cocks are laid in cradles of string and weighed against each other on a small Roman steelyard, still called *La Romana*. They balance exactly. All four spurs are measured. The betting opens.

Fernando lays five hundred pesetas on the tray. 'A hundred bottles,' the assessor announces. A bottle, the commandant tells us, is five pesetas—a euphemism surviving from some brief period when it was illegal to bet in money. He explains that since the cocks are the same in weight and armament, and only hidden courage and fortitude are in the balance, the betting is even. Bicicleta's owner will have to match the amount that is wagered on Tranquilo, or his cock will be retired. But if even money cannot be reached, two-thirds may suffice.

Bicicleta's owner can put down only fifty bottles. He addresses the ring, seeking backers. It is not, he says, that he lacks confidence in his champion—far from it. But he is a man modestly situated and with many children. Had he a thousand bottles—nay, a million— they would lie there on that tray. He does us the favour of advising us to back Bicicleta with our all.

The commandant begs Dr. Johnson and me not to back Fernando's cock. Bicicleta will have his work cut out to rise to a hundred bottles, and if we increase the sum he has to meet, by raising the ante on Tranquilo, there will be endless delay. Tranquilo is a known killer; Bicicleta is a dark horse. Oh yes, the commandant says, they both look good, identical, in fact. But Cruz Guerrero has race and blood and caste in his cock house. This other fellow—this peasant— has three cocks and a lot of cheek.

Bottle by bottle, Bicicleta's pile rises until it reaches sixty-eight. The president then decrees that the fight begin. The peasant protests—even money or home he goes! Fernando, holding Tranquilo gently over the ring with both hands, swings him gently to and fro and turns his eyes up to heaven, seeking patience.

The president quotes the ancient rule: a cock must fight if his backing reaches two-thirds of the leading stake. The peasant remarks that it is a funny thing that the rules, like the laws, are always invoked against the poor man. At this, everyone looks up at the commandant, but he is staring up at the sky.

'The rules! The rules!' comes from all sides, but 'To hell with the rules!' shouts the peasant, hugging Bicicleta under his arm. Then suddenly, hispanically, he gives in, and thrusts the cock into the president's hands. The president impales his half lemon on each of the cock's spurs in turn, and twirls it vigorously. Tranquilo's spurs are similarly treated, and the two cocks are placed carefully in the ring by their owners, each cock pointed at his adversary, and re-leased with a final pat of encouragement.

Now a tight circle of anxious faces bends towards and over the cockpit. A foot below the noses of the ringsiders, the cocks crouch on the mat, necks stretched, wings hanging, beak to beak. They weave with their necks, each trying to get a little 'side' on the other. Tranquilo strikes first, with a jump into the air, a flick of hard wings, and a double blow with spurs almost too fast to follow. Bicicleta rolls over once, lands on his feet, twitches his fiery head, and runs back to battle.

'The head,' says the commandant. 'They die by the head. You will see.'

In the next ten minutes that brief action is repeated fifty times. Thirty times Tranquilo leads; twenty times it is Bicicleta. In the cockfight, I decide, there seems to be no variation and very little luck. True, says the commandant—rarely a lucky knockout, and hardly ever an unexpected recovery. It is a war of attrition, in the manner of modern heavyweights, hammering each other's damaged eyes. Indeed, it is duller, for the cocks fight by reflex only. They fight to win and kill, with no dash, no undue risks, nothing but a dull and deathly fortitude.

Now the birds are beginning to tire. Their relative quality be-comes more exposed, and the betting reopens. Even I can see that Bicicleta is tiring faster than Tranquilo. 'Blood tells,' whispers the commandant. 'And look at the spurs.' Tranquilo's legs are blood-stained right up to the feathers; Bicicleta's are yellow and clean. Both heads are bloodstained; the wounds there do not show. It is the weapons that tell the story.

The birds are striking less often, but with even more effect. The aim is surer now, and the target more fixed. They stand sparring, trying to catch each other by the stumpy comb—to catch, hold and strike. Every blow now is patiently manœuvred; no strength remains to be wasted. Both beaks are open, both crimson heads are glistening with blood. Tranquilo's nostril is torn. Then Bicicleta loses an eye.

'It's criminal,' says the commandant. 'But they are born to fight. What can we do?'

'We could separate them,' I suggest, hopefully.

'And the money?' he asks, laughing. 'Who would get the money?'

Tranquilo is keeping on the blind side of the enemy—by cunning, they say, but to me it seems that by mere trial and error he has found the blind side safer. He seizes and strikes incessantly, pressing his advantage. Bicicleta pecks the air, his remaining eye filled with blood. When he feels the foe, he strikes, but he does this rarely and wildly, throwing his feeble funds away. He runs here and there, bleeding, fumbling, groping for a target. Alert and confident, Tranquilo trips along after him and hits him when he turns. I find a deep pathos in the contrast. No one will bet any more on the result. Bicicleta's owner, the modest man with many children, watches in dull despair.

Soon Bicicleta is pushed against the spattered canvas wall and cornered. Tranquilo holds him there and cuts him rhythmically twenty times. The blind bird strikes back once or twice, but misses. He clinches, and tucks his head under his tormentor's wing. Tranquilo twists away, breasts him to the wall, steps back, flips Bicicleta's head up, and hacks him in mid air. Bicicleta's head droops downwards in jerks, lower and lower, until his bill rests on the matting. But even that will not do. Tranquilo plucks his head up by the stump of comb, steadies it at the correct level, and strikes again.

'If he let him alone,' says the commandant, 'Bicicleta would put his breast on the canvas and end it. But while he's attacked, his legs won't bend—that's his instinct and training.'

'What's the point of keeping him there?' I ask.

'The money, sir, the money! If he stands on his feet for forty-five minutes—keeps his breast off the mat—then it's a draw, and they'll all get their money back.'

'How long has he stood it?'

'Sixteen and a half minutes now. He'll never make the time. Too sick too early.'

'Why doesn't his owner take him out?'

'Cheek, sir, I told you. Also, he has nothing to lose—the cock cannot live. He thinks he has some chance to gain—say Tranquilo goes to sleep, or some such thing!'

But Tranquilo has no intention of going to sleep. He will leave nothing to chance. He flicks the head up again and again, until a hook catchesBicicleta inthe ye socket and rolls him on to his back. He lies there, cycling feebly in the air with his yellow legs. Then he dies.

Tranquilo stands eyeing the corpse. There is nothing in his wild, hard eye but a wary curiosity about the enemy's new position. Perhaps he does not recognize this prone and grotesque creature as another cock. He waits, watching for the slightest movement, but sees none. Then he draws in a little breath, throws back his bloody head, and crows a short, cracked crow. A ripple of laughter runs round the cockpit, and the fight is over.

There are five more duels to come, but Dr. Johnson and I decide that we have seen our cockfight, our first and our last. I have found it more wearying than historical research. Our host, Fernando, is busy presenting Tranquilo to the president and collecting his winnings, and the commandant accompanies us out into the spring sunshine. He has seen many fights in Madrid, he tells us. This is only country stuff. So long as he is in again for the fourth bout—his own cock, heavily backed. . . . Meanwhile, will we do him the honour of drinking a bottle of sherry with him?

So we share half a bottle of fine sherry out in the yard, with the caged game cocks crowing all around us, and the Spanish commandant beaming at us across the table.

'Well, gentlemen? Good? Or not good?'

'Very interesting,' we say. 'A great tradition in our own country.'

'Ah, in all the world!' he says. '*There* is bravery, single-mindedness, and fortitude! Now, a nation with soldiers like that . . .'

But the Doctor wants to know the purpose of the half lemon the president applied to the spurs. The commandant says it is used to remove all possibility of poison. What kind of poison? The commandant says there are many kinds, but he does not know their names, because, of course, he has never given a thought to such methods himself. He has lost money at the cocks, much money, but a man has to face his own honour; there is no hiding from that. No. The lemon removes every known poison, and keeps the grand old sport clean and pure—thank God!

'I know one poison it wouldn't remove,' says the Doctor.

'Which is that?' asks the commandant.

'Curare,' says Johnson. 'Curare would permeate the spur. And it would be deadly, too. It paralyses the muscles—just in the right place, and not too obviously.'

'What colour is it?'

'Colourless.'

'Spell it, please.'

The Doctor's Spanish is not equal to this, so he writes it down on a piece of paper. The commandant puzzles over the writing; then he asks Johnson if he will be so good as to print the name in capitals. Johnson does so. The commandant reads it, nods, and tosses the paper on the table.

Before the bottle is finished, we escape. Dr. Johnson says he must get back to Gibraltar; he has a patient to attend. The commandant is very sorry that we have to go, but he understands—none better— the stern call of duty. He walks with us to the yard gate, shaking hands and slapping shoulders. There we part.

But I find that I do not have my camera with me, and run back to see if I have left it on the table—run back just in time to see the commandant in the act of snatching up the little paper with the name of the poison in block letters and thrusting it into his pocket. He bows briefly and hurries over to the cockpit.

On the drive back I tell Johnson what I have seen.

'Presumably to prevent its falling into irresponsible hands,' he says. 'A pity. It could have let some of them die a little faster.'

14

ROUND THE RUGGED ROCK

Britain took Gibraltar in 1704, repulsed three counter-attacks and consolidated the conquest over a period of eighty years. They were years of Britain's youth as a great power, and of Spain's senility.

During the long period of consolidation military considerations must have excluded all others, and one would not expect much immigration or civil development. There was some of each, nevertheless, and it is of special interest. The oldest roots of the British Gibraltarian people were put down at this time; from here we can trace the stock of the modern crop of people. Of interest, too, are the motives which drove or drew those early settlers to this place of discomfort and danger.

According to Dr. Howes, who has made the only study of the complicated ethnics of Gibraltar, the civil population remaining after the conquest amounted to thirty families of Genoese—about one hundred and fifty people. There is no evidence of any Jews or Moors being there at that time. The Spaniards, as we have seen, walked out *en masse*, leaving only a few invalids and an old priest to bury them.

The Spanish population waited and watched from their temporary quarters on San Roque hill, just out of gunshot, wishfully believing that right would prevail and that they would soon be home again. After the convincing repulse of the first counter-attack, such few realists as there were among them must have begun to doubt their country's ability to oust the invaders. A few of these Spaniards, probably the most practical and least principled stole back into Gibraltar and so put themselves under British rule and, possibly, recovered some of their possessions.

Thus, although only a few of the Spanish citizens returned, and although many of these had to leave again before the siege of 1727, it is still possible for a Gibraltarian with a Spanish name to claim a long history in the place. In fact he might claim, as a descendant of the pre-British settlers, to have a longer association with Gibraltar than anyone there with a British, Jewish or Italian name.

A muster roll of 1721, when the second siege threatened, lists the civilians able to bear arms:

45 English
96 Spaniards
169 Genoese.

If I may consider these as heads of households and assess their families at four persons each, the civilian population at that time would have been about one hundred and eighty English, four hundred Spaniards, and some six hundred Genoese. In the face of the renewed threat from Spain, the Spaniards in Gibraltar were very naturally suspect, and many of them left—or were expelled—before the siege began.

The English were nearly all civil employees of the army and navy, but a few sharp-nosed merchants were already in operation. The Genoese could not have quadrupled their numbers in seventeen years by natural increase, so I assume that some of them were new immigrants, paying a sincere compliment to Britain. Spanish or British government made little difference to them, for they were expatriates on sufferance in either case, but it is noteworthy that the changed sovereignty of Gibraltar did not deter them.

The muster roll does not list any Jews as able to bear arms, but this does not indicate that there were none there. There were, in fact, twenty-eight Jewish shops in Main Street as early as 1712, all paying rent—and a Christmas levy!—into the pocket of the governor.

Thirty-two years later, in 1753, the first census found a civilian population of 1,816 persons, made up as follows:

434 British
597 Genoese
575 Jews
185 Spaniards
25 Portuguese.

The broth thickens. The British population has doubled, and since it is too early in history to apply Parkinson's Law about the growth of bureaucracy, we shall seek and find other reasons for this increase. The Genoese and Spaniards have remained static in numbers, the exodus of some of the latter having been replaced by natural increase. The Jews have multiplied rapidly, and by 1779 they will make up one-third of the population. What could be attracting these peace-loving people to this bare, embattled Rock?

The Gibraltar Jews are all Sephardim, of that branch of the race which takes pride in having entered Europe by the front door rather than the back. They were carried along, all the way from their homeland, on the waves of Arab conquest, appreciated—however grudgingly—for their innate abilities. The conquering Moors in their heyday in Spain, had five hundred different names for a sword, which seems to indicate an insane obsession with warfare and violence. Their attendant Jews, with no such fruitless preoccupations, quietly proceeded with the necessary work of empire, with finance, supply, commerce and trade. They found time, too, for creative endeavour in the arts and sciences. One can judge their value by the fact that they were tolerated by Islam, that least tolerant of all faiths, and that many of them, in the face of every disability, acquired great wealth and distinction in Moorish Spain. That value, those innate abilities, continue to be handed down from careful father to dutiful son and ensured to each new generation by painstaking discipline and instruction. Even in these relaxed times, there is no carefree, rowdy youth for a Gibraltar Jew; life is all sober work and duty.

'Gibraltar is full of Jews,' is one of the many misapprehensions one hears about this place. It is not full of Jews, nor one-tenth full of Jews. But the small percentage there are all descendants of early birds and exceptionally able and, therefore, prominent citizens.

After the reconquest of Spain the embittered Moors would not have had much generosity or tolerance for their Jewish companions in disaster. In the shrunken circumstances of Morocco there could not have been much scope for Jewish enterprise. The Sephardim were uneasy and unhappy there, and the boldest of them must have been on the watch for an opportunity elsewhere. That opportunity came when, under their very eyes, the British captured Gibraltar.

After the first siege, from 1705 onwards, the British garrison depended on Morocco for fresh food and water and for necessary building materials. The Moorish emperor permitted this commerce on the condition that his subjects could trade freely on The Rock. The early governors of Gibraltar, stuffing their pockets with license fees, let them all come. Provided that they paid, it did not matter who they were nor whence they came. The traders flocked in from Barbary, Leghorn, and Portugal. From nearby Morocco came Jews and Moors, but mostly, we may be sure, Jews. Some of these Jews had arabic names but they were none the less Jewish by race and religion.

Gibraltar was in effect a free port right from the beginning of the British period. Desperately in need of all kinds of supplies, with Mother England forty days sail distant, there could be no question of levying import duties. Every passing ship, of whatsoever flag, had to be tempted to the port, if possible, and greedily unloaded there.

Britain recognized this privilege in 1706, and Gibraltar was visited by merchantmen of all nations. Whatever it may have done since, in those days trade followed the flag, and The Rock soon became a place of brisk and constant commerce—and not merely the commerce needed to support a few thousand soldiers and a few hundred civilians.

Spain, even then, was a duty-bound country, with high tariff walls to protect royal and privileged monopolies, and so inevitably, she had a well-established smuggling industry on all her frontiers. The whole of the southern branch of this industry turned its attention eagerly to the new, independent and convenient off-shore depot, Gibraltar. With its keen new merchants all fully protected by greedy governors indirectly profiting from the trade, with a complete lack of sentiment regarding the revenues of the neighbouring enemy, Gibraltar rose at once to the occasion. The first thing the British did in Gibraltar, as it happened, was to open it up for a smuggling base to Spain, so that it must have looked almost as though they had seized it for that purpose. Thus they laid the foundations for a trade and a reputation both still strong to this day.

Gibraltar's governors, at this period, used to make up to £20,000 per annum from traders' licenses, ground rents, fees and fines, and what would now be called protection money. For this they permitted and even encouraged the development of a sordid plague spot on The Rock, a haven for malefactors, a nasty gold-rush port which became a bad neighbour to all others.

To recognize the *status quo*, well believed to be necessary for the supply of The Fortress, and also to rival Leghorn, the only other free port in the Mediterranean, Queen Anne formally ratified Gibraltar's Free Port status by order in council in 1712. From that date onwards it was a free-for-all and a free fox in a free henroost. The greatest sufferer, of course, was neighbouring Spain. The Spaniards, who had held The Rock almost sacred, saw their worst fears realized by this surge of sacrilegious commercialism and lawlessness, and so began their implacable hatred for British Gibraltar and all that it represents. In place of their convents, warehouses; in place of churches, whorehouses; in place of religious austerity, profligate greed; and the brutal British heretic with his accursed Jews and Moors treading the streets of this holiest part of Holy Spain! Unkindest cut of all, this polyglot raggle-taggle was rapidly growing in strength and riches, whilst Spain grew poorer year by year. It was considerations like this, they say, which so tortured the Spanish king Philip V that he spent his whole life going mad about The Rock and scheming to regain it. His successors are still going mad about it two hundred years later.

*   *   *   *

Conn, in his *Gibraltar and British Diplomacy in the Eighteenth Century*, says that 'the corrupt and arbitrary administration of The Rock led the English merchants to avoid it, and so most of the local trade was handled by Moors, Jews and Genoese'. He points out that the open roadstead, with its sandy bottom for anchorage and dangerous east wind, had an inhibiting effect on trade. Nevertheless, there was a growing group of British merchants—not so much English as Irish—who, without going there for trading purposes, had found themselves there with the ball, so to speak, at their feet. Some of these, with the advantage of the English language, forged ahead even faster than the Jews. The Moors never made much of the situation, and have long since died out on The Rock, but for one old survivor and a pitiful vestige of a family mosque which remained there until about 1950.

By a clause in the Treaty of Utrecht, 1713, Britain agreed to exclude Jews and Moors from Gibraltar. This is one of the clauses since quoted by Spain to indicate that the cession was only conditional and temporary and that it never gave full sovereignty, but was rather in the nature of what is now termed a 'base'. A subsequent British treaty with the Sultan of Morocco, in 1729, permitted Moors and Jews to sojourn on The Rock, for trading purposes, for up to thirty days at a time. Needless to say, they stayed as long as they wished, as long as they paid the Governor.

The Utrecht Treaty had provided for a specified commerce between Gibraltar and Spain, but the Spaniards often revoked that privilege on the pretext of quarantine. In 1728 Spain forbade all commerce between her subjects and Morocco; since Gibraltar had to trade with Morocco, this had the effect of isolating The Rock from Spain. In 1748 commerce between Spain and Gibraltar reopened, and an uneasy friendship continued until 1763.

The population grew with the trade. There were censuses every ten years, and they tell their own tale:

	1767	*1777*	*1787*
British	467	519	512
Roman Catholics	1,460	1,819	2,098
Jews	783	863	776
	2,710	3,201	3,386

The Spanish historian, Ayala, wrote in 1766: 'It is difficult to conceive how so many persons can be maintained by trade in so small a space . . . there being neither manufactures nor agriculture wherein to employ themselves, nor vineyards, nor herds to be attended to.' His surprise was directed at a population of about 2,500 people. When, through time, that population rose to 25,000 it became obvious to the most innocent observer that Gibraltar had hidden assets. Alas, long before it reached that figure, the population was so heavily dependent on those assets that, clandestine and disreputable as they were, they could not be cast aside—not even in the cause of international goodwill and legality.

Modern British attitudes to bribery and corruption are, of course, exemplary. The civil service—and I have been a sharp-eyed member of various branches of it for over twenty years—is wellnigh incorruptible. Even the politicians have high standards of honesty. We tend to take this state of affairs for granted, to presume that it was always so in England. In fact, it is only a century old. In the eighteenth century our politics and administration were fields for ruthless plunder, and were not expected to be otherwise. Neither the Governors of Gibraltar nor those who appointed them could see anything wrong in the spoils system of the times. Occasionally some disgruntled officer, dismissed from The Rock for complaining of abuses there, would publish and expose the state of government in Gibraltar. No public action would be taken to improve matters; perhaps the erring Governor would be warned to be more tactful, to control his rapacity a little, but his fees and private ground rents would continue as before.

The neglect and exploitation of the civil population of Gibraltar had effects which have lasted to the present day. It worked both ways, neglect of the poor gave license to the rich—or better, since none of the early settlers arrived rich, let me say that there was license for the shrewd, bold and ruthless. Without guidance, aid or even security and justice, the poor grew poorer and descended into sordid squalor. Without let or hindrance on their nefarious practices, the rich grew richer, and cautiously began the consolidation of their property and power. Whilst the devil took the hindmost the foremost were free to advance. There was a minimum of what businessmen call 'Government interference'. So long as they made enough money to pay off the authorities, the dealer and grafter were in their paradise. Before the end of the century, great fortunes were already founded in Gibraltar.

But great misfortunes were already founded, too. Terrible epidemics were soon to ravage the population. In the year 1800 one-sixteenth of the Garrison died; in 1804 nearly six thousand people died in four months; the disease returned in the year 1810 and in 1813–14 it claimed eighteen hundred lives. What was it? Yellow fever? Bulam's fever? Or just an intermittent fever? The doctors differed and argued, and the patients died. What caused it? Some held to the Theory of Noxious Vapours, others swore by straight contagion but all had to agree that destitution and dirt were the root causes. Those diseases were finally defeated in Gibraltar as elsewhere, but the social distempers of those bad times are less easily eradicable.

Britain's first cynical century in Gibraltar seems to me to have allowed the civil and commercial life of the community to put down twisted roots. Looking back on that first hundred years, I see the great fortress, noble as ever, but lonely no longer. Its head is in the clouds, but its skirts are seething with greed and graft, with privilege and poverty.

'Round and round the rugged Rock the ragged rascals ran. . . .'

15

CONTRABANDO

The word looks strange in Spanish, but it need not do so, for we took it from that language, just as we took our word 'tariff' from the port of Tarifa, Gibraltar's neighbour in The Straits. My region has an ancient history of fiscal forfeit and its inevitable evasion.

Down here at Gibraltar we have two continents lying face to face, nine miles apart. The rivals—'owners of opposing river banks'— were enemy nations, both of them greedily and autocratically governed and full of avarice and privilege. Neither Moor nor Spaniard will rob his friends, but with centuries of bad government behind them they do not hesitate to rob the State and all its institutions.

Bribery and corruption, the ancient and universal system of The Orient, was brought to this place by the Arabs, spread throughout Spain, and consolidated there for seven centuries. It remains an integral and ineradicable characteristic of the Spanish way of life, and flourishes, Islam's curse on Christendom, in every country where Spain held sway.

The Moor's first and last duty is to pay tribute to his overlord, his sacred as well as secular superior. The Spaniard's duty is to his Church and to his family. Without money neither can fulfil his duty. Whence the money comes, how it is won, is a secondary consideration in both countries. The Moor and Spaniard sat there, glowering at each other across the narrow sea, with a deep mutual distrust and disagreement but with two characteristics in common—a deep and dire need for money and a lack of scruple as to the manner of its acquisition.

Into this situation, geographical and economic, there suddenly intrudes the perfect catalyst, the ideal go-between and wheeler-dealer—the rich and ruthless England of the eighteenth century. Hitherto The Rock of Gibraltar has been a bastion of Spanish law and order, manned by the King to protect his revenues. Overnight, almost, it became a smuggler's den, able and willing to defy the King of Spain and all his men, happy and ready to injure the Spanish State and to protect all its enemies.

In command of this off-shore depot, this safe retreat under the eyes of Spain, with the Convent of the Holy Franciscans as his counting house, was the Master *Contrabandista* to whom all others paid tribute. So long as you paid your import duty to him you could export as you wished, and no questions asked.

It is impossible to describe Gibraltar without mentioning the smuggling trade, with its formative effects on the past, present and future of the place and the community. Having mentioned it, let us explore it thoroughly.

The freeing of the Port of Gibraltar had been forced upon Queen Anne's government by the King of Morocco. The Order in Council of 1715 was issued to emphasize a previous order and to prevent abuses by the Governor in Gibraltar. It was not very successful in either. All that the Governor had to do was find some new illegal means of raising the wind, from time to time accepting another mild rebuke. And so, throughout the eighteenth century, the government of Gibraltar proceeded.

By implication, Gibraltar ceased to be a Free Port when an Order in Council of 1827 put charges on hulks and pontoons in The Bay. These were all smuggling depots and their purpose was to evade import duties—import duties without proper legal sanction! Thus we had thieves robbing thieves at that time.

In 1848 wharfage tolls were imposed, and in 1858, tonnage duties. In 1865 the Privy Council ordered duties on wines and spirits. But the idea of freedom has lingered on, perhaps because the original grant was never totally rescinded. The majority of goods, from wheresoever they may come, still enter without paying duty, and the whole trade and commerce of the place is geared to that fact.

The trouble with freedom, of course, is that it soon degenerates into license, especially in the circumstances which I described at the beginning of this chapter. Without recounting the tedious growth and prevalence of smuggling in Gibraltar during the eighteenth century, let us look ahead to the later development of it.

There is a report from a Mr. Reade, Her Majesty's Consul at Cádiz, to Lord Napier of Magdala, Governor of Gibraltar, transmitted to the Earl of Carnarvon, Her Majesty's Secretary of State for the Colonies, in the year 1876, which proves that there was then four times as much tobacco coming in illegally through Gibraltar as the Spanish Government bought for legal distribution! It would be a stupid government, indeed, which would not feel a draught of that magnitude, and Spain complained constantly about the wreckage of her tax structure caused by the Gibraltar smugglers. It was one of these complaints which caused Mr. Reade to write to the Governor of Gibraltar.

That Governor, General Napier, was a brave soldier, but it would have needed a different kind of courage to attack the richest commerce of Gibraltar and upset the whole economy of the place in his charge. Besides, he would reflect, his predecessor General Gardiner had exposed the tobacco trade and censured it, appealed to Westminster, and been outmanœuvred and sacked. In fact, his immediate predecessor, General Sir Archibald Hunter, had just been sacked, after a deputation from the Gibraltar Chamber of Commerce went to London to complain of his martinet attitudes. It was clear to Napier, as to every other governor since his time, that the merchants of Gibraltar, powerfully backed by the Tory and Whig businessmen of Westminster, could do more or less as they wished. A most important element in generalship is to know when to retreat, and every general who has governed Gibraltar since Hunter's short sojourn has retreated from the smuggling problem.

From the Earl of Kimberley, H.M. Secretary of State for the Colonies, to the Governor of Gibraltar, dated 1873:
'Sir,

'I have the honour to acknowledge the receipt of your Despatch reporting the result of a conference between yourself and Señor Santiago y Perminon on the means of suppressing smuggling at Gibraltar.

'2. You state in regard to the first proposal made by the Spanish Commissioner that the question of imposing a duty on tobacco presents almost insuperable difficulties, and that "Gibraltar being a free port, no revenue of any sort is raised on goods imported into the fortress".

'3. As at present advised, I am inclined to think that this could not be regarded as sufficient answer, because as duties are levied on the importation of wines and spirits, Gibraltar cannot correctly be said to be a free port. . . .

'4. . . . I am not aware of any insuperable difficulty in the way of subjecting the article to a moderate duty such as is in force in some Colonies. . . . I have not, however, come to any final conclusion on this subject, and I shall be glad to receive any observations. . . .'

His Excellency the Governor never replied. The question of good relations with Spain were involved and on this occasion the Foreign Secretary agreed with the Colonial Secretary—perhaps he pressed him. Be that as it may, the matter meandered around Whitehall for fifteen months, until an incident at Gibraltar—one of a long and continuing list of such incidents, but particularly effective at this time—forced Gibraltar's tobacco back into the limelight.

From the Captain of the Port, Gibraltar, to the Colonial Secretary, Gibraltar, 1874:

'Sir,

'I have the honour to report, for the information of His Excellency the Acting Governor, that the British steamer *Cádiz* . . . left the anchorage at 8 o'clock last evening for Málaga, and stopped after passing the New Mole to take eight Spanish *faluches* in tow (laden chiefly with tobacco) with which she proceeded, four on either side. After passing Rosia she was suddenly attacked by the Spanish *guarda costas*, that had evidently been lying in wait for her. There was a smart firing of musketry and much noise and confusion. The *Cádiz* went ahead, and though no time was lost in despatching a boat from the "Samarang", as well as an armed boat from H.M. Gunboat *Pigeon*, neither could find any trace of what occurred.

'One thing is very clear, a British steamer has taken to sea eight smugglers straight from this anchorage. It is no unusual occurrence, and not contrary to any port regulation. . . .'

H.M. Chargé d'Affaires at Madrid was called into action to protest to the Spanish Government. They agreed as to 'the gross nature of the outrage', but, says the Chargé d'Affaires, apologetically:

'I cannot but express to your Lordship the difficulty I found in meeting the Spanish assertion so repeatedly made, that the contraband trade openly carried on at Gibraltar was the real cause of all these questions. . . .

'. . . my excuse must be the desire I have to see an end put to a state of things so injurious and offensive to Spain, and so discreditable to the British flag as the contraband trade openly organised at Gibraltar.'

This letter deserves some comment. The euphemism 'Spanish traders' for the tobacco-laden *faluches* is not mere polite double-talk. So far as Gibraltar was—is—concerned, smugglers are exporters. They smuggle nothing into Gibraltar; it is no part of British business to presume that they intend to smuggle elsewhere, nor to suspect and hinder them. No part of our business, unless, of course, in the cause of international goodwill and legality, we make it our business to see that we do not give them the means and facilities to smuggle. This is common practice between neighbouring nations, and the French have co-operated with the Spaniards on the northern frontier, just as the British co-operate with the Irish customs on the frontier I know best. But in both of those cases there is two-way trade.

At Gibraltar the British Government could say in all truth that it did not know the destination of the goods. There may be, somewhere in the Mediterranean, within the range of sixty-ton launches, some unknown island where hundreds of tons of tobacco may still be landed legally and duty-free. It is not likely, but it may be possible, and there is no burden on Gibraltar's government to inquire into it.

After this affair, the Foreign Office wrote to the Colonial Office with some firmness and requested consideration of a tobacco duty for Gibraltar. The Secretary of State for the Colonies, now in 1876 the Earl of Carnarvon, found himself without a leg to stand on, and replied that it was a complicated matter, but that it would be done. He then fell back on the delaying tactic. Later in the year he wrote to Lord Napier, the new Governor of Gibraltar, to introduce two Customs men, Mr. Chester and Mr. Barton, who were on the way to The Rock to study the situation and prepare for the imposition of the tobacco duty.

A month after the arrival of the experts we find Lord Napier writing home to tell the Colonial Secretary that he had had several consultations with them, and that they had all come to the conclusion that the proposed tax would 'entail on the port of Gibraltar nearly all the evils of an extensive customs tariff, and would most seriously injure if it did not destroy the freedom of the port'.

It is amusing to find the two customs officers so thoroughly brainwashed that they join in condemnation of the evils of the customs system—their own profession and *raison d'être*.

We can see what the Governor had in mind. He goes on to report that the people of Gibraltar are excited about the newcomers and that there were rumours and speculations about the mission of Messrs. Chester and Barton. In other words—this is my own observation—the merchants had got to work on the man in the street. The Governor goes on to wonder if he should inform the Exchange Committee—a sort of chamber of commerce—and obtain the benefit of their opinions.

Here we have an exceptionally able Governor, Napier, seriously proposing to ask merchants whether they think they should be taxed or not! He ended his letter:

'As there is no doubt that the illicit trade in tobacco has continued for years under our knowledge, if not tacit consent, it appears to me that the law which will put a stop to it should not be put in force without due notice, so that orders to distant markets for the supply may be corrected, and accumulated stocks disposed of before we enter on a strictly reformed Gibraltar.'

In other words: 'I admit it's illicit and wrong, but let it continue until the sin can be abandoned without inconvenience to the sinner.'

Lord Napier enclosed reports from the experts, who said, among other things, that the proposed tax—which was, of course, intended to wipe out smuggling by making it unprofitable—would deprive some thousands of people of their livelihood, and also that the expense of collecting and enforcing the tax would be very great, calling for bonded warehouses, staff, ships, clerks, and all the paraphernalia which we have, in our day, come to take for granted.

Their alternative scheme was simpler, aimed at putting down smuggling only and leaving the legitimate trade unhampered. They would restrict the importation of tobacco to packages of 80 lb., and the size of importing ships to 200 tons burden, require the registration of imports and exports of tobacco, control the movements of boats, hulks and so forth, limit the export of tobacco to ships of, say, 100 tons at a minimum, and make the master of each ship enter into a bond as to his destination, and prove delivery there to clear the bond.

The suggestion to prohibit small ships from exporting tobacco would have struck an even more effective blow at the smugglers. Small ships are always employed in this sort of business, for two good reasons. One reason is that they are not so easily detected; the other is that, if the ship is seized—as she frequently is—the loss is not so great. On the Port Register of Gibraltar at the end of 1962 there were seventy-four ships of under one hundred tons. Forty-five of these were sixty-tonners, mostly converted wartime M.T.B.s, long, low and swift; the other fourteen were nine-tonners. The numbers do not include pleasure launches, fishing-boats, nor utility craft for harbour work; all these are separately licensed under local ordinances. The seventy-four ships to which I refer are those licensed as sea-going, under the Merchant Shipping Act of 1894. Yet the Government Report of 1962 says 'Exports of goods of local origin are negligible,' adding 'but there is a flourishing entrepôt trade.' The Report of the Port Department for the same year says: 'Imports are mainly for home consumption as is shown by the slight export figures.' It gives, under 'General Cargo', 62,000 tons coming in, and only 5,000 tons going out—but there is a snag! The snag is that the export figure is for 'ships over 150 tons net register' only. A man in a hurry would presume that the exports in ships of less tonnage was negligible; the fact is that it is all-important.

While the Secretary of State for the Colonies was considering these letters and reports the Gibraltar merchants were not idle. Mr. Francia, the Chairman of the Exchange Committee there, had written to the Governor asking what was in the wind.

Messrs. Chester and Barton continued their researches as far as Málaga and Cádiz, and received much straight information from the British Consuls in those ports. They wrote in a further report:

'The smuggling of tobacco into Spain is mostly from small ships in various parts of the coast where the Government officials have been made secure by previously agreed rewards,'—they could not bring themselves to use the right word—'and the tobacco after landing is carried up the country on the backs of mules. This portion of the trade, so far as Gibraltar is concerned will be effectively stopped by the scheme we propose to prevent tobacco being placed on board small sized vessels. These small vessels usually leave under pretence that their destination is Oran, Melilla, or some other free port on the African coast. . . .'

Like all good civil servants, and particularly Treasury ones, these gentlemen are very careful not to give offence. They knew perfectly well, and could have pointed out, that there would be no point in shipping tobacco from one free port to another, and that all the talk about entrepôt trade was eyewash. They would have found out even more in Málaga and Cádiz but for the fact that Spanish pride inhibits the authorities from admitting that their own coastguards are open to bribery.

The Earl of Carnarvon, I think, flew into a rage when he received all this verbiage. The Experts had been sent to Gibraltar for one purpose—to set up a customs scheme. Now they were trying to blind him with science. They had evidently come under the influence of the Governor, the neighbouring consuls, and others, and had recommended something distinctly different. In his letter of introduction Carnarvon had written 'Her Majesty's Government have decided to impose a tax on the importation of tobacco into Gibraltar'. Plain enough—but Mr. Chester and Mr. Barton, mere civil servants, had decided to recommend otherwise, emboldened by the backing of this soldier-governor who was, doubtless, beginning to fancy himself as a statesman!

Carnarvon demanded the return of the Experts by telegraph, which was a dashing step in those days, and they sailed to London on the next ship. Like good bureaucrats they spent the journey costing their scheme and even drafting the law and the form of the destination bond. So thorough and so convincing were those good officers that within a month of their return to London we find Lord Carnarvon writing to Lord Napier at Gibraltar and enclosing a copy of the new law for publication in the *Gibraltar Chronicle*.

In reply to this letter, Lord Napier wrote to say that it was all right as a law, but that he still felt it would injure the trade of the place and deprive many of the poorer classes of their living.

The fact is that the authorities in London and in Gibraltar were, to some extent, at cross purposes. The Secretary of State had been told by his experts that the proposed law would not injure the legitimate trade in tobacco, but only the small-ship smuggler. That was the truth, but not the whole truth. The Governor knew, but could never say outright—not even to this day—that without the smuggler there would be scarcely any trade in tobacco at Gibraltar. There would be The Rock's few thousand smokers to supply and, perhaps, the occasional ship which had omitted to stock up with ex-bond tobacco at its home port—and that is all. About 100,000 lb. of tobacco would meet that trade, whereas the present trade (1876) was estimated at 12,000,000 lb. The anti-smuggling law would, therefore, cut the trade by approximately ninety-nine per cent!

Messrs. Chester and Barton may have seen this, but it was not their concern. The Governor saw it too and, being the man on the spot, it concerned him very much. Napier cast about for delaying tactics of his own.

The Attorney General of Gibraltar, the Governor's left-hand man, raised all the legal points he could in a long criticism of the proposed Ordinance. He even queried the Imperial Government's right to revoke Queen Anne's charter of freedom of the port, and here he went too far. He said that a clause in the Ordinance which empowered the authorities to fire on a ship or boat which failed to stop would have to go before Parliament, and was not within the competence of an Order in Council. That would set the cat among the pigeons, and set the Ordinance back for a few months, at least!

A memorandum published with the Ordinance gives some very interesting figures, for Messrs. Chester and Barton have been in Gibraltar again, busier than ever. They state that the total number of Gibraltar people employed in the tobacco trade is 1,450. They tell the Governor that the idea of a Bond of Delivery is not theirs, that they see many objections to it, and that the new law would be quite effective without it. They say that they have not been able to find out the extent of the trade in tobacco. Very large quantities come in from India, and very large quantities go out, on the face of it, to Oran. They hope that the legitimate trade to Oran may continue. They have found figures for all the more mundane imports and exports. One fact stands out strangely—that Gibraltar imported half a million pounds worth of Manchester cottons in the year 1875.

We may now expect to see the Manchester cotton lobby and other pressures groups of British manufacturers rushing to the aid of their agents and customers on The Rock. The Exchange Committee of Gibraltar called in the aid of the Manchester Chamber of Commerce, and as the fight developed they were able to call on the shipowners of London, the merchants of Glasgow and Liverpool, and other high-powered organs of the Nation of Shopkeepers. But the Gibraltar people fired the first shots themselves, and shrewd enough shots they were—too shrewd for the gallant old Governor and his 'civil' secretary, Colonel Baynes.

From Mr. Francis Francia, Chairman of the Exchange Committee, to the Colonial Secretary of Gibraltar, 14th March 1877:

'I have the honour to enclose for the information of His Excellency a copy of three resolutions passed at the meeting. . . .

'The Committee fully support the sentiments expressed in these resolutions, and feel convinced that if measures in the proposed scheme are carried out, it will cause most material injury to all classes of this community, destroy Gibraltar as a commercial centre and free port, and bring untold misery on a large proportion of its poorer inhabitants.'

The resolutions are wordy with indignation and I must paraphrase them. The first, proposed by J. A. Crooks and seconded by Judah Levy, declares that the proposed law is contrary to Queen Anne's Order in Council which made Gibraltar a free port. Time and again the merchants of Gibraltar have appeared to assume that Queen Anne made laws similar to those of the Medes and Persians, permanent and unalterable.

The second resolution, by Y. Bergel, seconded by Henry Thornton, points out that the inhabitants of Gibraltar, firmly believing in the freedom of its port, have invested their money here in many ways, and are now to be ruined to uphold the revenue of a foreign state. Here, I must remark, they admit by implication that their fortunes were based on the downfall of the revenue of the foreign state.

The third resolution, proposed by J. H. Recano and seconded by Richard Abrines, reiterates the danger to trade and livelihood, and gives full powers to the Exchange Committee to act and to use funds which may be raised by public subscription.

The Committee then called on the Governor in deputation and asked him to hold up the return of the Draft Ordinance to Lord Carnarvon pending a memorial from the Committee, which was in preparation. A fortnight later the memorial was sent to the Earl of Carnarvon, by the Governor of Gibraltar.

The Humble Memorialists left nothing much unsaid, and their document is a potted history of the trade and commerce of The Rock. The target which they displayed may have been too expansive for their own interests, for the Colonial Office was able to score many hits on it—none of them, however, mortal.

First of all, the merchants complain that they have not been consulted—overlooking the fact that they are being consulted now, by a preview of the Draft Ordinance sent especially to them.

Passing on from that, they refer to the Capture of Gibraltar and to Queen Anne's famous Order in Council making it a free port. 'And your Memorialists respectfully submit that the Sovereigns of England have neither by their own acts, or with the advice of the Privy Council, at any time done anything to affect the validity of the provisions of the Order in Council thus constituting Gibraltar a free port.' This was patently untrue. As Colonial Secretary Lord Kimberley had told the Governor of Gibraltar in 1873, duties had been levied there by Order in Council both long ago and frequently —to be exact about it, in 1827, 1848, 1858 and 1865. No one would be more aware of those duties than the merchants of Gibraltar, and they must have damaged their case gravely by beginning their Memorial with a blatant and obvious lie. In any case, even had the Monarch in Council not done it before, there was no reason on earth why he should not do it now.

The Memorialists then cast up the sad case of Sir Robert Gardiner, whom they had so signally defeated twenty-five years before. 'He entertained the erroneous idea that the sale of merchandise in Gibraltar to Spaniards was illegal . . . and unjustly interfered with the free actions of merchants and traders.' They tell how they went to London to wait on the Duke of Newcastle, and how his Grace hauled Gardiner over the coals, saying that there was no law forbidding the merchants to sell to Spaniards. 'The question as to the legality of the trade was therefore settled. . . .'

Poor Gardiner ruined his career on this point of principle, condemning the whole ramshackle structure of the smuggling trade and not merely the point raised in the Memorial. He kept harping on Britain's disgrace at Gibraltar even after his dismissal, but the times were not with him. Those were years of ferocious commercialism.

However, the Memorialists next cited the Duke and the other authorities to the effect that one nation is not bound to protect the revenue laws of another, adding that to do so was, therefore, 'at variance with international law'.

They went on to ask if there was one solitary instance of a Destination Bond system in any other British Dominion.

They said that Her Majesty's Government, if it imposed this law 'would virtually be upholding the monopoly of the Spanish Government in the sale of tobacco', and that the proposed restrictions would amount to prohibition. This is clear enough, to me. It states, as I have already calculated, that there was no tobacco trade worth considering *except* the smuggling trade. It admits that the target of the trade is Spain—not Oran as stated to the Customs experts.

Four thousand persons, the Memorialists claimed, being the wage earners in tobacco and their dependents, will be 'inevitably reduced to indigence and starvation'. These British subjects would suffer and the Spanish state would gain.

Lastly, the Memorialists said, the great ocean-going ships would cease to use Gibraltar, with its new restrictions, as a port of call. But they did not say why they should, and one would have thought that a Destination Bond would not embarrass the P. & O. Line or its predecessors.

As I see it, a sixth-form schoolboy could have shot this Memorial to pieces in ten minutes. I was tempted to do so above, but I have left some of the fabric untouched for Lord Carnarvon and his back-room boys. They studied it for six weeks before replying to it.

The reply disposed of the claim to freedom of the port with ease, citing all the measures which had been passed to limit it and to impose duties on Gibraltar. Queen Anne was dead.

Of course there was no law to forbid the merchants of Gibraltar to sell to any customer. Nor was there any such provision in the present Ordinance. The only innovation is that the customer will in future be required to conform to certain regulations in removing the goods.

Of course there is no law which requires one country to uphold the revenue laws of another. But it does not follow that a country may not so frame its municipal laws as to prevent its ports being used as bases of systematic smuggling into a neighbouring and friendly country. It is nonsense for the Memorialists to say that any such law, framed to prevent fraud, is 'at variance with international law'.

Yes, the system of bonds has been used many times before and in many places. The proposed bonds are 'not of a character to which an honest exporter ought reasonably to object. If his trade is lawful, he incurs no penalty'.

As for amounting to prohibition, 'that they will amount to a prohibition in the case of the Spanish subject who lives by defrauding his country, I am not concerned to deny'.

As for the starvation of the 4,000, 'I trust that those who may be thrown out of work will have no great difficulty in obtaining other and more legitimate modes of employment'. If that proves difficult, H.M. Government will take care of them.

So that's that, Lord Carnarvon must have said, having shot off that broadside. One would not have thought there was much of the great Memorial left intact. Nor was there, but his Lordship did not get long to rest on his laurels. A curious document landed on his desk from no less a personage than the Right Reverend Dr. Scandella, Roman Catholic Vicar Apostolic of Gibraltar, in effect, the Bishop.

This letter was easy enough to answer in one way, for the Bishop was evidently innocent of commercial knowledge and had sought no one's advice. It was a naïve document, honest even in its dishonesty, a plea for the welfare of his parishioners, an attempt at mediation, at casuistry and compromise.

In another way, it would be hard to answer. Gibraltar was about ninety per cent Catholic, yet the Bishop's position was not officially recognized. According to law, the Bishop of Gibraltar was the Anglican one, even though he did not reside there, and had very few parishioners. This Scandella could not be addressed officially as Bishop, and in the circumstances it would be only too easy to give offence to him, to his Church, and hence to his adherents, and so add the flames of religious controversy to the fumes of Gibraltar tobacco. A snub—and it would have been well deserved—would have suited Scandella admirably, for he could then have harnessed the religious grievance to the commercial one, yoked God and Mammon, and thence, perhaps have strengthened the position of his Church—and of himself.

Dr. Scandella opened by proposing an alternative scheme for putting down smuggling. Let smugglers of both countries, he said, be declared criminals and subject to mutual extradition. He appears to be all for law and order, but on the next page he fears that the present scheme—i.e. the hindrance of the small smuggler and his shore supporters—'would cause deep irritation throughout the great neighbouring towns . . . whose inhabitants depend, in a very great measure, on their trade with Gibraltar. . . . It is unquestionable that The Lines, Campamento, San Roque,

Algeciras, Marbella and Estepona will be almost ruined'.

The Doctor goes on to say how much he fears for his people in Gibraltar if the Ordinance is passed and the smuggling put down—already unmindful that his alternative, to subject all smugglers to extradition, would have just the same effect! England, the Doctor continues, has never thought to prevent smuggling from the Channel ports into France, so why pick on Gibraltar? At this stage of his letter he is belligerently pro-smuggling.

Now Dr. Scandella raises a new consideration. 'It is to be feared lest such zeal on the part of England may wound the Spanish national dignity. . . . Were the many enemies of Don Alphonsus and his Government to use such measures on our part as an argument against the present political state of things, such procedure would not be in the least surprising.'

He then proceeds to put his foot in deeper. In trying to show the extent of the tobacco trade he states that 1,000 tons are brought in yearly, and says 'it is clear that, with the exception of the small quantity consumed in Gibraltar together with that which is disposed of among visiting seamen for their own use, all the rest goes to Spain, even what is apparently shipped for Oran, Melilla and Ceuta. The embarkation of tobacco for the said free ports is but a pretext and pretence'.

The bond system, says the Bishop, is 'totally unknown in other countries, and contrary to the rights of free ports'. He ends by claiming that should the Ordinance be passed then the merchants should be compensated, since they have been 'relying on Queen Anne's august Royal Word'. He cites the Protestant Irish clergy and the West Indies slave-owners—strange bedfellows these—as two precedents of payment to those who lost a dubious livelihood by legislation.

Lord Carnarvon, who was not unacquainted with the perennial Irish problem, immediately recognized the politico-religious pincer. As we say in the vernacular of that country, he was too old a cat to be raped by a kitten. He replied with reserve, but he could not resist a mild tug at the episcopal leg where it was most temptingly extended.

As to 'why pick on Gibraltar?' he pointed out that the measures now proposed were based on those already in use and effective in the Channel Islands, where they had been imposed, as in the present case, as a gesture towards good order and international goodwill.

He pointed out that no representations from King Alfonso, as to the danger of his opposition making political capital out of the proposed Ordinance, had been received, and added: 'I need not say that any such representations would receive the most careful attention.'

As to the irritation of neighbouring Spaniards, 'it must be plain that the possible irritation of the subjects of a foreign state, which is due to their losing the opportunity of breaking the laws of that state, is not a feeling which Her Majesty's Government can so far take into account as to induce them to depart from a line of policy which is enforced by very serious considerations of justice and expediency'.

The Secretary of State notes, with surprise, Dr. Scandella's statement as to the Oran trade being false, for 'the intervention of Her Majesty's ships has more than once been sought in cases of seizure where the ship was apparently bound for one of the ports mentioned. If, however, Dr. Scandella's assertion be well founded, then the intervention of the British Government has been sought in cases unworthy of countenance'.

As for the entry and clearance system being totally unknown elsewhere, 'as far as I am aware similar provisions are in force in every well regulated port in the world'.

As for Queen Anne, upon whose 'august Royal Word' so many worthy merchants have relied for so long, it cannot be too often repeated that she is dead.

That, on the face of it, was the end of Dr. Scandella's intervention. But the British Government would remain aware that it had another very formidable antagonist, the last one in the world to retire from the fray just because its case had been discredited.

The Secretary of State now turned his guns on the Attorney General of Gibraltar, shot his sails to ribbons, and exposed him as a mere smart aleck. No doubt he had very much more experienced lawyers available to him in Whitehall.

He wrote to say that he was sorry that such a word as 'Charter' had been used, 'as it is one tending to encourage such mischievous misconceptions'. Once again, Queen Anne was dead.

As for that one about firing on a ship trying to escape, for which the Attorney General had stated that the penalty if caught was £20, if not caught, death—Nonsense, Sir! 'I am of the opinion that death could not correctly be termed a penalty in such a case. The danger would be voluntarily incurred, and the death would be his own act as far as the offender was concerned, and an accident as far as the Law was concerned.' This reply was conclusive and incontrovertible, and the Attorney General of Gibraltar, having marred his career through loyalty to his Governor, was knocked out of the controversy for good.

At this juncture the redoubtable Chambers of Commerce of Manchester and Liverpool, alerted by their Gibraltar agents, weighed in with heavy Memorials. So did Messrs. Pirrie, Foote & Company, Glasgow merchants engaged in the Gibraltar trade. The Chairman of the General Shipowners' Society, London, wrote in, and several deputations were received. British Big Business—then the biggest in the world—was on the move.

On the 26th July 1877, the main antagonists confronted each other in London. Lord Carnarvon received a deputation at the Colonial Office, introduced by Mr. Hardcastle, M.P., and led by Mr. Francis Francia, all the way from Gibraltar.

Mr. Hardcastle, as is the way of M.P.s, said that he ought not to occupy his Lordship's time, and proceeded to do so. He put the case that Gibraltar was being sacrificed to save Spain from her own smugglers and from her own revenue officers who were in league with them. He said that Gibraltar should not merely be occupied, but treated as a colony in the full sense of that word. The basic logic of his speech—though he did not say so—was that two wrongs make a right; since there were Spanish smugglers, Britain was none the worse for helping them. He finished, and presented Mr. Francia.

Francis Francia spoke as never before. He said at the outset: 'We assure your Lordship that we have no sympathy with the smuggling into Spain, and we are not here to defend that practice. We fully agree in the necessity of avoiding all possibility of such suspicion of complicity, but we are convinced that the fiscal system of Spain and the administration of the Spanish revenue service are such that no measures taken by the British Government can diminish smuggling into that country.' But all that he had really said was, in effect: 'Since there will always be smuggling into Spain, let us have our share of it.'

Mr. Ashworth, President of Manchester Chamber of Commerce, backed him up, speaking of shipping generally, and of how Customs delay and hamper it. He was of the formidable Free Trade Lobby, the Liberal Party's secret weapon. He asked for a year to try out other measures before the dreaded Ordinance was applied. He said:

'We pass by the front of The Rock more than one hundred million pounds worth of British property every year, in and out, and we say that in negotiating these matters with the Spanish Government and complying with their request that we should aid them in collecting their revenues, we recognise a submission to the rule and authority of the Spanish Government which may lead to very serious political complications hereafter; and if they should ask, with a view to getting rid of the difficulty, that you should cede The Rock to them, I am quite sure that it would be a very difficult matter indeed for this country.'

He was speaking for British export trade, most of it, in those days, from Lancashire. He was, no doubt, deeply involved in this trade himself and, like most men when they are deeply involved in self-interest, his arguments were worthless. Time has shown how worthless they were. He said, in effect, that if we helped the Spanish Government in this neighbourly way it might lead them to renew their claim to Gibraltar. The reverse has happened. Britain, on this occasion, as on all others before and since, refused them this co-operation. This persistent refusal, and the smuggling resulting from it, are to this day the basis of Spain's hatred of Gibraltar and her lust to lay hands on it and control it.

Mr. Smith, merchant of Gibraltar, told Lord Carnarvon: 'On the part of the merchants of Gibraltar, that everyone there would be perfectly ready to give unreserved and honourably straightforward information upon the subject, and everything in their reach would be placed at the disposal of any Commissioner, should your Lordship consent to name one.' Thank you, Mr. Smith, but his Lordship had already named and sent two—Mr. Chester and Mr. Barton. They were told, by the merchants of Gibraltar, that most of the tobacco goes to the free port of Oran, but we have a letter from your Bishop to say that none of it goes to Oran at all!

Now it was the turn of Mr. Mundella, M.P., who had a Spanish name. He said he had no direct interest in the Gibraltar trade, but he knew Spain of old. He said that Britain might make what engagements she wished, and keep them, but the Spanish Government could never do so. We could not protect Spain against smuggling, for she did nothing to protect herself. 'From what I know of Spanish officials, I should very much doubt whether there is any one of them, from the Prime Minister down to the very lowest subaltern, who would not, for a consideration, wink at smuggling.' No comment from me, for I know nothing of the Prime Minister of Spain in 1877.

Mr. Pirrie, London merchant, pointed out that Spain had always put penal duties on British goods. For instance, one hundred per cent duty on cotton goods at present. They had asked for it, their own people were against them, so were their officials, so let them have it!

Lord Carnarvon replied, making all his points over again. Mr. Mundella punctuated him, with agreement and comment, in a way that no one else there would have dared to do. All that his Lordship said anew was that Gibraltar was to be considered as a fortress, rather than as a colony, 'which I must conceive to take precedence of anything else'. He made some minor comments on the present recommendations. Then, in conclusion, he gave way. He said that he would lay it all before Parliament when time allowed, and that might not be soon. Meanwhile, he would be glad of all kinds of criticism, from whatsoever source. . . .

Francia, Smith and Thompson, thus invited, wrote again, a very long letter, from their hotel in London before they sailed for home. They replied, at last, with renewed confidence, to Lord Carnarvon's reply to their first Memorial. Drunk with words and facts they spent another month in London, talking, thinking, comparing notes. At the end of this time they sent in yet another letter proposing certain regulations for the patrolling of Gibraltar's coastline and frontier, which would make the smuggler's task more difficult and, at the same time, remove all appearance of British complicity. But their proposals, as they well knew, would not stop the smugglers, for in Spain the harder it is the higher the price. Smuggling is never impossible in such circumstances.

Six months later the Governor of Gibraltar wrote to Whitehall to say that 'smuggling has apparently very materially diminished of late'. He has made certain local orders to hinder it—trading hulks to be deprived of their licenses if found loading boats in the night without permission; guards at Europa to warn off boats passing close to The Rock. Also, the Port Department had increased its vigilance. He asked for a new steam launch, a cliff path, authority to impose some heavy fines, all means to keep smugglers at least offshore—off Gibraltar's doorstep. No doubt the merchants, after their scare, were helping in their way.

Lord Napier ended his letter cautiously:

'If these measures could be carried out I believe an effectual check would be given to smuggling in The Bay, with the least possible distress to the commercial community, and that the proposed Customs Ordinance might be postponed pending the result of the experiment.'

It was postponed. It still is. Why? You may wonder. When scarcely a sensible argument was put forward against it, when all the written representations were so speedily demolished, when the oral representations were scarcely worth answering, why should this legislation have been postponed? Why should Lord Carnarvon, after stating and reiterating his determination, let it go by default?

Looking back, you will remember that he did not initiate the matter. No Minister seeks trouble in his own department. This business had been forced on him by the Secretary of State for Foreign Affairs. Carnarvon had promised, reluctantly, to look into it. He did so, through Messrs. Chester and Barton, and he saw enough to convince him that something must be done before the smugglers of Gibraltar provoked a war with Spain. He had to proceed, or, since international relations were not his responsibility, he had at least to make a good show of proceeding. He soon found himself confronted and opposed by at least three strong forces, all ill-armed with argument, but heavy with prestige and influence.

Baron Napier of Mágdala, the Governor, was a national hero in England—and these were Jingo days. Dr. Scandella was to be presumed a national hero, or something more, in Catholic Gibraltar, and held the pride of that colonial community in his hands. The big business of Gibraltar, backed by the far bigger business at home, was an invincible force in those times. Carnarvon knew well—he proved —that none of them had anything valid to say, but he also knew that, with the final intervention of members of the British Parliament, he had enough opposition to frighten the Foreign Office off his tail. He could now return to his colleague the Foreign Secretary and say: 'Well, I've tried. The entire business community is against us. Do you wish me to lay the matter before Parliament? Do you mind if I say that it is a Foreign Office policy, in the interests of international relations? Will your chaps back me up? Better still, would they like to lead?'

The Foreign Secretary must have agreed to let the Ordinance go by default, to let the smuggling at Gibraltar continue, to pass this most critical problem of Anglo-Spanish relations down to his successors in office, one of whom is trying to deal with it as I write this account, almost one hundred years after the events I have described.

16

THE TRUE TRAFALGAR

Gibraltar has two naval harbours lying side by side. One of them is two and a half miles long by half a mile wide and appears, on the map, to be almost as extensive as the land area of the whole territory. The other harbour, after a careful search, may be located just beyond the southern tip of the great harbour. It is about one hundred yards in diameter, and appears as a tiny circular indentation in the ragged coastline.

From my study, six hundred feet above it, I can see that this little bowl is surrounded on the shore side by massive walls of cut stone, pierced with numerous embrasures, and that a few fat-bellied guns lie there still, idly threatening. This is Rosia Harbour, once the hub and headquarters, if not the birthplace, of Britain's command of the sea and, for a while, of the world.

The contrast between the two harbours, the new one thirty times bigger than the old, provides the tersest possible comment on Britain's growth during the nineteenth century. No normal growth, this, but what the modern Chinese might call 'a great leap forward'. The leap forward in naval power trailed trade in its wake and dragged Gibraltar into the centre of the world stage.

We pull down our barns and build bigger, like the optimist in the parable, and in the night we hear a voice saying 'Thou fool . . .'. Rosia Harbour, in the eighteenth century which it served so well, was completely secure. It was shielded and hidden from the nearest Spanish territory, a mile and a half distant, by a rocky headland. It lay four full gunshots from Algeciras across The Bay. Against naval attack it was surrounded by the biggest guns in the world, far bigger than any ship could carry.

The great new harbour, on the other hand, with its three dry docks and vast installations, was completely commanded by foreign gunfire almost as soon as it was built. Had Spain joined our enemies in either of the World Wars—and in the second one she very nearly did so—and used the long range guns installed all along her encircling hilltops, then Gibraltar Harbour and base could have been put out of action by a day's bombardment. In fact, the threat and certainty of such a bombardment would have rendered the base useless, for Britain would not have dared to concentrate ships in it. The bigger they are, the harder they fall. . . .

We used Rosia Harbour as a swimming club, and many a sunny evening I have spent lying there like a bull seal, surrounded by the bikinied females of the Garrison, my mind wandering from the old stones to the young flesh, from history to biology and back again.

Into this tight little pool, on the 23rd October 1805, limped Nelson's battered fleet of twenty-seven ships, towing four prizes from Trafalgar. Thirty-one ships, the whole Mediterranean Fleet of Britain, crowded into or close to this harbour, where you could not fit one modern destroyer. Those were the days of small ships and big men.

First, they carried off the wounded, which too often meant, in those days, the dying. The dead, all but one, had been committed to the deep. They carried the dying up the steep hill to the Naval Hospital, and there, in spite of—or, perhaps, because of—medical attention, they duly died, of shock, gangrene, septicaemia and loss of blood. They buried them in a special plot called Trafalgar Cemetery, just outside the South Gate of the town. Visitors are disappointed to find that only a few of the tombstones there carry the word 'Trafalgar', but this is easily explained. The great battle did not acquire its name, in those days of slow communications, until some time after it was fought—more time than it took the survivors to die.

Admiral Lord Nelson, the first and, to my mind, the greatest of British popular heroes, died on the job. His body was brought back to Gibraltar—'this dark corner of the world', as he had called it, with strange foreboding, as he left it to sail out to his last battle. Nelson had no great love for The Rock, but great use for it. From here he mounted his greatest battle. Cape Trafalgar at the western entrance to The Straits, is but one day's sail from the Gibraltar base, given the right wind. It is safe to say that without possession of Gibraltar, Britain could not have mounted such an operation at that place and, thence, Napoleon would have stood a better chance of making Britain a province of France. Without becoming involved with the pros and cons of that possibility, I will say that after Trafalgar there was no more talk of trading The Rock for advantage elsewhere.

After Nelson's death, pious and official legend tends to take over. To assess him accurately, one must read between the lines. It is known that his body was brought back to Rosia Harbour, and it is said that it was laid out in a certain fine house, which is still there and occupied, in Rosia Parade. But a contemporary report, not so well known, tells how his broken body was casked in cognac for want of the more proper rum, and how, when the expanding stomach gases added their pressure to the vapours of the spirit, the admiral blew his top for the last time and terrified the night watch by his Polyphemus glare over the rim of the cask. They rammed him back and battened him down, and the first task at Rosia Harbour was to drain off the volatile brandy and replace it with the more viscous rum. Since the voyage, upwind and stormy, had taken four days in the warm month of October, I doubt if the body was ever laid out in that house. If the more popular and circumstantial tale is not true, then it ought to be.

During my time in Gibraltar, in 1955, we celebrated the one hundred and fiftieth anniversary of the victory, with suitable religious services and a British Council exhibition of Nelsoniana. I was a contributor to the *Gibraltar Chronicle*, a small daily which was founded in 1801, and which takes pride to this day in its first and greatest scoop—the report of the Battle of Trafalgar. I was asked to stitch the occasion together with a piece on Nelson and his victory.

The task was not to my taste, for great occasions and heroes tend to be written threadbare. Casting about for something new to say on the subject, I read all the Nelsoniana and a great deal more besides, and made myself, for the time being, a master of it all. I think I succeeded in finding some fresh interest in Nelson and his background.

I travelled overland to Trafalgar. You take the Cádiz road from Gibraltar and turn off to the left at the ancient fortress town of Vejer de la Frontera, fifty miles westwards. The sign reads 'Meca' and points to Islam across The Straits, and you pass a village called Zahara, so that for a moment you may begin to wonder if you have crossed the narrow sea into Africa without noticing it. But you keep on down the dirt road with giant aloes and prickly pear towering over your car, until the mountains drop down into sand-dune country. There are some miles of this, miles stolen from the farmers by the Atlantic winds. At the end of the road there is a lighthouse perched on a flat rocky headland. You reach this by a causeway, with a beach at either side of you. You can see that Cape Trafalgar was once an island, a big rock out in the sea, and that the winds and tides, here as at Gibraltar, have made it into a peninsula.

I asked the lighthouse-keeper about Trafalgar, but there I made a mistake. He knew little of it and cared less. The Spaniards, like ourselves, forget their defeats and concentrate on their victories. From the promontory I looked out over the waters of the great battle, and it looked like any other part of the sunny sea.

'The tunny aren't running today,' said the lighthouse-keeper. 'The wind's wrong for them.' He could think of nothing else likely to bring me out on to that limb of land.

No, there was nothing to see, but I had seen Nelson's little flagship, the *Victory*, and pictures of naval battles long ago, and I could imagine the scene here on the 19th of October 1805. There were twenty-seven British ships of the line—which seems a grand title for the tiny top-heavy cockleshells which they were—waiting for the enemy fleet to put out from the safe landlocked harbour of Cádiz, twenty miles down the coast. They would not appear to be waiting, for it was far too deep to anchor, and they would have had to sail to and fro incessantly. It would look like a yacht race out there—and it had gone on for weeks. Nelson knew that there was a big concentration of French and Spanish ships in Cádiz. He did not know their numbers, which turned out to be thirty-four. He could not be sure that they would ever come out to fight. If not, well and good, he was holding them there and preventing them from doing harm somewhere else.

But Villeneuve, the French admiral in command, knew that he would have to come out sooner or later—and he hoped, later. He had direct instructions from Napoleon himself to take that fleet up to Toulon and to engage and defeat any fleet that stood in his way. Villeneuve was between the sword and the wall and it made him cautious. He was waiting for a strong west wind, which would carry him into the battle—and out of it again—at top speed. After three weeks of waiting he heard that Napoleon's patience was exhausted and that another admiral had been appointed to take over his fleet and was on the way. Thus it was that Villeneuve came lumbering out of his harbour on a day of light breeze, a day so hopeless for manoeuvring—which was all that he was good at—that it took him four whole hours to bring his fleet about when he sighted the British. I know little of naval matters, but I should think that one would have to do it in four minutes today.

Nelson did not care whether the battle was to be fast or slow. He had no brilliant tactics up his sleeve, and only the skeleton of a plan, for the enemy were making the running. When he sighted their fleet, and saw that the wind was of no help to anyone, he realized that the battle would go to the better slogger. Good formations could neither be made nor held in that weather, so all the theory, all the books, might go overboard. It was to be a test of courage, doggedness, and stoicism. His last important order to his captains told them to use their own initiative—which is pure Nelson touch. This is how he put it:

'Something must be left to chance. Nothing is sure in a sea fight, above all others. No captain can do very wrong if he places his ship alongside that of the enemy.' After the exhortations of our own times, about tearing the guts out of soft underbellies and so forth, it is good to read these laconic and powerful phrases of pre-Victorian style.

The ships had to get within a mile of each other before they fired a shot. When, soon after that, they met and mixed it, the watcher on the Cape would have seen complete confusion, as though two huge, cumbersome and disorganized regattas had become entangled. In all that vast expanse of water, here were sixty ships trying to get as close together as they could, and every one of them unable either to keep still or to go fast. But the watcher could tell that there was furious activity out there by the incessant rumble of the guns, by the puffs of smoke along the sides of every ship, and by the pall of it which soon formed and drifted over the scene.

They did not sink each other in those days—at least, not often. Sometimes, but rarely, they set each other on fire, or hit a magazine and blew each other up. Mostly they just pulled alongside, right into the fusillade of broadside guns, and let off everything they had, cannon, grapeshot, muskets and, finally, men with cutlasses who boarded the enemy ship and overpowered her crew. That is what transpired on this occasion of Trafalgar, and continued for four or five hours. But it was always a case of the British boarding the French and Spanish ships, the enemy surrendering ship by ship under the fury of Nelson's guns and men.

After five hours the watcher would have seen some of the French ships break from the mêlée and sail slowly away from the scene. Much later, after a period of rounding up and patching up, the British fleet set sail for Gibraltar to the east, with eighteen captured ships herded or towed in its midst. Then a sudden storm blew up, and there was no more to be seen. The watcher would not know until long afterwards what had happened out there on the calm and gleaming sea, and would walk away shaking his head at such a waste of good gunpowder.

But it is all clear now, for the Battle of Trafalgar was recognized as one of the decisive battles of our era, and it has been analysed almost shot by shot. Horatio Nelson defeated the combined fleets of France and Spain and broke Napoleon's sea power decisively and finally, just as, ten years later, Wellington broke his land power at Waterloo. Nelson won the battle in spite of the fact that wind and weather conditions gave him little chance to use to the full his skill in manœuvre. The enemy were slightly superior in ships, but about equal in gun power. The weather favoured neither side. The British won because they put more cannon balls through the same number of guns, and because they were not quite so ready to submit.

The question arises—why should this have been so? To find the answer we must lay aside any myths of racial superiority and examine the leadership.

David Garrick the great actor, with royal patronage in mind, appointed himself cheerleader of the Navy in 1760 or thereabouts, when he published 'Heart of Oak', that stirring sea shanty which British schoolboys learn by heart. It is worth reading with care, with its background and motive in mind:

> 'Come, cheer up, my lads! 'Tis to glory we steer,
> To add something more to this wonderful year;
> To honour we call you, not press you like slaves,
> For who are so free as the sons of the waves?'

The fact is that they *were* pressed like slaves. Dr. Johnson, with his feet more firmly planted on the ground, replied:

'No man will be a sailor who has contrivance enough to get himself into a jail; for being in a ship is being in a jail with the chance of being drowned . . . a man in jail has more room, better food and commonly better company.'

Unpaid, unfed, flogged and tortured at whim by officers, the miserable sailors had suffered for a century or more. The 'shacombe filthies, raggamuffings and scovies', as one of their own captains had described them in the time of Rooke, were waiting for a chance to mutiny, and for a leader.

In 1797, just eight years before Trafalgar, Captain Pigot of H.M.S. *Hermione* threatened suddenly to flog the last man down from the yards. Two topmen, in their terrified anxiety, fell to the deck and broke their limbs. 'Throw those lubbers overboard,' ordered Pigot, and it was done. That night the sailors rose and murdered Pigot and his officers. Since that day there has been a stand of arms available in the officers' quarters.

A little later, at Spithead on the Channel, in the face of Napoleonic threat, Seaman Valentine Joyce took over the Channel Fleet and put the officers courteously ashore. Edmund Burke told Parliament that he was 'A seditious clubbist from Belfast'—in other words, a pressganged United Irishman. Joyce ruled his Fleet well enough with the help of his Executive Committee—Patrick Dugan, Reilly, Patrick Glynn, William Anderson, and Denis Lawlor from Kildare. Meanwhile, at the Nore, Charles McCarthy and another Irishman called Hawkins seized the North Sea Fleet. The erstwhile Royal Navy became 'The Floating Republic'.

The leaders were educated men, fugitives through their political activities. They were able to treat with the Lords of Admiralty, and finally handed the Navy back on certain promises and conditions. The Admiralty did not feel itself bound to honour the surrender terms, but something had to be done. Among the officers, heads rolled, and they were mostly fat old heads. Young officers had to be promoted. One of the latter was Captain Horatio Nelson who, thanks to the Irish Revolution in the Royal Navy, rose rapidly to become an Admiral.

Nelson, as one might expect, spent the great years of his career under constant sniping from the discredited Naval Establishment. But the more he was criticized the more battles he seemed to win, until even the scandal of his sex life could not injure his position.

Coolly regarded, Nelson's liaison with Lady Hamilton demonstrated his good qualities rather than his defects. Instead of whoring round the ports in true naval style, he showed discrimination, affection and steadfastness. Once he had compromised the lady he stood by her, even at the risk of wrecking a splendid career. He could easily have thrown her back at her husband and laid a false trail with some woman less prominent. The fact that he did not do so seems to show his sincerity and honour. It may be that the very qualities which underlay his brave and loving affair with Emma Hamilton were those which, in other form, impressed and endeared his officers and men and called forth the heroic efforts of Trafalgar.

We know that Nelson was, by nature, informal and democratic. We know that he appealed, in his pre-battle signal, to 'every man'. That was a new approach to the despised and brutalized conscripts of the Royal Navy, and it proved to be effective.

Facing him was Villeneuve, a frightened aristocrat, a separate species from his men, whose decision to fight had been forced upon him and imperilled every man in his own fleet. His sailors did what they had to do; Nelson's did a little more—enough to turn the balance on that deadlocked day.

When Nelson's coffin, containing his small, thin, one-armed, one-eyed, broken-backed body, arrived in London, the common people downed tools and gatecrashed the state funeral. They seemed to sense that Horatio Nelson was their man, the first great popular hero of modern times, the first great democrat in action.

*   *   *   *

The British Council exhibition showed portraits of Nelson at all ages. They showed the usual divergence of opinion as to how he looked, various artists seeing him differently. But their common denominator is a face of fine-drawn strength and calmness. There is an unmistakable warmth of heart shining from his eyes—even from his surviving eye—from first to last, a quality which most high commanders are at some pains to disguise. No wounds, apparently, could embitter him. No honours, nor power, nor fame could make him thrust out his chin, lower one eyelid, or design himself a fancy hat. He had an inner certainty which seems rare in the great commanders of our own times.

The face declares this essence of his character, and the despatches underline it. His letters, some of them painfully yet jokingly written with his left hand, confirm it all. The recent and best-documented biographies all speak of Nelson's 'pranks', and throw new and endearing light on the man. I grew up believing that he was a sombre and dedicated, almost a tragic hero. Now, it appears, even his famous Duty Signal was flown, in his own words 'to amuse the Fleet',—and, incidentally, to take the edge off pre-battle tension.

I found ample evidence that Nelson had been poor, sickly, reviled, and, of course, horribly wounded. His personal history would have aided his natural gift of sympathy for the unfortunate, for the unfortunates under his command. This sympathy, with his carefree manner and his obvious personal courage, must have been known to every man in his Fleet—a far smaller and more intimate Fleet than a man could command today.

After the battle, and the tragedy, some of Nelson's men tried to write about him. 'I'm but a saucy foremast Jack,' scrawled one humble survivor, continuing:

> 'But now Lord Nelson is no more,
> It grieves me for to say,
> And he always lived victorious until that very day,
> For on that great and glorious day
> It was his lot to fall,
> And his memory shall be ever dear
> To British sailors all.'

You can lead a horse to the water, but beyond that you cannot go. A man under orders does as he must, but no one can order a British seaman to express himself in verse. This Jack loved Nelson, and so did thousands more, which adds up to the Nelson Touch which has become proverbial in our language.

Nelson's Pillar in O'Connell Street, standing before the General Post Office of glorious memory, was the pivot of Dublin city. From time to time there have been suggestions by fervent but misguided patriots, to remove the Admiral's effigy and, replace him by some Irish hero. But so stands Nelson's stock, even in this country, so cruelly treated by his country in his time, that a majority of Irishmen wished him to stay put. It is as though they knew—although I am sure they do not—that Nelson owed his promotion to Irishmen.

Had the Dubliners voted to remove Nelson from his Pillar and known all that they should know about him, they might have put Valentine Joyce, United Irishman and Naval Reformer in his place. But the question was rashly and finally answered, whilst I was writing this book, by an explosion in the small hours, the work of a militant minority of Irishmen, and Horatio Nelson lay shattered in O'Connell Street. Long may he continue to lord it over London.

17

VICTORIANA

The history of Britain in the nineteenth century resounds to the cry of 'Glory' underscored by the quieter but more convincing note of 'Gain'. The armed forces of the Crown, with their new gunboats and Gatling guns, were used by successive governments of financiers and manufacturers as their advance salesmen—the highest pressure salesmen yet seen by a startled world. America, Africa, China, India, Russia, Arabia, Egypt, Ireland and Japan, to name but a few, still bear the scars of those sales campaigns of rising England, of her wholehearted attempts to sell her tea, opium, coal and textiles to reluctant purchasers, or to seize and safeguard the sources of her raw materials.

Sir Francis Drake, forerunner and pioneer of colonialism, not only made signal contribution to the physical foundation of our world-wide buccaneering but also attempted to advance it in theory. He it was who wrote:

> 'Their gain shall be the knowledge of our Faith,
> And ours such riches as the country hath.'

What he recommended, in plain prose, was to force the new and disputacious anglican religion on to the conquered and, that done, to rob them.

I was taught in school, in front of a map all covered over with red, that the British Empire was a hard-won and well-deserved heritage and a sacred trust. At the same time I was taught that it had voluntarily surrendered itself into our hands in accordance with God's will and in admiration for Queen Victoria. Of that great lady all I knew was that she was in favour of trade and against sex, and I never doubted that, with these attributes, all the peoples of the world would be tumbling over each other in their anxiety to be ruled by her. Many years later I discovered that whereas trade doesn't suit everyone, sex undoubtedly does so.

I came to the conclusion that the British Empire was not only a highly dubious affair, but that it was sinister, sham and, finally, harmful, which is a view widely held throughout the modern world and applied to all empires or subordinations of one country to another.

On wider acquaintance with the colonies and in maturer wisdom I came to revise my views once again. I came to believe that the British Empire was less harmful and more magnanimous than almost any other; that its defects were all due to ignorance, to the untrained administrator who has brought Britain to her knees at home and abroad, and that malice had no part in these defects, and greed, in the latter phase of empire, very little part. In some respects and in some places British rule was positively and demonstrably beneficent.

Gibraltar, smallest and strangest of our overseas possessions as well as one of the oldest, may offer a key to this problem of assessment, as she does to so many others. Gibraltar provides what biologists call a 'control', a free and isolated sample wherein stress and change may conveniently be studied. From their effects on this tiny sample it may be possible to infer their manifestations in a greater mass. In a similar manner, the history of the British Empire, the development of Britain's overseas policies and attitudes and actions, may be assessed, to some extent, by observation of her treatment of Gibraltar. To some extent only, because Gibraltar was—still is— unique in several respects. The most important of these is that The Rock was the only British military outpost in the Continent of Europe, and has thus spent much of its time under threat of war. The effect of this has been that the civilians there have been relegated for two centuries to the position of second-class citizens, necessary nuisances in a garrisoned fortress.

*   *   *   *

From the year 1805, with Nelson dead and England in command of the seas, to the year 1815 when, with some timely aid, we won our Waterloo, must have been a very unsettled period for Europe and, as always, for Gibraltar. The French had occupied the whole of Spain, right down to our Straits, and the Spaniards uneasily accepted British aid to oust them.

Waterloo ended this time of hesitation and strife by ending the Napoleonic and all other threats and challenges to Great Britain. From 1815 onwards for almost a century she was undisputed

Top Nation, a greater power in the world than either the U.S.A. or the U.S.S.R. in our own times.

France was defeated and full of internal strife. Germany and Italy were struggling towards nationhood. Russia was a daft and distant tyranny. The United States was preoccupied with the winning and consolidation of her own wide territories. Japan was, from the British viewpoint, nothing more than a cheeky child, and China a comic-opera country. India, most of Africa, Canada, Australia, New Zealand, the Middle East and much of the Far East were all in the British bag.

Britain's century of power and peace was disturbed at will only, by such foolish gambles as the Crimea and by what would now be called police actions against Boers and Boxers, Hindus, Afghans, Fuzziwuzzies, Zulus, and anyone else who talked or acted out of turn.

The British Victorian era as we have come to call it, was characterized by strength and stability—strength of all kinds, military, monetary, and, it was claimed, moral. The resultant developments were unprecedented.

At home there was amazing material progress, based on the work of a half-dozen of brilliant engineers and a million work-hungry Irish immigrants, and giving rise to unheard of prosperity and poverty. Abroad there was a vast extension of Empire, to cover every part of the globe, literally from pole to pole and including the ice floes of Baffin Bay and the lost atolls of the Pacific—or, as Kipling put it 'dominion over palm and pine'. Trade, indeed, followed the flag, and if it did so reluctantly, as, for instance, in Hong Kong and Japan, there were gunboats galore to speed up the process. But for the effective use of gunboats there must be overseas naval bases.

There is only one other nation which merits mention in the list I have given, and that is Spain. That country was in a state of steady and inexorable decline, not to say decay. Spain lost her overseas possessions one by one, until, by the turn of the century, all that remained were some small and unenvied patches of Africa. Great Britain, by an uneasy alliance in the Peninsular War and by a subsequent royal marriage, kept on apparently friendly terms with Spain for a hundred years, snapping up her South American markets as fast as they shook free of the Spanish yoke.

I say 'apparently' because it was always suspected, and ultimately declared that the friendship—on Spain's side, at least—was reluctant, forced and insincere. Over a period of three hundred years Great Britain had steadily defeated, disgraced and discredited Spain throughout the world, pulled her down from her erstwhile supremacy, supplanted her influence and appropriated her trade. Always amply aided by the fatal flaws in Spanish character, Britain had pushed Spain down into the position of picturesque impotence which she occupies so gracefully to this day.

The Spaniards are careless of many things, but one thing they cherish is the memory of past wrongs. I know of no nation less likely to forgive and forget. Once a Spaniard comes to hate you—it takes time, for he is noble and magnanimous in his fashion—he will watch and wait for his revenge like a wounded bull in its *queréncia*. They have a proverb which says: 'He will put out one of his eyes to make you blind.'

Meanwhile, full of guns and ships and soldiers, with the subdued Mediterranean before it and smiling, silent Spain behind, The Rock of Gibraltar begins its century in the sun. Not a nation in Europe, nor in the world, dare threaten it, and our Fortress can give its whole attention to the furtherance of British power and prestige and prosperity, and, if its rulers see fit, to the constructive development of the place itself.

The practical developments at Gibraltar, those of a warlike nature, were all, as one would expect, on a spectacular scale. The harbour, with its big dockyard and graving docks, military buildings and installations of all kinds, roads, reservoirs, magazines and tunnels, proceeded fast and early and were once the wonder of the world. I can think of no place which owes so much to human ingenuity, to the engineer. Without artifice Man could not eat or drink there, supply, defence, shelter, and all the modern refinements necessary to human life have been grafted on to this inhospitable rock by successive generations of technicians. The list of achievements runs from Tarik's fort through twelve hundred years to the radar controlled airstrip. Gibraltar will not see any more miracles of engineering, but it is well to remember that it was a pioneer place in the development of harbour works, water catchments, artillery and tunnelling, and that the British Royal Engineers, still called

'Sappers' and, to the best of my knowledge, the first such corps in any army, were born in this place.

Britain had unlimited funds in the past century and there was no opposition to expenditure on the extension of Empire. The Tories were patriotically promoting the Flag, with a shrewd eye to their high finance, their shipping and insurance shares, and the profitable placement of their younger sons. The Whigs, later Liberals, were all for Trade and the freer the better. The small band of reformers and radicals, the conscientious and humane, supported the British régime in the belief that the country had a civilizing mission, to confer upon the 'lesser breeds' the benefits of English Christian Victorianism. So, for a hundred years, money was lavished on Gibraltar, as a fortress and as a naval base, but not, alas, as a colony or community of human beings.

The last heavy bombardment of Gibraltar took place in 1781, towards the end of the Great Siege. The destruction of earlier sieges had scarcely been repaired because the place was under threat and its future uncertain. Breaches in the defences were, no doubt, made good, but the town itself remained damaged and dilapidated. By the 19th April 1781, according to Benedict R. Miles in his brief *History of Gibraltar*, 'the town was almost a heap of ruins'.

As a result, only a few eighteenth-century buildings survive. There is The Convent, which is Government House, and which was built in 1531 for the Franciscan Friars, but very little of the original building remains. There was the Cathedral of St. Mary the Crowned, but it has been renovated and reconstructed so that only a shred of the old fabric survives. A few old towers in the town area were tough enough to resist the rain of iron balls, and the walls, gates and bastions withstood it well. Explosive shells were used, but they contained only gunpowder and are not to be compared to high-explosive missiles of our own times. Gibraltar has never yet been shelled, in the modern sense, but merely battered by iron balls.

The South District was out of sight and out of range of the enemy guns a mile or more to northwards. Miles states that 'the inhabitants, panic-stricken, retreated to the southward of The Rock'. It is regrettable that there was not much eighteenth-century development in that part, for such as there was is still with us. Like every other part of Gibraltar, except the inaccessible heights and precipices, the

South District has been marred by expedient excrescences—stores and warehouses, strongpoints, barbed-wire enclosures, iron tanks, masts and aerials, all the usual military paraphernalia past and present. There are even some hutments left over from World War I, for such is the army system that it is more difficult to write material off than to obtain it. But, in the midst of this clutter, some fine buildings remain, enough to suggest what the town might have been like before its destruction and unfortunate rebuilding. South Barracks, with its long double colonnade of white stonework, was built for use, and its resulting economy achieves a sort of beauty. Rosia Harbour with its surrounding embrasured ramparts, all formed of massive blocks of silver stone closely cut and fitted together, has a satisfying solidity and honesty. There are some fine old houses, like The Mount where the Flag Officer lives, but they are mostly buried in their trees and gardens and not visible from the roads. Visiting them as a guest I found fine Georgian and Regency fenestration, well-cut masonry, graceful proportions and even, here and there, the original fireboxes in earliest cast iron, bearing the cypher of King William IV.

But the physiognomy of the city of Gibraltar is predominately Victorian, and Colonial Victorian at that. The period, in architecture as in other arts and matters of taste, had inescapable and fatal faults. It was competitive, grandiose, individualistic, vulgar, gimcrack and eclectic. The governing philosophy of the era, that of success and riches, does not readily transmit into aesthetic forms.

The faults of Victorian architecture are seen at their worst in streets and cities. The individual buildings, ill-proportioned, false-faced, fussed up with pretentious and senseless detail and adornment, are bad enough in themselves. But when rows of them are slapped together, regardless of each other, the overall result is chaotic, hideous and ultimately depressing. It is in studying such a street scene that one recognizes the essential error of the period, the undue emphasis on individual wealth, with its corollary—devil take the hindmost. The basic bad manners and inhumanity of our golden century are enshrined in our Greek railway stations, hatters' castles and gothic cast-iron urinals. Only in such a conservative culture as the English could such a school have lingered for half a century at home, and far longer abroad, after wise voices were raised against it. They are still defacing the English countryside with what Osbert Lancaster so aptly labelled 'Stockbroker's Tudor'.

But bad as the Victorian street scene is at home, in Britain, it is far worse abroad, in British colonies. Gibraltar never saw a fully professional architect until very recent years. Throughout the century of its development, of the building as you see it today, design was in the hands of military engineers, at best. At best, because they would have some education and common sense, and some pressure on them to economize. At worst, that is in the case of all civilian building, the designers were very often the builders themselves, who did what they liked and what they could.

The final result is that Gibraltar gives the visitor an impression of fustiness, of backwatered Victorianism, of the shabby-genteel, and of unjustified pretentiousness. Such impressions have frequently been published, and the Gibraltarians, believing that the epithets are applied to themselves, very naturally take offence. The fact is, our visitors do not know what has hit them. Very few people look closely at architecture or attempt to analyse it, yet it cannot be ignored. If the conscious mind rejects it, the eye still receives it and, I suppose, implants it subliminally on the subconscious. A city of grandeur, like Paris or New York or parts of London, impresses and inhibits its visitors so that in a sense, they lower their voices. A provincial town is inhibited by its visitors, who stroll its streets in shorts and suntops, laughing and shouting. The streets of Gibraltar, in spite of the noble history of the place, are unimpressive. At best they promote a sense of intimacy and security; at worst they are depressing.

My advice to visitors would be that they should concentrate their gaze on the shop windows of Gibraltar—and in this the shopkeeping citizens would concur. To raise the eyes to the tiled façades, the florid iron balconies, the grim and narrow windows, the general lack of paint, the grotesque disparities in scale and style between each building and its neighbour, is to be aesthetically inflicted and dismayed. The mind simply picks up the atmosphere of obsolescence, squalor and decay. On street level, in shop fronts and bars, there has been much modernization which is, at least, lively rather than moribund and, in the commercial sense, inviting.

The Gibraltarian of today is not to be blamed for his inherited architectural environment. Provincial people lag behind their metropolis in matters of taste and fashion; colonial people, up to recent years so widely divorced from the sources of inspiration, lag far further. The Gibraltarians are behind the times—London standard—in architectural taste as in many other matters, but they are not so far behind as the face of their town implies.

When the Government brought out a brilliant and daring young architect, native son Mario Sanguinetti, English trained to membership of the Royal Institute of British Architects, he and his work received ready and general acceptance and admiration.

Building heights and sites have always been limited by the requirements of military lines of fire. Now, at last, these archaic restrictions have been removed and Gibraltar is building upwards. There are groups of fine new apartment buildings below the Moorish Castle and on the flat land at the foot of the cliffs, and sixteen-storey blocks are under construction as I write. The Gibraltar of the future—if all goes well—may become a miniature Manhattan Island.

But when it does so Main Street will remain as it is, narrow, crooked and irregular, just as curving Broadway survived the rectilinear rationalization of the Manhattan street plan. Their high frontage values defend such streets against alteration, but what gives such streets more value than the straight and sensible? The answer may be that man prefers to promenade on a curving street, with the vistas changing as he proceeds. Or, perhaps, we are just devious.

I have described the shell of Gibraltar, that ornate and ugly carapace of Victorian growth. Now I must proceed to examine the oyster itself.

The census of 1814 tells me that there were then 1,657 houses, with 5,804 rooms. There were 10,136 civilians, so that there may have been about 2,500 families. Hence, the average Gibraltar family had a two-room habitation, but since there were already a few rich people occupying many more than two, it is to be assumed that there were many families with one room only. There are still many one-room families in Gibraltar as I write, but they have every hope of receiving better accommodation soon. At the beginning of this golden century of Victoria's the prospects of the poor, had they known it, were those of deepening poverty.

The garrison at this date, including wives and children, added up to 6,754, so that the total population of The Rock was 17,000 people. But for the epidemics, the population would have been close to the present-day figure, for no less than 7,000 people had died of yellow fever in the ten years preceding the census. It is difficult for us, in our clean, spacious and healthy cities, to imagine the effects of plague in a small, closed town. The disease was undiagnosed and incurable and came to be regarded with superstitious drèad. There was no escape from it, for Spain put up a *cordon sanitaire* and no ship's master would take a suspect citizen aboard. The people of Gibraltar had to wait and watch, in unrelenting dread, until the plague, having killed something more than one out of every three of them, chose to abate. We can assume that every survivor had had his nose rubbed in disaster and death, and that we begin the nineteenth century with a community of sombre and apprehensive people. The citizens of Gibraltar are, by British standards, highly hypochondriac to this day. To know their sad history is to forgive this idiosyncrasy.

This census, 1814, divides the civil population into racial groups as follows:

Genoese	886
Portuguese	650
Spanish	527
Jewish	489
British	403 (including Irish)
Minorcans	138
Italians	104

It is noteworthy that the Spaniards have returned, so that they now outnumber the British. The Portuguese and Minorcan elements at the base of the modern population are often overlooked. The Genoese and other Italians, then of separate nations, add up to almost 1,000, and emerge as the numerically dominant race in Gibraltar. They still do so, one hundred and fifty years later.

It should be remembered that those Genoese and Jews, who suffered as much as—maybe more than—the soldiers, were the ancestors and progenitors of the Gibraltarians of today. They it was who set the tone of the early community, the morals and aspirations which have been handed down to the modern Gibraltarians.

What held them, these Italian Roman Catholics and Sephardic Jews, in this strange, bullying British garrison, exposed to constant danger and insult, lacking all comforts and that elementary security which is the strongest desire of commercial people?

The inescapable truth is that Gibraltar rapidly became so in-ordinately profitable to its civilians, such an easy goldmine to those who could tolerate its oppression and restriction, that the civilians could not see their way to leave it. The early merchants, before a semblance of democracy arrived, and faster communications to en-force it, were men who put gold before personal pride, and even before their personal security and safety.

I have defined this attitude because it may shed some light, later on, on the values and aspirations of the representative Gibraltarian of today. Those values are pragmatically and unashamedly com-mercial, more so even than those of Victorian England. The rich men of The Rock, and they are many, are not the gay and graceful inheritors of aristocratic funds, the chief adornment of England's oligarchy. They are the time-toughened descendants of a harried and displaced peasantry, knocked down and robbed by history time and time again. Each one still on his feet has built around himself and his clan, brick by brick, a close wall of personal security and well-being, and he will fight for the last brick of it.

The group called British in the 1814 census were the merchants or agents of United Kingdom firms, with their families. This census gives the occupations of the citizens, as well as their races and reli-gions. Of the British, ninety-one of them described themselves as merchants, and if I put the family size at four, I find that nearly all the so-called British residents were either merchants or aspiring to become merchants. In so far as one could lead, in a military dictatorship, these were the leading people of the place.

There were a few professionals, for the first time, some lawyers and medical men. There were about fifty citizens who called themselves cigar-makers, and almost a hundred fishermen and boatmen. Al-though only two citizens were so simple as to put themselves down as 'smugglers', it is evident that the tobacco trade was well on its way.

The Genoese came to fish, proceeded to the more profitable and less arduous trade of market gardening on the Neutral Ground be-tween The Rock and Spain. Out there, finding themselves in close contact with the customer, they took to smuggling. From that risky trade, some of them graduated to become merchants in tobacco, suppliers rather than carriers. The early British merchants dealt in cotton cloth and other manufactured goods, all heavily taxed as legitimate imports to Spain, and therefore highly profitable as contraband. The tobacco business, which has proved to have more staying power, fell into the hands of the Genoese and remained in their hands down to the present time. The principal names in Gibraltar tobacco are still Italianate—Russo, Stagnetto, Povedano, with one Spanish name, Vasquez.

The first thirty years of the nineteenth century were a period of boom for Gibraltar. The steamship had not yet arrived, but sailing ships, in hundreds, used to put in at Gibraltar to wait for the right wind to carry them out through The Straits. At times, according to contemporary reports, the whole Bay was crowded with ships waiting for the wind to change. Here we had a huge haven, safe from weather and from pillage, and placed at the only door to the busiest sea in the world. Those years were Gibraltar's heyday, in maritime matters, at least. They laid the basis of some great fortunes there.

One dark cloud still hung over The Rock. In 1828 the population was decimated once more by yellow fever. In three months, 1,667 people died. As a result of this, the 1830 census shows little advance on its predecessor of sixteen years earlier. It found the total population to be 17,024, and categorized them as follows:

Roman Catholics	(Native)	7,392
Jews	(Native)	1,340
Roman Catholics	(Alien)	6,305
Jews	(Alien)	603

The aliens were either recent immigrants or else those who had neglected to apply for British citizenship.

It was in this year, 1830, that the Civil Magistracy was established, tempering, and to some extent replacing, the Governor's judicial powers. Up to this date, Gibraltar was, in effect, under martial law, and the best trial a citizen could expect must have been something in the nature of a drumhead court martial. This new charter of justice was the first step towards the recognition of a civil community, of civil rights for the inhabitants of Gibraltar. It was, no doubt, aimed at offering some protection and encouragement for the merchant class, the colonial offshoots of men who were beginning to entrench themselves in power at home in Britain. The concession may have been, however, in the good old tradition of too little and too late.

The first steamship arrived in Gibraltar in 1823, and was greeted, here as elsewhere, with some amusement. But the advantages of a ship which could travel where and when it wished, plan its movements, keep to its schedule, and so earn its keep three times as well as a sailing ship, soon became obvious. The changeover from sail to steam, backed by heavy funds, was very rapid. Gibraltar soon began to lose her callers and her passing trade, for the steamers could go through The Straits without delay.

Much later, the steamships began to use Gibraltar as a coaling station, but in this, as in other matters where risk and enterprise and foresight are called for, Gibraltar missed the boat. When coaling did, tardily, begin here, it was all done by hand labour, and so it continued to be done right up to 1933. The hundreds of men who heaved the coal in small hand baskets, in arduous and hopeless competition with the machinery in more progressive ports, were to develop into the spearhead of Gibraltar's labour movement. One hundred years after the need—and the opportunity—arose, acres of massive gantries and grabs were installed on the North Mole, at great cost, to give the process of coaling the speed which ships had long demanded. Alas, by that time the ships were changing over to oil-firing, and as with the previous changeover, the coal-burners soon vanished from the seas. In 1958–9 I saw much of this fine coaling machinery pushed aside, all of it in new condition but scarcely saleable elsewhere, to make room for a necessary transit shed.

By 1833 the new dockyard at Malta began to assume importance, with injurious effect on Gibraltar's naval business. After 1834, the figures prove, the population grew only by ingress of Spaniards. No one who could easily choose otherwise would come to The Rock, with its horrible record of disease—revived in 1834 when a cholera epidemic claimed 380 victims—and its declining trade in both naval and mercantile shipping.

In 1842 England began to use The Rock as an outlet for her surging stream of convicts and transportees. Many of these, as I keep assuring my Australian friends, were the best of Englishmen, who had fallen foul of the multifarious and restrictive laws of the time through their courage, principles or sincerity. The Tolpuddle Martyrs, founders of rural trade unionism, were among them. Be that as it may, their influx did harm in Gibraltar. They were put to work on the massive masonry of the naval dockyard and military fortifications. One immediate result must have been that the native labourers were laid aside and compelled to live on their wits. Another bad result, and an even more lasting one, was that manual labour was degraded to criminal level in the eyes of the Gibraltarians.

After the setback of the 'thirties The Rock began to enjoy another boom in trade. By 1844 the French wars had had the effect of excluding British shipping from all ports on the continent—except Gibraltar. The local merchants made full use of their opportunities and the turnover of Manchester goods grew to immense proportions. The tobacco came and went as never before and in 1844 there were 2,000 avowed cigar-makers, about one breadwinner in two of the British inhabitants. Let us look at the census for that year.

The total civilian population was touching 16,000, which shows the decline which I have explained. Of these, 12,000 were British subjects, categorized as follows:

British Isles, including Service families	995
Natives	9,802
Jewish Natives	1,385

The remaining 4,000 made up of those who had not yet received British citizenship and those who did not seek it, comprised nearly 2,000 Spaniards, most of whom were women; 800 Genoese, presumably new immigrants; and over 500 Portuguese. There were a few French, Moors and Italians, and 240 people described as 'Foreign Jews'.

The good times lasted until the 1850s, when the interfering Governor, General Gardiner, threw a spanner in the works. He pointed out that the smuggling trade, by then undeniably the chief business of Gibraltar, was in direct contravention of the Treaty of Utrecht, the basis of Britain's tenure of Gibraltar, that it was ruining the good name of the colony and of Britain, that it was endangering our relations with Spain and hence, our base, and—new and unpopular idea—that it was simply wrong!

Such had been the progress, the growth in influence and power of the merchant class both at home and abroad, that Gardiner was overruled, defeated and disgraced. A mere fifty years earlier he could have had his adversaries whipped through the town at the cart's tail.

Now, in 1852, money talked. It talked louder than the Governor, louder than the clergy, louder, for that matter, than the Queen herself. On The Rock the merchants heard it talk and saw it talk, and turned to each other with gleeful congratulations. From now on, they knew, under British flags and guns, they could do as they pleased in commercial matters. This was the heyday, the apogee and high tide of Victorianism.

18

ALBERT MEMORIAL

In the second half of the century Gibraltar had its ups and downs, commercially speaking, but the general trend, thanks to Britain's policy and pre-eminence and to The Rock's special position and privileges, was upwards. Upwards for the few, that is, for the shrewdest and least scrupulous who, under this system of unbridled acquisitiveness were sure to rise to the top. The period in the United Kingdom is noteworthy for the beginnings of reform, for the amelioration of the terrible social conditions which the competitive system had caused. The voice of the liberal and religious rebel was loud in the land—Shaftesbury, Chadwick, Wilberforce, Nightingale, Fry, to name a few. But none of these voices were heard on The Rock. None of the new social legislation of Britain applied there. Nothing at all was done for the Gibraltarians, British though they were, except to protect them and police them.

Not even the merchants, those sacred cows of the Victorian era, could win themselves a hearing in our Colony. Over and over again they asked to be taken into the confidence of the Governor and consulted on forthcoming legislation. Over and over again they were refused. They could win, with the aid of the hard-faced Manchester lobby in Victoria's parliament, commercial victories over the Government, as they did in 1853 and 1878, but more than that they could not do. The control of The Rock, the Fortress, was to remain firmly in the hands of the military Governor until the end of the Second World War.

Nevertheless, great fortunes were made and, as one might expect, great poverty was created in their wake. The poverty was relieved by public charity. The scale and persistence of public charity in Gibraltar is Roman, almost oriental. The idea of a civic duty to the less fortunate, to the victims of the competitive system, is a comparatively new one. It was scarcely accepted in England until the Labour Government of 1945 began to build the Welfare State, although it had been promulgated in that country many years earlier. In the United States the burden was officially accepted in

1964. In colonial cultures, such as Hong Kong and Gibraltar, the rich will fight to keep the collection and distribution of charity in their personal and private hands. One obvious reason for this is that it avoids taxation, it is also, of course, a source and show of power, but there is a far older and more subtle motive behind it—the idea of acquiring merit by charitable works.

In Victorian times which, in my view, still linger in our outposts of Empire, poverty was a symptom of indolence and thriftlessness rather than of natural disadvantages, since even the most ignorant of men could and did make money. Divine favour had been withdrawn from you, and left you, though not a miscreant, an object of some disdain. The cure for this public disease, which was inevitable and endemic, was the pleasant device of public subscription. Since there was no public duty to feed the hungry—to any greater extent than God, in His wisdom, had decided to do—one could acquire merit by the disinterested and altruistic action of feeding them. A rich man could thus help his own soul—which he may have felt to be much in need of it—and the poor man's belly at the same time. Added to that sensible transaction, he could stave off unrest, revolution, and taxation, and keep his town safer and cleaner too.

To this day, Gibraltar is full of fortuitous charities, and proud of them. The Catholic organizations are many, from St. Vincent de Paul downwards, and they find plenty to do. There is a Jewish Poor Fund and a Protestant Poor Fund, whose targets would now be hard to define. There was one Trust Fund, in my time, which had been left to house the poor, within certain definitions. Since the particular type of poor ceased to be forthcoming, the houses were let to the rich, quite legally, in the hope of keeping the Fund strong in case the special poverty arose again. The Red Cross is active and provides the major social occasion of the year with a ball at Government House, from which, they tell me, Messrs. Dior and Balenciaga make rather more than anyone else. The Royal Society for the Prevention of Cruelty to Animals is to the fore here, as in all British colonies, and attention which it pays to thirsty hens in the market and to donkeys left in the sun, causes the Spaniards endless surprise. Quaintest of all the charities is, perhaps, an organization called The Ladies' Needlework Guild, which meets under the auspices of the Governor's wife to take tea and sew smalls for the deserving poor. Any lady in it—and you have to be a lady to join—could write a cheque in five minutes to cover the annual production. But let me revert to the Victorian roots of these strange plants.

In 1829, to celebrate the end of yet another epidemic, they raised $27,000 Spanish, 'for the relief of the poor encamped on the Neutral Ground'. The King of Spain gave 10,000 *fanegas* of his wheat, it is recorded, which must have given someone a headache working *fanegas* out in ounces. But charity at best is only a temporary expedient and poverty in Gibraltar grew inexorably.

In 1865 they raised $14,000 and set up soup kitchens. In 1901, to celebrate a visit by the Duke and Duchess of York, the Chamber of Commerce felt it wise to give the poor of Gibraltar 1,000 lb. of meat and 2,000 lb. of bread. A year later, to celebrate the coronation of Edward VII, Messrs. Bland & Co. went it alone and distributed 3,000 lb. of beef, 6,000 lb. of potatoes and 6,000 lb. of bread. The word 'poor' had gone out of fashion by then, and the gift was addressed 'to the indigent of Gibraltar'.

In 1903 they were at it again. A visit by the new king, who left £100 out of his privy purse for the poor of The Rock, was the pretext for collecting 5,000 pesetas from local sources. In 1905 Queen Alexandra came alone and left another £100 for the poor. It must never have occurred to anyone, least of all to the Administration, to consider why this problem was so persistent. Nor did it occur to them to consider themselves responsible for it, much less disgraced by it, for they seem to have had no hesitation in bringing the sad condition of their people to the attention of the King and Queen.

During World War I very large sums were readily collected in Gibraltar for the Red Cross and other wartime charities. The place was, through circumstances rather than by design, a war profiteer on the grand scale, and trade had never been so good. Thousands of pounds of conscience money were thrown eagerly into the hat. 'Our Day' in Gibraltar, 12th October 1917, raised £5,011 for the Red Cross, most of it from the untaxed and thriving merchants of the Exchange Committee. Just four years later, on the 17th November 1921, the Red Cross, in response to a request, sent £5,000 back to Gibraltar towards the cost of a maternity ward at the Colonial Hospital. Thus the merchants saved their souls, stalled off taxation, and got their money back as well.

In 1920 a meeting of the Sanitary Commissioners—mostly local merchants and lawyers—proudly informed the Governor that a Poor Law was not wanted in Gibraltar. This was after a full century of extreme poverty, growing and persisting right under their noses and relieved only by occasional and arbitrary hand-outs. In the same year the Emergency Food Supply Committee, which had been issuing cheap food for the accredited poor on a ticket system, decided to discontinue the practice. It is on record that, so obvious and dire was the need, some grocers continued the issue of cheap food at their own expense.

Throughout the Victorian era, including its straggling aftermath, the social conditions in Great Britain were, by all accounts, horrible. But strong voices called out incessantly for reform and improvement and they were, ultimately, successful. Conditions in the colonies were far worse, and no voice could be raised. In booming Hong Kong, as I saw there last year, it is still perfectly easy to die in the streets or to sell your little daughter to an old man. Gibraltar, perhaps because it is a Christian community, is much further forward, but social welfare is of recent growth there.

In the very bad times of last century, and on into the present one, there were only three or four voices, apart from the Governor's, which would be heard at all. The strongest, potentially, was that of the Roman Catholic Church. But the Church looks after souls rather than bodies, and its uneasy acceptance in The Fortress may have robbed it of any courage it might have had. Another potential voice was the official Anglican Church, sometimes irreverently known as 'The Tory Party at Prayer'. But it had, in Victorian times, very little to say on any social problem, as is indicated by the rise and spread of the Methodist movement. I am aware that the Wesleys were pre-Victorian, but the era, in my view, is not precisely coeval with Victoria's reign. The Jewish church might have spoken out, but here, as elsewhere, it was exclusive and discreet. It felt, no doubt, that it had better be so. Further, it had enough to do to educate and cherish its own people. The strongest voice was that of the merchant class of rich and well-connected men. But, since these were the very men who would bear the weight of social improvements, in the form of taxation, it is not surprising that this voice was raised only to oppose them, to protest against public expenditure in any shape or form. The Gibraltar Chamber of Commerce made this age-old protest once again as late as February 1965.

Not that there was, in the worst times, much occasion for such protest, nor much danger of progressive and expensive government. Military governors, all elderly generals, with radical or even liberal views, are as rare as three-humped camels, or holy water in an Orange Lodge. Typically, they had no views at all, except as to their rank and profession. Should, by some mischance, a Red General happen to be sent to Gibraltar, the merchants knew by experience that he could probably be defeated and dismissed as the freak purist General Gardiner had been before.

The outcome of these circumstances was that the social and material development of the Gibraltar civil community was sadly and shamefully retarded. The Army and the Navy had their own hospitals, doctors and scavengers, and looked after their own health and sanitation. They even had—still have—their own water supply and sewerage systems. The civil community had no such protection until recent times.

The Sanitary Commissioners, charged with keeping the place clean and reasonably safe from plague and pestilence, were appointed in 1865, after an epidemic which killed 572 people in three months. Chadwick, in England, had pointed out that sanitation was good economy. Epidemic diseases, quite apart from their toll in human life and suffering, cost more in hard cash than did sewers and refuse collection and reasonable housing. At the same time, advances in medical science made the rich man aware that diseases could not always be contained in the slums. In the light of these arguments the rulers of Britain grudgingly voted money and subjected themselves to municipal rates and taxes. The rich men of Gibraltar where, hot and crowded as it was, the need was even more urgent, fought a long rearguard action against such public enterprise and expenditure. But it was an action which they were sure to lose, for the Army doctors kept up a constant pressure, and the Governor and Commander-in-Chief had a duty to protect his troops.

The first public waterworks, in advance of a village supply, was inaugurated as late as 1865. Up to then the public drew water from a three-hundred-year old conduit, laid by the Spaniards, from the Red Sands along what is now Rosia Road. The Red Sands, the source and collection area of the town's water supply, was used as a cemetery. 'The death rate', says Mrs. Ellicott, Gibraltar's leading resident historian, 'increased enormously, and people blamed the Levanter.' She does not say for how long it had been increasing. I can see a vicious circle of peculiar horror. The more people the water killed, the more corpses would there be in the Red Sands, and the more people the water would kill! A War Office Sanitary Commission, sent out in 1861, found the water highly contaminated and ordered the fountain closed and, it may be, told the Governor that he had better set up a permanent Sanitary Commission and force it to enlist some knowledgeable officials.

Even the improved water supply which ensued only brought water to central points, thence it was carried by donkeys to such householders as could afford it. To this day there are hundreds of Gibraltarian citizens without running water in their homes. In this electronic age, water is still bought by the gallon at the municipal fountain and carried upstairs to apartments in ancient wooden kegs.

One of the earliest public utilities in Gibraltar was, rather typically, a gasworks. But its product must have been far beyond the purse of the majority of the inhabitants. Right up to the outbreak of World War II the Gibraltarians were cooking on primitive Spanish charcoal stoves. In fact, many of the resettlement centres, for evacuees returning to The Rock in 1945, were equipped, in that year, with such cooking arrangements, and I had the pleasure of tearing out many such Don Quixote dingbats ten years later when the people were rehoused. The post-war flats all have electric cookers, but tradition dies hard and the Gibraltarians still refer to their electricity supply as '*la luz*', because for so many years it was used only for lighting.

Sewerage and main drainage were not effectively installed until the 1890s, which may help to explain why a cholera epidemic struck as late as 1885 and killed twenty-two people.

The main sewage outfall of Gibraltar is in the best possible place, at the southern tip of the promontory and a little to the Mediterranean side. The prevailing current should carry the sewage far away into the middle of the sea, the sump of the world. But, such are the strange eddies that swirl around The Rock that obdurate and buoyant exemplars of the sewers' contents occasionally bob home to roost on the leeward side. The Army's chief medico, an *ex-officio* member of the City Council in my time, once announced the presence of such undesirable intruders into the Harbour. The City

Council had a majority of elected members—Gibraltarians—long before the Legislative Council, with the result that it was always trying to prove that it was the more efficient of the two councils and, indeed, that it could do no wrong. It could certainly not admit to any error or inefficiency, and I never knew it to do so. The medical colonel was simply told that he was mistaken.

For a full colonel to be told in public that he could not recognize one of the most common objects in the world was not to be borne. With true British persistence this colonel took the first opportunity to swim in the Harbour, suitably equipped, and to capture an outstanding specimen of trespassing sewage. He enclosed this, in salt water, in a glass pickle jar.

At the next meeting of the Council he repeated his statement, waited for it to be denied, then unwrapped his jar and waved it aloft. Alas, the exhibit had disintegrated, and the contents of the jar were unidentifiable—except by means which the Mayor could not permit. The protest disintegrated too, amidst laughter, and the good colonel was ever afterwards known to the Gibraltarians as 'The Big Fisherman'.

With the constant and widespread poverty in Gibraltar, so often publicly acknowledged by charitable collections, it must have been obvious that a majority of the inhabitants were unable to buy, build or even rent proper accommodation. As the population increased and land values rose, the poor were huddled into smaller space at higher rents. The census of 1814 indicates the existence of many one-room families; later censuses could have indicated for more. There were hundreds of such families as late as 1955, and hundreds more living in old Nissen huts, at two families to a hut. The Government had never done more than begin to play with the provision of houses, and the home life of the Gibraltar citizen had always been, typically, one of crowded squalor.

Such circumstances were, as the army medical officers came to recognize and often declared, a fine field for the spread of diseases arising from foul water, open cesspits, rotting garbage, flies, bedbugs, fleas and lice—all of which flourish in this frost-free climate—and from the rats of all nations which are carried to Gibraltar's port.

After yellow fever and cholera had been conquered, less dramatic killers were found to be widespread. Gibraltar's tuberculosis problem, a direct result of overcrowding, was a serious one, and was only brought under control in the 1950s.

It was not until 1930, after the *sursum corda* of World War I, and more than half a century after the appointment of the (merchant) Sanitary Commissioners, that any action was taken to house the poor. The first publicly built tenement block was opened in 1930. The Commissioners, later City Council, built a few middle-class houses between that date and the outbreak of World War II, but the task was never to their liking and the Government had to take it over from them after the war.

In 1936, the outbreak of the Spanish Civil War—which took place in the towns of the Bay, at the gates of Gibraltar—drove about 2,000 Gibraltarians back to their native Rock. All these possessed and now claimed the right to live in Gibraltar, and they had to be housed in barracks, hutments and encampments. Up to then, and to some extent up to 1965, Spain had been shouldering a considerable portion of Gibraltar's housing problem.

Since World War II—these catastrophes make their creative contribution—some thousands of good modern apartments have been built in Gibraltar by the Government, and the time is approaching when every Gibraltarian family will be housed. There will still remain the unending task of rebuilding the slums and the substandard. There is local political pressure in these matters now, and the humble people of the place can see, all around them, what good housing standards ought to be. Much has been done, and the work continues. But it must be said that most of this post-war housing has been paid for by grants from Colonial Development and Welfare Funds, that is, from the tattered and torn pockets and purses of the hard-pressed United Kingdom tax-payer.

The amount of the grant for 1961 was £304,770, and it had been of that order for many of the previous years—a free gift from the most heavily taxed man in the world to the man most lightly taxed! Added to this, the British tax-payer pays for the defence of Gibraltar and, through the Overseas Aid Scheme, for some of the expenses of the civil administration.

I should add that these facts do not necessarily reflect the generosity or altruism of the British tax-payer. It is my belief, gathered through conversation and by the lack of public complaint in the United Kingdom, that the average Englishman has not the faintest idea of where his taxes go nor of how they are spent. He is far too busy trying to avoid taxation to study a subject as complicated as overseas aid. Even his representatives in Parliament must be but vaguely aware of the uses to which British funds are put in colonies overseas. If they did know, we should certainly hear more from them on the subject, for the overseas distribution and administration of hard-won British money would provide any ambitious opposition M.P. with a strong stick to beat the Government.

Electricity arrived in Gibraltar in 1897. Telephones and taxis came in the 1920s. There was a Committee on Unemployment in 1927, some twenty years after the setting up of Labour Exchanges in the United Kingdom. The first Board of Education was set up in 1921 to dispense small grants in aid to existing religious schools. A new civil hospital was founded in 1880, and a very poor and unsatisfactory one it has proved to be. One wonders what kind of an institution it could have replaced. In 1884 they opened the first lunatic asylum, an institution which was put to most appropriate use some thirty-two years later when, at the triumphant end of the First World War, the Governor decreed that a gala dinner should be fed to the inmates.

One social service which came curiously early to Gibraltar was the civil police force. This was inaugurated in 1830, is the oldest of all colonial police forces, and only a few years younger than Sir Robert Peel's original London force. I have heard it suggested that the establishment of this service made possible the neglect of many others. In the past century, in Gibraltar as in Ireland, the main duty of the police would be to preserve the peace and protect property. The more property a man had, the more protection he would need, and receive, and the man of no property, in those times, could expect neither protection nor respect. But I can see other reasons for the early introduction of the force.

All contemporary accounts agree that The Rock in 1830, and up to then, was a potentially unruly place. It was full of hardened smugglers and mariners, mixed races, prostitutes, fugitives, and—not least dangerous—drunken and violent soldiers and sailors. I do not doubt that thorough policing was urgently needed and, if I am to take the Duke of Wellington's word for it, the British soldier of those times was not the man to be entrusted with such duties.

The Gibraltarians criticize their police force, not for harshness, nor even for officiousness, but for timidity and gentleness. I must say that The Rock has the kindest and most considerate police that I have encountered anywhere. From the tourist point of view, at least, this is a virtue.

I have not yet decided whether the police or the churches should get most credit for the fact—the demonstrable fact—that Gibraltar is singularly free from serious crime. The press reports of the magistrate's court usually deal with such minor matters as traffic offences and hooliganism. When theft and violence occur, as they rarely do, they are found to be committed by young servicemen, newly escaped from home influences, and beating it up as young men will.

It seems greatly to the credit of the Gibraltarian people that in the face of scanty education and of all the difficulties and deprivations of their environment they developed in their social, if not their commercial behaviour, into a decent and docile community.

The curious colonial time lag—in social ideas and fashions, as well as in more material manifestations—is well seen in the given names of the people of Gibraltar.

During World War II, when women were evacuated from Gibraltar, a certain citizen whom I will call Vengali had a son born in Málaga. He went there to arrange the baptism with the priest. Mr. Vengali, in accordance with the attitude which I have outlined, wanted his son christened James—plain James.

'But this cannot be,' said the Spanish priest. 'It must be a saint's name. That is the law of the Church and of the State.'

'But James *is* a saint's name, Father! An apostle! One of the foremost saints!'

At last they consulted a dictionary and found therein that the English James could be rendered into Spanish in three forms—Jaime, Diego, or even Santiago. The priest, having discovered that 'James' was a doggerel form of the name of the holiest saint in Spain, was all the more determined not to apply it.

'Look at the richness of our language!' he said proudly. 'All you have to do is choose one of these three noble names.'

'But I have chosen, Father,' said the Gibraltarian. 'I want him called James.'

'In English? But the law says nothing about translating the holy names into foreign tongues. And English! Are you aware that the English were the betrayers of our Holy Faith?'

Poor Vengali must have seemed perverse to the point of perdition, for how could he explain to a Spanish priest that British nationality meant, to him, almost as much as the Catholic Church? He had a long fight and a long wait, but he won in the end and carried his little James Vengali back to The Rock, leaving the priest scratching his tonsure.

There is more than mere sentiment behind Vengali's actions. The last I heard of James he was at a great British public school. Had his father accepted Diego, the swarthy son would, with unanimous accord, have been dubbed 'Dago' and damaged in the process.

19

A LITTLE LEARNING

When we arrived at Gibraltar, in 1952, we were inclined to send our eight-year-old daughter, Eve, to the nearest Government school. At a truly public school, according to our experience in Northern Ireland, she would be practically and democratically educated up to secondary or high school standard. We did not wish to claim or buy the privilege of private schooling, which is a doubtful one, anyway, in my experience. We did wish our girl to mix with the local children, to make friends with them and learn their ways as part of her education. That is what we ourselves were trying to do in our adult life.

But I was very soon advised, on the best professional authority, that to send my daughter to a Government school would be to put her at a sad disadvantage. When I learnt of the past history and present—1952—condition of education in Gibraltar, I had to agree that no amount of good principles would compensate Eve for the setback she would suffer.

Public education in Gibraltar, I discovered, was actually half a century behind the British model, and had been starved and retarded ever since its very tardy introduction. School buildings were disgraceful slums, furniture makeshift and battered, books few and filthy, and the great majority of teachers were officially categorized as 'unqualified'. Twelve years of steady improvement have not overtaken this terrible backlog, nor will twenty, nor, for that matter, will forty years, for it must be said—and many Gibraltarians have said it to me and published it in their own newspapers, that the vast majority of the community are ill-educated, by British standards, and bound to remain so for life. Further education is non-existent on The Rock, and adult education has made only a feeble beginning.

The pace of social progress in Gibraltar, and of all reform, improvement and development, will be governed by that fact for at least another generation. Whose fault is that?

Public education, so heavily emphasized since 1945, is a com-

parative newcomer to British colonial territories. The class which
invariably provided colonial administrators has never believed in
public education; its whole faith has been pinned on private and
exclusive education, as provided by the misnamed 'public' schools
which produced it.

It may be that the amateur administrators simply did not concern
themselves with education. It may be that they were understaffed,
short of funds, preoccupied with the even more urgent issues of law
and order and public health. It may be that the Colonial Office
deliberately held back, envisaging a premature and prevalent crop
of Gandhis and Nehrus, Nkrumahs and Bandas, Kenyattas and
Mboyas. It takes a very magnanimous man to educate people to
outwit and usurp him.

Whatever the reasons, up to the end of the First World War, the
education of our colonial peoples was left in the willing hands of the
Christian missions in the colonies, with results which we shall have
to consider.

State-aided education in Gibraltar, where the people were European, highly civilized in their way of life, and well disposed to learn,
began in 1917, which is fifty years later than in the Mother Country.
It would not have begun then but for a daring agitation led by the
leaders of The Rock's first trade unions, and carried by them right
to London. Compulsory education was not introduced until 1945.

There is a book to be written—by a specialist—on educational
missions and their cultural, political and historical effects. In my
own small country, Protestant and Catholic education have produced two diametrically different types of men, and the same in-
tractible results appear to have been developed in India and Cyprus.
There is an ever present risk in shared mission territories of the
simple native taking his indoctrination too seriously, of his swallow-
ing it whole and putting it into the literal and terrible interpretation
which tortured Europe for so long. If a fiery priest—and mission
priests are not appointed for their qualities of moderation—tells a
Micronesian that his Protestant neighbours are heretics and on the
road to hell, he may feel it his duty to set about their forcible
conversion. This is not fanciful. A few years ago a couple of priests
who tried to land on one of the Protestant islands of the Ellice group
were stoned and driven back to their boat. In fact, such things

happen in Northern Ireland at every election, every Twelfth of July.

There is a story, apocryphal but possible, of a simple citizen of my native Belfast, where schisms and sects proliferate most fiercely. This man, they say, met an obvious Jew on one of the city's bridges. He promptly seized him by the throat and thrust him half-way over the parapet.

'What's this for?' gasped the poor Jew. 'I have done nothing!'

'You killed Christ, you bastard!' shouted the Belfast man.

'But—but—' the Jew spluttered, 'that was two thousand years ago!'

'It doesn't matter a damn!' said the Irishman, pushing him further. 'I only heard about it at the Mission Hall last night!'

Such damaging dichotomies never arose in Gibraltar. Catholic and Jew live there in amity and mutual respect. What they have in common, perhaps, is the Spanish language, thought pattern and temperament, for all the Jews of The Rock are of the Sephardic branch of the race, Levantines, long exiled from Spain, but persistently Spanish-speaking for centuries. Three of the leading politicians of the place are Jews married to Spanish Roman Catholics, and, far from disapproving, the people vote them back to power at every election. I have to criticize the people of The Rock in some respects, so it is pleasant to record that in religious toleration and co-operation they are an example to the world. When Dublin, that Catholic city, elected a Jew as its Lord Mayor, the citizens boasted of their forbearance. Catholic Gibraltar has elected a Jewish mayor for the past twenty years or so, and no one there thinks it worthy of remark. He is simply the best man for the job.

The population of Gibraltar, since 1785 at any rate, has been predominantly Mediterranean and hence Roman Catholic. At the date of writing about ninety per cent of the people belong to this church. The small minority of Jews, Sephardic and orthodox, carefully educated their own children by private tutoring in the old days and, latterly, in state-aided Jewish schools. They have no objection to sending their children to any good school where they are acceptable, for they look after their religious indoctrination in their own way.

The Jews, of course, never proselytize; the Christian faiths know better than to attempt to convert orthodox Jews; no Protestant sect of any weight or wisdom attempts to convert Roman Catholics. A fringe group, its roots deep in northern England's industrial jungle, does make some attempt to call the faithful of Gibraltar to divine revelations in its corrugated iron tabernacle, and is treated with kindly toleration and amusement. The only dynamic factor in Gibraltar's religious situation is provided by the recent arrival of the Jehovah's Witnesses, who appear to be offering some novelty value to the humbler people there.

Yet Gibraltar has her missions, for The Rock is part of the Irish Mission Field of the Roman Catholic Church. Before I proceed to probe this strange phenomenon, I must mention that the Anglican Bishop of Gibraltar is responsible to Canterbury for the spiritual welfare of the whole population of the northern coast of the Mediterranean, from Gibraltar to the Caspian Sea, and that His Holiness the Pope is one of his parishioners. It would be not only quite correct, but also in the line of strict duty, for our Anglican Bishop to call on the Pope in the Vatican and inquire after the state of his soul! Meanwhile, the Anglican Bishop of Fulham—God help him— is responsible for all the lost sheep along the southern coast—North Africa. Neither of these reverend gentlemen is strenuously active, which is just as well, since Britain's gunboats are mostly in mothballs.

To return to Gibraltar . . . it amazed me to find that the Irish Mission was responsible for the souls there. Modern Gibraltar is as soundly Catholic as Ireland—more so, maybe. It is almost as well educated, and certainly far richer, man for man. I can only assume that this was not always the case. There was a time when the Catholics of Gibraltar, mixed strays and rootless refugees, were seen as an orphan congregation. They may even have been considered to be in spiritual danger, for the English built a big cathedral, (the only Anglican cathedral built in Moorish style), and the Presbyterians and Methodists erected sound churches for their soldiers and merchants. For a period, Spanish priests came in and ministered to the Catholics of Gibraltar, and the old Cathedral of St. Mary the Crowned was known as 'The Spanish Church'. Such an arrangement could have pleased no one. The commanders of The Fortress would lie awake thinking of Spanish fanatics within the gates, influencing and suborning the natives. The leading opinion among the Gibraltarians was anti-Spanish and pro-British, and they could not have enjoyed being British all week and Spanish on Sundays.

I do not know how it was done, or whence the move originated, with the governors or the governed. It may be that they were in agreement. But we turn the page, and find an Irish Roman Catholic as Lord Bishop of Gibraltar. There is an ancient Irish College at Salamanca, where the banished priests of occupied Ireland studied and trained, an historic meeting-place of the Irish and the Spanish Churches. Bishop Fitzgerald, who was in Gibraltar in my time, had been at Salamanca, and he spoke Spanish as he spoke English, gently and perfectly. He loved Spain as he loved Ireland and, rendering unto Caesar the things which were Caesar's, he harboured no animosity for Britain, nor, so far as anyone could discover, for anything else, except The Devil. Indeed, there was no reason at all why any Catholic bishop of Gibraltar, Irish or otherwise, should harbour any animosity for Britain, for the British Government there was falling over itself to please and placate the Catholic Church. The Bishop was consulted about everything which could possibly concern him; he was *ex-officio* chairman of the official Education Committee; and he was treated—to the point of incorrectness—as the religious leader at every state ceremony and function. I say incorrectness because the Anglican Dean of Gibraltar would be the senior clergyman if the British Constitution were strictly observed, and even the young Presbyterian incumbent would be senior to the Roman Bishop. But for reasons of expediency—thoughts on Malta, Cyprus, India, Ireland, where religious leaders had often been tactlessly insulted—or for reasons of courtesy, or for reasons of rank, the Catholic leader being senior, on the face of it, to the leaders of other churches, or for mere common sense, the British Government treated the Roman Catholic Bishop as the Pope of Gibraltar.

As part of the Irish Mission Field, Gibraltar attracted two Catholic teaching orders, the Loreto Nuns and the Christian Brothers. The Jews, as I have said, looked after their own education within their small, closed community. The armed forces of the Crown had their garrison schools, and a good technical school attached to the Naval Dockyard. The British officers sent their sons home to boarding schools. The rich Gibraltarians sent theirs to the Catholic schools, Downside, Ampleforth and Stoneyhurst.

I would not blame the Church nor the other private educators in Gibraltar for the sad shortfall in education there. The situation is that any Gibraltarian over sixty, (i.e. who left school before 1918), has gone through life ill-educated, unless his parents happened to have the ability to pay fees. Fortunately, many parents had this ability, but a majority had not. When public education began here in 1918 Gibraltar stood at the stage of Britain in 1870. The system had to be built, staffed, equipped and developed from that starting date, and its effectiveness would not begin to be felt until fifteen years later.

Right up to 1945 primary education in Gibraltar was left in voluntary hands, state-aided by a small *per capita* grant only. Secondary education was utterly unaided, and was only made possible by the fact that the teachers in the two secondary schools were nuns and Christian Brothers who do not receive full professional salaries. Even with this economy, fees had to be charged, and only fee-paying pupils accepted.

If I am permitted to assume that one-third of Gibraltarian families could pay the fees—and that seems to me a generous assumption—I find that two out of three of the valid candidates for secondary education had to be cast aside with no more equipment for life than a dubious primary education. This leads me to the conclusion that in the generation of Gibraltarians now in its prime—all those over thirty-five or so—two out of three have not the education they deserved, and might be said to have very little education at all. Since Gibraltar is a commercial community, living by its wits and brains—its manual work is largely in the hands of commuting Spaniards—the loss of brain power is even more serious than it would appear to be. It is particularly grievous at this critical period of Gibraltar's history.

There was, and is, in this matter of education, a special difficulty to be overcome—the English language. Since it is, by common consent and by law, the medium of teaching, every subject is stultified by the Gibraltarian's limited vocabulary in this language, by his difficulty in using and comprehending it. Everything one says in Gibraltar is half understood; everything said to one is half expressed. Every Gibraltarian you meet is using his second language, and you will know from your own experience that more than half your ability remains with your first. My Spanish is fluent, but I cannot write this in it—at least, not readily. In Spain I am regarded as a quaint and convivial ass, which is all that I deserve in that language, but which does not represent me fully. So a Gibraltarian will appear in English.

Unfortunately, English and Spanish, the two languages of Gibraltar, are highly incompatible. They have divergent roots, the one Teutonic, the other Latin. Spanish is regular, phonetic, pure, simple and logical. English is so irregular in its behaviour and pronunciation, so obscure in its idiom, so richly various in every respect, that a Spanish speaker has to learn it a word at a time. The perversities of English are proverbial and I need not waste time in illustrating them further, except in so far as they affect the Gibraltarian.

'You will get us into a scrape,' a Gibraltarian Head of Department said to me, when I suggested some bold action. 'And if we get into a scrape,' he went on, 'who is the scrape-goat? Me!'

'Why do we employ such people?' the Governor asked another Head of Department who was on the mat to explain some minor dishonesty among his clerks.

'Because, Sir,' said the Gibraltarian, 'at the salaries we are paying, who can I recruit? No one, Sir, except the riff and the raff!' Since the Rif lived just across the Straits and the R.A.F. was stationed on The Rock, he left the Governor scratching his helmet.

No sooner does a Gibraltarian begin to feel some confidence in his English than it lets him down and makes a fool of him. Like most colonial people, he cannot bear to feel foolish, and his resulting anxiety makes him flounder more deeply and frequently. He is too proud to ask for help or explanation, so he proceeds on instructions but half understood. Muddle and inefficiency result. No business can be done easily there, no transaction is simple and straightforward. Sometimes I try to transact my business in Spanish, but most Gibraltarians will have none of it. They speak it with their compatriots, but never with an 'Englishman'. They will answer my Spanish question in English, and often with some curtness, for I have implied that they are not educated men, not thoroughly British.

The lack of language limits everything on The Rock. No one reads much beyond illustrated newspapers and magazines, and I have seen grown men—even senior civil servants— engrossed in lurid 'comics'. The first bookshop opened about six years ago, and there is no public library in Gibraltar up to the time of writing.

The Gibraltarians can do little with English and nothing without it, now that they are turning their backs on Spain. In this matter, as in others, the older generation is less able than the younger; it is the leaders of Gibraltar, those who left the worse schools of long ago, who are least competent to lead. They will remain for years to come dependent on Englishmen to guide them—the Permanent Secretary, the Chief Justice, Attorney General, Commissioner of Police, will remain posts for ex-patriates. For the future, there is a generation of people now in their thirties, educated post-war and sent to Britain on scholarships. Some of these would be rated as highly intelligent anywhere in the world, but the the British system being as it is, they will have to wait their turn.

This transition, this slow development of competence, should have taken place whilst the community was immature and tucked firmly under Britain's sheltering wing. But, through the backlog and neglect of education, Gibraltar now has to face the world with a crippling handicap. The complete confusion of tongues stopped the works on the Tower of Babel; the partial confusion in Gibraltar cuts the works to half speed.

Further to that, the Gibraltarians are in danger of falling between two stools, linguistically and culturally, and becoming—some would say, remaining—second-rate imitations of Englishmen. Only a full generation of intensive and extensive education can save them from that fate. 'The human mind is our fundamental resource,' said President Kennedy of his own great country. How much more strongly this applies to Gibraltar, which has scarcely any other resource at all.

Joan and I took Eve along to the Loreto Convent Private School. We had certain misgivings. As Ulster Protestants we had been conditioned to regard nuns as limited human beings and teachers, as women with more grace than gumption. We had known the old Church to stamp on curiosity and to censor creative thought. There might be, we thought, an undue and unhealthy emphasis on 'purity', with the consequent growth of prurience. There might even be, for all we knew, some subtle attempt to lure our small daughter into the Church, with all its duties, prohibitions and inhibitions which press particularly hard on women.

We were wrong on all counts. The Irish nuns were cultured, sophisticated and charming, so that, in the presence of the Mother

Superior I felt like a red-necked Orange savage, a black northerner, rude in speech and thought.

Eve throve happily at her Convent for ten years and passed all the examinations we could wish, including her G.C.E. at Advanced Level. She left it with three languages, a good knowledge of history, and enough mathematics to add up her change. She learnt nothing of horses and hockey.

*   *   *   *

It is the practice of most residents, and the dream of the rest, to leave it all behind once a week, to drive from under the Levanter cloud, past the two frontiers, and away into the sunny spaciousness of the Spanish countryside. From the slopes of those bare hills, with the wide *campo* spread below you, The Rock of Gibraltar is seen in a truer perspective. All the artificiality, all the ugly excrescences, have disappeared with distance, with the clamour and the crowds. There is our home as it was in the beginning, a silver mountain, serene and lonely, sleeping in the sea. And here comes a simple man, uncrowded and unhurried, an ancient Spaniard of the *sierras*, surely a man with no learning and great wisdom, who may have time to soothe us, to lead us back a little way towards the truth.

'If it will not molest you,' said the old man, 'I will sit down here beside you for a little while.'

'Please do,' I said to him. 'It is hot for walking.'

He swung his pack to the ground and sank down stiffly on the hard, warm clay, and sponged his brow with a wisp of bark fibre.

'It is hot for walking up that accursed hill. January is not always as hot as this. It is a fine day for you and your family to take your food here in the country, eh?'

'A fine day and a fine place.'

'A fine place to look at,' said the old man, glancing round the pink mountains and down over the olive groves to Gibraltar Bay. 'Oh, very fine to look at! This would be a lovely country to live in, if you only had to look at it—if you didn't have to eat!' I offered him some sandwiches and, after three refusals, he began to eat.

'Eating can be a pleasure too,' he said, chewing rapidly, nose to chin. 'But for me, I would have been happier without the necessity of it. I have had more trouble finding the food than pleasure in eating it!'

'*Como come el mulo caga el culo*,' said I, which means that as a mule eats so it dungs. The old man slapped his legs and laughed.

'You know Spanish very well?'

'I am learning it. It is a very handsome language.'

'So they say. As for me, I cannot very well judge, because I know no other. But I have a daughter in England and she knows two languages, the same as you. She's married to an Englishman, a lorry driver he is. Is that a good trade in England?'

'Very good. Hard work, but good money.'

'That is my information. He makes fourteen pounds a week, I heard once, which is, they say, about two thousand pesetas! It makes one's head swim! He must be carrying legal gold!'

'It's good pay.'

'Good pay, man? It is incredible. But then, of course, the English pay very well. Even the Spaniards who go to work on The Fat Rock over there, they make big money. And my son-in-law is better than that—he is an Englishman! Johnson, he is called.'

'And they live where?'

'In London. Do you know it? It is a very big city.'

'I know it well. It is very big indeed. It holds out great opportunities.'

'You mean for lorry drivers?'

'For everyone who works hard. London is a place where one can live well.'

'Thank God for that. You have not, by any chance, met my son-in-law, the lorry driver Johnson?'

'Up to the moment, no—on account of the great numbers of people in London.'

'Ah, yes, naturally. But I understand that it is an old family, that Johnson is a name well thought of in England, a name of which you may have heard?'

'I have heard of it frequently. They are very good people. There is no doubt of that.'

'Thank God again! That is my information too. The mother and I were anxious, for we never met the man. My daughter went to England nine years ago, you see. She went with an English lady, as her maid. My daughter used to send me a pound every year, near the end of December. I suppose it was what she had saved in a twelvemonth—money she had left over. It came always at a good

time for us, I can tell you! The winter is bad up here in the *sierras*—
as she knows well, poor girl!'

The old man shook his head and chewed grimly for a little while,
but soon he brightened up again.

'Ah, the trouble I used to have getting pesetas for those pounds!'
he said. 'That was a caper, I can tell you! But it was worth it. The
pound put us round the corner of the year, and up the January hill.
Then she got married, the daughter, in England.'

'When was that?' I asked him.

'Six years ago. She did not send the pound that year—or if she
did, it never arrived. But I do not think she could have sent it,
because there was none the next year, nor the year after that, nor
any year since. We did not like to ask her whether she had sent it
or not, do you see? We always thought that the pounds, maybe, had
got caught up somewhere on the long journey, and might arrive all
together. This year the pound has not come, either. Of course, it
may be that she will send it yet, but we are in January now, and
it always came in December. But it may be that there is some good
reason. Now, as I walked up that hill I saw you and your beautiful
wife and children and I said to myself, 'Strangers!' Then I saw your
fine car, there, under the olive trees, and I knew it was an English
car by its letters. So, said I, this gentleman will know England, and
he will, for sure, have learning.'

'Very little,' I said.

'No, sir. I saw you and I said, 'Here is a man who knows English—
the first I have met for a long time—and, please God, he knows some
Spanish, too!' You see, I have a card here . . . here . . . no, somewhere about me. . . . Ah, here—this card! Now look at this card,
sir. Is not that a pretty card?'

'Very beautiful. This shows a church in the snow.'

'A rare-looking church, that!'

'Protestant—a church of England.'

'True? Now, my wife, there, she said it was a church, and I, old
fool, said it was a storehouse. She was right for once—and that will
keep her going for a long time! And these birds, then,—these will
be holy birds?'

'Not holy, exactly, but sympathetic. There are some of these birds
in Spain—*petirojo*, you call them.'

'If they are in Spain then I have never seen one. But they may have more sense than to come up here. They would get better pickings down near Gibraltar there! We thought, perhaps, they were some kind of holy symbol—their breasts stained by Our Saviour's blood?'

'It may well be so. There is no doubt that they are good birds. They represent courage and kindness and goodwill.'

'There you are then! Isn't that enough? But open it—open the card. Don't be afraid of it! Now, my daughter sent it two months ago. The postman from Estepona had to carry it right up here—that is the Law. You should have heard the language of him! Now, there, you see, is my daughter's name, Carmela. La Señora Carmela Alvarez y Cirugeda de Johnson—she wrote that with a pen. She has learnt to write in London, and that is a very great advantage in life, let me tell you!'

'She sends her loving embraces to you and to her mother.'

'She does indeed! She is a true daughter. We have only one living child, but thank God we have a good one! That part, where she wrote with a pen, being in Spanish, we had no difficulty with it. We had it read out to us by a little girl who has been down to the coast to school. It says fourteen pounds a week, does it not?'

'Yes.'

'That confirms it then! There was always a chance that the child might have been mistaken. But see the other side of the card—here. This poem is printed—it is a poem, is it not? It is said to have the shape of one.'

'Yes, a poem. In English.'

'Ah, now that is what no man in the village—no man, woman nor child—could tell us. And that—since she has had it printed— will be the most important part. Now, when I saw the car, that English car, the card jumped in my pocket. Now, I said, now, please God, this riddle will be solved, after two months!'

'You wish me to translate the poem?'

'The poem, please—the poem she had printed for us!'

'I must first explain to you that my translation will not be poetry.'

'Oh? How is that?'

'I can give you the sense of it, but the composition of poetry is a task for specialists.'

'Well, well! I should have thought—but no matter. It is the

meaning, it is what she wishes to say to us, of her love for us, perhaps, and her life in London—that is what the mother hopes for. Be so kind as to begin.'

'Very well. I shall read it to you first in English, so that you may hear the poetry, and then I shall give you the meaning in Spanish.'

'Stupendous! Please begin, sir!'

'It starts:

> "The snow lies thick,
> But hearts beat quick,
> And joybells ring out clear . . ."

in Spanish', I told him, 'you would say: "*Hay mucha nieve, pero pulsan bien los corazones*," which means "there is a lot of snow but the hearts are beating well".'

'I am glad!' said the old man. 'I am glad! The weather is cold, naturally, but they are, thank God, in good health. Is that it?'

'Yes. To continue . . . "*Y tocan las campanas . . .*".'

'Bells? Bells? Why the bells? No one dead, I pray?'

'It is the custom in England to ring the bells at this time of the year. Joybells, you might call them.'

'So? And a very pleasant custom, too. She is fortunate to live amongst these bells. Please go on.'

'In English:

> "Old Santa comes
> With sugar plums,
> And gifts from far and near . . .".'

'That sounds very fine to me!' the old man shouted. 'Reading is a gift from Heaven. And English is a very pretty language to listen to!'

'It may not sound so well in my bad Spanish, but it means:

> "*Ya viene San Nicolas el viejo,*
> *Con frutas—er—cristalizadas,*
> *Y regalos de lejos y de cerca . . .*".'

'Saint Nicholas? Who the devil is he? He is not in the calendar to my knowledge. And what does he want with these glassified fruits, eh?'

'Here is his portrait on the card.'

'That one! We wondered who that could be—in his red coat and cap. He appeared to be too old for the lorry driver Johnson. What a droll face he has—and that great belly—from eating those fruits, no doubt! Thank God I have been spared such malformation! Perhaps he is ill of the dropsy, and so cheerful in the face of this affliction that they canonized him?'

'Maybe so.'

'Anyhow, he is well dressed for the weather, and looks content enough, so we need not pity him. And presents, you said? Is that sack of his full of presents?'

'It is.'

'Well, he can come here to Spain if he has any left over! He can come up here, any time, to our village. He'll be welcome up here, any time, bells or no bells!'

'To continue this poem:

> "I hope, like mine,
> Your Christmastime
> Has merriment and mirth . . ."

which means to say, in Spanish:

> "*Espero que pasen bien lus festividades*
> *Contigo, como pasaran conmigo,*
> *Con muchas diversiones y alegria . . .*"

—I fear that this poem does not go very well in Spanish?'

'Do not say it! It carries great beauty! She is full of fun and joy, as befits a young wife, and she wishes the same for her mother and me. That is a fine thing, a very fine thing indeed, in any language whatsoever! The thought graces her! Pray continue, if there is any more?'

'There is a little more. It says:

> "And of goodwill,
> You'll drink your fill,
> With joy and peace on earth!" '

I translated that, too, and the old man leapt up in excitement.

'Harken to that!' he shouted. 'A prayer! A holy prayer for us and for all the rest of the world besides! And in poetry! And printed, too! There is a pious girl, and a good girl for you! Wait till I tell the mother about this! She has had her fears, the mother, with all these Protestants in England. But now we shall set all these doubts at naught! Is there any more, sir?'

'No. Nothing more,' I told him.

'I see a very small thing down here, right at the bottom. It did not escape your notice?'

'No—it is only the name of the man who printed the card.'

'And a very good job he made of it, too. What would his name be?'

'Er—Jenkins. A Señor Jenkins and his son.'

'Good for them,' said the old man. 'And now I will molest you no longer. I will go in gratitude and tell all this to the mother.'

'But will you be able to remember it?'

'How shall I ever forget it, man? I have it all stored here, thanks to you—all here in the head. The very greatest thanks to you, sir, and blessings on the wife and family. May she have many more before she is too old.'

'It was a privilege and a pleasure.'

'You will be repaid in Heaven.'

The old man writhed into his pack and strode away up the hill with his staff jabbing at the stones. At the crest he turned and waved the white card and shouted something about God.

20

THE GOODNESS AND THE GRACE

> I love the goodness and the grace
> Which on my birth have smiled,
> And made me, in this distant place,
> A little English child.

This is a version of a poem which the children of Ireland used to chant, monotonously by rote, in the old 'National' schools. No doubt the Gibraltarians would have been taught it, too, had they had schools there in the nineteenth century. In contexts like this the more inclusive word 'British' has superseded the more racial 'English', and with that amendment the Gibraltarians could sing that song today. An oft repeated slogan on their walls, as I write, declares 'British we are; British we stay'.

The blatant and aggressive patriotism of the Gibraltarian is not merely based, as the Spaniards claim, on self-interest. A more important cause of it is the momentum, fifty years maintained, of the great Victorian epoch. The views and values of the Gibraltarians, and of their spokesmen and leaders particularly, were forged and formed during the nineteenth century, and such is the colonial time-lag that they do not tend to change. These people were cast and conditioned in the Victorian mould and, since their only remembered history is their British history, they have never known any other influence.

The social system and values of that era lasted in England far into the present century. In the outer provinces—in still puritan Wales and Scotland, for instance, and my own bigotted bible belt Ulster— the Victorian era began late and ended late. It may not have ended even yet. Further afield still, further from the central growth point of British culture, the time shift is far greater.

It was during Victoria's century when her England was top nation, that the Indians, Hong Kong Chinese, Africans and Gibraltarians became not only British *de jure*, but also anglified *de facto*. In backward nations, as we learned to call them—those like India with ancient and unchangeable cultures of their own—only the leaders acquired this Victorian varnish. In Gibraltar, where the citizens had no corporate or recognizable history, there was a cultural vacuum to fill. Queen Victoria filled it, once and for all. In all British colonies, or ex-colonies, you find pockets of extreme anglification. I have observed them from Dublin to Fiji, clubs, corners and cliques of people who appear thus because their original anglification was Victorian and has so remained, whereas the English at home have changed, and changed greatly. The colonies were, for a century or so, politically static, a century during which the home population fought for and won a full democracy. The colonies remain socially static, not to say stagnant, for the simple reason that dynamic factors did not exist in them. Colonial education, as I have shown, is something new—not much more than twenty years old.

Great Britain's overseas officers, civil and military, appeared to me as professional perpetuators of high Victorianism. It is not only that the senior selection boards of Whitehall had an instinctive preference for the conservative and traditionalist type (their key adjective is 'sound') but it is also true to say that colonial service has tended to attract such men. The 'local' civil servant, rising slowly towards senior rank, would proceed in studied imitation of his superiors, and end up talking like an off-beat Bertie Wooster. The Latins in Gibraltar, in official employment, even submitted themselves to the tortures of cricket in their efforts to be British, and blushed if one hailed them at the bullfights across the Frontier.

The leaders of the Overseas Civil Service, as it is now called, are men who were recruited thirty or forty years ago, prior to Britain's post-war revaluation of her household gods. Most of them, I found, were passionately devoted to the myths of the Victorian Empire. Gunboats, firm hands, corporal and capital punishment, the stiff upper lip, the inflexibility of formula, routine and protocol and ceremonial, distrust for learning in all its forms and especially for the fine arts, all these were, to these men, the very rubrics of religion. It is scarcely believable, but none the less true, that Colonial Administrators still wear the discredited solar topee and a little tin sword with their Victorian dress uniforms. Governors are allowed to garnish this headgear with a plume of white cock's feathers, an adornment which, in my presence, reduced even the innocent Polynesians to helpless laughter. One of my Colonial Secretaries at Gibraltar, on instructions, turned out for a ceremonial parade in full tropicals, as I have described them. At his appearance in that

civil and European colony in this Darkest Africa outfit there was a
rare muttering in the ranks. 'Who the hell does he think we are?'
a Gibraltarian colleague asked me. 'A lot of bloody Hottentots at a
corroboree?'

By such worthy and unalterable people—the wives, as you would
expect, are more conservative than their husbands—we have the
example of our nineteenth-century civilization constantly presented
to the culture-hungry colonial. At the same time, little or no modern
information to correct the impression, to present Britain as she is and
as she is becoming. The result is inevitable. Gibraltar is, in every
aspect, personal and environmental, commercial and cultural, a
Victorian backwater. Lest this be thought too harsh, let me hasten
to add, so is Bombay, so is Singapore, so are Hong Kong and Suva.
I would even go so far as to say, so are Melbourne and Belfast. I
add, too, that Victorianism had and has its values and virtues, and
is not to be considered a purely depreciatory term. If it seems so to
me, I remind myself, that is because I am a middle-aged provincial
myself, and thus a refugee from the Victorian epoch.

As with most statements about the Gibraltarians, one has to
qualify, at once. There are Gibraltarians, young professional men
educated and trained in England, who are as modern as tomorrow.
There are others, older and poorer, who could pass for Spaniards,
and would never dream of attempting to anglify themselves in any
mould, ancient or modern. Such men have a timeless quality, and
a certain integrity. Generally speaking, the higher you rise in
Gibraltarian society, which means the richer it becomes, the more
Victorian it is in taste and outlook.

One dangerous corollary of Victorianism—dangerous in these
times, at least—was a patriotism which went to the length of saying
'My Country right or wrong'. The Gibraltarians, with no other
example before them, and with everything to gain commercially
through the spread of British supremacy throughout the world,
swallowed this chauvinism whole. Britain's colonial wars had their
home critics, but the Gibraltarians excelled the most jingoist English
in wagging the flag. One basis of this exaggerated loyalty is a purely
pragmatical preference for the 'divil you know' over the uncertain alternative—in Gibraltar's case, ill-governed and stressful
Spain. My own people in Ulster, for a similar reason, harbour
similar sentiments, and their brash and hysterical loyalty to the

British crown is an embarrassment to the cool-headed English.

Throughout the nineteenth century Gibraltar vociferously applauded every feat of British arms. When Palmerston sent a gunboat to threaten Greece into paying insurance money to the aggrieved British Gibraltarian Jew, Don Pacifico, The Rock went wild with joy.

The Prince of Wales, later Edward VII, was of a wandering disposition and had good reason, at times, to absent himself from the supervision of his august mother. He paid occasional visits to The Rock—which has, in fact, remained to this day a favourite hideyhole of harassed royalty—and every visit was an occasion for public hysteria with guns, huzzas, fireworks, parades, tattoos, flowers and unnecessary addresses of loyalty. It must have bored the gay Edward painfully to hear it all over again, and one suspects that he longed to return to his champagne on the royal yacht. The troops were bored too, it seems. On one such occasion the Fortress Order of the Day contains the stern instruction—'Cheering will be spontaneous and prolonged.'

The full flowering of Victorian patriotism extended into the present century and its most fulsome blossoms appeared at the time of World War I. After that futile four-year massacre, wars were not to be greeted so gleefully again.

The outbreak of World War II was not so cordially welcomed, although the Gibraltarians left no doubt that they were in full support of Great Britain. There were obvious reasons for this support, such as common interest, but there were others not so obvious. The Jews of Gibraltar had enjoyed equal citizenship since 1878 when they were admitted to the Jury Lists, and this may have a bearing on the Gibraltarians' ready acceptance of a dangerous war against the Jew-baiting Nazis.

At the outset and on the face of it, World War II was perilous for Gibraltar. The long-range bomber had removed the advantage of remoteness. Franco, successfully concluding his conquest of Spain, was in full sympathy and military association with the two dictators. The forces of the Axis Powers, German and Italian, had been in Spain for years, and were at the very gates of Gibraltar. It was highly likely that Germany would be allowed to pass through Spain and attack The Rock—if, indeed, she needed to seek permission. It was even possible that

Franco would attempt to take Gibraltar of his own accord.

As it happened, Gibraltar never had to suffer from direct on-slaught during the War, but the community suffered greatly from the complete disruption of family life. All women and children and old people were sent away from The Rock. The men—'essential occupations only'—remained as uneasy citizens in a fortress stripped for action and run like a battleship. This state of affairs lasted for the whole length of the hostilities.

Now the century of patriotic indoctrination proved its efficacy. In spite of hardship the loyal people of Gibraltar raised no complaint until the war was practically won. Then they let it be known—to a surprised British Government—that they had not enjoyed the situation and that they did not wish to be so treated on any future occasion. And so their long delayed political emancipation began.

Immediately after World War II Great Britain was forced to take a new look at the citizens of Gibraltar—the 'Gibraltarians'. I have used this generic name for convenience throughout this book, but it is of recent coinage and application. These people are, of course, British, but they cannot simply be called British—not without con-fusion with the garrison there and with the population of the United Kingdom and others who are British but not Gibraltarian. Among themselves, they referred to the ex-patriate officers on The Rock as '*los ingleses*',—'the English', quite regardless of the fact that many of us were Irish, Scots or Welsh. They could not call us '*britanicos*', for in Spanish that word is an adjective rather than a title—besides, the Gibraltarians would classify themselves a '*britanicos*' so the adjective would not serve to distinguish us from them.

Gibraltarians are closely defined by statute as citizens of the place, with certain rights and duties. They have, for instance, the right of residence and of trading there, which my son, although he was born in Gibraltar of British parents, can never have.

My wife and I were categorized as statutory aliens, even after ten years of residence in Gibraltar. But then, so was His Excellency the Governor and Commander-in-Chief, and about two thousand other officers and men of all the forces of the British Crown and of Her Majesty's Civil Service. Our right of residence was limited to our tenure of office. When that ended, by virtue of recent legislation, we might be granted the right to live in Gibraltar, if we were rich and independent, but not the right to take up employment there or to start a business. Gibraltar, with its bluntly named 'Trade Restriction Ordinance', is a closed shop in the interests of the legal Gibraltarians. Such legislation has cramped the spirit of initiative and of competition, lowered the standards in every kind of business activity, and left Gibraltar bereft of external capital, interest or assistance. It has enabled a very few to make easy riches, but has faced the community with ruin. The damaging Ordinance is still in full force and likely to remain so.

As well as statutory aliens, there were the mere aliens, those who did not qualify by British passport for the adjective 'statutory'. These were the Spanish workers, most of them commuting daily from their own country, plus a few foreigners licensed for special reasons— 57 Portuguese, 18 Moroccans, 11 Germans, 11 Italians, 9 French, 7 Israelis, 4 Americans, one lonely Swiss, and a couple of hundred Indians and Pakistanis.

With this new name, then, and its legal status, but always with the unspoken word 'British' behind it, the Gibraltarians began in 1945 to make representations for constitutional advancement. But never, be it noted, were their protests anti-British. India, Ireland, Cyprus and all the rest of the erstwhile Empire mustered both internal and external support by claiming the dignity of full nationhood. Little Gibraltar, safe and subsidized under Britain's wing, had the delicate task of claiming human and political dignity without pressing the claim any further. If the Gibraltarians were aware of any past injustice or oppression, they did not recite it. 'How can I be anti-British?' my friend Mauricio asked me, flashing a blue passport. 'Look at this! I am as British as you are!' To which I felt like replying, as an Irishman, 'You may be rather more so.'

At the time of the Suez Adventure he, and every other Gibraltarian I met, was passionately on the side of what we have almost all come to see as erring Britain. I found myself, with a couple of senior officers who were my friends, the only dissentients to that abortive essay in commercial colonialism. We, the supposed standard-bearers, were hanging back ashamed, whilst the 'lesser breeds', were beating the big drum and baying for Egyptian blood. When it was over, General Sir Charles Keightley, who had led the British forces at Suez and was said to be a justly angry man, was quickly appointed Governor of Gibraltar, and thus effectively silenced.

Now I must turn back to deal with other factors in the forging of the Gibraltarian people. As well as its natural increase, the basic population of Italian, Briton and Jew received recruits from three other sources. First of all, there was a constant infiltration of Spaniards, those who sought and—in the old days—won residence and British nationality for purposes of gain, and also those who sought political asylum. Gibraltar was admitting political refugees right up to 1939, but not many as a result of Spain's last upheaval, for the reason that the Gibraltarians were, in the majority, in favour of Franco—or, better say, the leading opinion of the community ran against the Republic.

Another important source of immigration was Malta. The Maltese began to stray to Gibraltar in mid-century, to tend goats on the Upper Rock and sleep in the caves. But they soon discovered the Free Port goldmine and by 1870 some of them were on the way to fortune and sending home for their relatives. In 1878 the leading citizens of Gibraltar, including their religious leader the Vicar Apostolic, Dr. J. B. Scandella, petitioned the Governor to prohibit the entry of more Maltese. The petition stated that their numbers had doubled during the preceding seven years and that they were 'the scum of that people' and mostly ex-jailbirds. It seems to me that the leading Genoese, by this date all very British, mainly English-speaking and already very rich, resented the late intrusion of yet another group of refugees to share their prosperity.

The petition may have checked the flow, for there are not many Maltese names in Gibraltar. Such as there are stand out starkly and strangely—names like Mifsud, Zammit, Xerri, Wahnon and Azzo-pardi.

The Maltese have been easily and completely absorbed into the population and hold some of the leading positions on The Rock. As the most ardent Roman Catholics in the world—in spite of the Vicar Apostolic's opposition—they have given strong support to the Church in Gibraltar and, indeed, have provided some of its leading priests.

There is one remaining constituent of Gibraltar's strange popula-tion which I had better mention at this point. The Indians, we call them, although they include Pakistanis, were admitted during the present century for the specified purpose of selling their own goods—that is, products of their own country which, they claimed, no one else could sell for them. At the time of their admission, before India's independence, they were all colonial subjects, with exactly the same British nationality and status as the Gibraltarians. The Government of the time—in which the Gibraltarians had no say—acceded to their reasonable request to trade in this colony as they did in many others—East Africa, Singapore, Fiji and Aden, for instance.

The Indians opened their curio shops in Main Street and throve greatly. By shrewdness and single-mindedness, by the low prices based on the tiny wages of their homeland, by accepting money in any shape or form, they soon beat the Gibraltarian shopkeeper at his own game. I once watched an Indian shopkeeper produce his own cheque book and accept a signature for £40 from a tourist whose wife had fallen in love with a wrist watch in his shop. After the happy couple had gone back to their ship I asked the shopkeeper if he lost much by such risky transactions. He told me that he lost about two per cent in bad debts, adding with a wink that his profits were much in excess of that. Only unrelenting insistence by the Gibraltarians on the limitation of the Indians' commerce has kept them from capturing the retail trade completely.

The Gibraltarian shopkeeper and his assistants kept themselves at a disadvantage by a surprising abruptness and discourtesy of manner. Visitors from Spain—surely one of the world's politest countries—are shocked by the minimal, unsmiling service at the counters of Gibraltar. The shopgirls will finish their conversations before attending a customer, or even serve them with one hand and no attention, shouting Spanish over their shoulders as they do it. This demeanour is so widespread that it is frequently referred to by the Gibraltarians themselves in their press, and last year the Chamber of Commerce issued handbills exhorting the shopkeepers to train their assistants to say 'Good morning' and 'Thank you'.

It is a demeanour curiously out of character, for the people of Gibraltar are, in fact, expansive, affectionate and generous. Even those of them who do not have these qualities are nevertheless glad to see visitors and to make profits. The explanation of this rudeness lies, with most of the Gibraltarian's defects, in his language problem, in his deficient education. The average shop worker and the older shopkeepers are uneasy in English and so inclined to make minimum use of it. To invite conversation would be to risk showing ignorance and hence losing that self-esteem which is the most precious and fragile possession of a colonial subject.

The Indians have a different attitude. They are true professionals in shopkeeping, members of a merchant caste from which they can neither rise nor fall. They are secure and happy in their work and position in society, and this makes them enviably insult-proof. They will sell a customer a smile and a sense of superiority gladly—so long as there is enough profit in the deal. I think it was Confucius who said: 'If you can't smile, don't keep a shop.' The Gibraltarians must learn to smile, or go out of business.

The Indians, with their gaudy and exotic goods, dominate the facade of Gibraltar's Main Street, so that visitors exclaim: 'The place is full of Indians!' In fact, there are only a few hundred of them, including their populous families, but they stand at the entrances to their numerous and showy shops and so capture the tourist's attention.

One or two of the great Indian tycoons, like Chellaram and Dialdas, have set up successful branches in Gibraltar and must bring money to the place. Now that Gibraltar is facing grave economic difficulties and finding herself short of development capital, these Indian millionaires might save the situation. But they are unlikely to be asked and, after opposition, ill will and distrust, it is unlikely that they would respond. The Indian has no reason to cherish or trust the white man and his whole aim and object is to make money and return with it to his own great country. Several of them have left Gibraltar already, as soon as her situation worsened, to set up shop in Málaga and Algeciras. There is no sentiment in any business, least of all in theirs.

By the end of the nineteenth century the civil population of Gibraltar had risen to 20,000 people. With a garrison and naval establishment of about 6,000 the total population of The Rock amounted to much the same as it does today—which is to say that the place was overcrowded by any standards. But Spain was friendly and co-operative, the frontier lay wide open, and the surplus population overspilled into La Línea and the surrounding Campo area. There, rents, food and everything else were far cheaper than they were in The Fortress.

Victorian patterns of property and poverty had been firmly established in our colony. The rich were richer, the poor poorer than they had been before. God had picked His winners. A cast-iron class system had been imposed upon the community, a stratification even more rigid and obdurate than that of the Mother Country. In addition to the criteria of accent, income and occupation which govern the English class system, that of Gibraltar had the written and recognized protocol of a seat of Government and a Viceregal Court, of military rank and of race. Its main divisions have been defined as British officers, Gibraltarian traders, and Spanish workers, but it seems to me much more subtle than that. In my time, the 1950s, the order of precedence was as follows:

1. The Governor, senior officers and officials, all of them ex-patriates, with a select few of the richest of English-educated Gibraltarians. The latter paid their way in the rarified social atmosphere by lavish entertaining. They were politely, but never intimately accepted in it.

2. Less senior ex-patriate officers, with selected, English-educated rich Gibraltarians or members of the liberal professions there.

3. Non-commissioned officers and Gibraltarians of moderate means.

4. Soldiers, sailors and airmen and most Gibraltarians, including the local working class and small shopkeepers.

5. The Spanish commuting workers, the hewers of wood and drawers of water, and the Indians.

Just as the class system of England is primarily based on accent— on the manner in which one speaks—so that of Gibraltar was consolidated by language barriers. It applied a heavy and unremitting pressure on the Gibraltarians to become proficient in English, but such English as they might acquire on The Rock would not admit them to the higher echelons of society. Only the 'home-educated', meaning those very few who had been sent to boarding school in the United Kingdom, could achieve the accent and idiom of the ruling class. To such men as achieved this, there remained the problem of their wives. Only very rarely was a girl sent to school in England, for her parents, however rich and aspiring they might be, would be mainly preoccupied about her virtue. Female virginity in Gibraltar, as in Spain, is guarded like gold dust, and not only for its intrinsic value on the marriage market. An erring daughter or sister, no less than a wandering wife, is held to furnish all her male relatives with invisible but risible horns. Since the English, as is well known, no longer hold such views, it is to be assumed that they are all cuckolds long since. He who sends his young daughter into such a country might as well get measured for his horns beforehand. Be that as it may, the end result of this quaint survival is that very few Gibraltar girls are fluent in the English language.

The class system in Gibraltar, like most other Victorian institutions there, remains intact to this day, a living museum piece for sociological study. The people are frankly and openly class conscious, to the extent of saying, without any sarcasm or rancour, 'He is higher class than I am,'—a shocking statement to an Englishman. The open discussion, or even mention of class distinctions has become embarrassing to polite English people, but I can remember when, forty years ago, no one was ashamed of the system and everyone knew and accepted his place in it. So it is still in Gibraltar. The class system is taken for granted there. It is all part of being British.

21

BEYOND THE PALE

'Who were the first inhabitants of Spain?' the Spanish priest asked
the little peasant boy.

'Adam and Eve, Father.' Laughter in class and then, with heavy
sarcasm—

'And what makes you think that Adam and Eve were Spanish,
may I ask?' (Never ask.)

'Because, Father, they went ill-clad and barefoot, and yet believed
themselves in Paradise.'

During the 1950s up to 13,000 Spanish men and women came to
work in Gibraltar daily. They earned much more than they could
have done in their own country at that time, but much less than
a Gibraltarian in parallel employment. By and large, they were
content.

Only once, in my ten years, did they go on strike. They were
temporary men, working for a British contractor on a great tunnelling project, and the dispute was about shift pay. The Spanish press,
naturally, made much of the strike, ignoring the fact that it would
have been illegal in Spain, but was quite permissible and, indeed,
sympathetically treated in Gibraltar. They strove to prove that the
British were *negreros*—slave drivers—and that, by implication, Spain
was a workers' paradise. The Gibraltarians, with their special, ironic
wit, put out a story on the subject.

'How much do the cruel British pay these abused, deprived, despised Spanish tunnellers?' the Spanish Minister of Labour asks the
Governor of Algeciras.

'Seven pounds fifteen shillings a week, Your Excellency, or about
one thousand pesetas—er—excuse me, Your Excellency, you are
leaving?'

'Right now!' said the Minister. 'I'm off to Gibraltar to get myself
a job on those tunnels!'

But there was more to it than pay. Every man and woman carried
back into Spain, every day, some small tolerated or hidden quantity

of contraband, as much as he dared. Such was the tradition of this traffic that if his funds had run out, towards pay day, he would stoop on the Gibraltar side of the Frontier, pick up a pebble and carry it into Spain. These people did live in Paradise, for it has been said that Spain would be a paradise if you did not have to eat. They carried their sustenance in with them.

All the hard and much of the skilled work of Gibraltar was in the hands of these Spaniards, and they were well liked and respected on The Rock. Man for man, it is difficult not to like and respect a Spaniard. The lowliest of them have a grave courtesy and a sense of duty and, although they have only to see an institution to itch to rob it, in personal relations they are as honest as the day. We believed that they liked us, too, although they had no great respect for the Gibraltarians. They regarded them as soft—*mimao*—spoiled in the sense of spoiled children, and *apatético*, apathetic and, by Spanish standards, insincere. But they liked and admired the British system and, within certain limits, the British ex-patriate officer. Our system offered them freedom of contract, some protection against industrial injustice, and even a voice on local industrial councils. Their grievances were heard at once, and if possible redressed. This was not only for fairness and courtesy, but also because they were valuable assets to Gibraltar—and more, in fact, for we could not afford to lose them. Their compatriots, those who could not get passes from the Spanish authorities, called them with rueful envy '*Los Especiales*'—the favoured ones.

La Línea de la Concepcion, Gibraltar's sister city, was elevated to city rank by the Spanish State in 1913. Its growth is not well recorded. Spanish statistics, when they can be found, are not to be quoted with full confidence, for the governments of that unhappy country have always been so resented and embattled that their published information contains strong elements of propaganda. I have studied some old photographs and plans of La Línea, and read what I could find, and talked with old men who live there. I believe that the growth of the place covers much less than one hundred years. Today, they say, the population is more than three times that of Gibraltar and, comparing city area to city area, it is three times more extensive.

La Línea spread from its focal point which is the Customs barrier

facing Gibraltar, and sprawled inland over the dry sandflats below
the red foothills of the Sierra Carbonera. It grew without plan,
enlarging sporadically to meet the labour demands of Gibraltar and
the fluctuations of the smuggling trade. It grew without pride or
style or sense of place. Its name means simply 'The Lines', where
the besiegers drew up their ranks; a little inland there is the village
of Campamento, the nearest camp out of eighteenth-century gunshot. No one came to this cul-de-sac of Spain from free choice, and
no one stayed here because he liked the place. Everyone came from
necessity—or rapacity. The site has no natural features, no river, no
woods, no good land, no beach worthy of the name. The town has
no history nor traditions except reprehensible ones, no *raison d'être*
except *La Piedra Gorda*, the Fat Rock with its work and wages and
its opportunity to subsidize the latter by constant, cautious smuggling.

Spaniards are absurdly and endearingly patriotic, not only about
their country—'All the world is in Spain,' they say—but also about
their region, then their province, its capital, and finally and fiercely,
their home village.

But what are the *Linenses* to say about their city of La Línea,
Gibraltar's poor relation and east end? We all work for the British,
man. We have to do so. We do a bit of smuggling to supplement
our wages. The British like us to do it because it helps trade. The
authorities let us carry it in, because we give them a share of it. Even
when we get fired we still go to Gibraltar every day on our passes,
pretending to work, or to seek work, and living on our contraband.
Look at their building industry over there. See those blocks of flats?
Every brick of them laid by Spanish hands. Yes, every brick. Without
us, their building trade would stop at once. However, we are not
to be proud of our contribution to the British Fortress, for it is an
affront to Holy Spain. We would rather work in our own country,
if we could find work there. If we could find work, that is, with the
same pay—that is, the pay plus the profits from the tobacco we
carry.

Such is the attitude of the *Linense*, Gibraltar's Spanish neighbour,
deprived as he is of that civic pride which bolsters up the hard-
wrought communities of Spain. As you would expect, his city is a
sordid and uncherished place, a town where men live because they
must, rather than because they choose. Here, they used to tell me,

is the only city in Spain whose citizens feel ashamed of it. A mile away they can see The Rock towering up to its cloudy plume, the Fat Rock where people make money so easily, form political parties and trade unions, criticize the Government, demand fair play, demonstrate and protest about this and that, argue with their tame, unarmed police, enjoy goods from all over the world, pay neither taxes nor bribes, and regard every privilege as a right.

But here in La Línea, where the real workers live, there was in the 1950s a dire and drastic contrast. It had been far worse; it is now far better. The Spanish State has just bestowed almost a million pounds in aid to La Línea, whose shopkeepers are suffering from the Frontier blockade and the consequent Gibraltarian boycott. But I describe it as I saw it during my ten years in Gibraltar—as I saw it several times a week, and as I knew it, intimately. It was the most destitute and wretched place I had ever seen, worse than the worst of Dublin, the Gorbals of Glasgow, the slums of Manchester and Liverpool. I had to go all the way to Hong Kong to see such living conditions again.

There in La Línea in 1953 the very essences of squalor lay everywhere in the ill-lit streets—broken bottles, nettles, ashes, excrement, the all-pervading odour of urine and rancid oil and rotten fish and cabbage. There were unpaved streets flooded with filthy water or, in the hot summer, swept by dust storms. Beggars, cripples, children and stray dogs begged at every café table. Boot-blacks and little boys pimped at street corners, and there was a district full of formidable harlots leering from their white-tiled dens with paper flowers in their hair.

This city was the sump of Spain. The magnet of the Fat Rock had drawn the displaced poor of Spain's poorest region. Here were more prostitutes, pimps, touts, beggars, *gitanos malos*, and tramps than you could find in Seville or Málaga. 'La Línea is not Spain, señor,' the good workmen of the town used to say to me, 'and don't you think it is, please.' I knew they spoke the truth.

The queue of cars re-entering Gibraltar every Sunday evening had to run a long gauntlet of outstretched hands, the hands of the blind, the maimed, the mad, the hungry and the greedy. Near the *Aduana*, where the lights stayed on until the small hours of the morning, a little girl slept every night, wrapped in sacks, at the foot of a dirty wall. Above her head there was an ancient tourist poster. In cracked

English it read: 'Spain! The dreamy hope of an artist come to life!'

It may seem that La Línea was in a position to share the riches of Gibraltar, and that it ought to be a prosperous place. But one has to remember that the prosperity of Gibraltar was, still is, restricted to the very few. It has never been shared by taxation and re-distribution, nor even by fair wages. Badly off as were the workers of Gibraltar, these foreign workers were in far worse case.

By its geographical and political position rather than by any Machiavellian tactics, Gibraltar has practised for over a century a policy of Apartheid. The labour reserve of the helots is not only far removed from the bossman's city, as in South Africa. In Gibraltar's case it is in another country and under another administration. The Spaniards in Gibraltar could be employed at any wages which— taking into account the hopeless poverty of their own country, and their opportunities of smuggling—the employers saw fit to offer them. The effect of this was the same as that when the starving immigrant Irish came to England in the early years of the Industrial Revolution. It kept local wages down to a minimum, and in fact, below anything which would be called a minimum anywhere else.

In my time there were hundreds of Spaniards entering Gibraltar daily for no wages at all. These were men who had been laid off, redundant through no fault of their own but through the inevitable ups and downs of the ship-repairing and building trades. They came in for the contraband alone. A working man once housed, however indifferently, will suffer great privation before he migrates. He may never find the cash to clear his debts and pay for his removal. He dreads upheaval and insecurity and leaving his friends behind him. In Spain, a removal is complicated further by laws which demand permissions, documents and good-conduct certificates for every change of residence. Thus, in La Línea, Gibraltar had what is known in another context as 'a captive audience', a large pool of tied and hopeless labour waiting for work at any rate of pay. With this threat outside, those within the gates could not be exigent in their demands.

Gibraltar has, in effect, made La Línea its 'east end', what the Americans call 'the wrong side of the tracks'. All the social evils of a modern city and port have been exported from Gibraltar to La Línea, which is to say, from British territory to Spanish. Overcrowding, unemployment, poverty, consequent diseases, vice and crime, all these have—ultimately—been banished from The Rock and tossed over the Frontier into the sister city. Most cities have a west end and an east end, and the west, through rates and taxes, has to look after the east. But such responsibilities never arose in Gibraltar, with its proletarian quarter cut off by an international boundary.

When there is redundancy in Gibraltar—and it used to be frequent—the Spaniards were fired first. It was not a question of merit; the pay came from British funds and if you paid off Gibraltarians they could go and claim a welfare benefit. No employer in Gibraltar is allowed to hire a Spaniard if there is a Gibraltarian available. The Gibraltarian building contractors themselves refused to employ Gibraltarians, and used to wait and watch until the official employers—my Department and the Services—had taken them off the lists of unemployed. Then they would swoop rapidly into the Labour Exchange and snap up the Spaniards.

The effect of this and other similar regulations was that the worthiest Spaniard might have to wait for weeks before a Gibraltar employer was permitted to offer him a job. This had two certain effects; one was that it reduced his annual income; the second was that it ensured that he depended on smuggling during his waiting periods. Whatever happened to such a man, Gibraltar could not lose.

To fix the perspective of Gibraltar's wages, I must add that for supervising these workmen my salary was well over £1,000 a year. Since I had a wife and two children this was practically tax-free. I used to supplement it with about £500 of literary fees, and so average a total and net income of almost £40 a week. That is to say, I had ten times as much money as the working Spaniard, plus a subsidized house rent and an allowance for running a car. One of my children was receiving her secondary education free. In spite of this, my wife and I had constant difficulty in making ends meet, and such were our straits that I begged year after year for transfer to a 'richer' colony. When I finally received that transfer, to the tiny, bare atolls of mid-Pacific, my salary was doubled.

Looking back on it and summing it up, the wage system of Gibraltar was grossly inhuman and unfair. Its perpetration was made possible by two unique factors. The Gibraltarian worker was conditioned to submission by generations of autocracy; he was also misled by his 'popular' party, the AACR. He was told by his leaders to wait, not to rock the boat, to be patient, to eschew 'class hatred', and so forth. As for the Spaniard within the gates, his even lower wages were made possible by the prolonged distress and poverty in Spain.

The employers, from the Government right down to the housewife with her pittance-paid domestics, have had it all their own way. But the ball is over now. Whatever way Gibraltar is driven in the future, one thing is certain, her people will have to work and her employers will have to pay them wages.

The unfortunate effects of this cheap and available foreign labour were more dramatically displayed in the past, before the Gibraltar Government concerned itself with wages. In my time there was a close liaison between the Labour and Welfare Department of Gibraltar and the Spanish *Sindicato*, which looks after the workers within certain limits. Wages and conditions on The Rock were reasonably satisfactory to both sides. All Government contracts contained a 'Fair Wages' clause, necessary to ensure that contractors did not undercut each other in wages, for had they done so it might have caused trouble with the Spanish authorities. But in the nineteenth century it was pure jungle warfare.

Old men in the Works Department—Gibraltarians of working class—have told me how they spent the day as navvies on the works and the whole night heaving coal, in their efforts to support a family. They put in sixteen hours a day of the heaviest labour and were glad to get it. This was not only in the past century, but well on into the present one. There was no effective trade union in Gibraltar until the Transport & General arrived in 1919, but the coalmen formed a rough and ready association and struck at their persecutors time and time again.

In 1890 three coalheavers were sentenced to three months imprisonment for intimidating other workmen. Working-class indignation was such that a detachment of troops had to escort the men to jail. The Governor read the Riot Act, and the merchants shivered in their shoes.

In 1898 the coalheavers went out on strike and it is recorded that 'Mr. James L. Imossi and other merchants were illtreated and severely injured.'* Once again, the troops were mobilized. The Governor settled this dispute by mediation, but under the threat of armed force.

In 1919, the war over, there was a general workers' demonstration, led by the indomitable coalheavers, to protest against the high price of food—not to say the low rate of wages! The Governor addressed the people with soothing words, with his troops drawn up behind him to emphasize the reasonableness of his address. Out of ingrained respect for him, or fear, the people went home quietly.

But one week later they were out again. His Excellency's reassurances as to better times ahead had been so tamely received that he had thought it wise to give immediate permission to his merchant friends to meet their own cost of living problem by raising rents throughout the Colony. The people's protest was 'noted', in civil service terminology, and the increased rents remained in force.

Two months later the coalheavers came out on strike once more, and this time they stayed out for four months. They were forced to capitulate by the importation of Moorish labour from Tangier, which set to work under military protection. Once more the forces of the British Crown were used to further the interests of the few against those of the many. Thus did bad government lay the basis of social resentment and suspicion which, to this day, shouts and sneers from the pages of Gibraltar's opposition press, and which militates against agreement and co-operation in the community.

The degree of distress in Gibraltar at this period has not been recorded and I can only assess it by its manifestations and by what I have been told. The *Gibraltar Chronicle* was more concerned with royal visits and birthdays, and the *El Calpense*, a daily paper in Spanish which had begun in the 1860s, was on the side of Respectability. The workers were all Spanish-speaking, which in Gibraltar amounted to being inarticulate, and they had neither person nor press to present their case.

Old workmen have told me that they were in desperate case, utterly deprived and destitute. Only those strong enough to do a double day's work could support their families without charity. But for the fact that charity was, as we have seen, readily forthcoming, there would have been a large emigration from The Rock, and the Spanish commuters from La Línea would have taken over the work

* *The Gibraltar Directory* by Benedict R. Miles.

of the place. Such an outcome, had it gone so far, might have suited the Gibraltar employers in two ways. The labour would have been more docile and, added to that, an increased corps of unofficial exporters would increase the lucrative turnover of tobacco, coffee and everything else in short supply in Spain.

However, poor men stay put, preferring the devil they know to others they may meet. The Gibraltarians are fond of their Rock and proud of their nationality. Many emigrated to South America, many more to the United Kingdom, some even to Spain, but the majority suffered on in the hope of better times.

By 1927, with the great post-war depression hitting England, the people of Gibraltar were even worse off than ever before. In that year the Government had to set up a Commission to inquire into the problem of unemployment. We may be sure that the victims had been pursuing their own inquiries into the problem for some years previously. Not long before this date, soon after his wife had founded the Needlework Guild to supply clothes to the destitute, His Excellency the Governor, General Sir H. L. Smith-Dorrien, G.C.B., G.C.M.G., D.S.O., published his thanks for 'the generous and loyal response made by the inhabitants of Gibraltar to the Prince of Wales National Relief Fund'. The merchants had contributed no less than £2,365 he said, which was sent off to England as a drop in the bucket, to wash their faces there. With such people neither charity nor loyalty begin at home, for that sum would have been a week's pay for every hard-pressed workman in the Colony.

A year later the merchants told the Governor that no Poor Law was needed in the Colony, which advice he gratefully swallowed. There was no poverty in *his* Colony! He dismissed the Food Supply Committee, established in 1918 to run the breadlines, withdrew the 'cheap food' tickets, removed the flour subsidy, and increased the price of bread.

The best thing I can say about General Sir H. L. Smith-Dorrien is that he was unwittingly the dupe of knaves. His credulousness put a generation of Gibraltarians at the mercy of the merchants so ensuring and acerbating their poverty, and harming the social outlook and climate of the community. The bitter cynicism of the ordinary man, his scepticism of all governments and administrations—including, today, his own elected—may be traced to the 1920s, the cruel youth of the leading men of this present decade.

The coalheavers struck again in 1928, in the face of unemployment. They were replaced and kept out for four months. How they lived for that period has never been disclosed. They came back to work at the Governor's request, but their grievances were never met and they were driven to strike again in 1932. By this time the Transport Workers' Union, backed by strong funds from the United Kingdom, would have given them support and practical aid. But they still lacked the sympathy of the rich and powerful of the community. That, they could see, was lavished daily upon the dogs and donkeys in the streets. The Royal Society for the Prevention of Cruelty to Animals, rich in funds and influence, had been founded sixty years before.

Bad as conditions in Gibraltar were, they were at all times and in all ways, worse in La Línea de la Concepcion.

Another social problem, prostitution, was banished from The Rock about half a century ago, and Gibraltar became, the sailors tell me, the only whoreless port in the Mediterranean Sea. Can we give the churches and their earnest adherents the credit for this reform? Catholic countries around the world seem well furnished in this respect. Can we credit the British administration then? I think not, for the world's supermarket for whores is Hong Kong, where the anglican British are in undisputed authority.

As I see it, Gibraltar was simply too small, crowded and intimate to contain the trade. The brothel quarter was right in the heart of the city, naturally known to every citizen, regardless of sex or age. A local septuagenarian told me, without remorse, how he used to go there as a little lad on his way home from school and see an impressive peepshow for a penny. His point was to let me know what good value there was, in all things, in the good old days. So notorious a place, hemmed in on all its approaches by respectable private houses, could have been of little use to the manly citizens. It served only as a magnet for soldiers and sailors, and became a resort of drunkenness and noisy debauchery, with the inevitable fighting which attends such occasions. Complaints and scandals made the trade intolerable, and it was ended easily, like Gibraltar's other social problems—by export.

When the law was passed the professional ladies, some Spanish, some British, moved to La Línea. The frontier was not much restricted at that time, and their clients could find them. The migration covered not more than a mile as the crow flies and in the circumstances, as they knew, he flies fast and straight. In La Línea the girls colonized a whole street, a street which points straight at The Rock and, perhaps for that reason, but some say for nostalgia, was called *La Calle de Gibraltar*. I do not say that there were no prostitutes there before the new exiles arrived, but be that as it may, Victorian Gibraltar could now point across the frontier and say: 'There are no such women in my dominions.'

Before prostitution was made illegal in Spain, in the 1950s, I often visited this street with my wife and friends in search of true *flamenco*. It was to be found there in three gaudy saloons of Dawson City vintage, each known to the Spaniards as a *'venta animadora'*, literally 'an encouraging pub'. I admired the ancient Latin wisdom in this frank description, when I thought of the short shrift we would give in Belfast or Glasgow to 'a public house for the encouragement of vice'. The Spanish police—and La Línea is full of them—were happy, as police are everywhere, to have the vice of the city well centralized and easy to supervise.

In the saloons there were girls old and young, hideous and pretty, acting as oriental hostesses. They joined men's tables and solicited drinks of green cordial, on which they were paid commission. Some of them wore ball gowns, if that is the proper term, and these were employed by the management and could not be taken out until the place closed at 3 a.m. The prettier girls, rather more of them, wore short dresses and were free agents. They could, and did, come and go every half-hour.

These, on public display, were the *élite* of the profession, and I was told that they could earn up to one hundred pesetas for a consultation—about twelve shillings an hour, being as much as their fathers might earn in Gibraltar in a day. In the houses on each side of the street, each with a tough old madame sitting at the receipt of custom in the white-tiled hallway, were the tried and true professionals, fit to be seen only in a dim, religious light. These women went down to twenty-five pesetas—about half a crown—for their brief ministrations, but made a good living by the swiftness of their turnover.

None of this shocked me, nor does it yet. I am well aware that where there are troops and sailors and migratory labour there will be fornication. I am in favour of having it legal, professional and controlled, rather than—as in Victorian England—clandestine, amateur and attended by such calamities as rape, seduction, illegitimacy and disease. I saw what Paris suffered when that earnest woman deputy closed the *maisons tolerées* and filled the streets with blatant and greedy women; I have also seen how discreet, well ordered and even artistic is the brothel business of Japan and Hong Kong. It was in Japan that I learnt that the 50,000 well-esteemed brothel-keepers had formed a society called The National Association for the Prevention of Venereal Disease, and that they were subsidizing prophylaxis as keenly and generously as Standard Oil does fire prevention. I saw some sense in that.

But what about the poor girls, I am asked. One has to remember that these are, in one sense, the rich girls, as Bernard Shaw pointed out so long ago. Money is not everything, of course, but in society as we and the Japanese and the Spaniards choose to run it, it is a very great deal. The alternative for girls of the prostitute class is hard work and poverty. It used to be held that they had no alternative, that they were all tricked into the business, after being ruined by villains with long black moustachios and doped champagne, but no one who has spoken to a modern prostitute is going to believe that one.

At the same time, it is evident, that in any European city, prostitution breeds squalor, misguides the young, encourages perversions, attracts crime and vice of every kind, and is often attended by violence, and blackmail. It was these undesirable symptoms which Gibraltar banished, sending them to her sister city, La Línea de la Concepcion.

Before leaving this ever-interesting topic I must tell the tale of Gibraltar's solitary surviving whore. Well over fifty, all passion spent, this poor woman showed her British passport, claimed residence and returned to The Rock, leaving her disappointments behind in La Línea. In Gibraltar she found life stale, flat and, above all, unprofitable. When, under the NATO Agreement, the great warships of the U.S.A. began to call, a percentage of their crews— unofficially reckoned by the police at ten—ranged the town late at night looking for women. Since they were not to be found there, and the frontier was closed, the single superannuated harlot found a new scarcity value and put herself back into circulation. Without proper premises, she used to take her occasional suitors up the mountain, past my house, and entertain them in the roadside thickets. The benign climate of Gibraltar lends itself to all outdoor activities.

The Gibraltar Police soon got to hear of this enterprise—not from me—and decided to lay a trap at her lair. They focused a fine camera on her *al fresco* couch which, they told me, was well impressed and unmistakable. Then they strung the surrounding trees with flashbulbs and lay there in wait in the darkness, like tiger hunters on safari.

They judged their moment by the cessation of light bilingual conversation, pressed the button, cast a fierce glare over the scene and caught a U.S. boatswain and the lady, both blatantly *deshabillés*.

Since I was a responsible official and the nearest neighbour to the love nest, one of the police officers called on me to see if I could add any corroborative evidence. Had I seen her passing? and so forth. He could not help boasting to me of the technical achievement, for this was the first miscreant caught by the new photographic unit of the force. It was no secret, anyway, for it was to come out in court next day.

'What are you going to charge her with?' I asked him. As an Irishman, my first instinct is to defend the fox. It could hardly be a soliciting charge, nor obstruction, nor insulting behaviour, nor keeping a disorderly house, nor any other of the mealy-mouthed British charges against prostitutes. The woman could say that this was her long-lost fiancé from America, if she thought of it, and if she knew that there was no law against petting, however advanced, so long as it does not offend the presently disengaged and disenchanted.

'Oh, we have her all right,' said the policeman. 'We've found the right charge. To take your clothes off within twenty yards of the public highway, that's indecent exposure! That's the charge for her!'

'I thought you told me it was pitch dark?'

'So it was,' he said. 'That's why we chose last night, sir, and that's how we caught her! Dark as Egypt, it was, sir!'

'Well, then, how could she have made an indecent exposure?'

'Eh? Look at this photograph! If that's not indecent I don't know what is!'

'I've seen it. But no one could see that, man, in the dark, could they? As a matter of fact,' I told him, 'you and your flashbulbs made the exposure indecent. The police made the indecent exposure, man!' I told him. 'Maybe she'll counter-charge you with that—and with possessing pornographic photographs, too!'

He left me, perplexed and dismayed, and I think I gave him a bad half-hour. But back at the station they laughed and decided to go ahead. The unfortunate woman, caught in the heavy hands of Authority, had neither the knowledge nor the will to argue. She bowed to the charge and surrendered a morsel of her earnings into the court funds.

That was the end of her public career and, so far as I know, the belated end of prostitution in Gibraltar.

22

GIBRALTAR ADOLESCENT

Dr. Henry M. Field, an American visitor, published his sketch *Gibraltar* in 1889, close to the heyday of the place. According to him, the garrison at that peaceful time numbered five or six thousand men, which is to say that the Fortress was crammed full of troops. The fortifications, mile upon mile of casemates, bastions, redoubts and galleries, ranging from sea-level up to Rock Gun on the peak, impressed him mightily. Unlike the troops, these are still there for inspection. But most impressive of all, he says, were the guns.

'The latest pets of Gibraltar are a pair of twins—two guns, each of which weighs a hundred tons! These are guarded with great care from the too close inspection of strangers.'

A footnote states that these guns were built by Armstrong, were nearly 33 ft. long, of over 17 in. bore, and that they fired 450 lb. of powder and a 2,000 lb. shot. Their maximum range was eight miles and their muzzle velocity was such that the shot would penetrate 25 in. of wrought iron. One such gun may still be seen lying above Rosia Bay at Gibraltar. Such has been the speed of development in military equipment that, after a mere ninety years, it appears prehistoric. Once held in awe, the pride of The Rock, the old gun now evokes only facetious comments. From the little I know of such things it seems to have been a misguided effort, for at eight miles trajectory the winds of The Straits must have veered that big ball hundreds of yards off target. There seems little point in penetrating 25 in. of iron if you cannot hit it.

'With such a range,' says Dr. Field, 'it would reach every part of the Bay, and a brace of them, with the hundreds of heavy guns along the Line Wall, might be relied upon to clear the Bay of a hostile fleet, so that Gibraltar could hardly be approached by sea.

'But', he goes on, 'these are not the whole of the defences; they are only the beginning. There are batteries in the rear of the town, as well as in front, so that, if an enemy were to effect a landing he would have to fight his way at every step. As you climb The Rock it fairly bristles with guns. You cannot turn to the right or left

without seeing these open-mouthed monsters and looking into their
murderous throats. Everywhere it is nothing but guns, guns, guns!

'It is the Queen's birthday, when the Rock Gun, mounted on the
highest point of The Rock, 1,400 ft. in the air, gives the signal; which
is immediately caught up by the galleries below, one after the other;
and the batteries along the sea answer to those of the mountainside,
until the mighty reverberations not only sweep round the Bay, but
across the Mediterranean, and far along the African shores. Nothing
like this is seen or heard in any other part of the world!'

What the 20,000 peaceful citizens thought of this cannonade has
never been recorded for the good reason that they were never consulted on this or any other military matter. They were completely
conditioned to the role of camp-followers or, at best, tolerated
civilians in a military cantonment.

'Of course,' says Dr. Field, 'in a garrison town the military
element is first and foremost. As there are five or six thousand troops
in Gibraltar it is perhaps the largest garrison town in the British
dominions, unless the troops in and around London be reckoned as
a garrison. Very different from London is a garrison town where a
large body of troops is shut up within the walls of a fortress. Here
the military element is so absorbing and controlling that it dominates
the whole life of the place.

'Everything goes by military rule; even the hours of the day are
announced by gunfire; the morning gun gives the exact minute at
which the soldiers are to turn out of their beds, and the last evening
gun the minute at which they are to "turn in", signals which, though
for the soldiers only, the working population of the town find it
convenient to adopt; and which outsiders *must* regard, since at these
hours the gates are opened or shut; so that a large part of the non-
military population have to keep step almost as much as if they were
marching in the ranks, since their risings up and their lying down,
their goings out and their comings in, are all regulated by the fire
of the gun and the blast of the bugle.'

That is the authentic picture, as written by a neutral and intelligent observer, of Gibraltar at the close of last century. It was more
or less the same for many years before and after that date—a fortress
with strangers within the gates, accidental intruders, a naval base
with incidental commerce. The map of the place tells the same tale.

Nine-tenths of the land area was—still is—in the hands of the War Department, or the Navy or Air Force. Of the sea area enclosed in harbours, nine-tenths was reserved for the Navy. The armed services, as was their duty, jealously held on to every last inch of land and water, with the result that the growth of the town was cramped and twisted. Not until 1960 could a large merchantman come alongside the commercial wharfs, and even yet there is only room for one or two ships alongside the North Mole, so that most callers have to anchor out in The Bay and unload by tender and lighters. Meanwhile the huge naval harbour, with its miles of wharfs and dry docks, lies empty and deserted. The priorities of Gibraltar are still written on its face.

In 1922, and not before, the Governor appointed an Executive Council. This brought Gibraltar, after more than two centuries of British rule, into a new stage of colonial development. It is on record that, soon after the new Council was called, the tide rose and fell four times in two hours.

Yet the innovation was not of earth-shaking consequence. The Governor's appointees were of the calibre and quality already described, men who would nod their heads in eager assent as soon as His Excellency opened his august mouth. The officials, a majority of the Council, would do so for promotion, or for fear of bullying and humiliation. That last is an outcome especially to be feared in dealing with a military governor, for some of them take as much pride in making an aggressive noise as normal men take in keeping the peace. I have had to witness such outbursts on several occasions. The nominees would go with the Governor, right or wrong, for the social prestige of remaining on the Council, and for the possibility of future honours. One way and another, their advisory services would influence the Governor about as much as Stalin's Central Committee or Hitler's General Staff influenced those potentates. The actions and attitudes of post-1922 governors, those with benefit of Executive Council, were not demonstrably influenced by collective wisdom, and still less by any new considerations of civilized government. The widespread poverty persisted and increased, so that new soup kitchens—those symbols of social bankruptcy—had to be opened within one year of the Executive Council's first appointment.

Meanwhile the only politics permitted in Gibraltar were pursued in the City Council. The *ex-officio* members, representatives of the armed forces and Governor's nominees, were all sticklers for sanitation and safety. They were ex-patriate officers to a man, known locally as *importados*. Most of them did a two or three-year tour of duty on The Rock, so that they had no need to take a long view of local problems. They would seek to make immediate improvements, and since they were not themselves rate-payers, or at least, not directly so, they had no need to worry about the cost. Gibraltar's rates were ridiculously low, anyway, to British eyes. Nevertheless, the rates were strongly felt and resented by those who had to pay them, the more so because there was not and never had been any other form of direct taxation in Gibraltar. Every increase in rates— and they had to increase as the improvers strove to overtake the negligence of centuries—was naturally blamed on the irresponsible *importado* majority on the City Council, with its fancy foreign ideas. Given a majority of local businessmen, men from the rate-paying community, the process of improvement could be controlled and decelerated, and the rates diminished. The Gibraltarian merchant's idea of a high rate was, as he had shown, 2s. 8d. in the pound.

In 1926 the elected councillors appealed to the Governor to ask the Secretary of State to reconstitute their Council and to give them a majority on it. In effect, they raised the cry 'No taxation without representation'. Let the rate-payers representatives fix the rates.

But the Governor had responsibility for the health of his garrison, so often, in the past, infected from the sores of the city. With this history in mind, his chief medical officers were permanently planted in the Council. He showed the ancient distrust for the efficiency and good intentions of the local moguls and told them that he would not recommend their request.

In 1929, when there were four elected members and five appointed on the Council, the request for a reversal of these proportions was sprung on a new and, apparently, liberal Governor. But the City Councillors received the same old answer—No.

The import duty on tobacco had been increased in 1922, prior to the appointment of the Executive Council. In 1926 the new Governor, Sir Alexander Godley, raised the duties on wines and spirits and imposed a new duty on perfumery, which had become an important staple in the smuggling trade. The Exchange Committee and the Chamber of Commerce petitioned him not to levy further duties and asked for a reduction in the expenditure of the colony. The Governor, up to the neck in public distress, unemployment, homelessness and free soup, had mooted the beginnings of a small and direly needed scheme for public housing. He had to find the money somewhere and the obvious place was in the vast imports of luxury goods, mostly destined for contraband. He rejected the petition.

Before passing on, I must remark that the public expenditure of Gibraltar was, at that date, infinitesimal. As late as 1935 the total clerical staff of the Civil Service amounted to thirty-three, all male because Gibraltar girls were not permitted, by their fathers, to go out to work until very recent years. The pay of these clerks was penurious, such that about £10,000 paid the whole staff, at an average salary of £330 per man. There were four clerks in the Lands & Works Department, always the biggest spender, five in the Treasury, fewer in other essential services, and they must have been hard put to it to keep up with the work. Even as I write, in 1965, the public service in Gibraltar is demonstrably underpaid, and the lowest salaries in any British territory are to be found there. Heads of Departments, Surgeons and such people are in receipt of £1,750 per annum, about one-third of what they would receive in Great Britain or in a generous colony. In 1958–9 the Government of Gibraltar recruited a young but fully qualified architect and set him to work reforming the whole face of the town. His salary for his first year was £750; I calculated his fees on the work he designed and executed in that year, at the fixed rates of the Royal Institute of British Architects, and found that they would have been in excess of £20,000. The attitude of the dominant businessmen, then as theretofore, was enshrined in the local proverb '*No llora; no teta*', meaning 'If you don't scream, you won't get the breast', or 'Devil take the hindmost'. The leaders of Gibraltar affect to regard every pound spent on the public service as a waste of money at their expense. The legend runs that all civil servants are idle loafers, afraid to face the competitive world of business, and that they spend their time polishing the seat of their pants. The working man, somewhat envious of the security of the Service, backs his boss in this assessment, and the result is that the civil servant has not a friend in the place. The inevitable outcome is an underpaid, unattractive and, ultimately, inefficient Civil Service. Since it is held to do nothing but prey on the business community, the less effective it becomes, the merchants hold, the better! A return to anarchy would suit some of them very well indeed.

Throughout the decades of distress the tempo of protest accelerated. The year 1935 is a typically busy one on the political front. The Exchange Committee and Chamber of Commerce allied themselves, for the first time, with the Transport Workers' Union and offered their views to the Governor on the subject of a new Estates Duty Ordinance. The Governor rejected all their advice.

Soon afterwards they all joined forces again and petitioned the Governor to restrict his appointees to the citizenry of Gibraltar. The petition was 'noted'.

At that they held a public meeting of protest, closed the shops, and collected 3,000 signatures to a memorial addressed to the King himself, over the Governor's head. The subject was the old one, still untouched by concession, of more local representation on the City Council, but it hinted, for the first time, at greater developments in local responsibility in Gibraltar. It reached the lengths of a parliamentary debate at Westminster, but the ultimate answer was, as ever, a firm and definite 'No'.

Now we enter the years of fear, rearmament, threats and appeasements, of Abyssinia and the Spanish Civil War, of dissension, duplicity and double-cross. Gibraltar's warlike propensities were, in those times, not merely uppermost, but the only considerations accorded to the place. The advance of the civilian community of The Rock was postponed for ten whole years.

The Executive Council, the Gibraltarian's only pretence to guide his own destiny, was revoked for the duration of World War II. Even the City Council, on which he was but feebly represented, was suspended. His press, such as it was, was closely controlled, and public protest was unthinkable in wartime. The ineffectives of the community, as they were officially called, being women, children and inessential men to the number of 16,000, were peremptorily and, as we have seen, unfortunately evacuated. Rationing, price control, and a host of irksome security regulations were hastily imposed. The last vestige of civil liberty was extinguished by the exigencies of war. Gibraltar was no longer even a subject and primitive colony; it was a fortress containing, in a phrase used long years before 'the civil acolytes of military power'.

But the civil acolytes of the 1940s were a people very different from the illiterate, polyglot rabble of hucksters, pedlars and refugees of a hundred years before. The few thousand men who were permitted to remain in Gibraltar throughout the war were the 'effectives', which is to say, the cream of the community. Amongst them were men who had spent their youth in English public schools, graduates of great universities, ex-officers of famous regiments, barristers of the London Inns of Court, and merchants of untold wealth and influence. '*Se obedece pero no se cumple,*' runs the famous proverb of the eternal Spanish resistance, 'We obey but we do not comply.' The Gibraltarians are well aware of it, too. Cooped up in The Fortress, voiceless and voteless, subjected to every petty restriction which the military mind could invent, treated as second-class citizens in the city which they had to come to think of as their own, these people inevitably drew closer together and began to forge a political instrument for use after the war.

The first, only and, perhaps, the last political party in Gibraltar was founded in 1942, and has been in complete domination of the community for the past twenty-four years. The triumphs of the community in its advance towards self-government must be accorded to this party; and so, to a great extent, must be the present and future tribulations of The Rock.

The Association for the Advancement of Civil Rights, as this party is cumbersomely called, did not begin life as a political party. No politics were, officially, permitted in 1942. Its title was not intended to be grandiose, to claim political liberties in general. Gibraltarian English is literal rather than idiomatic, and this association's original purpose was to advance civil, as opposed to military rights, the rights of civilians living under military domination. It seems doubtful to me if any of the founding fathers, whose immediate concern was the alleviation of senseless and irritating restrictions, had any idea of how far their flag would lead them.

The AACR, with a programme so simple, so obviously needed, and so generally acceptable, immediately embraced a wide panel of Gibraltarians. The cultivated millionaires of The Rock, men of wide experience and heavy responsibility, and the humblest workman there found themselves in the same position of frustration. The London-trained lawyers, capable men in other professions, trade unionists, Gibraltarians of whatsoever ability or function, all suffered under the exigencies of the martial régime and, to some extent, smarted under an implied suspicion and disdain. I know of several Englishmen, civilian ex-patriates who lived in Gibraltar in managerial positions, who joined this association, or, at least approved of it. 'We called it', one such told me, 'the Anti-Bull Club, and blessed the day it began!'

The founding father was a trade union leader, Albert J. Risso, an impressive, dignified and honest man, full of solid strength of purpose. He commanded general respect in 1942 and still does so today, after twenty-three years or more in the Latin and parish pump politics of Gibraltar. More than that, no man could do. Risso was, remains, leader of the Gibraltar Confederation of Labour, which has absorbed the Transport & General Workers' Union and all other trade unions in Gibraltar except some inconsiderable splinter groups. It is typical of the man that, finding a surprising amount of support for his new association, he recognized his own limitations and consulted a lawyer to draw up a constitution and rules. His choice for this task was Joshua A. Hassan, thirtyish, Jewish, clever, courageous and unhampered by great possessions. There were senior lawyers, some of them sympathetic, but they were richer and busier than Hassan and, from choice or caution, held themselves aloof.

By the end of the War the AACR was two or three years old and had acquired shape and strength. The Government, faced by several different forms and causes of popular discontent, may have been glad to have such a body to consult. The old merchant gang, which had been able to evacuate its families to Málaga or Tangier at its own expense, and to keep them in safety and luxury throughout the war, could scarcely have spoken for the men whose wives and children had faced the Flying Bombs of London or the rigours of the Northern Irish climate. The Association soon became recognized as being the chief platform of Gibraltarian opinion, and thus assumed political functions.

Risso, the labour leader, had the voices, which were soon to become the votes; Hassan had the organizing ability, the necessary command of English, the legal knowledge, and some gift of oratory. He had something even more valuable, although less tangible. He had inherited, and he knew it, all the respect and prestige which the British authorities, even at their most oppressive, accord to lawyers in circumstances such as these.

The AACR, like all political parties, had its teething troubles. The merchant class—'*Los Millonarios*'—who could, as they knew, look after themselves in any case, cast suspicious eyes on it as soon as it began to assume political proportions. A party run by an ambitious young Jew and a principled workman, with a majority following of horny-handed and Spanish-tongued toilers, had no appeal for the sanctimonious commercialists of Gibraltar. They withdrew into a scattered and individualistic opposition.

Others who withdrew from the dominant AACR did so either on principle or for personal reasons. S. A. Seruya, graduate of economics of St. Andrew's University, and a far more prescient politician than Hassan, left the AACR over a dispute on Gibraltar-Spanish relations. In 1954, in the face of some Spanish obstruction at the frontier which resulted from the Queen's Coronation visit, Seruya suggested that Gibraltar should try to co-operate with Spain rather than to defy her and aggravate the situation. This was impolitic, since the simpler Gibraltarians were incensed against Spain, but it has since proved to be the only possible and sensible course to take. Hassan, trading on the unpopularity of Seruya's moderate views, was able to oust him from the party, and he became the chief vote catcher in the ineffective opposition. Hassan retained the party and the votes. Trade unionist A. J. Baldorino went into opposition with his own—minor—trade union when he saw the AACR, inevitably, co-operating with the Big Business lobby.

Three young lawyers sit in opposition in the present Legislative Council. They are all men with stronger social pretensions than Hassan, and scions of the high income group. Since it is fair to say that no immigrant to Gibraltar ever came in with rank or wealth, social pretensions are based on nothing more than a rich father or grandfather, but they are taken very seriously none the less.

Peter J. Isola, second-generation lawyer and ex-minister of Education and leader of the official Opposition, has accompanied Hassan twice to UNO to make Gibraltar's case. He is able, fair-minded and sophisticated, and it is these qualities, added to his youth and kindliness which, in spite of his wealth and social superiority, have kept him popular at the polls. But Joshua Hassan, whilst he remains sufficiently a man of the people to retain the trade union support of the AACR, will stay far ahead of all his rivals in popular estimation, and only disaster will oust him from the saddle in Gibraltar.

Since these words were written disaster, in the form of Spanish frontier obstruction ruinous to Gibraltar's tourist trade, has forced Hassan into an uneasy coalition with Isola's Opposition group. But there is no doubt as to which of the two wields the real power. For better or for worse, Sir Joshua Hassan remains the leader of the Gibraltarians.

23

GIBRALTAR'S COMING OF AGE

The peak point of Gibraltar's contribution to World War II occurred in 1942. By clawing down one and a half million tons of rock—which hardly left a scar—and dumping it in the sea, the Allied engineers were able to make a runway long enough for the fighter aircraft of that time. As well as providing General Eisenhower with a strong headquarters, The Rock became the greatest and safest aircraft carrier in the Western Mediterranean, and provided full and effective air cover for the Allied landings in North Africa.

Here, by hindsight, we can see that the war turned towards its final result, for this was the first successful counter-attack on the hitherto invincible enemy. General Franco recognized the fact by foresight, and withdrew from further negotiations with Hitler. Gibraltar, packed with American and Commonwealth, as well as British troops, was an impossible objective for Spain, both physically and politically. The Rock was no more troubled with any threat from the mainland.

After 1942 the tide of war receded from Gibraltar, which assumed the role of a naval base, supply depot and rest camp for campaigns in North Africa and other parts of the Mediterranean. Once the time of maximum danger had passed the few resident Gibraltarians could give their full attention to business and, a little later, to politics.

Price control and rationing were no more successful in Gibraltar than in any other Latin community, and there is said to have been a great leakage of foodstuffs into the black markets of starving Spain. Britain kept Gibraltar lavishly supplied with food throughout the war, with the result that there were surpluses for trafficking. The effect of this trade, and the general devaluation of money and rise in world prices, was to cause a dramatic increase in the cost of living in Gibraltar. Before the war the cost of living had been very low, a fact which must have helped to stave off civil unrest. 'You could get your hair cut for a penny,' an old Gibraltarian told me. After the war prices here were more than doubled, and salaries and wages lagged far behind. Added to all the other factors which I have examined, there was a new economic pressure on the people.

But the strongest of all the causes of unrest was the evacuation of wives and families. It had, in the event, proved unnecessary, since Gibraltar suffered scarcely any attack throughout the war. It had also proved—or appeared—to be mismanaged, careless and inconsiderate. The evacuees had been thrown straight out of Casablanca by the Vichy French, perilously ferried to London to be boarded out under a rain of bombs, and held there for too long, while their menfolk lived on The Rock in anxiety and dread.

After their baptism of fire the evacuees were shipped to the wet fields of Ulster, where the psychological climate is anti-Catholic and the physical climate is anti-human. Wandering in the wilderness the tribes elected leaders and mounted protests and demands and, finally, won themselves a hearing.

By 1944 the Axis Powers were contained, and there was no longer any reason to keep the Gibraltarians away from their homeland. The Repatriation Plan was to send back 500 people every month, to a total of 4,000 during the first year, but the poor exiles were not yet out of the wood. Mustered in London to await shipping, they found themselves under the worst of all attacks—the Flying Bombs. The Government accelerated the Repatriation and sent 9,000 people back to The Rock in 1944, and the rest of them soon afterwards.

They had said, these good people, as you and I would say: 'We know it's going to be difficult there, but let us back home and we'll put up with anything.' They poured into a grim fortress girt for war, littered with concrete gunposts and air-raid shelters, wreathed in barbed wire, devoid of amenities, full of restrictions. Many of them were plunged into sudden poverty. They had earned good money in Britain's wartime industries; they left that income behind and came home to find prices at heights unprecedented. But the worst of all hardships was in housing.

Accommodation had been strained before the war by the return of some thousands of Gibraltarians from Spain. There had been no civil building during the war. There should have been housing units for the whole population minus the 1936 influx and the few new families formed during the four years' exile. The fortunate returned to their old homes, such as they were, but there were thousands of families without any kind of accommodation. Decades of neglect of this problem, of the people's welfare, caught up with the Government of Gibraltar almost overnight.

This, then, was the social background against which the Gibraltarians played out their little struggle for self-government. It is not difficult to see whence the AACR drew its strong support. The people of Gibraltar knew, from their enforced peregrinations, how British citizens ought to live. Back home at last, they found matters worse than ever. They had nothing to lose and everything to gain by agitating for self-government and progress.

The Colonial Government, casting about in bewilderment to save its face and proclaim its belated good intentions, had an elaborate but ineffective Town Plan drawn up, and consulted Professor Hayek, eminent conservative apologist and advocate of self-help, for a comprehensive social survey. I do not know if this survey ever came to light. It is usual in Gibraltar for the Government to keep such economic reports secret, as they are doing now, in 1965, with the Selwyn Report, probably because it deals with the subject of smuggling. Be that as it may, Hayek could only have told the General and his gentlemen what Sydney and Beatrice Webb could have told them sixty years before. What they had to learn, and learn fast, with the help of the leading Gibraltarians, were the simple facts of life, the ABC of public administration—that government must be creative and not merely restrictive; permissive and not merely repressive; democratic rather than aristocratic; and, in all things, responsible.

In 1945 the City Council of Gibraltar was reconstituted with its long-awaited local majority—one elected member. With a new pride in itself, as the first forum where a Gibraltarian could say, and prove, what was good for Gibraltar, the Council went ahead boldly and efficiently. In my time, in spite of the many practical difficulties peculiar to the city—in water supply, roadworks, cleansing and so forth—it was a model of what a municipal council ought to be. In many respects, for instance in the treatment of its officers, it was far ahead of the Colonial Government. It did not, however, hold responsibility for the greatest of all civic problems, that of public housing.

A deputation to Westminster in 1945 suggested that The Rock should be integrated with the United Kingdom, and some sections of Gibraltarian opinion are calling for that as a solution to current difficulties. Integration was once, briefly, offered to Malta, but a great sigh of relief must have arisen in Whitehall when the Maltese foolishly rejected it. In my opinion Britain will never offer integration again, nor accede to any pleas for it. The Mother of Parliaments remembers too well how a handful of Irish Nationalist M.P.s could freeze all parliamentary business, horse-trade its support for sectional and national advantage, make and break the governments of Great Britain. The British Labour Party is only too well aware, in these days of political see-saw, of the automatic election of a dozen Tory backwoodsmen from integrated Ulster. These people, not one of whom has ever distinguished himself in Westminster except perhaps as a nuisance, are elected on the archaic and irrelevant religious issues of old Ireland, and on promises to 'Keep the Pope out of Portadown' and suchlike constructive proposals. As you might expect, they are loyal and unswerving conservatives, and their added weight could obstruct or defeat the Government of Great Britain. Thus, at its worst, Great Britain might get a Tory rather than a Labour Government simply because His Holiness the Pope is unpopular with the addlepated yokels of Portadown.

Let there be no doubt that M.P.s from Gibraltar would be highly conservative, too, and would so vote at Westminster on the acute economic problems which are Britain's main concern, and maybe swing the balance. They would not be elected to do that, but on some such local issue as the strength of their record of defiance of Spain.

At Westminster today the most acute of all problems, as the Speaker keeps commenting, is the lack of parliamentary time. Narrow majorities are another feature of our times. A caucus of impassioned and voluble Latins claiming time to raise their small and remote affairs would be about as welcome at Westminster as a hole in the head, and whoever seeks it is patently wasting his time.

Instead of accepting the compliment of integration with Gibraltar, the British Government had offered her colony a new constitution with an element of indigenous representation. The proposal of 1944 included the reconstituted City Council, with six elected and six official members, and an Advisory Council to be comprised of the City Council plus the Colonial Secretary, (i.e. the chief official of the Government of Gibraltar), and the Attorney General, chief law officer of the Crown. Slipped into the prospectus, in such a way as to represent a compliment was a proviso that the Chairman of this Advisory Council must be an elected member. Since chairmen do not usually vote, the official side would still retain a majority of one!

Every shade of opinion in the community, from the *millonarios* down to the humblest workman, from the Chamber of Commerce to the Transport Workers' Union, accepted the leadership of the AACR, for the first time, and rejected the proposal out of hand.

The London *Times* rumbled faintly at this situation. 'A people,' it euphemistically stated, 'which lives by importing a commodity and selling it to someone who is on the spot or comes to fetch it, had not hitherto developed racial or national characteristics as do tillers of the soil or fishers of the sea. There is, therefore, a certain irresponsibility and lack of discipline which needs to be recognized.'

To this *The Times** added an understatement so exquisite that it reads like a straight translation from the Japanese:

'The method of selection of the Governor, by the appointment of a general whose army career had earned him a high appointment or a baton, for neither of which a vacancy existed, cannot be said to conduce to the progressive treatment of colonial social problems.'

In 1950 the first Legislative Council was inaugurated in Gibraltar, by the Duke of Edinburgh, with all due pomp and ceremony. It consisted of the Governor as President, three *ex-officio* members, (the three senior civil servants), two nominated members, (of whom both might and one must be an official), and five elected members. On the face of it, this amounted to a fifty-fifty line-up, for the nominated members, just as much as the civil servants, were the Governor's men. But in the event of a deadlock of opinion, the Governor would have the casting vote. Indeed he had, still has, more than that. He has reserved powers to override any or all of the advice and opinions of his Legislative Council, and to make such laws as he deemed necessary, regardless of the elected representatives.

It is evident that at this stage we are still playing at politics for, in spite of the semblance of democracy, of representation of local interests and opinions, all the power lies fairly and squarely

* *The Times*, 4th January 1946.

where it had always lain—in the hands of one man, the Governor.

For election purposes it was arranged and agreed that The Rock should not be divided up into constituencies on the British pattern. A system of proportional representation was adopted. Each elector had three votes, to fill five (later more) seats, and he was to use these in his own order of preference. There is much to be said for the proportional representation system, and the Liberal Party of Britain would be far more fairly represented at Westminster had this system been in operation there. But in Gibraltar it was taken to be a device of the Government's to prevent the election of one party, or of five men of like mind. The AACR, which is to say, Hassan, saw through this trick too. They put up the full number of candidates, told the electors exactly which three to vote for—this three at this polling station, that three at that—and so managed to win either all of the seats or a strong majority of them. Thus, the Government side found itself with an opposition stronger, and more easily united, than it had anticipated.

This stage of constitutional development, with a handpicked Executive Council and a semi-representative Legislative Council, proved to be an impossible state of affairs, satisfactory to no one. All that can be said for it is that the members are being trained, gaining experience in procedure and debate. The said members would indignantly deny that they stand in need of such training.

The local minority on the Council cannot effect anything; all that it can do is complain and criticize. The officials retain all the power and all the responsibility of government, as well as all the secret information which helps to motivate it. They are, in effect, an executive thrust into the sphere of legislation, in spite of the fact that all experience and good sense has long since separated these two functions in all the civilized countries of the world. To combine them is only to create confusion.

Throughout this period the Colonial Secretary, Financial Secretary and Attorney General find themselves in a most anomalous position, and one which they are unlikely to be fitted to fill. Instead of proceeding quietly with their various duties, behind closed doors, as is the habit of civil servants, they now find that they have to explain most of their decisions and actions in public, to submit them to frustrated, disgruntled and half-informed critics, all anxious to score political points. Apart from the Attorney General, they are unlikely to have had much experience in public speaking. They are further disarmed by the style and traditions of the Service, which has a form of expression moderate, vague and non-committal, with much verbal timidity and modesty false or real, and by the secrecy which surrounds some areas of their work.

All the force and vitality, all the dynamic, is on the other side of the House, with the new politicians who have manœuvred and fought at the hustings. Yet the Opposition is so placed that it can make no concrete achievement. The Legislative Council only debates such matters as the Governor—The Executive—chooses to submit to it, and when it offers its advice the Governor need not accept it.

Some power lies with the Executive Council, which meets in camera with the Governor. At this stage, it has one or two senior elected members, likely to be of opposed local factions, and heavily outnumbered by civil servants and appointed yes-men. But since there is no occasion for politicking behind closed doors the advice offered will be sincere, or at least more sincere than that paraded in the public forum, and I do not doubt that Governors tend to respect it and, when possible, to accept it. At the same time it must be said that a Governor is unlikely to invite trouble and delay by selecting members of strong convictions and views far divergent from his own. The elected zealots and reformers can shout and sneer in the Advisory Council as they wish, playing to the public gal'ery and the local press; but in his private Executive Council the Governor wants only gentlemen and 'sound chaps', which is to say, the most static and orthodox men he can find. Even should a liberal or a progressive man slip into this august cabal, the cabinet atmosphere has a taming effect, and so, of course, has the Honours List.

The Colonial Honours List, an archaic and curiously English institution, is not as vain and foolish as it may appear to be. It is, in effect, an implement of government, and an effective one at that. If we reduce the control of men to the simple system of punishments and rewards, the old ass-driver's stick and carrot, it is the Honours List which provides the carrots.

In an emergent colony the stick must be laid aside and, with an eye to future relationships between the Mother Country and her grown-up child, goodwill must be cultivated assiduously. At this stage, honours are scattered thick and fast on the hitherto humiliated community, as compliments not only to the recipients but also to those whom they represent. Those who have received honours are grateful and mollified, disposed thenceforth to dignified and moderate behaviour. Those who have not received them may hope to do so, and guard their tongues and actions so as not to prejudice their chances.

The smaller the community, the larger honours loom. A knight in London may pass through the streets unknown, open like the rest of us to the insolence of taxi-drivers and lavatory attendants. A knight in a tiny town like Gibraltar will be reminded of his eminence by everyone he meets, and I have seen one seated on a window-sill in the Main Street, basking in the sun and in the admiration of his fellow-citizens.

There are no less than eight knights living in Gibraltar at present, and I can see at least two more who may shortly join them. This works out at one for every 3,600 people, or every 2,000 adults, and is as though Great Britain had 17,000 of them, or two for every three doctors. Lesser honours, such as C.B.E.s, O.B.E.s, and M.B.E.s, lie thick on the ground. These honours are doubtless well earned, and it would be ungracious to devalue them, but, at the same time, the sight of eight knights congregated round a parish pump demands some explanation, lest the uninformed visitor believes himself to be in medieval Malta. It must be admitted that British honours are far more easily acquired abroad than at home.

A colonial subject is honoured for being a good boy, to encourage him, and others, to remain good. It is a matter of benign blackmail. To win the same recognition in Britain a man must be distinguished in his field, outstandingly excellent. To be unaware of these relative values, and of the cause of and reason for the system of colonial honours, is to proceed in unnecessary confusion.

The first problem of government is finance, and in an emergent colony, highly charged with aspirations and led by such makeshift governments as I have described, the problem may be an acute one. As a child of the Mother Country the colony has been nourished and supported by grant and subsidy; as an adult it will be expected to become self-supporting; meanwhile, as an adolescent, it will need more money to meet new and growing responsibilities. The young nation's allowance may be temporarily increased; at the same time it will be called upon to increase its own earning power, that is, its internal revenue.

Gibraltar has received many millions of pounds from Great Britain since the war ended, in the form of grants for specific purposes—mostly for public housing. In justice and common sense, however, the community had to raise some extra revenue by means of new taxation. The new voice in government, the voice of the Gibraltarian, called impatiently for reforms and improvements. Britain answered, in effect, 'You may have them, and we shall help you. But you must not expect us to pay the whole bill.'

The principle accepted everywhere—in theory, at least—is to apply taxes where they hurt least and to re-distribute the money where it is most needed, to alleviate want and promote the welfare of the community. Such a process is not only democratic and Christian; it has also been proved practical. Disagreement arises over the question—Where do taxes hurt least?

Here is where political immaturity, that lack of a settled and responsible middle class, may display itself. The leaders who, outside parliament or within it in irresponsible opposition, have called loudest for social justice, may prove unwilling to tax themselves and their friends to provide it. Up to this stage, their solution has been to demand more and more aid from Britain, but you cannot be a big boy and remain tied to your mother's apron strings.

The shaky little half-government of Gibraltar, in 1950, inherited three main sources of revenue. To my mind, they were all dubious expedients, unfortunate in outcome. The main contribution came from import duties, applied and increased in the past in the face of fierce opposition. Since these were almost all collected on the stuff of contraband they had the effect of giving the Government a vested interest in smuggling. They had the side effect of leaving the Colony's economy at the mercy of neighbouring nations. Should any of the victim countries decide to tighten its fiscal defences, the tobacco, whisky and so forth would pile up in the warehouses of Gibraltar until the merchants ceased to bring it there. That is what ultimately happened, in 1964.

At this date there was no income tax at all in Gibraltar, a fact which seems incredible in the modern world. Income tax is widely agreed to be the fairest of all forms of taxation. There is even a good biblical godfather for it, as 'the first fruits of every man, as God hath prospered him'. The only strong criticism of it is that it is a tax on ability and energy, and the answer to that is that it is not profitable nor practicable to tax incompetence or sloth. If income tax is ever unfair it is unfair to the salaried man as distinct from the self-employed or the man who lives by independent ownership. The salaried man cannot avoid or evade the tax and must pay it promptly and fully. The previous forms of government in Gibraltar—and even this new one in 1950—were dominated by salaried officials, including the Governor himself. Perhaps for this reason, and also for the widespread protest which income tax would be sure to evoke in a place which had never suffered it, the Government had laid it aside. In its place they proposed a Trades Tax, a tax on business profits.

The short-lived Trades Tax infuriated the merchants of Gibraltar. The brasher among them attacked it frontally, raising the old cry that they would never have come here and given The Rock the benefit of their business but for the fact that it was a tax haven. This might have made some sense in the old days of wars and hardships, but now, with hundreds of the rich and retired knocking on the gates for right of residence—tax-free, sunny, scenic residence—it made no sense at all. A couple of centuries tax free is as much as any businessman can claim. The main attack, from the leaders of the *millonarios*, was oblique and peculiarly Gibraltarian. They did not mind, they claimed, paying taxes like every other modern man in the world. It was just this one that they found objectionable, for the civil servants, (on their lips, almost a term of abuse), would be permitted to pry into their business affairs.

In the face of furious outcry, then, this Trades Tax had been imposed and briefly collected. The third important source of revenue was less direct, more subtle, and strangely popular.

The Gibraltar Government Lottery, instituted at the end of 1947, was a great success from the start. By 1964 the net profit from it, after paying out the expenses of printing, administration, and widespread and generous prize money, was about £150,000. That is to say that it taxed the adult population of The Rock to the tune of about £20 per head. But what a fine way of raising the wind a public lottery appears to be! Fun, excitement, anticipation are thrown in free; Lady Luck alights once a week with £3,000 for her chosen citizen, £1,250 for another, £50 for many. Hundreds more get their money back, a tax-free week for them. There is no pressure to lay out more than you can afford, nor to gamble at all if you disapprove of it—or of the Government! What objections, you may ask, can there be to a state lottery? Why does not every country in the world have one, and let its people pay their taxes with a smile?

The sad fact is that a state lottery is a deeply immoral device for raising revenue. It raises it unfairly and from the wrong source. The greatest gamblers, everywhere, are the poor. It is in the under-privileged segments of society that one finds financial frustration, ignorance and improvidence, all the potent factors in the gambling urge. The more fortunate people do not need pie-in-the-sky, pipe dreams about wealth and ease; they either have them already or they can see their way to them. The well educated are not so foolish as to put their money to hazard, except strictly within their means.

I was responsible for some years for the mechanics of the Gibraltar Lottery, and I attended, on duty, every Saturday draw. It was, like all other Government activities there, fair and straight—within its terms. As a gamble it was generous, offering better odds than football pools or horse-race bets. Yet it robbed the poor, and the fact that they chose to be robbed does not, to my mind, justify it.

I have no moral objection to gambling. For me, the last word on the subject was said by the great Dr. Johnson in the eighteenth century. He said it was not wrong, but merely unprofitable, since money changed hands without producing goods or benefit. My objection was to the practice of the responsible authorities promoting gambling, recommending it to ignorant people.

I used to pay one shilling a week for one-tenth of a ticket, to co-operate with my staff who clubbed up for one, and to give myself an interest in the long draw which I had to witness. One of my labourers, and friends, lottery mad because he knew a man who had won a large prize, spent ten shillings each week on a whole ticket. Since I earned eight times as much as he did, I reckoned that his contribution to the funds was, proportionately, eighty times as much as mine. I also reckoned that it was because of this contribution, multiplied many thousands of times, that I had no income tax to pay. My friend, on the other hand, lived out his life in crushing debt, hounded and exploited by the abundant money-lenders, at the pin of his collar to keep his children fed. Over his destitute but hopeful head, as he stood and watched the bright balls spewing out of the state gambling machine, waved the Government's banner— 'Invest in the Gibraltar Lottery!'

You get rich quick, or you get poor slowly. The twenty thousand one-ticket supporters of the lottery were what are rudely called, in racetrack parlance, 'the mugs'. There were, here as elsewhere, the professional punters, men of means who would buy fifty tickets more easily than my labourer could buy one. Very naturally, the prizes usually fell to such men. Later, when income tax was introduced, any sudden access of obvious wealth could be ascribed to a win in the lottery, which was tax-free. 'To him that hath shall be given' is a precept well honoured on The Rock for two and a half centuries.

When the Government of Gibraltar, in 1953, dropped the Trades Tax and imposed an Income Tax in its place, there was some grumbling but no strong opposition. Many potential tax-payers had disarmed themselves by declaring that the Trades Tax was the only one they would reject. Others had enough sense to see that to howl out against taxation, as heretofore, might draw down the attention of the British Government and its hard-wrought tax-payers to their sunny tax haven. The tax was a small fraction of British income tax, and the lowest in the British Commonwealth. The shrewd man, and he is not in short supply in Gibraltar, was thankful for small mercies.

'*Hay que pagar algo para los monos,*' a small businessman shrugged at me, on paying his income tax for the first time. He had in mind the old saw that whilst the apes remain on The Rock, so will the British; hence, he thought, one has to pay something for the apes— that is, to remain British. He did not like it, but he paid it, which is, I suppose, the attitude which most of us have to taxation.

By 1955 the Government's expenditure was increasing rapidly. There was heavy pressure for acceleration in the provision of public housing, for many families had grown up, over ten years, in the rusting and rotting Nissen huts. Education, so long neglected, was beginning to make strong demands. Added to these, there was the urgent need for improvements in amenity, for Gibraltar was in transition from a fortress with tourists to a tourist centre with fortifications. As the army and navy withdrew, Gibraltar discovered and appreciated for the first time, that the community had been very largely sustained by military expenditure and employment. That income, all of it provided by the United Kingdom tax-payer, had to be replaced. The Rock, immemorially designed for repulsion, had to make itself attractive.

In July 1955 the Government proposed an *ad valorem* import duty of ten per cent on a few specific luxury articles—automobiles, cameras, watches, lighters—and on one apparent necessity, razor blades. To avoid speculation the proposal had to be submitted suddenly to the Legislative Council, without pre-publication as a bill. It had, one presumes, already been discussed in secrecy in the Executive Council, where the officials and nominees were certain to carry the proposal. The elected men in the Executive Council, there on the Governor's invitation and not as of right, were enabled to make their plans, but prohibited from a premature outcry.

When the matter was put to the Legislative Council in public, the Financial Secretary faced loud complaints that there had been no prior discussion. This was, therefore, dictatorship! No taxation without representation! Free Port! What did Queen Anne promise?

The Government side pointed out that this was standard budget procedure, and necessary, and that the House could discuss the proposal there and then. But the protagonists of this sensible viewpoint, being civil servants and lacking practice in political polemics, failed to carry the debate. The vote, such was the constitution of the Council at that time, resulted in a deadlock, with the officials and yes-men for the proposal and the same number of elected, members —five—unanimously against it. The Governor, cavalry general Sir Harold Redman, promptly and properly cast his presidential vote for the measure, using his constitutional powers to pass it into law.

The immediate result of this was the resignation of all the elected members from the Legislative and Executive Councils. They resigned on the ostensible grounds that the Governor's action was undemocratic, disrespectful to the Council, to the People's representatives, hence to the People of Gibraltar. They went on, some of them, to say that to increase the price of those articles of commerce, all of them goods of high turnover, was to ruin the economy of Gibraltar. They even said, some of them, that to tax razor blades was to attack self-respect and to penalize the poor man, whose beard was as tough as, or tougher than, that of the rich.

As I saw it, all these arguments were specious ones. The Governor, as everyone knew perfectly well, had acted within his powers—powers given to him to meet just such an emergency. To postpone the imposition of the tax once it had been mooted would, as everyone knew, result in a hurricane of speculation and profiteering. To increase the price of, say, a Rolleiflex camera from £50 to £55 would, as everyone knew, have very little effect on its sales, since its price in taxed countries was about £100. Tourists would not be aware that watches had once been a little cheaper, nor would they care. The duty was no hardship at all, for the merchants would simply pass it on to the purchasers, the vast majority of whom would be visitors to The Rock.

'But what about the razor blades?' I asked a Treasury official at this time. 'By touching those, surely, you gave the opposition a stick to beat you with?'

'Something you don't know,' he told me. 'Gibraltar imports and sells enough razor blades to shave half the population of Spain.'

It was a sad sight to see the newly elected democrats, led by Joshua Hassan and his AACR henchmen, withdrawing from public duty on such a meretricious case. The facade of the protest was not improved by the fact that one of his closest colleagues in the AACR representation was a leading merchant in cameras and watches. Yet the results of this questionable defection were amazingly successful.

Mr. Lennox Boyd, as he then was, the Secretary of State for the Colonies, flew out from London, scolded and conciliated all those concerned, and reduced the tax from the proposed and necessary ten per cent to eight and one-third per cent. The members were completely mollified by this reduction, which seems to indicate that, in spite of all the declarations of principle and invocations of Magna Carta, money was doing most of the talking. They stood for re-election and were all returned unopposed, which proves that, rightly or wrongly, the people of Gibraltar approved of their action.

But what the people voted for was the twisting of the lion's tail. They did not stop to think—they were not encouraged to do so—of the economics of the matter. The affair cost them, the majority of humble people who are the recipients and beneficiaries of public disbursements, a one-and-two-thirds per cent cut on the vast luxury trade of Gibraltar. The sale of these luxuries, predictably, languished not at all. More and more visitors kept coming as prosperity spread and grew elsewhere, and bought watches and cameras 'duty free'. It never seems to occur to anyone that duty must be paid when the plunder of The Rock is carried home to Britain or America. The luxuries of Gibraltar are duty free—or nearly so—to the residents only. The Gibraltarian purchasers of new cars and cameras, the few, saved one-and-two-thirds per cent on the deal; and that is just what the majority, those outside the class of luxury buyers, lost. The AACR representatives had, for the first time, sold out on their supporters. Or, possibly, to be fair, the long frustrated people felt that it was worth the money to knock the General and his gentlemen into a cocked hat.

From that day onwards the elected members of the Gibraltar legislature knew that they could do whatsoever they liked, and that all their demands would be met by Britain. Succeeding Governors, and their civil servants, must have realized that they were, in the last resort, helpless. The only thing to do was to drift with the main stream. Not long afterwards, almost as a reward for their irresponsible actions, the politicians were granted a majority on the Legislative Council, with seven elected members against five Government appointees. The main power remained with the Executive Council, but the leading representatives were there, too, and now as of right. Although they were in a minority on Exco, numerically speaking, their voice, as they well knew, was as strong as that of Her Majesty's Secretary of State for the Colonies. They did not fail to use it.

At this time the newly powerful politicians were delegated something of ministerial power. They were designated 'Member associated with So-and-So', but the Spanish-speaking citizens, impatient of English double-talk, bluntly called them *'Ministro'*. Without any real responsibility, for the professional Head of Department remained responsible for the execution of the work and answerable for the financial votes, they were enabled and encouraged to sit in, supervise, and interfere with the work of the civil service. Utterly inexperienced as they were, and given the Gibraltarian attitude to public service, they were, at best a nuisance and a brake, at worst, a spanner in the works. Immediately, discipline was put in jeopardy. If a junior defaulted and was reprimanded or dismissed, he would go straight to his *'Ministro'*. Since the plaintiff was a voter, the Head of Department might be asked—or told—to reconsider the case. If reinstated, the employee was, of course, a great deal worse than useless.

A typical case of the period concerns a perambulating politician passing through a mean street in the traditional baby-kissing mood. He hailed a woman at her door, the wife of one of his known supporters. He praised a child she had with her, and then it occurred to him that the child should be at school. When he asked her if it was well, she told him that she had made frequent applications to get it into school, but that 'They' had no place for it.

Back in his office, the politician telephoned the Director of Education, an Englishman, and complained to him about the case. The Director investigated it, and soon found that the woman had not only never made any application to enter her child in school, but that she had been prosecuted previously for withholding an older child. He called the politician and told him.

'Dear me, what are you going to do now?' asked the politician.

'I'm going to prosecute her again,' said the Director. 'There's far too much of this in Gibraltar.'

'Oh, I wouldn't do that!' said the legislator, alarmed.

'I have to do it,' said the Director. 'Now that it has been brought to my notice it is my duty under the Law.'

'As a favour to me, don't do it,' said the politician, who could see himself losing all the votes in the street as a '*chivato*', or informer, the most hated man in the community.

'I have to do it,' said the Director.

'Very well,' said the politician, lowering his voice, 'but if you do so, you may expect to find things sticky in some other way.'

The Director, a bold man and due for retirement, did his duty in this case, but not every Head of Department would have had his strength of position or of character.

I myself had to intervene in three cases, at the risk of my post and promotion, to protect junior civil servants against political pressure and discrimination. It would be invidious to detail these cases here, and they are not so much different from the one I have described.

England and her instructed agents had two good reasons—possibly three—for letting the new politicians have their head.

In 1954 the Queen visited Gibraltar on her Coronation Tour. Once the visit was announced, the Spanish Government protested strongly, but to accede to their wishes and exclude the Queen would have been tantamount to admitting that they had some sovereignty over The Rock. The Queen came, and her visit inevitably irritated the Spanish situation. She came for the reason which I have just given, and for other reasons even stronger. The royal yacht *Britannia* brought her past Kenya, threatened with insurrection, past Aden, reckoned to be dangerous, past Cyprus, known to be perilous, and past Malta, highly disaffected. Gibraltar was her only possible and peaceful port of call in several thousands of miles. It was the only place in the whole of the Mediterranean where the old *Pax Britannica* still survived, and the British Government were fully determined that it should be placated at all costs, and remain a contented and exemplary colony.

The attitudes of the United Nations, with a growing membership of ex-colonies, brought strong pressure to bear on Britain, as on all other colonial powers, to speed the self-government and self-determination of remaining dependencies. They pursued this end without rhyme or reason, so that only Britain and four other countries had voted against a proposal that all colonies should be granted self-government forthwith and regardless of consequences.

An uncle of mine and my father, both long dead, once went hunting in a remote part of Ireland and shot and wounded a wild cat. The cat took refuge in some gorse and turned at bay. My uncle, less circumspect, was encouraged by my father to go in after the animal. Squeals of rage and screams of pain soon emanated from the bushes. 'Shall I come in and help you to hold her?' my father shouted. 'No,' yelled my uncle. 'Come in and help me to let her go'!

The possible third reason for the British attitude to Gibraltar at this time is my guess, only. I suspect that, once the value of Gibraltar as a military and naval base was obviously diminished and headed towards its end, the British reassessed the place in search of other values. What they found there was a liability—they were subsidizing it heavily—and an embarrassment, for the smuggling and the minor naval incidents went on unabated. In view of these two factors the British Government, importuned, beleaguered, embarrassed and milked at many parts of the world, was glad to see Gibraltar hurrying towards self-government. Like my uncle and the wild cat, Britain seeks no aid to hold hot colonies.

Well, we had been warned. It was exactly a century earlier that the merchants said: 'The taxation of Gibraltar is a subject of great delicacy,' and went on to hint that, if they were not consulted on it, then they would oppose it. They, and their dupes or henchmen of the AACR, did no more than they promised. They won far more than they expected. They won more than a one-and-two-thirds per cent reduction in taxation; they were awarded a strong pat on the back, as well, which accelerated them sharply towards full responsibility for their own affairs.

We were also warned, by many precedents elsewhere, that a legislature with an elected majority is sure to clash fast and frequently with an unrepresentative executive.

At this point I might be asked—What about the U.S.A.? The President's immediate executive consists of nominated officials of his own choice. They do not, however, claim free seats in the legislature, and I imagine that they would get very short shrift if they did so. They face considerable suspicion and criticism as it is.

Then what of Great Britain herself? There the Cabinet—analogous to an Executive Council—is composed of members of the legislature. But they are, one and all, elected, and thus answerable not only to the House, but ultimately to the People.

The untenable and indefensible qualities of this stage of colonial development lie in the fact that the Governor and his gentlemen face no electorate, but remain in office, whatever their incompetence or unpopularity, 'during the Queen's pleasure'. The will of the People, newly recognized, respected and encouraged in public, may be frustrated in private by men who represent only the distant Crown, and that may be a very temporary Secretary of State taking time off from his family business to get himself a peerage.

This anomalous situation is usually worsened by the contrast between the opposing forces. On the one hand, the People's compatriots and chosen representatives, by now politicians of some experience, professional conciliators of viewpoints, shrewd and articulate manipulators of public opinion and, in a small place like Gibraltar, intimately approachable by every citizen. On the other hand, remote, austere and 'foreign' placemen, well paid out of public funds, secure, safe and unapproachable, and utterly unpractised in the political arts and their expression.

In twenty years in the British public service, at home and abroad, I met many a classified administrator who disdained such fancy subjects as economics, sociology and political science, and took permanent pride in his arts degree in forgotten Latin, lost Greek and Middle English. In recent years the would-be administrator took a short course after he had taken his degree—a scrap of law, a dash of sanitation, a glance, perhaps, at some colonial language, and a scamper over the Rules and Regulations. Up to recently, and still, perhaps, the real test was a country house week-end under the tutelage of a senior 'administrator'. The object of this was to ensure that the candidate could eat, converse and comport himself like an old-style English gentleman. Where folklore might have helped them, they devoted their studies to forklore—a branch of learning which sensible people take for granted.

'They did very well, considering . . .' says Dame Margery Perham, in effect, in her *Colonial Reckoning*. But how much better they—and Great Britain—might have done had they been compelled to make some small study of the subject in hand? This we shall never know.

Such was the confrontation, then, here as elsewhere. It could not last for long. Gibraltar accelerated down the slippery slope towards full, internal self-government.

24

OUT OF THE FRYING-PAN

'Britain is proud and happy that Gibraltar should wish to continue an association which has lasted over 250 years,' said Mr. Duncan Sandys, Secretary of State for Commonwealth Affairs. He put this in a letter which, in July 1964, conveyed the Instruments of State which granted Gibraltar's present—and controversial—constitutional position, a form of internal self-government.

As is so often the case with these resounding pronouncements of statesmanship, this one defies exact interpretation. It can hardly be that Mr. Sandys meant The Rock itself, when he used the name 'Gibraltar'. If, by 'Gibraltar' he meant the community, he should have known that it simply was not there 250 years ago, but grew slowly since then. Its association with Britain, up to very recent times, had been that of servant to master, and since the early immigrants had been driven there by fear or necessity, scarcely a matter of choice.

But the Gibraltarians so addressed were in no mood to look a gift horse in the mouth. The new Constitution was, at first glance, a great advance, a concession, a compliment and a privilege. It prescribed a Legislative Council of eleven elected members, completed by two senior civil servants who would sit as Officers of the House and support the Government majority. There would be a Chief Minister, who would be Leader of the House, vested with responsibility for the direction of Government business. He would appoint, from his majority of members, Ministers to control and answer for the various departments of Government, and to sit in a Council of Ministers.

'While the Governor in Council', quotes the *Gibraltar Chronicle*, 'will be free to refer to the Council of Ministers any matter on which its advice is desired, matters within the responsibility of Ministers will normally come direct to the Council of Ministers without such reference, and its recommendations on matters of purely domestic concern will, as a general rule, be endorsed by the Governor in Council'.

The Governor in what Council? His own, private, picked Executive Council—the mixture as before. But is a Council of Ministers not tantamount to a Cabinet? It is, and in Great Britain, by slow evolution, the Cabinet came to be the governing body of the State. But there is another council, even there, and one which, in theory, is senior to the Cabinet. It is called Her Majesty's Privy Council, and its members may or may not be the elected representatives of the people. They are, on the face of it, chosen by the monarch, who may personally preside over their deliberations when—and if—she seeks their advice. It seems unlikely, almost unthinkable, that in modern Britain the Privy Council would attempt to overrule the Cabinet, but it *might* do so, constitutionally. The Cabinet has no long history, nor stated rights, nor written constitutional status; the Privy Council has all these and more besides—it is a development of the monarchy, of sovereignty itself, without which there is, in Great Britain, no authority over the people.

In an emergent colony, as here in Gibraltar, this ancient pattern is followed, and no one can object. If the British at home—those of them who know of it—will put up with a Privy Council, then the Gibraltarians have no complaints. That is the way it is done, and they know of no other way. But there is a certain difference between the systems at home and abroad. Her Majesty the Queen's Privy Council may be a harmless, picturesque, and apparently ineffective survival, its duties confined by custom to legalities and ceremonies. His Excellency the Governor's Executive Council is, as heretofore, and as its name implies, an effective if not an omnipotent force in the direction of all public affairs. With its name changed from Executive Council to 'The Council of Gibraltar' to give it a new image, it presently comprises:

The Governor	
The Deputy Fortress Commander	Five Elected
The Permanent Secretary	Members of the
The Attorney General	Legislative Council
The Financial Secretary	

The members on the left of my line are all officials, appointed and not elected. It is noteworthy how far, in the matter of majority, this inner and secret and ultimate council lags behind the public and window-dressed Legislative Council.

The Council of Ministers is junior and subsidiary to the Council of Gibraltar, which is, in fact, the Government. The 'Government', as the simpler citizens call it, in the Legislative Council can only make representations to the Council of Gibraltar, and hope for its approval. The Governor—let us add, in parentheses, (in Council),— retains the real power, reserved until he considers it necessary or desirable to use it. His is the overriding authority in Gibraltar under the new—the present—constitution. All that has been granted to the citizens, in cold reality, is the right to debate their local business— and local business only—freely among themselves, and pass their decisions up to the Governor in Council for approval. What happens to their ideas may for ever remain obscure, for the upper Council, unlike the Legislative, is not conducted in public.

In theatrical terms, which are helpful in this context, because they compare the importance of various elements by using letters of different sizes, the credits for legislative achievements might be stated thus:

BY ROYAL WARRANT

HIS EXCELLENCY THE GOVERNOR

AND COMMANDER IN CHIEF

WITH

HIS EXECUTIVE COUNCIL

AS

FULL SUPPORTING CAST

in a charade entitled

"THE STRAY DOGS ORDINANCE"

BY

HIS HONOUR THE ATTORNEY-GENERAL

ADVISED BY

HIS HONOUR THE FINANCIAL SECRETARY

PRODUCED AND DIRECTED BY

HIS HONOUR THE PERMANENT SECRETARY

BASED ON AN IDEA BY

THE ELECTED LEGISLATIVE COUNCIL

REPRESENTING THE PEOPLE OF GIBRALTAR

GOD SAVE THE QUEEN

It should be mentioned that the Chief Minister and such of his henchmen as the Governor, or the Westminster authority, chooses, will be in the Executive Council, and therefore in the cast of this charade. But they are not in there, behind those guarded doors, as the direct representatives of the people who elected them, and they are not answerable to anyone but the Governor for such advice as they privately offer him. They could, in fact, put or agree to views diametrically opposed to those which they have previously expounded in the public forum. They will certainly trim their views to suit the environment.

The chief character actor in the play is our old friend the chief civil servant—sometime called Colonial Secretary, later, Chief Secretary, now at last, Permanent Secretary. In case this last tame title may appear to relegate him to the cautious anonymity of the Civil Service, as it would do in Britain and elsewhere, it is laid down in the new Instruments, or in Mr. Sandys's instructions which accompanied them, that the Permanent Secretary is 'designated to perform the functions of the office of Governor in the absence or incapacity of the Governor'. That is to say, he is to be, in effect, civil governor or deputy governor, and that this civil servant—and not, as you might expect, the Chief Minister—is second-in-command of Gibraltar. In the not impossible case of a Governor who recognizes his own chronic incapacity in civil affairs, the Permanent Secretary could become not only the power behind the throne, but the effective ruler of the community.

Just in case the Council of Ministers should try to turn themselves into a Cabinet, to deliberate in private and, perhaps, in opposition to the real Government, it is laid down that 'The agenda and minutes of all meetings of the Council will be sent to the Permanent Secretary, the Financial Secretary, and the Attorney General'. The elected representatives must tell the civil servants what they are going to talk about and what they said. Not for nothing has the British Cabinet, which passed through some such stage of development long, long ago, dispensed with minutes altogether; a legislator whose private opinions are recorded and forwarded to higher authority is gagged and hamstrung before he starts.

Small as was this advance towards full self-government, it was dressed up to appear impressive. Both sides had their reasons to publicize it, to magnify it into a matter of historical significance. Britain was concerned with her image at the United Nations and in the World, and anxious to publicize yet another colonial concession. The Gibraltarian leaders were proud to progress, and happy in their increased dignity, they forebore to denigrate the concession. In addition, the Gibraltarian delegates to the UNO Committee of Twenty-four, some months before, had been authorized to state that Gibraltar was on 'the eve of self-government'. That statement had to appear to be fulfilled.

There was no public examination of the new constitution. No one seemed to notice that the application of the proverbial checks and balances had been such as to render it all check and no balance. It was received, or swallowed, with reciprocal backslapping and mutual congratulations.

But the people of Gibraltar were to see their birthright endangered in return for this mess of political pottage, for Spain chose to take the new constitution at its proffered face value, as a grant of self-government and a precursor of independence—an independence which would be in direct contravention of the Treaty of Utrecht.

The new 'Government', elected on the 10th September 1965 for a five-year term, was embattled even before it met. When Chief Minister Sir Joshua Hassan took over the reins of domestic administration he took over, with them, the fourteenth siege of Gibraltar, a siege of attrition far more subtly dangerous than any that had gone before. Before describing that, let us look at the new leaders and their possibilities for withstanding this siege.

Sir Joshua Hassan, leader of the broad-based Association for the Advancement of Civil Rights, won the 1964 election with an impressive personal majority, which confirmed him, after twenty years in the hot limelight of his tiny kingdom, as the undisputed leader of the community. Yet there were some signs that the people were beginning to tire of him, for his triumph was not complete.

There were fifteen candidates for election, the six with the AACR label and nine standing as Independents. When the votes were counted Sir Joshua found himself with A. J. Risso, the Labour leader, A. W. Serfaty, architect and wealthy merchant, A. P. Montegriffo, a pious businessman with some political experience, and a pretty newcomer, Mary Chiappe. But, with five seats out of eleven, he had no majority and could not form a Government.

Others elected were Baldorino, representative of those left left; Peter Isola, lawyer and ex-'Ministro' of Education, held in the highest esteem; Sir Peter Russo, a reputed millionaire, hitherto favoured as a nominated member, and standing for his first LegCo election now that nominated members were abolished; the brilliant but, some said, too shrewd Solly Seruya, rich merchant and successful ex-'Ministro' of Tourism; Guy Stagnetto, lawyer, whose name, like Russo's, was redolent of tobacco, a tough and unflappable man; and the ebullient, active, eloquent and handsome Louis Triay, yet another lawyer. This amounted to a political Noah's Ark with no Noah to take the helm, or even to keep order while the ship drifted.

Had these six stalwart Independents been able to compromise sufficiently they would have been able to form a Government and push Hassan into opposition. But it proved impossible; their panel was too wide. Russo, who had described himself—predictably—as 'extreme right wing', and Baldorino, bitter opponent of privilege, could never sail in one boat. Isola and Seruya were both possible leaders, so that neither would readily subjugate himself to the other. Stagnetto and Triay, both of rich families and therefore conservatively inclined, might have jumped on a bandwaggon if one had been forthcoming. But bandwaggon there was none, for it was beyond the ingenuity of man to fit the pieces together—the ill-assorted pieces of six separate do-it-yourself kits.

For six days the elected politicians wavered to and fro, seeking advice and, perhaps, making tentative offers to trim their principles and promises. There was extreme urgency in sorting things out and forming a government, for the ancient and implacable enemy, Spain, was knocking on the gates. The new leaders, once defined, would have an immediate and crucial task before them—to go and put the case for Gibraltar to the Special Committee of UNO, the anti-colonization Committee of Twenty-four, and this had to be done before a certain date. The press and public began to complain, and there was talk of another election. The AACR had the votes and the mandate; the Independents had the seats. It became evident that someone must sacrifice principle, abrogate his recently declared intentions, walk away from his electors and cross the floor of the House. Who was it to be?

Sir Peter Russo was the man. He accepted an offer of the portfolio of Housing and Economic Development, crossed the floor, and joined his old enemy Hassan and, in effect, the ranks of the AACR, the party which, in the past, he had consistently opposed.

A public outcry followed this move. Here was a man elected as an Independent, which is to say, as anti-AACR, immediately kicking his platform to pieces and carrying 'stolen' votes into the enemy camp. The merchants, as *Vox* had pointed out, would do anything and sit with anyone to remain in control of taxation and expenditure, both of which now fell into Russo's already loaded hands!

In an interview with Nancy Vaughan, published in *Vox** a few days before the poll, she had asked Sir Peter Russo:

'Anything in the report that you are AACR biased, even though you stand as an Independent?'

Russo: 'No.'

Vaughan: 'You wouldn't say that a vote for P. G. Russo was a vote for the AACR?'

Russo: 'No.'

At the end of the interview Sir Peter declared: 'I want to be there because I think I can help—but through the straight road. I am stupidly honest, as honest as a human being can be.'

In the subsequent storm of statements and counter-statements, Sir Joshua Hassan, now, thanks to his fellow-knight Russo, the Chief Minister of the Government of Gibraltar, revealed that he had offered a Ministry to Peter Isola as well. Isola, on votes the leading member of the Opposition, as it now became, wisely and properly declined to cross the floor. He suggested a coalition government, in view of the emergency circumstances, but Hassan said that would be impossible. Isola said he had tried to form a government under his own leadership—as indicated by the poll—with the other assorted Independents. Such is his standing that they all agreed, except Sir Peter Russo.

Mr. Isola, who became official Leader of the Opposition, issued a statement on behalf of himself and his deserted colleagues. It details the six days of horse-trading, deal by deal, and concludes:

'On Wednesday Mr. Isola held a further talk with Sir Peter Russo in an endeavour to persuade him to join an Independent government. This appears not to have been acceptable to Sir Peter Russo

* *Vox*, 21st August 1964.

who has now agreed, despite his assurances to the contrary, to serve by himself in an AACR Government.' On the previous Saturday, further to his public assurances, Sir Peter had promised the Independents privately that he would not serve with the AACR.

The statement continues: 'The Independents believe that the electorate by their votes determined that there should be an Independent or Independent-led Government. The wishes of the people have, in our view, been frustrated by the act of a member elected as an Independent.

'In these circumstances it would seem to us that Sir Peter Russo should resign his seat in the Legislative Council and allow the people in a subsequent bye-election to determine the matter. Meanwhile we shall accept the role of Opposition with dignity and responsibility.'*

To face a by-election, after displaying himself as a political contortionist, was the last thing Sir Peter Russo would do. The poorest view of the case is that a government formed by a switch of allegiance, in defiance of the will of the people as expressed at the polls a few days before, is neither democratic, representative, nor even valid. Hence the present 'Government of Gibraltar' should resign and seek re-election or, at least, regurgitate Russo and let the people say what they think of him. But this Government has been embattled since its formation, and its present position is so fraught with difficulty and danger that it has had no time to seek public confirmation. The people can see that, and they too have much more to worry about than the constitutional niceties at the present time.

Ten months after the election, the matter of the Government's mandate had been laid aside. I have reviewed its formation because it will remain in office for another four years, and those will be the most eventful and fateful years in all Gibraltar's stormy history.

The Committee of Twenty-four was sitting in New York and actually waiting for Gibraltar's petitioners to arrive, as promised. The Spanish petitioners were already there, sharpening their knives. Hassan and Isola, fully, officially and hurriedly endorsed as leaders of Gibraltar opinion, had to fly out to UNO within hours of the Government's formation—of Sir Peter Russo's switchover. A few

* *Gibraltar Chronicle*, 18th September 1964.

hours later they were fighting for the very life of the Gibraltar community, and winning for it a form of reprieve.

I have to lead the reader a little further into the devious labyrinth of Gibraltar's politics and personalities. In a country so small, those two concepts are completely inseparable. In the Legislative Council every member carries the voice of, say, sixty M.P.s at Westminster, for the numerical proportions are 630 voices to 11. On this small scale, policies are subordinated to persons, and principles to people.

'There are no politicians in Gibraltar,' a wise political correspondent told me, after he had had talks with the leaders. 'There is not one of them who knows or cares a thing about political theory or science. They are only personaliticians!'

I found that to be fair comment. Of all the Gibraltar politicians there is only one, to the best of my knowledge, who has made a serious and successful study of any subject germane to his public activities—Solomon Seruya the economist—and he, too, in this restricted environment, is forced to be a personalitician.

But the field is, to my mind, none the less interesting and significant. In it one might find answers to such questions as: 'What happens when an undefined and uncommitted "popular front" party drags its right wing so much that it pivots round on it and swerves right?' 'How would our politicians behave if they were completely free from all preconceived ideas and ideals and party labels and traditions?' Recent field research on free-ranging gorillas has discovered more in one year than the previous twenty years of observation of captive specimens. . . .

This hot little political cockpit may demonstrate some important principles. Parish-pump politics are the grassroots of statesmanship. In the U.S.A., in Britain, in the Soviet bloc as well, it all begins at parish council level. From down there a man may work his way up to be Premier or President. In Gibraltar it scarcely rises above parish-pump level, but where else could you find a parish council, eleven men strong, in control of a unique and detached community, economically besieged and facing bankruptcy? That is the precise position in Gibraltar today.

The active democrat, on the wide field offered by nations of normal size, lobbies his colleagues for support, forms blocs of votes, and proceeds to press and carry his point. On the village scale, in Gibraltar, each politician—or personalitician—is a bloc in himself. The most powerful and interesting, and the most truly representative of these, is Sir Joshua Hassan, Chief Minister of Gibraltar and Mayor of the City, sometimes called 'Mr. Gibraltar'.

The Gibraltar Question—whether The Rock remains British or becomes Spanish—will be settled one way or the other within the next few years. Hassan, elected and appointed in September 1964, will be in charge for the next four years. Whatever the settlement, and whatever the events which lead up to it, the voice of Sir Joshua Hassan will speak for the people of Gibraltar. Already known slightly on the stage of world politics for his two competent appearances before the Committee of Twenty-four at the United Nations Organization, Hassan's name may well become a household word in the near future, in Britain, Spain and further afield. From circumstances alone, he will surely acquire the significance of a Mintoff, a Jagan or a Bustamente. The pressures of our times, those of them which bear so heavily on Gibraltar today, will soon thrust his tiny country up into a brief world prominence.

'Self-determination!'

'End Colonialism!'

'Rights of Small Nations!'

'*Arriba España, Una, Grande, Libre!*'

'God Save the Queen!'

'*Viva Franco!*'

These are some of the ideals and slogans which are echoing around the battered Old Rock, and keeping its 25,000 inhabitants in a state of intolerable insecurity and nervous tension, some fitting out their lifeboats, others digging in their heels. Indeed, the greatest of all political issues is in the balance here—Should men be allowed to vote, or not? Just free of one military autocracy, newly enfranchised, are the Gibraltarians to be embraced by another such, surrender their brand-new democracy, and celebrate henceforth as their Liberation Day—as do the cities of Spain—the day they lost the vote?

25

INTO THE FIRE

Over a period of ten years in Gibraltar, as a senior civil servant and sometime acting Head of Department, I came to know Joshua Hassan well. I sat with him, usually under his chairmanship, on various public committees. I have watched him at the hustings, orating in English and Spanish and listened to him in Legislative Council, speaking in a soberer style. In my opinion, he would rate as a clever man anywhere; in Gibraltar, with its limited human resources, he appeared as a genius and a word wizard. Among the simpler citizens he had, indeed, something of the kudos of a witch-doctor. As mayor, he was responsible for the municipal water supply, always a cause of anxiety in Gibraltar. In times of drought, which occur annually there, he used to announce the remaining resources of water to his Council, calling on the citizens for economy. Should the supply fall dangerously low, the city was put to the expense of importing water from abroad. Hassan would wait until the drought had run its course, or had lasted so long that it was likely to break soon. Then, and then only, would he raise the subject in Council, and soon after that, inevitably, the rains came. He was wise enough to make no claims nor promises, and accepted all the awed congratulations with a modest smile.

I had—still have—great admiration for his intelligence, for his fast assimilation of a new subject, and his rapid assessment of an issue. He is one of the few Gibraltarians who speak English well, without errors in grammar or oddities in stress or intonation. At the same time, I would not say he had a full command of the language. Since the scope of his vocabulary does not seem to cover the wide scope of his mind, I came to believe that he wisely confined his speeches to the well-tried words and phrases which, by trial and error, he had long since made his own. The loquaciousness of Spanish shows in the interminable length of his periods and para-graphs. In his last New Year Message, no doubt carefully compiled, and printed in the *Gibraltar Post*, a weekly which provides him with a platform, he said:

'If we are determined, as I am absolutely sure we are, to do whatever is necessary to safeguard our liberty and the way of life which we hold so dear, and of which you gave such manifest proof on the 10th October, on our return from New York, then I am certain that whatever difficulties may lie ahead will be endured with firmness and with the certainty that once again in the long history of Gibraltar its people with the help of Great Britain, will weather the storm and succeed in preserving what we most cherish.'* In his next paragraph he proceeds to say it all over again—whatever it is that he has said. I do not wish to leave the impression that he talks mere double-Dutch or gobbledygook. It is simply that he is pedestrian in speech, so that there is no joy in listening to him. Judged by the highest standards of oratory—those which one wistfully seeks but rarely finds in a political leader—he lacks verbal felicity and boldness, invention and inspiration. In private conversation he sometimes permits himself a shaft of sardonic wit, but his public utterances suffer from the lack of such illumination.

I cannot judge Hassan's command of Spanish. It is not necessarily complete, because Gibraltarians pick up their Spanish—the local dialect of it—casually, and very few of them bother to study the language. But I presume that, since it is his first language, and since his utterances in it are for popular rather than for official consumption, he uses it more dashingly than he does English. I can say that when his curiously high tenor voice rings out with '*Nosotros, el Pueblo de Gibraltar . . .*' a thrill runs down the stiffest English spine and a murmur rumbles through the Latin crowd.

One speaks good English, my Spanish tutor pointed out to me, through tight lips, leaning back in a chair, legs crossed, arms folded. To speak good Spanish, he said, sit on the edge of your chair, lean forward, assume a maniacal expression, raise your voice one octave and as many decibels as you dare, and let those arms fly. The manic-depressive curve of politics in every Spanish-speaking country—from anarchy to dictatorship, fascism to communism—bears witness to the extreme and immediate effectiveness of Spanish as a political language. Joshua Hassan, since his mass following is the Spanish-speaking working class of Gibraltar, makes full use of this hispanic extravagance to win election; once elected and in the Council

* *Gibraltar Post*, 1st January 1965.

Chamber, he has to change down to English, which amounts to a change of personality. It must be like leaving a bullfight to attend a cricket match—I have seen him at both—and it is to his credit that he makes the dramatic transition so well.

So much for how he talks, but the essential quality of a politician lies in what he says. In Hassan's case, this is difficult to define. His overriding policy—and it is one that is shared by all shades of political opinion in Gibraltar—is to keep The Rock British. In the early days of the AACR, the days of struggle, he used to talk about social reform and attack the black spots of housing, wages and education. There was no need then to be constructive, to state long-term aims; the first and obvious objective was the urgent repair of the social conditions of a community long neglected.

As time went on, as Hassan and his AACR consolidated themselves as the almost undisputed leading faction, and as he gradually acquired more and more power, he moderated his statements. Faced with responsibility—and this is the pattern of politics everywhere—he spoke less and less of reform, dropped the attack and assumed the defensive. By 1960 *Vox* was roundly accusing him of moving to the right and supporting the economic policies of Big Business. When pressed by his Labour supporters, or by such Liberal opposition as existed, to speak out in favour of the workers, he frequently warned them not 'to foment class hatred', a derivative and captured phrase which sounded good but meant very little. There was not—never has been—any communist party in Gibraltar; as staunch and obedient Catholics the people would not even commit themselves to democratic socialism, 'the thin edge of the wedge'. There was no danger whatsoever of violent or dangerous class hatred in the place, and even the vilest living conditions and the worst of exploitation never caused more than an orderly strike or a respectful demonstration.

Hassan is far too intelligent to be unaware that poverty, even if suffered in silence, is the ideal forcing bed for class hatred, and that the poverty of the people—in wages, homes and schools—was the creation of the untaxed and untaxable merchant princes of the place, as much as of the amateur imported administrators.

As Chief Member, up to the 1964 election which made him Chief Minister, Joshua Hassan was in constant daily association with P. G. Russo, then a senior nominated member of LegCo and ExCo, and presumed to be the representative of the merchant interest. Both of them, naturally enough, were in close association with the then Chief Secretary. The Chief Secretary, representing Governor and Government and, for that matter, Westminster too, could keep the peace whilst he kept this ill-matched pair—the capitalist and the popular leader—under one yoke. The right horse would pull for privilege and to protect his stores of fodder; the left horse would pull for the pure joy of feeling his power and, maybe, of being yoked in such noble company. But what was the yoke that held this spirited pair so docile and so diligent? After some years of joint labour, on the recommendation of the Chief Secretary, they were both knighted.

Now I have given the impression that the official side held full control of the situation. But, here as everywhere, political motivations are complex. There is no doubt that the official side tacitly held out the strong inducement of honours, but it, too, was under duress. The defeat of the Governor over the ten per cent import duty, following the visit, cap-in-hand, of the Secretary of State, and the resulting compensatory constitutional advance, had given fair warning that Great Britain would do anything, or leave anything undone, rather than expose herself to international opprobrium as a colonial bully. That Governor and his successors, and their subordinate officers, must have had clear instructions that the Gibraltarians must be kept happy.

It would not serve this policy of Peace-at-any-price to placate one side and infuriate the other. Hassan had an overwhelming majority of votes, but the merchant group, represented by Russo, had proved its power and influence long ago and several times. During the 1950s the government of Britain was in the hands of the conservative party, traditional conservers and protectors of wealth and privilege. A colonial governor must, above all, keep the peace, and if he can do so by keeping an extreme Tory in harness with a retreating radical, then he is achieving his highest function. Besides, such caucus coalitions can be very effective.

The change from fortress to tourist resort was very largely guided and prodded by the Government, for the Gibraltarians, in this matter as in other matters of enterprise, were inclined to hang back and keep their hand on their ha'penny.

There was considerable progress in Gibraltar, both social and commercial, during this transition period, 1950 to 1964, and the officials, with Hassan, Russo, and *'Ministro de Turismo'* Seruya, may share the credit for it. But there was nothing like the progress that there might have been, and the major challenges to the Government were either ignored or, at best, tackled in a half-hearted manner.

Port Development was one such challenge. Fraught with the vested interests of *Los Millonarios*, it was emasculated to suit them, and has never produced the promised and expected results. The vast majority of freight and passenger ships calling at Gibraltar had always stood off and anchored out in The Bay, to be serviced by tugs, ferries and lighters. There were a few berths within the great naval harbour available to regular callers, but matters were so arranged that goods unloaded there had to be reloaded into lighters, towed a long distance round to the Commercial Wharf and unloaded for the second time. Such a system was obviously inefficient and, indeed, quite indefensible, the more so because a few individuals, the owners of the tugs and lighters, made high profits from it. A handful of families—Thompson, Imossi and Gaggero—had inherited what amounted to a stranglehold on the imports and exports of the whole community, by means as legitimate as those of The Bay Street Boys of the Bahamas, but none the less unfortunate. By early investment in tugs, tenders and barges, all so costly today that no one else could enter the field to compete, these three or four long-founded family firms were—and still are—able to levy a tribute on everything that enters or leaves the port. The importers pass it on to the consumer, and it is felt most on cheap goods. Luxury goods absorb the cost of such imposts; sixpence on the price of a camera is nothing, but twopence on a packet of cornflakes is a heavy duty. The net effect of the Gibraltar Docks system is that *Los Millonarios*, almost untaxed themselves, are collecting a tax on the food of the community. At the same time, as employers of labour, they are to the fore in opposing wages increases.

In defence of their position the beneficiaries claim that there are handling charges everywhere, that they are providing a public service, that they are entitled to a return on capital invested, that their charges are not unduly high, and that private rights must be respected.

The answers—far better known to the Government than to me—are as follows. The handling charges were in fact, ridiculously high—there was nothing to prevent their being so. It cost, for instance, about £25 to carry an automobile out to a ship, a charge which must have had some inhibiting effect on Gibraltar's tourist trade. As for the investment, a glance at the ships and gear proved them old and obsolete in the main, which was, no doubt, a factor in the high operating costs and consequent charges. As for the just return on investment, none of the firms concerned seemed to publish their profits, but the great wealth of their owners was flaunted in Rolls Royces and country estates in Spain.

In failing to meet the challenge to rationalize the port the Government showed either a lack of moral courage or, worse, a subservience to the private interests of the few, who would then be, in effect, the true rulers of Gibraltar. The history of the place as I have written it shows good reason for either or both of these fatal weaknesses. The sad fact about the administration of the port of Gibraltar is that whilst legitimate trade suffered discouragement, the illegitimate trade was put to no difficulty at all. The smuggling launches used to tie up and load at the town end of the harbour, in full view of passing tourists; when, about six years ago, the Admiralty released part of its idle harbour to the civil authorities, the smugglers were the first to be given new berths, far up the mole and out of sight of the general public.

The Government showed a further lack of courage, or subservience to private interests, in failing to increase income tax to a realistic level. With rich revenues lying untapped, the Government spent most of its time pleading poverty. Its Civil Service was the worst paid in the Commonwealth, with the result that valuable people—particularly schoolteachers—were constantly leaving it, to be replaced, one must presume, with others less qualified and experienced. School building proceeded at snail's pace. The hospital service was run on a shoe string so that many patients would not eat the food provided. Private patients were, still are, forced to pay, no matter how ill they are, before they receive treatment.

Government economy in Gibraltar is insensate and descends to ludicrous levels. When a good colleague of mine fell off his Government motor-cycle in the execution of his duties, and tore his trousers, he claimed the modest sum of fifty shillings for a new pair. After much delay and debate he was awarded thirty shillings, the reduction being made on the grounds that the ruined trousers had been part worn. The decline in the quality of his service after that insult could have cost the Government many thousands of pounds.

In the provision of public housing, which was given priority over all other expenditures because of its high political potential, the position was, roughly, that either (*a*) the ordinary man could not have a house because the Government 'could not afford it', or (*b*) that if he must have one, then the United Kingdom tax-payer must pay for it. Fortunately, consciously or unconsciously, the U.K. tax-payer did pay for it. Thus the rich Gibraltarians kept their potential income tax in their pockets.

Governors come and go; in my ten years on The Rock I served under four of them, and they were only distinguishable by their physical differences. Chief Secretaries, whatever they are from time to time entitled, are civil servants, and as such can disown responsibility for policy. Until last year's election, Sir Peter Russo was a nominee of Governors, and might be held to have reflected and expressed the views of his nominators. The continuous guidance of Gibraltar's affairs throughout those fourteen fateful years would appear to have been very largely in the able hands of Hassan. How does he emerge from this long test of leadership?

My answer must be, neither well nor badly. There was a King Hassan on each side of The Straits, one in Morocco and one in Gibraltar. King Hassan of Morocco, by one means or another, threw the money-changers out of his temple and the notorious smuggling trade out of Tangier. King Hassan of Gibraltar permitted that trade to be harboured in his kingdom.

But there are essential differences between the two kings. The Moroccan was empowered absolutely by his inheritance and his religion; the Gibraltarian had neither to aid him. Democracy is King Hassan's plaything; Joshua Hassan is the plaything of democracy. In Gibraltar, his tiny, personalized parish, he could either trim his sails to every puff of politics or else sink into oblivion, with twenty wasted years to rue. He chose to trim. The first duty of a politician, in his own view, at any rate, is to stay in politics. To do that he cannot be much better than the people he represents, otherwise he would not represent them for long.

'Not many years ago,' says the Gibraltar paper *Vox*, 'the London *Daily Telegraph* quoted Mr. J. A. Hassan, (as he then was), defining himself as a Liberal politically, but in Britain probably a Conservative. A few years later the *New Yorker* quoted the same Mr. Hassan . . . defining himself as a Liberal in politics and a Socialist in economics.'

'It is well for our Chief Minister', *Vox* comments, 'that he does not live in Britain, where, presumably, he would spoil his ballot paper at every election by voting for all three candidates.'*

But it only amounts to being a good democrat. Hassan waits, as he is doing in the present crisis, to find out what the people of Gibraltar are about to say—and then he smartly says it for them. He is 'outer-directed', and fairly and fully represents the ideals and aims of most Gibraltarians. These aims are—here as in most human communities—

(1) to stay alive and in business

(2) to get rich and be happy, and

(3) to remain both.

Like his people, Hassan has no fixed, overall pattern to his politics, except to remain British, which in Gibraltar means to remain protected, aided, privileged and untaxed. 'The poor think he is a friend of the poor,' as was said of an American President, 'the rich know he is not.' Leaders of great nations may achieve a pinnacle of aloofness, and take their instructions, as Moses did, directly from God. But the leader of Gibraltar is up to the neck in clamouring humanity every hour of his day, and he would be superhuman if he could ignore it and retain its vital support.

All that I have said applies to mere politicians, a role to which any man may aspire. The private aim of politicians, as they writhe and twist to suit the pressures and fashions and whims of the moment, is to ascend to statesmanship, and in that lofty realm to act with fearless intellectual honesty. Few of them reach those heights, and when they do they are sure to find that the means has vitiated the end. The Perfect Politician arrives at his full powers with his ideals sapped by their years of suppression and dissipation, his position

* *Vox*, 22nd May 1964.

suborned by the promises and compromises which we—his constituents—have forced upon him.

Sir Joshua Hassan can never rise to greatness, but he is as good a man as little Gibraltar is ever likely to find. If he fails in the crucial tests which lie before him he may find comfort in the thought that any other Gibraltarian would have failed more certainly and sooner.

26

CONTRABAND CONTINUED

From *Vox* (Gibraltar), October 1960:

'The 57 ton British motor launch *Alamoana*, registered in Gibraltar and owned by Mrs. Esther Mellul of Tangier, sailed from our port on Monday night after having been cleared by her agents . . . with six tons of cigarettes, whiskey and nylon, manifested to the vessel's destination, Bordeaux. . . .

'Shortly after leaving Gibraltar, at approximately 1 a.m., and when one and a half miles off Europa Point, the *Alamoana* was ambushed by the armed launch *Vega*, a Spanish patrol launch which is based on Ceuta. The *Vega*, believed to be the ex-M.V. *Express*, a British vessel previously seized by the Spanish Authorities, was without lights and appeared to be marauding in the area.

'Without the slightest warning, with no sort of indication whatsoever, the *Vega* machine-gunned with explosive rounds the defenceless *Alamoana* and continued her merciless attack for nearly an hour. A passenger aboard, Mr. Melgar Tallez, was shot dead, whilst Captain Rouse received bullets in both legs, and deckhand Gonzalez Martin was seriously wounded in the abdomen.'

Vox headed its report 'THE BAY MURDER', with a sub-headline 'Unprotected British vessel attacked by Spanish Armed Launch in British waters'. The verb 'to maraud' which they used, means, according to the Oxford Dictionary, 'to make a plundering raid' or 'to go about pilfering', and seems a curious term to apply to official preventive officers. The press and public of Gibraltar were somewhat incensed by the report, and called for some action on the part of their Government or of the Royal Navy, but no protest—at least, no public protest—was made in this case either by the Government of Gibraltar or by that of Great Britain. Nor was there any visible official action in the many previous cases of seizure of Gibraltar-based vessels by the Spanish Customs. The *Pring*, the *Andromeda*, the *Dallas*, the *Seaflower*, the *Knuckleduster*, the *Mariola*, the *Hild Dover*, and the *Sevril*, good British bottoms all, lay in the Spanish harbour of Algeciras under the furious eyes of their erstwhile owners, whilst the gunboats of the Royal Navy, lying in Gibraltar harbour a mere four miles away, pretended not to see them.

The motor-launch *Kim* was captured by a Spanish Customs gunboat on the 3rd March 1965, near Adra, and taken to Almeria, where I have seen her lying alongside the mole, awaiting auction. She was manifested 'Gibraltar to Genoa', had been loaded at Gibraltar and cleared by a Gibraltarian shipping agent. Her cargo was 900 cases of tobacco. The Captain, one Juan Martinez Rios, was naturalized British; the crew consisted of four Spaniards; the owner was a British Maltese. The ship's complement appeared on Spanish Television, confessed their mission and intentions, and named a Gibraltarian as owner of the cargo, but they subsequently stated that they did this under duress.

Vox, (of 5th March 1965), recognized at last that this trade was hammering down the lid of Gibraltar's coffin. Now, in the face of blockade and danger, it published a protest, thus:

'If these launches are trading legitimately then their capture on the high seas must be accepted as nothing short of piracy. In this case, every protection should be afforded to them, if necessary in the form of an armed escort.

'If, on the other hand, there is reason to believe that Gibraltar is being used by these aliens (sic; both owner and captain of the *Kim* were British subjects) for any illicit trading, then it is high time those concerned are kicked out of The Rock. Gibraltar and the Gibraltarian's reputation is at stake.'

In view of what we have seen of 1865, and, indeed, of 1765, the expression 'high time' is a striking understatement. To answer *Vox's* agonized, if tardy, inquiry, let them seek answers to the following questions:

(i) Is there a legitimate landing for Gibraltar tobacco in the port of Genoa?

(ii) Is Italy's tobacco supply to any extent dependent on fast sixty-ton launches, manned by Spanish-British and operated by Maltese?

(iii) Why and when did Captain Martinez Rios seek British nationality? And does he hold a British Master's Certificate?

(iv) What regulations are there in Gibraltar to ensure that a ship goes to its manifested destination? And are these regulations, if any, ever enforced?

Once again, in this latest case, no official complaint was made to the marauding Spanish. There was good reason for this official indifference. Britain, and Gibraltar, have no case, no valid cause for complaint.

It is very doubtful if Gibraltar possesses any territorial waters. By courtesy, by custom and usage, she patrols and controls the immediately inshore waters of The Bay, but they are never strongly claimed for legal rights to them are unsound. Clause X of the Treaty of Utrecht, that oft-quoted and operative document, states 'that the above-named propriety be yielded to Great Britain without any territorial jurisdiction'. It may be pointed out that this is double-talk, self-contradictory, for to own a place, implied by 'propriety', is surely to have some, if not total, jurisdiction over it. But British Governments have been well advised not to attempt to push this tenuous claim out to sea. Even in her bullying days Britain has been chary of claiming the usual marine jurisdiction. She has certainly not claimed it to protect Gibraltar's smugglers, for that would be to give a bad case a worse start.

The British press, in its innocence, used to make some stir about these cases of seizure, and the *Alamoana* case, in which a man was killed and an Englishman badly wounded, caused a considerable flutter of indignation at home. But the Government of Gibraltar had nothing to say. They might have said: 'We have no official knowledge, confirmation, nor concern. The alleged incident took place outside our jurisdiction. No subject of this Government has been involved. We have no responsibility for international affairs, in any case.'

To this the hard-pressed British Foreign Secretary might have replied, as his predecessors did: 'No, but you are going to involve a lot more than Gibraltar, one of these days, if you go on permitting ships to load tobacco there and manifest it to Bordeaux, where the French would not welcome it, and then go wherever they wish, and return to do it over and over again, year in year out, using Gibraltar as a home port for smuggling attacks on four or five friendly countries and carrying your contraband under the British flag!' If he did say any such thing, it had no effect in Gibraltar, for five years of busy and profitable smuggling lie between the capture of the *Alamoana* and that of the *Kim*. Maybe such a warning was never issued; there are reasons why it should not have been.

The smuggling trade, like all illegitimate business, is very difficult to assess. Figures are suppressed and distorted by both sides, even when they are known. Most of the traffic must be completely hidden and unknown, leaving it open to anyone's guess, and to polemical publication.

The Malaga newspaper *Sur* stated in March 1965 that 300 smuggling ships cleared the port of Gibraltar in 1959, a peak year, carrying an average of 800 cases of tobacco. There is no reason why they should not know the number for, as was subsequently discovered, the Spanish authorities had radio-equipped informers on The Rock to keep them in daily touch with such shipping movements. Due to vigorous action on the part of the Spanish revenue launches, claims *Sur*, the number of voyages was reduced to 130 in 1963, and to 70 in 1964. Of the five tobacco manufactories in Gibraltar, two of them rebuilt since the war, they have succeeded in closing three and the remaining two are now idling along with only a handful of employees.

The last of these claims, at least, is quite true, but it is also true that the main smuggling traffic has turned to American cigarettes which are not, of course, manufactured in Gibraltar.

Señor Fraga Iribarne, the Spanish Minister of Information, gave some very startling information during an interview on B.B.C. Television, early in 1965. He claimed that 'very nearly 1,000 smuggling boats have been operating near Gibraltar, and 40 such boats have been captured by us in recent months and 20 by France, Italy, Morocco and Algeria'. The Gibraltar shipping registers have never listed more than about 60 possible and potential smuggling launches, so it would seem that the rest of his 1,000 must be crowded into Tangier. The Tangier smugglers, now that that port is no longer 'free', are said, by the Spaniards, to carry their contraband from Gibraltar. Sr. Fraga stated that Gibraltar had 're-exported more than a thousand tons of cigarettes to Spain during 1963, and half a million motors'. None of the re-export, he implied, was legal.

Sur bewailed not only the loss of lawful revenue, but pointed out that the ill-gained *pesetas* were dumped in millions among what we have learned to call 'the gnomes of Zurich', and that this upset Spain's balance of payments and tended to devalue her credit and currency. Thus the Spanish case, very naturally put at the very worst estimate, amounts to accusing Gibraltar of being a national problem and a serious danger to the Spanish economy.

Neutral observers go some way towards confirming the Spanish assessment of the Gibraltar smuggling trade. In the *Gibraltar Chronicle* of 19th July 1961, an article by a Mr. John Reed describes the new boom in the traffic caused by certain changes in the régime at Tangier:

'In one six-month period last year,' he writes, 'the statistics of the American Department of Agriculture noted that Gibraltar imported 841 million American cigarettes. A remarkable number, indeed, for in the previous six months a mere five million cigarettes were shipped to Gibraltar.' He went on to give the reason for this sudden and astronomical increase:

'Another page of the American document . . . showed that the imports of cigarettes into the nearby Mediterranean port of Tangier had dropped by 850 million. One doesn't need Scotland Yard training to deduce that the cigarettes which were being channelled through Tangier were now being passed through Gibraltar.'

'Similar research would show', he adds, 'that not only cigarettes but a multitude of curiously assorted goods were coming into Gibraltar in great quantities, for the first time.' He states that one-twelfth of the output of a Japanese radio factory was sent to The Rock, and I can add that there were a score of different makes of Japanese radios on sale in Gibraltar. Mr. Reed concludes:

'Gibraltar has become the operations centre for smuggling organizations. Gibraltar is not a free port, but it is the next best thing. Imported goods are put into bond, for which a modest fee is charged. They can be removed and shipped out whenever the owner wishes. As long as they are not smuggled back into Gibraltar, the Customs authorities do not worry too much where they go.' Some three years after this report was written a Gibraltarian was caught smuggling bonded watches from the portside Government stores into Gibraltar. The watches were the property of three local merchants, and the object of the enterprise was to avoid the small *ad valorem* import duty. The value of the goods was high, and the magistrate applied a penalty equal to three times the value, as laid down by law. To everyone's surprise, the Governor-in-Council made a great reduction in the fine. The owners of the watches, some of them honoured citizens, explained that they had simply sold the goods at the bonded stores, for 'export', and that they had no knowledge of their destination.

Although the *Gibraltar Chronicle*, which is published by the Committee of the Garrison Officers' Library, under the patronage of the Governor, is something of an official gazette, this article of Mr. Reed's was never officially denied or even questioned. The reason is that, although an unfortunate publication, it is undeniably and demonstrably true. At the time, 1960, the Government was increasing its bonded storage, and dividing bulk stores into small, individually rented cubicles, so as to let everyone have a stake in the new goldmine. As the Official Report for 1962 blandly puts it, (on p. 19): 'A substantial portion of the export trade in dutiable articles was conducted from the private bonded stores area at Waterport.'

The Gibraltar Chamber of Commerce Report for 1960 was so foolish as to put on record that the Government had made these arrangements for the purpose of facilitating the smuggling trade. Since the direct beneficiaries were the outside syndicates, based on Tangier and elsewhere, and the Indians, as the most prominent local dealers in Japanese radios, the merchants of Gibraltar were inclined to be envious and critical. The Report told the members of the Chamber:

'Several discussions took place with the Financial Secretary. Government's view is that the *type of organization* which is making the bulk of cubicle sales has the *contacts among the buyers*. Government does not consider that the local dealer has either the business acumen or the resources to take over these sales. The Chamber's view is that Government is blinded by exaggerated figures of estimated income based on profits made on turnover at the cubicles.'

The italics are mine and, in their gangster phrases, they tell their own tale. The Government of Gibraltar never made any public denial of this responsible and printed statement, nor offered any alternative explanation to what appears to be an allegation of its deliberate policy to aid and facilitate wholesale smuggling.

Among Sr. Fraga Iribarne's accusations was the dangerous one of trafficking in marijuana. There have been occasional seizures of this drug in Gibraltar, and at her frontier with Spain. In August 1960, the *Gibraltar Post* declared: 'The peddlars have been corrupting local youth in a big-time spread of marijuana cigarettes', but this scare headline was based on the apprehension of one supplier and one small group of teenagers. There was, however, a seizure of marijuana in Gibraltar as recently as September 1965. It is not surprising, given the geographical position of the place and the smuggling traditions, that narcotics are occasionally to be found there.

The long overdue and very proper reforms at Tangier may well have doubled the import-export trade of Gibraltar, but it was a very dubious inheritance. As you would expect from the arabic country closest to Western Europe and the U.S.A., hashish and marijuana were among the staples of Tangier's smuggled exports. In Tetuan, in 1960, I saw hashish or *kif* on sale or in course of consumption at almost every café.

Gibraltar, Government and people, is strongly opposed to this deadly traffic, and the few dealers and pushers who have been caught there have turned out to be aliens—usually Spaniards. The fact remains that it was possible, and even easy, to bring narcotics into Gibraltar from nearby Morocco, and there is, therefore, some substance in Spain's accusations on that score.

In recent months the Spaniards have arrested several Englishmen for carrying drugs from Tangier and Ceuta into Algeciras, no doubt *en route* for London. In the most serious case a car's upholstery was stuffed with hemp. It may well be that these people were diverted to Algeciras by Spain's present tight grip on her land frontier with Gibraltar. In any case, the presence or possibility of narcotics in Gibraltar furnishes Spain with a strong excuse or pretext for stringent Customs at La Línea.

Gibraltar's reply to all these allegations is, quite naturally, to minimize them. Sr. Fraga Iribarne's appearance on British television—'the face that launched a thousand ships'—caused bitter amusement on The Rock by its self-evident exaggerations. It also served to convince some British parliamentarians that all Spain's accusations against Gibraltar were impossible and mendacious.

Responsible Gibraltarians will admit that there was smuggling in the past, but add that there is none today. They do not add that it continued in full spate until the Spaniards forcibly stopped it in 1964, but they will agree to this if it is put to them. They will not fail to tell you, and truthfully, that most of the smuggling was always done by citizens of Spain, and much of it in collusion with Spanish officials. They will also tell you, as though seeking to lay aside the blame and to find some shelter from the blast, that 'the British Government did not seem to mind the smuggling'.

The Gibraltar Government's reply to charges of wholesale smuggling is to refer the accuser to its official reports. It is the duty of those who compile such reports to hide all damaging information without actually perpetrating falsehood. The biennial Government Reports on Gibraltar, which may be obtained at H.M. Stationery Office by anyone with a few shillings to spare, give import and re-export figures for dutiable goods, but as one report follows another and the world becomes more sophisticated, these figures become more obscure. The technique is to group dubious commodities with innocent ones, so that the former cannot be subjected to separate assessment.

The 1949 Report, in more innocent days, gives the total imports of tobacco as 1,418 tons, which, with a population of 25,000, retails out at 10 ounces per day for every adult on The Rock. Since few Latin women smoke, the men would appear to be smoking 15 ounces a day each, or about 300 cigarettes. But the Government has a permanent loophole here. Some tobacco is bought by ships and tourists, and you will never discover how much—or how little.

The imports of coffee for 1949 totalled 4,234 tons, to the value of more than half a million pounds sterling. Spain's legitimate imports, at that time, were very narrowly limited, although Spaniards cannot live without coffee. There was a coffee famine throughout Europe, indeed, as there was of cigarettes, and Gibraltar was one of the very few places able to import these precious drugs without restraint. The quantity of coffee brought into Gibraltar works out at a daily one pound per head for every man, woman and child in the place. Since the tinned milk imports for the same period work out at three ounces, one might presume that the Gibraltarians liked their coffee black! In the case of this commodity it can hardly be claimed that much was sold to ships and tourists.

Obviously, these vast quantities of tobacco and coffee were re-exported, but this 1949 Report does not list re-exports. Even if it did so, one would have to ask—Re-exported to where? What country officially, openly and legally depends on Gibraltar for its tobacco or coffee? Is there any country, anywhere, which would not import its own tobacco and coffee from source, directly, and so avoid Gibraltar import duty or bond storage charges, or double handling?

The latest available Government Report for Gibraltar groups total imports of 'Wines, Spirits, Malts and Tobacco' under one heading, extending their quantities in two units—tons and gallons. Appendix IV, which covers re-exports, deals with each commodity separately. The effect of this is to prevent a direct comparison between the two sets of figures. A man on a galloping horse could not tell, from this Report, how much of any imported commodity was re-exported, nor learn anything at all about the dramatic relationship between Gibraltar's imports and exports.

But I am not on a galloping horse. I took forty cubic feet, or two hundred and fifty gallons to the freight ton, and thence I found a direct comparison, as follows:

Wines, Spirits, Malts and Tobacco
1962	In	£3,000,000
	Out	£2,654,400
	Consumed in Gibraltar	£345,600

This is to say that ninety per cent of the import of these goods is for re-export, and it checks with my hypothetical heavy smoker and his 300 cigarettes a day. One-tenth of that—thirty cigarettes a day—would be just about what he *does* smoke. The remaining 270 cigarettes pay their tribute to the revenues and the merchants of Gibraltar and then sail away to be smoked in foreign lands.

The said Appendix IV, Summary of Re-exports, is clearly headed 'Dutiable Goods only'. From this heading, a man on a galloping horse would be led to believe that it was a full list of dutiable goods. But it is no such thing. Motor-vehicles and spares are not included in this list, nor are radios, lighters, cameras, razor blades, watches and fountain pens, all of which—and nothing else, except liquor, tobacco, petroleum and coffee—attract import duty on entering Gibraltar. All of these things, except motor-cars, were imported and re-exported in vast quantities, and it was for this reason that the import duty was laid upon them. Appendix III groups them all under the blanket 'Manufactured Goods', and so prevents us from seeing some fantastic figures. One Gibraltarian shopkeeper once told me that he was selling one-sixtieth of the total output of one of the world's most famous fountain pens. When I asked him how this could be, he replied: 'By supplying the whole Iberian Peninsula.' I do not mean that he was a smuggler. He simply sold the pens, taking both wholesale and retail profits, to the ten thousand Spanish commuters, who carried them into Spain at the rate of one per day per man. Another Gibraltarian, and a very decent man he is, made himself independent for life, at this time, by selling saccharin alone. All he had to do was order it up by the barrel, break it down into tuppenny packets, and sell it to the Spanish workers. There was no end to the business and the money made, in those ten first post-war years, for Spain was short of everything, except perhaps sherry, olive oil, oranges, and bulls.

Razor blades present an interesting and amusing facet of Gibraltar's trade. In Spain the strongest beard in the world met the weakest blade—the home product is said to be of tenth-rate quality. Imports were prohibited or strictly controlled, to protect home industry and trade balance. Spanish men are very vain of their appearance. Once one of them had tried a British blade on his chin he would never look back to Bilbao. One shave a day does not suffice him, but, in most cases, it was all that he could afford. Rather than waste it on his workaday hours, he goes out in the morning unshaven, growing more villainous-looking as the day proceeds. He shaves at the beginning of the evening, so as to appear at his best for the *paseo*, the social parade. *Buenas tardes empiezan con Gillette*—Good afternoons begin with Gillette. Since nothing is easier to smuggle than a packet of razor blades, Gibraltar, with the aid of her ten thousand daily carriers, gladly undertook responsibility for half the chins of Spain.

Whenever accused of supplying the smuggling trade, as she so frequently is, Gibraltar points to her two unimpeachable channels of re-export, both of which are emphasized in the official reports. The first is the supply of visiting ships.

In the year 1962 the total number of merchant ships which called

at the port was 4,389. The re-exports of tobacco totalled £2,222,897.
To clear this, the ships would have had to purchase £506 worth
each. But since a majority of these ships were tankers, with 'No
smoking' regulations, I turn to listed passenger ships. Three hundred
and twenty-nine of these visited The Rock, and to re-export all that
tobacco they would have had to buy about £7,000 worth each. In
fact, I doubt if any passenger ship, except those of Italy, loads her
tobacco at Gibraltar. There would be no point in her doing so. Be
she American, British or Russian, she can surely load cigarettes
ex-bond and duty-free at her home port and carry them herself.
Such transactions are arranged by advantageous bulk contracts with
ships' suppliers, and not by shopping around for bits and pieces
at this port and that. Any purser who overlooked to include
his tobacco with all his other supplies, and had to stock up at
Gibraltar, paying freight to there, as well as import duty, storage
and double handling, and possibly delaying his ship, would
scarcely do so twice!

The other legitimate outlet is in sales to landed passengers.
Cigarettes are cheap in Gibraltar, no doubt, but they should be even
cheaper on board ship. They pay some duty in Gibraltar, whereas
ship's supplies ought to be duty-free. This outlet would seem to be
negligible.

The other main channel of re-export, as stated in the 1962 Report,
is also a dubious one. 'The alien daily labour force is permitted by
the Spanish Authorities to spend twenty-five per cent of their wages
in Gibraltar,' in official phraseology. The said labour force is a
vanishing asset, because the Spanish Government has issued no new
passes to its nationals for the past ten years, since the quarrel over
the Queen's visit in 1954. But it still stands at, or near, 10,000 men
and women, and twenty-five per cent of their total wages amounts
to, at least, £5,000 per day, or almost £2,000,000 per annum. The
Spanish workers, up to October 1964, carried this value of tobacco,
coffee, cloth, lighters, blades and other manufactured goods back
into Spain, in small daily quantities, and without paying duty to
their Customs.

It used to be true that the Spanish Government allowed these
people to spend a quarter of their wages in Gibraltar, where they
earned the money. But this allowance, as the writers of such Reports

should be aware, dated from the post-Civil War period, when Spain was short of food and Gibraltar was a well-stocked shop window. Now, and for many years back, there is plenty of food in Spain, as well as all other necessities and many imported luxuries, often at prices lower than those of Gibraltar. Thus the only profitable merchandise to carry home was that which was supposed to be taxed on entering Spain. The bulk of that two million pounds was, therefore, carried in contraband, at the loss of revenue to the Spanish Treasury.

This loss could be prevented by one of two methods. Spain could withdraw all workers' passes, but she would then face the problem of re-deploying and re-employing about 10,000 people. Alternatively, the Customs could apply a body search to every man and woman at the gates, and cancel the passes of all those caught smuggling. The latter was laborious, but very practical from Spain's point of view, for it had the effect of diminishing the labour-smuggler force gradually, and of leaving the unemployed with no one to blame but themselves. It is the course which Spain took in the autumn of 1964 and maintains up to the moment of writing. Large oil refineries are being built at Algeciras and at Campamento, close to La Línea, and Gibraltar's commuters are encouraged to find employment on these and other nearby works. Since the new restrictions on smuggling have the effect of bringing their income down to Spanish level, they no longer have any incentive to travel to Gibraltar.

The La Línea Customs also make a thorough search of every vehicle passing the frontier, with the result that it takes several hours to enter Spain by that route.

The measures are completely effective. The labour force is being depleted daily, and the survivors dare not smuggle anything. Very few cars attempt to enter Spain from Gibraltar, and those which must do so do not now carry any contraband. Smuggling on the land frontier has ceased altogether.

Marine smuggling from Gibraltar, fully professional and backed by strong funds and interests, has always been a far more formidable problem than that of the land frontier. In recent years, as we have seen, the Spanish authorities have been suppressing it with ruthless vigour, shooting up and seizing British ships on many occasions. In view of these violent international incidents in the shadow of The

Rock, and the constant, grave risk of their becoming even worse, it seems amazing that nothing was done, either by the Government of Gibraltar or by Whitehall, to discourage Gibraltar's role in international smuggling, or to improve and protect the Colony's—and Great Britain's—reputation.

To limit the questionable imports of Gibraltar, the tobacco, coffee and other known commodities of Spanish contraband, would be to cause a drastic reduction in the Colony's revenues—about one-third. All those things which are heavily imported, down to the humble razor blade, bear a small import duty. These are, of course, the goods destined for re-export, and such is their bulk that the contribution to the local exchequer is very considerable. The Colony's Estimates for 1964 give import duties at the figure of £800,000, and it has been something of that order for several years back. Nine-tenths of this sum, as I have shown, is the import duty on goods for re-export—and for illegal import into Spain and other neighbouring countries. The gain to the Gibraltar community works out at £32 per head of the population, or about £140 per family, from the public funds. The sum is more than twice as great as any other single item in the Estimates.

In addition to this public profit from the smuggling trade there are, of course, very high private profits from the sales of tobacco, coffee and manufactured goods, for their turnover, as we have seen, is normally both voluminous and rapid. Nothing was done to limit or control this entrepot trade, as it is termed. The past twenty years have been tricky times for Colonial Powers and no British Government, neither Conservative nor Labour dared risk stirring up a hornets' nest in Gibraltar.

Let us consider the rates of income tax in the Colony. I take a married man, wife and two children, as an average family, and consider him at three ordinary income levels, thus:

		£
1	With £700 per annum	
	Tax payable in U.K.	14
	In 20 British Colonies, average	11
	In Gibraltar	Nil

2   With £1,500 per annum
    Tay payable in U.K.   226
    In 20 British Colonies, average   108
    In Gibraltar   12

3   With £2,500 per annum
    Tax payable in U.K.   547
    In 20 British Colonies, average   369
    In Gibraltar   75

I have taken all these figures from a Colonial Office Publication entitled 'Appointments Overseas', and published in the year 1960. The position has changed somewhat, but not much, by a small increase in Gibraltar's income tax rates imposed by an emergency budget in the summer of 1965, but it remains the lowest taxed of British colonies, and the only other in the same category is that other notorious smuggling centre, Hong Kong. A citizen of the Gilbert Islands, where I spent the past two years, pays four times as much income tax as a comparable Gibraltarian, plus heavy import duties, (seventeen per cent, for instance, on cloth and clothing), on all his imported food and other necessities, plus a twenty-five per cent export duty on his only product—copra. They never had a merchant lobby to protect them out there!

In spite of the million-pound windfall from dubious imports, and lavish free grants of money from the tax-payers of the United Kingdom, Gibraltar's social services still lag very far behind those of the welfare states of Europe. The education service, in my opinion, is just beginning to convalesce from a state of moribund starvation. Wages and welfare payments are at a minimum, and there is no free family health service. From all this it is evident that the present revenues of Gibraltar are not excessive; they cannot easily suffer a sudden, overall reduction.

To control the outflow of dubious goods would have been to diminish their import, and so injure import duties, the richest source of revenue. To balance this loss, income tax would have to be raised to a realistic level, to somewhere near the level accepted by every other colony and country in the modern world. This solution seemed obvious, but who would apply it?

The first Gibraltarian Government of Gibraltar, the fully elected

Legislative Council and Council of Ministers empowered by the new
Constitution of 1964, found itself faced with two alternative courses
of action in this matter of smuggling. Both of them were difficult,
for the merchant interest—and, in fact, the tobacco interest—was
strongly represented in the Legislature.

To prohibit or limit certain imports (which, one might ask, and
where do you stop?) would be to lose or diminish that one-third of
the total revenue which resulted from them. To replace this loss by
direct taxation would be to raise a riot, lose an election, and commit
political suicide.

To allow imports to remain unchecked and re-exports facilitated,
would be to perpetuate and aggravate bad relations with Spain, and
so put Gibraltar's whole economy and existence in hazard. Such a
course would furnish the now strong and vocal Spain with a real
grievance, impressive and convincing to the majority of law-abiding
nations. This would afford a strong subsidiary reason for putting an
end to Gibraltar's questioned status as a separate statelet.

The decision was made urgent by Spain's growing stature and by
the overwhelmingly anti-colonial sentiment of the United Nations
Organization. From the U.S.A. right across the chamber to U.S.S.R.
with all the liberated colonies in between, the voice was unanimous:
'Colonialism must be ended.'

Gibraltar's birthright, unanimously treasured there for good
reasons and bad, is membership of the British Empire. This had, at
last, materialized in a free press, a democratic system with full rights
and safeguards for everyone, the beginnings of social justice and the
promise of more to come. Should she risk losing all this for a mess
of pottage? Even for a mess of pottage of £800,000 per annum, or
£140 per family? The choice had been postponed for the first century, then for the second, then for half a century more. Finally, it
had been put off for the fateful decade 1954–64, in spite of grave
warnings from Spain.

At the end of that period it proved too late to choose, to make
amends or promises of future good-neighbourly behaviour. Spain
drew a noose round the neck of Gibraltar and forcibly stopped the
smuggling by land and sea.

The morals of smuggling do not trouble me. I am not one of that
infinitesimal minority of mankind which can lay its hand on its

breast and swear that it never smuggled anything. But governments, which expect and demand that their own laws shall be obeyed, should show a higher standard of responsibility than private persons. Governments whose moral standards are no higher than those of their citizens have, surely, no guidance, no leadership to offer.

To fail to stop the smuggling traffic, to facilitate it in the narrow and immediate interest of Gibraltar's finances, to make easy money by yielding to the unspoken pressures of the untaxed millionaires and the hot-headed tax-resisters, leaves the Government of Gibraltar open to accusations of cowardice, lack of principle and responsibility, and a dangerous lack of foresight and common sense. By coasting down those last fourteen rich and easy years, unheeding the good advice and warnings given by successive Financial Secretaries, that Government steered Gibraltar into the treacherous shoals where she wallows today and put the livelihood and the birthright of the community in peril.

There is, as always, a case for the defence. It hinges on the fact that the clean and dirty trade of Gibraltar were almost inextricably intermingled. What is the difference, say, between selling tobacco to a Spaniard who will smuggle it into Spain, and selling a watch to an English tourist, who may or may not intend to smuggle it into England? How can a shopkeeper be held responsible for the disposition of his wares once he has sold them? So runs the plea, and it is valid so far as it goes. But it does not cover the provision of private bonded stores, of special harbour facilities where sea-going launches openly loaded tobacco and whisky, or the studied laxity in port regulations. Devices such as these condemn the main commerce of Gibraltar, and cast a shadow over even its legitimate trade, inviting such a distinguished press as the London *Observer* to state (in its 1964 handbook, 'Time off in Southern Spain') that 'smuggling is the Colony's staple industry'.

Since October 1964, when Spain suddenly intensified her anti-smuggling cordon, Gibraltar's import duties dwindled rapidly. Simultaneously, her tourist trade diminished, for fifty per cent of her visitors used to come by the overland route. The Costa del Sol traffic, delayed and annoyed by the Customs at La Línea, switched from Gibraltar airport to that of Málaga. The crowds vanished from the streets and shops, and the stocks stayed on the shelves. The only remaining sources of custom were the local people, few of them rich, the passengers of calling ships, and the servicemen of the greatly depleted garrison. All three of Gibraltar's main sources of income were seen to be either stopped or in swift decline—the soldiers withdrawn, the tourists hindered, the smuggling stopped. At long last, with no other possible recourse in view, the Government was forced to do what it should have done so many years earlier—increase taxes.

On the 24th June 1965 the Financial Secretary of Gibraltar introduced an emergency budget, increasing the standard rate of income tax by twenty-five per cent, and raising the duty on petrol, liquor, tobacco and some other commodities. The increases were small, and the community remained very lightly taxed by modern standards, but such is the reaction to taxation in Gibraltar that *Vox* published the dread news under a headline incoherently furious:

'ON THE WAY TO HELL WITH MID-YEAR STAR!'*

The Leader of the Opposition, Mr. Isola, let his common sense waver for once. Instead of taxing themselves, he said, they should ask Great Britain to make a contribution to balance their budget. He overlooked the fact that Britain had been subsidizing untaxed Gibraltar throughout his lifetime, and was, in fact, still doing so.

Sir Joshua Hassan, for the Government, said, in effect, that they must make some little effort and sacrifice themselves before asking Britain for more.

The taxes fell fairly enough on a wide cross-section of the community, on the income of the rich and on the poor man's cigarettes. But they probably will raise only a small fraction of the revenue which is being lost. The Financial Secretary said that he would meet this loss from two other sources, in addition to the tax increases, being by economy in Government expenditure—which I have already shown to be at rock bottom and far below where it ought to be—and out of the accumulated funds of the Colony, which are, by the way, mainly invested elsewhere. This latter resource is, of course, spending capital. The only effective recourse may prove to be a two-fisted capital levy. Let the main beneficiaries of the long years of license make some amends for the disaster which they have brought down on the community of Gibraltar.

* *Vox*, 25th June 1965.

27

QUESTION TIME

The Gibraltar Question, complicated and confused as it is with side issues, is basically one of sovereignty over The Rock. Should Gibraltar belong to Britain or to Spain? There is no easy answer, except from the uninformed or thoughtless.

The simple Englishman may be excused for saying, as he will, 'It's always been ours, hasn't it? For centuries, anyway. What are the Spaniards moaning about after all this time?'

For almost a century after the Great Siege, from 1783 until 1870 or later, the question seemed to be settled. Britain had taken the place, on the invitation of a Spanish faction and with the aid of the Dutch, but taken it, rightly or wrongly, and nevertheless. Whether British interests were rooted there by straight conquest, as is believed in Britain, or by subsequent intrigue, is of no great account. The former enabled the latter means, as I see it, and it amounts to conquest however it was done. Furthermore, in that age conquest was counted a fair means of seizing anything. Until very recent times, might was right in all international affairs. Even today, in our international tribunals, violent means are only criticized by such nations as are not currently using them.

Certain rights in Gibraltar were ceded to Britain by the Treaty of Utrecht in 1713, and confirmed by two subsequent treaties. In British estimation, the Utrecht Treaty amounts to a deed of freehold. But the fact that Spain never accepted Britain's valuation of the Treaty is clearly demonstrated by her attacks on The Rock in 1727, in 1779 and, indirectly, in 1805. Her quiescence in the matter throughout the nineteenth century should not be taken as condonement of the British occupation of the place, nor of any intention to recognize British tenure by default of opposition to it.

The fact is that Spain lost ground all over the world as fast as Britain gained it. I would go further and say that the rulers of Spain were unable to govern their own people at home, let alone keep their overseas colonies, much less regain a colony from the clutches of the most powerful empire in the world. For a hundred years, then, Queen Isabella's holy bequest, 'The Key to Spain', was bewailed only in occasional literary laments.

But why, you may ask, should Spain even consider raising the Gibraltar Question again? Was it not ceded to Britain once and for all by the Treaty of Utrecht?

Unfortunately, it was not. Certainly, not clearly. The British Government's White Paper of 1965, (Cmnd. 2632), is somewhat coyly entitled 'Recent Differences with Spain', as though to suggest that the sovereignty of Gibraltar had been settled centuries ago. As a basis of settlement, of British sovereignty, the paper publishes as 'Document No. 1' the crucial Article X of the Treaty of Utrecht, or as much of it as is considered relevant. It is stated to be translated from the Latin. I have studied, in the subsequent Spanish *Red Book* in reply, the same Article in Spanish, which might be closer to the original Latin. I found no significant difference in meaning or intent. Here, then, is Britain's Deed of Freehold to Gibraltar, the whole basis of her claim to sovereignty:

'X. The Catholic King does hereby, for Himself, His heirs and successors, yield to the Crown of Great Britain the full and intire propriety of the Town and Castle of Gibraltar, together with the port, fortifications and forts thereunto belonging; and He gives up the said propriety, to be held and enjoyed absolutely with all manner of right for ever, without any exception or impediment whatsoever.'

So far, so good. It seems clear enough. But you have to watch these Spaniards . . . does 'propriety' mean 'sovereignty'? My house is my property, but I have not full sovereignty over it—to fortify it for instance, or turn it into a brothel or a thieves' kitchen, or even a fish-and-chip shop. Let us read on, to see if this language is clarified later in the Article. It continues:

'*But that abuses and frauds may be avoided by importing any kind of goods, the Catholic King wills, and takes it to be understood, that the above-named propriety be yielded to Great Britain without any territorial jurisdiction, and without any open communication by land with the country round about.*'

The italics only are mine, the rest is exactly as it is printed in the White Paper. I state this because you may find it hard to believe, you may think that I have inadvertently misquoted. The Paper purports to state and strengthen Britain's disputed case to own, rule and do as we wish in Gibraltar, and cites this Article X as the main basis of our claim. The Article clearly and explicitly denies our claim. The subsequent arguments in the White Paper blandly proceed on the basis which has been legally refuted and nullified by the passage quoted in italics. Doubting Thomases will confirm what I say here by buying the White Paper for 1s. 9d. from H.M. Stationery Office.

In Document No. 4, for instance, of the White Paper, which is a note from H.M. Embassy in Madrid to the Spanish Ministry of Foreign Affairs, dated 11th January 1965, Britain complains:

'Her Majesty's Government regret that procedures should have been imposed on the frontier with Gibraltar which are altogether different from those in force on Spain's other international frontiers.' All that Spain had to say in reply was to draw attention to the clear clause in the Treaty, as I have done—'without any open communication by land with the country round about'.

Already, by 1713, a few years after the British had invested The Rock, the Spaniards knew that it was being used as a base for smuggling by land and sea. To prevent smuggling by sea, Spain retained the rights of territorial jurisdiction, which would include, with much else, the rights of inspection and the punishment of law-breakers—the importers of the stuff of contraband. It never occurred to either party to the Treaty that such importers should be regarded as British subjects because of residence in Gibraltar. Britain signed, in effect, to keep them under Spanish law—jurisdiction.

To prevent smuggling by land, right of land access was specifically denied in principle, although specifically empowered, in the King of Spain's gift, for certain purposes and in certain circumstances. But land access was never to be anything more than a matter of permission and privilege. Now Spain is saying that there is no formal frontier between Gibraltar and Spain. Those who have not read the Treaty, but who have seen the Customs Station at La Línea, boldly labelled '*Aduana*', consider this statement perverse. But when the facilities of that Customs Station, that passage, are abused, the Spaniards declare, irrefutably, that it has no legal necessity nor entity and is to be considered a mere police post. People may pass, with permission, but no goods of any kind. When they put, say, three preventive officers there, with instructions to search a queue of one thousand vehicles, the tourists and Gibraltarians will complain: 'This Customs Station is not properly run!' The Spaniards will reply: 'What Customs Station? There is none here. The proper entry to Gibraltar is by ship from Algeciras across the Bay.' And so they have frequently replied, intermittently in the past, and since October 1964, unremittingly.

In the terms of the Treaty, then, Spain may do what she wishes on this land frontier, even to the point of closing it completely and for good. It seems likely that she will close it as soon as she has re-deployed the remains of the commuting labour force—the 9,000 Spaniards who go to work in Gibraltar every day. The privilege of passage, the Spanish authorities say, and anyone who has been there could confirm, has been greatly abused for many years, centuries of 'abuses and frauds'. It has been abused by Spain's own citizens, homing loot-laden from The Fat Rock, by tourists of every nation-ality who have fallen for Gibraltar's 'duty-free' goods, by the Gibral-tarians and by me, carrying our week-end whisky, money and tobacco freely into Spain, in our cars filled up with untaxed petrol.

By new Spanish regulations there—special regulations for this special 'frontier'—tourists are forbidden to import any Gibraltar purchase into Spain, even if they declare it and offer to pay duty. Spanish workers are allowed to bring home a minute quantity of specified commodities on one certain day of the week. If they are caught with more, or on any other day, their work passes are can-celled. In the circumstances, and reading that clause in the Treaty again, how can we complain? Yet we do, as I have quoted above.

'Without any territorial jurisdiction', states the Treaty, the Treaty we quote and on which we take our stand. Later in the same White Paper, Britain writes to Spain: 'Her Majesty's Government cannot regard the question of sovereignty as a matter of negotiation.' On first reading, Sr. Castiella must have thought that we were admitting Spanish sovereignty, but he would be disappointed by another letter, sent on 22nd January, a couple of weeks later:

'Her Majesty's Government totally reject the implications . . . that Gibraltar is a British military base in Spain.'

'Then what,' Sr. Castiella should have asked, 'then what the hell is it?' Diplomatic language cannot meet such occasions.

The Treaty's phrase 'Without any *open* communication' strikes me as an amusing pre-Freudian slip. Since a closed communication is inconceivable, this appears to be an invitation to a hidden or clan-destine communication. That is precisely what arose, of course, but none of the smugglers has ever had the effrontery to justify his actions by appeal to the Treaty. Semi-literate diplomatic draftsmen did not arise in our day, it appears, but there may be less excuse for our contemporaries since they use their own language rather than Latin.

I must not be accused of giving selected parts of Article X to suit my own interpretation. Directly after what I have quoted there follows:

'Yet whereas the communication by sea with the coast of Spain may not at all times be safe or open, and thereby it may happen that the garrison, and other inhabitants of Gibraltar may be brought to great straits; and as it is the intention of the Catholic King, only that fraudulent importations of goods should, as is above said, be hindred by an inland communication, it is therefore provided that in such cases it may be lawful to purchase, for ready money, in the neighbouring territories of Spain, provisions, and other things necessary for the use of the garrison, the inhabitants and the ships which lie in the harbour.'

In other words, in case of siege, with sea access closed or dangerous, the British may be permitted to buy and import necessities from nearby Spain. The Catholic King *may* permit it. There is nothing slipshod about 'may' in Latin, and it does not mean 'shall'. It would depend on his relations with Britain when the time came.

In the ensuing two centuries, the kings of Spain, weak kings of a weakening country, did permit traffic between Spain and Gibraltar, not only in time of siege, and not only of necessities but of many other goods as well. But this, too, remained a privilege, withdrawable at any time the Catholic King might think fit to withdraw it—or might feel strong enough to withdraw it. Like the privilege of passage, like all long-established privileges, indeed, it came to be regarded as a right.

The Article continues with a warning, thus:

'But if any goods be found imported by Gibraltar, either by way of barter for purchasing provisions, or under any other pretence, the same shall be confiscated, and complaint being made thereof, those persons who have acted contrary to the faith of this Treaty shall be severely punished.'

This last clause clearly contains the purpose of the Treaty's retention of jurisdiction in Spanish hands. Also, it clearly confirms the King's intention, and Franco's contention, that Gibraltar was only ceded to Britain on a rent-free lease and never alienated from Spain at all. The clause went by default for the simple reason that Spain was too weak to enforce it, and for the less simple reason that a section of the Spanish population found a vested interest in Gibraltar and used it to defraud their King and country.

The next clause of Article X stipulates: 'And Her Britannic Majesty, at the request of the Catholic King, does consent and agree, that no leave shall be given under any pretence whatsoever, either to Jews or Moors, to reside or have their dwellings in the said town of Gibraltar.'

That condition was infringed almost from the outset of the British epoch. It was unreasonable, of course, arising from Spain's fanatical religious sentiments and her ancient enmity for the heretics across The Straits. But the British did not break the law for good reasons of charity or common sense. The Jewish merchants bribed the early Governors. However they came, we are glad that they did so, and not even Spain would raise objection at this late date. At the same time, their admission affords further evidence that the British never paid any respect to the Treaty on which their claim to Gibraltar was—and still is—based.

The next clause, a long one, permits trade between Gibraltar and Morocco, recognizing that this must be necessary at times, and evidently preferring it to trade between Gibraltar and Spain. There follows a stipulation that 'the free exercise of their religion shall be indulged to the Roman Catholic residents of the aforesaid town'. Article X then comes to a close with a condition of paramount importance:

'And in case it shall hereafter seem meet to the Crown of Great Britain to grant, sell, or by any means to alienate therefrom the propriety of the said town of Gibraltar, it is hereby agreed and concluded, that in preference of having the same shall always be given to the Crown of Spain before any others.' The property, in plain words, cannot be sold or sub-let without the landlord's prior approval of the prospective tenant and neighbour. It is certainly not to be inherited by the tenant's lodgers.

Yet now, says Spain, having filled the place with people from a dozen different countries, including some prohibited by the Treaty and many who have lived by acting 'contrary to the faith' of the Treaty, Britain has elevated them to the position of householders of

Gibraltar. These people are officially unknown to us; they are not mentioned in the Treaty, nor covered by it in any way other than prohibition on some and limitation on all. Yet Britain, they point out, appeared to be on the point—in 1964—of walking out of the now useless Fortress and leaving these unknown and irresponsible people in charge of it, to do as they wished with it.

Britain replies that she did not intend to go so far as that, but Spain does not believe it. Independence is the normal end of the process of constitutional reforms in these times. Spain says, in effect, we have caught Britain half-way out of the door, but she had better stay and talk it over with us, the Landlords. Britain, whatever her intentions were, has agreed to do so.

Strange to say, with what appears to be a cast-iron case based on the Treaty, Spain's claims are often based on less relevant grounds.

One such basis is the historical, with its immediate emotional appeal. Spain fought for the Holy Rock, hard, long and heroically, and then had it treacherously snatched from her hands by the barbarous and heretical British! Britain's easy answer to this one is that she has now owned Gibraltar for longer than Spain, and that she has made it rich and famous. She might add that the Moors held it for longer than their two successors added together. Spain snatched it from the Moors, who had snatched it from the Visigoths, who had snatched it from the Romans, and so *ad infinitum*. To follow this line to its obvious conclusion the earliest and strongest claim would be that of Neanderthal Man, who had left his corroded cranium on The Rock as mute testimony of his ancient occupation.

Right of conquest is, for better or for worse, recognized throughout the world—old right of conquest, that is—for there would be chaos and confusion if the nations abrogated it and everyone went back where he originally belonged. Britain has some right of conquest at Gibraltar, and something of a Treaty towards the ratification of it.

Then there is the geographical claim. Gibraltar is a part of Spain on the map, and on the land. Well, yes. . . . Although it is somewhat detached from the mainland, there is no doubt that nations have arguable rights to their offshore islands. Within the twelve-mile—or certainly the three-mile—limit, an alienated island becomes an insult, a nuisance and a threat. But this claim, in this case, lacks the force of sincerity, for a few miles away and in full view of Gibraltar, Spain holds the very similar peninsula of Ceuta, and beyond that again, Melilla, both of which are, geographically, parts of Morocco. The Moors, who are just as proud, religious and exclusive as the Spaniards, hate to see their land so occupied and have spilt a lot of blood in attempts to liberate it. An even quainter parallel is another Spanish 'province', Fernando Poo, which looks like an off-shore island of ex-British West African territory. The British never raised objection to Spain's presence there, perhaps because a little diversity is good for trade.

Sometimes Spain's claims are given something of an ethnical basis. The Gibraltarians, it may be said, are more Spanish than English. They speak Spanish first, and think in Spanish. They pray and eat in Spanish style. Many—perhaps most—of them have Spanish wives. Their babies leave hospital, a week old, with rings in their ears and tiny ribbons in their long, black hair. '*Mas Gomez que Smith*,' said the Spanish daily 'ABC' after studying the Gibraltar telephone directory.

All this is true, but Spain cannot have it both ways. They also call the Gibraltarians a false, prefabricated population, a mongrel race gathered up from the rejected scraps of others. Also, let us bear in mind the sad words of Spanish Premier Canovas del Castillo—'*Son españoles los que no pueden ser otra cosa*'—They are Spaniards who cannot be anything else. He had in mind the abiding poverty and social injustice in Spain. The Gibraltarians have only to look over the hedge to see this, and the past decade of amelioration has not convinced them that Spain's future peace and progress are assured. They choose not to become Spanish citizens, and few non-Spaniards would criticize that choice. The Spaniards are fine people, man by man, but their society attracts very few immigrants.

That is a hard truth for Spain to accept. The implications of Gibraltar's preference are that her people believe more in the future of Britain than in that of Spain; that they prefer democracy to direction; that they have more respect for and trust in British institutions than in Spanish. The Spanish reply is a furious one. It is all lies, they say. The Gibraltarians wish to remain British so that they can go on smuggling and idling, and so that their leaders can enjoy fancy foreign titles.

But even if the original Spaniards had stayed on The Rock and become British subjects, and so remained for two centuries or more, the fact of race would not seem to justify a forced change of allegiance and all that it would imply. The right or, at the least, the principle of self-determination, which is what the Gibraltarians are now claiming, is well recognized and respected. When your ground lease expires the landlord may claim your house, but not the furniture in it, and much less the people.

However amicable, on the surface, were their relations with Great Britain, the Spaniards have always kept their claim to Gibraltar warm. In 1870 they minted a silver dollar—five *pesetas*—depicting a lady, draped and crowned, reclining beside the sea. Beyond her rears the unmistakable profile of *El Peñon de Gibraltar*, and the lady, *España*, offers it in her extended hand the olive branch of peace. It is not clear whether this gesture meant that Spain would like it back, peacefully, or that Britain might keep it, peacefully. But the British of 1870 were the last people in the world to respond to gentle allegory and the hint was ignored. The Spanish Government then struck a copper coin of one-hundredth part of the value of the silver one, showing poor España with the olive branch held behind her back. A very close study of the two coins discovers that there are more olives on the first branch than on the second, and the wits of Spain have suggested that the Gibraltarians picked a few off the scorned branch whilst it was on offer.

Spain had no part in World War I, nor any say or claim at the settlement which followed it. After that war, up to World War II, Britain's hold on The Rock was stronger than ever, taking into account the fact that Spain was, as usual, in the throes of seeking a viable form of domestic government and in no position to make any international claims.

Early in World War II General Franco made some attempt to deal with Hitler on the basis of a passage through Spain in exchange for the return of Gibraltar. Like everyone else in the world, he had every reason to distrust Hitler, and very little to oppose him with should he turn treacherous in Spain. He hesitated to conclude the deal, and Hitler's patience became exhausted. Then the Germans involved themselves in Russia, and the tide of war turned to the other end of the continent. Franco never had any reason or opportunity to resume his dealings with Hitler, and confined his war aims to occupying the unarmed International Zone of Tangier.

Again, Spain had no voice in the settlement of World War II, in fact, she had to keep very quiet indeed. Britain had no reason to be magnanimous to a country ruled by a friend and colleague of the dead dictators. Russia had been indirectly attacked by Spain, by the volunteer 'Blue Legion' of Spanish fascists. The United States was mindful that the armies and air forces of the Axis had been trained and hardened in the cause of Franco. For about twelve years after the war Spain was isolated, barred from all the international organizations.

By 1954 this situation began to change. Great Britain had been divesting herself of colonies great and small, and seemed well on the road back towards the original Little England. Spain's sins had been forgotten with the passage of time, at least by the one great nation which mattered most to her—the United States of America. When father turns, we all turn. After Sir Winston Churchill's Fulton speech, when he almost made it appear that we had all been fooled into fighting a war to make the world safe for Russian communism, Franco was in a position to declare: 'That's what I said all along!' Thus, one way and another, Spain could raise her head once more, and her voice. She began to do so.

The British Queen's Coronation Tour, it was announced, would include a visit to Gibraltar. Franco objected at once. He had not been asked, nor even told. The visit would be an insult to Spain, designed to reaffirm and consolidate Britain's illegal hold on Gibraltar, a territory within Spanish jurisdiction. Further, it was said, or hinted, Spain could not guarantee the Queen's safety in Gibraltar.

Her Majesty's Government—Sir Anthony Eden, as he then was, was the Foreign Secretary—had evidently not foreseen such a reaction to the proposal. Previous royal visits to The Rock, in monarchist times, had been greeted and welcomed by representatives of the Spanish royal family. Franco had declared himself as something of a royal stand-in; for years back, he had been silent on the subject of Gibraltar. Nevertheless, he was noisy now, and the British Government faced a dilemma. To have sought Franco's permission beforehand, had anyone thought of such a step, would have been to raise a hare, to invite difficulties. To concede his point, now that he had objected, would have been to weaken Britain's hold on The Rock, and, perhaps, to lose face throughout the world. There was nothing to be done but press on with the visit and hope for the best.

In preparation for the great day the security of Gibraltar was drastically tightened. The numerous security men already there, under a high official called the Defence Security Officer, were reinforced by some shiploads of cloak-and-dagger experts from London. Floodlights and barbed wire surrounded The Convent, where the Governor was to give a state banquet for Her Majesty. There, as officer in charge of the fabric of The Convent, I made my own small contribution, by replacing an old toilet seat with a bright new one. Subsequently, and in spite of all security measures, I found the old one back in place and the new one stolen, to become, no doubt, a hallowed heirloom in some loyal home.

The security men were aware that there was not a single anti-British citizen in Gibraltar, nor a voter against Santa Claus. The four or five perambulating lunatics and tramps, all harmless but unsightly, were made Her Majesty's guests, under lock and key, for the duration of the visit. The only possible danger to the Queen would be from an agent, official or unofficial, of Spain. They began to screen the 13,000 Spanish commuters, male and female, and to check their entry and work passes.

Ninety-nine times out of a hundred, Kings and Presidents visit cities and escape assassination. The security men count these as successes. The fact is, of course, that ninety-nine times out of a hundred there is no danger. Where there is danger, where the determined assassin lays his careful plot, rents his high room and installs his telescopic rifle, there is nothing at all which the security men can do about it. But they have to go on trying. In Gibraltar, as I saw it, in 1954, the security measures were demonstrably absurd. The Englishmen directing the operation spoke no Spanish and, as in Cyprus and Kenya, were dependent on information carried to them. Such informers as there are are not usually the most respectable and dependable of citizens. In this case, since the Spaniards were the only object of suspicion, and since the British security officers could scarcely invade Spain to pursue their inquiries, the chief informers must have been the Spanish Security Police.

But if there existed a Spaniard likely to misinterpret his Government's warning as to the Queen's safety it would be a starry-eyed patriot, would it not? Some dedicated and crackpot *falangista* propelled by ardent love of The Fatherland and a bitter hatred for the heretical English who had desecrated Holy Gibraltar? In short, it would be one of those endorsed by the Spanish Security Service.

Thus, the secure was insecure, and vice versa. The smouldering reds and pinks of Spain, objects of police suspicion there, would not raise a finger in aid of Franco's régime, but would be happy to see it embarrassed by the Royal visit.

As you would expect, many of the passes were filthy, tattered, illegible, outdated, signed with X's, and otherwise unsatisfactory. The older, more decrepit and harmless the bearer, the worse his or her pass might appear. Some ancient crones had lost theirs years ago. Many an old washerwoman was sent back into Spain; many an illiterate workman was turned away to improve his credentials. When my work force began to suffer from this operation I made so bold as to point out that if there were a hired assassin in the queue he might be expected to have the cleanest and clearest of passes. My reward for this advice was a slow and superior smile, and the screening continued.

The immediate effect of this was to cause a queue of waiting workers about half a mile long, stretching from Gibraltar's gates across No Man's Land to La Línea. That sad, hot stretch of land, the soakaway of seven centuries of bloodshed, was to see many another queue in the years to come, but this was the first of all.

The second effect was that a considerable number of workers were prohibited from entering Gibraltar during the Queen's visit. The third effect—and this was my concern—was disruption in the useful work of the place. The fourth effect was to infuriate the Spanish frontier officials and their superiors elsewhere, and this led to the last and worst effect—retaliation. There is no end to the red tape game, as every bureaucrat knows, and in playing this game at the Gibraltar 'frontier' the Spaniards, as I have shown, held every trump card in the pack.

The Spanish Customs, well within their rights, began to search and so delay every car passing from Gibraltar into Spain. They had always waved us on, either to save themselves trouble or just to keep the traffic moving; now they held every vehicle for a quarter of an hour. If you were lucky enough to lie, say fourth in the queue, you had to wait for an hour in the blazing sun. On Sundays, when hundreds—later, thousands—of Gibraltar motorists wished to enter Spain, the last of them would have to wait half the day to enter the promised land. Coming back in the evening with a carload of tired children was a hazard which spoiled the day's outing.

A thoroughly efficient frontier force, such as the British at Dover, would have been causing much greater delays all along, and for far less reason. The Spaniards justified their searching frequently by confiscating minor contraband and charging duty on much else. There are few professional smugglers in Gibraltar, as the Spanish daily 'ABC' has recently admitted, but there are thousands of enthusiastic amateurs at the game. These are people like you and me, or, in these tempting circumstances, a little more developed.

There was, and is, an element of malice in these 'frontier' restrictions. But who is to prove that—or the extent of it? A preventive officer does not overstep the mark if he asks you to take your trousers down and strips the tyres off your car. He must have reasonable suspicion; very well, anyone who did not have suspicion on the Gibraltar 'frontier' would be most unreasonable. Now and then the La Línea Customs caught a car with a false bottom in its boot, or a dummy petrol-tank stuffed with tobacco. I have seen both of these devices myself, and many more. Every such discovery could justify the careful searching of cars for months to come. The effect of this was to lay a finger on Gibraltar's jugular vein.

This legal and lethal weapon, discovered almost by chance by the Spanish Customs in 1954, is being used today, twelve years later, to strangle the economy and destroy the amenity of Gibraltar, to hold the whole community up to ransom. It is lethal because Gibraltar has only one land entrance, one artery of trade and traffic, and one outlet to the hinterland. There stands Spain, angry, armed and implacable.

The Gibraltarians might have pointed out that it was the Royal Visit which brought them this dire visitation, but they raised no cry of protest or recrimination. They said, in effect, an insult to Great Britain is an insult to us. They gave the Queen the customary delirious welcome and then settled down to face their worsened situation.

Now Spain applied to Gibraltar two restrictions which are still in force. Their effect was not felt immediately; they are like wasting diseases, one can live with them for years but the end is inevitable. The Spanish authorities refused to issue passes for any further recruits to the commuting labour force. This had the effect of reducing the force by a steady 300 a year, and also of continuously raising its average age. The natural wastage will accelerate as time passes; the output per worker tends to decline; wages, through lack of competition, have kept on rising.

As well as this, Spain refused to permit any of her nationals to visit Gibraltar as tourists, and thus deprived her of the very considerable income from the rich and privileged Spaniards who were once her most constant customers. The immediate problem, however, was the strangulation of land traffic.

The Gibraltarians, led and advised by Joshua Hassan and his AACR party, instituted an unofficial boycott of Spain. There was some difficulty in persuading all the people to adopt this measure, because many of them had vested interests, country houses, or family ties across the frontier. The persuaders harped on the 'insult' of the searching, and proclaimed that the delays were an affront to *'nuestra dignidad'*,—our dignity. The possessors of dignity never claim it, and the Gibraltarians, like all other colonial subjects, are very touchy about their lack of it, their deprivation by the ruling power. The appeal was effective, and ninety per cent of the people ceased visiting Spain. Those with close family ties, or some other sufficient reason, were allowed to go there without criticism. Those who went merely for recreation were pilloried in the political weeklies of Gibraltar, called men without dignity, blacklegs and traitors.

I, and a few more ex-patriate officers could not agree with this policy, nor could we, as serving officers, express and reason our disagreement. I did point out to some furious Gibraltarians that the British Customs at Dover applied far longer delays than the Spaniards had ever heard of, and that they might well 'insult' a Gibraltarian suspect, or his wife, by calling a strange doctor to subject them to the most undignified physical explorations. I got no thanks for that, nor for pointing out that the border of Spain stretched for some six or seven thousand miles and that Generalissimo Franco was unlikely to be brought to his knees by a boycott on a quarter of a mile of it. The people of Gibraltar were angry, as they are again today, and common sense was left aside. In the summer of 1965, as though to tease them, the Spaniards brought their most famous matador, *El Cordobés*, to the La Línea bullring. Gibraltar's reply was to organize a cricket match for the same day and hour. Many a British wicket fell that afternoon when its unhappy guardian's ears caught the swelling roars of '*Olé!*' from the shunned Sister City.

Our attitude to the boycott subsequently proved to be correct. In 1965, in circumstances similar or worse, the Admiral of Gibraltar took some of his officers into Spain to play polo. On his return he was physically attacked by a local mob led by taxi-drivers deprived of their profitable privilege of driving into Spain. He had to flee and find police protection. The mob marched to The Convent and howled the Governor out of bed on to his balcony, where he made some placatory gestures. In Parliament, later, the Admiralty spokesman exonerated and supported the Admiral, pointing out that the Gibraltarian boycott of Spain had no official standing or authority. He could have added that it was irresponsible and obstructive to negotiations.

Spain's 'frontier restriction' and Gibraltar's boycott dragged on for some months. On The Rock, we organized 'Holidays at Home', but no one was happy. We were, as one Spanish journalist aptly put it, '*una colmena sin jardin*,' a beehive without a garden—thirty thousand beleagured and bewildered bees, cut off from all the flowers. Both health and temper suffered under the Levanter cloud.

Then, after a few months, tentatively and mysteriously, the restrictions slackened. Through mere boredom, through inefficiency or lack of determination, or—said the cynics—because the Spanish Customs chiefs were losing their rake-offs on contraband, the passage of the 'frontier' eased. The Gibraltar blockade eased cautiously, to meet the situation, and soon the bees swarmed back to their garden.

Last year, in Gibraltar, Mr. Julian Amery, now out of office but in the Colonial Office at the time of this first cold war, stated that Britain 'used a lever' on Spain in 1954, and so forced her to relax her restrictions. He refused to specify the lever, but it was presumed to be an economic one for there was no other in sight. At the time I asked a visiting politician if England would consider boycotting Spanish sherry, of which she was the leading consumer. He laughed in my face. 'What!' he said. 'Affect the interests of fifty million people for the sake of 25,000? Not on your life!' I realized that I had been thinking colonially, and that the colonial tail will never wag the British dog in any manner which really matters to it. To the same politician I remember mentioning the Spanish island of Fernando Poo, lying off what was then British territory. It was dependent for labour, to some extent, on commuting British subjects, which was the exact converse of the Gibraltar situation. If the

Spaniards closed the 'frontier' and withdrew the labour force, as seemed likely, could Britain retaliate at Fernando Poo?

'Young man,' said the politician, 'that's all very clever. But the first and last principle of diplomacy is not to tangle up one problem with another and so get two on your hands.' I was glad to hear that there were some guiding rules in our diplomatic practice, and I accepted this at once. Why put the poor West Africans out of work for the sake of Gibraltarians—or vice versa?

Round One—not to count all the rounds of ancient fights—ended with honours even. Or, perhaps, Spain was winning on points. She had shown and proved that Gibraltar was highly vulnerable to such a simple and available weapon as mild frontier restrictions. Gibraltar should have taken warning. The ordinary man, however, lives from hand to mouth and from day to day, especially if he lives in the relaxing climate of the Mediterranean. The ordinary Gibraltarian, once the pressure was removed, reassumed his carefree way of living, did not alter his ways nor tighten his belt, turned his back on the little cloud which continued to hang in the blue Spanish sky. Governments, on the other hand, have a duty to look and plan ahead, to ensure the continuing welfare of the community they govern. After the clear warning of 1954 the Government of Gibraltar had ten years—which might have been far less—to make Gibraltar self-sufficient and independent of Spain's complaisance and co-operation, and to stop the persistent smuggling which was Spain's chief complaint and the pretext for her attacks. Very little, if anything was done, so that the renewed attack of 1964 found The Rock more vulnerable than ever before.

As Europe grew in affluence more and more ships called at Gibraltar, including all the NATO navies, the whaling fleets of Russia, luxury liners from Italy and fishermen from Japan. More and more tourists, about fifty per cent of the total of visitors, came in overland, by Spanish permission. Gibraltar and Spain both reaped a rich harvest from the development, by British, German and Scandinavian capital, of the famous Costa del Sol. It was a boom time for The Rock, as for most other places in the sun, now the balconies of an affluent Europe.

Slowly, but inexorably, the commuting labour force ran down. Building workers and domestic servants became scarce, so that we had to bring them in by the roundabout route—Algeciras–Tangier–

Gibraltar—on well-paid three-month contracts. But there was plenty of money in Gibraltar to pay for that, and for new cars and caravans, speedboats, couture clothes, silk, silver and champagne, and all the world's greatest gadgets. Easy money met untaxed goods, and the people went on a ten-year spending spree. Only the Government, and its servants, remained poor, only the schools, the hospitals and the other essential and responsible services. The thrifty British taxpayer kept on paying for the housing programme.

It was a good time for everyone. For Joan and me, with our blossoming daughter and our growing son, with our fine, free house and our meagre Government salary well subsidized from the bounty of the B.B.C. and the great American magazines, it was the best time of our lives.

My son Paul, three years old, had been out all day, stripped in the sun, helping the Royal Engineers to lay a cable. When he came in for tea he carried an envelope with three pennies in it, his 'wages' for his first day's work.

'Oh, you clever boy,' said his mother. 'Are you going to work for the soldiers again tomorrow?'

'No,' said little Paul sadly. 'There'll be no bloody cement tomorrow.'

Nor, indeed, was there.

28

THE DEBATE CONTINUES

Spain renewed her claim to Gibraltar in 1956 at the United Nations Assembly. No one paid much attention then, to the grievances of this backward and dubious nation. Great Britain made neither admission nor concession. It was clear that Spain had always in view the ultimate concession—the restoration of Gibraltar to Spanish sovereignty. Or, should I say, the recognition of unbroken Spanish sovereignty over Gibraltar?

From 1958 onwards Spain made great strides. A devaluation of currency, a pump-priming new economic policy forced on Franco, at long last, by circumstances and by the aid and advice of the United States, laid the foundations of progress. The boom in tourism, the general overspill of European affluence, brought Spain from the brink of bankruptcy to a new prosperity in the amazingly short space of five or six years. She found a new confidence and optimism which continue to grow.

Concurrently, Britain has flagged and lagged, and continues to do so. Her economic problems, beset with inherited, archaic industry on the one hand and intransigent trade unionism on the other, seem insoluble by democratic means. Spain, by way of contrast, had a clean slate industrially and docile and directed labour at low wage rates, the perfect landfall for floating foreign capital. Britain had been retreating with all possible speed from the expensive embarrassments of her erstwhile Empire, but catching her coat tails, here and there, on the barbed wire as she went.

The next chapter in the Gibraltar story, although only a few years after this reopening shot, finds the opposing parties reversed in their attitudes. Spain has become aggressive, proud and determined; Britain somewhat hangdog, anxious to placate, to court the good opinion of the nations.

'In September 1963 the Committee of 24, in pursuance of its mandate to put a speedy and unconditional end to colonialism in all its forms and manifestations, turned its attention to Gibraltar.'

So begins a pamphlet entitled 'The Future of Gibraltar', published there by the elected members of the Legislative Council in 1964. It goes on to tell how the official petitioners went from Gibraltar to New York to address the Committee. They told the Committee that whereas Gibraltar was indisputably a Crown Colony of Great Britain, it was one in which the evils of colonialism no longer existed, and one which was on the verge of achieving self-government.

The petitioners were Sir Joshua Hassan, then Chief Member of the Legislature and leader of the AACR Party, and the independent member Mr. P. J. Isola, who represented the Opposition.

As one would expect from experienced legal advocates with a carefully considered case, they comported themselves very well. They returned home to a tumultuous welcome, with the whole population of Gibraltar, an army with banners, assembled in John Mackintosh Square to greet the conquerors and hear their report.

'*Venerunt: viderunt: vincerunt!*' said one banner. Another, more typically '*llanito*', or truly Gibraltarian, put it in outmoded cricket parlance: 'Well held, Gents!' Yet a third, in yet a third language, shouted '*Muera Venezuela!*'—Death to Venezuela, the nation whose delegate, either through spontaneous *hispanismo* or prompting from Spain, had hit Gibraltar hardest. The innocent Honorary Consul for Venezuela, a Gibraltarian businessman who had accepted the little sinecure for social reasons, actually had his house attacked by the mob, and had to retreat into Spain for a few days to await the subsidence of hysteria.

Those three banners speak for the three classes in the community. The Spanish-speaking workers, tough, hot-headed and direct; the white-collar workers, shopkeepers and civil servants, uneasily bilingual and *babu*; the rich who had been 'Home' to English public schools and carry the old badge of dog Latin; those are the three voices of Gibraltar. Everyone, of every class, was behind Hassan and Isola on this occasion, and was to remain so as the dispute accelerated towards disaster.

In the cold light of dawn it could be seen that the *conquistadores* had brought back no agreement or reassurance, nothing, in fact, but a postponement of the day of judgment, one year's reprieve. The UNO Committee did not challenge their statements. It merely said to them: 'Your colony has not yet achieved self-government and it is the duty of this Committee—a duty owed both to the United Nations and to the people of Gibraltar—to satisfy itself that your self-government will be no longer delayed. When it is achieved, we shall consider your case again.'

'What case?' Sir Joshua might have asked. 'If we become self-governing, isn't that the end of it?'

To which Dr. Diaz Gonzalez, delegate from Venezuela, his dark eyes ardent with *hispanismo*, might have replied: 'Not quite. There is a little matter of settlement with Spain.' But then again, he might not have said it, for it might have sprung the trap into which the British Government, and Gibraltar, now proceeded to walk.

A few months later, in the spring of 1964, the British Minister of State visited Gibraltar for constitutional conferences. The result, which we have studied already, was an advancement in the emancipation process to what purported to be internal self-government. Gibraltar achieved, or was granted, a fully elected Legislative Council, (but with two seats reserved for necessary officials), a Chief Minister, a Council of Ministers, and a Council of Gibraltar. The Gibraltar pamphlet, which I have quoted, rashly claims that there is an elected majority in the Council of Gibraltar. This is not strictly true, for if the Governor votes with his officials and all the elected members vote against them, then there would be deadlock. In that case, the Secretary of State for the Colonies—Britain again and still—would settle the matter. In practice, whilst there remains an Honours List, the Governor could always bring an elected member to his side in any dispute. One way or the other, Britain remains Cock of The Rock.

However, to a man in a hurry, it looked as if the Chief Minister and his cabinet were in supreme command, as they effectually were, under similar titles in the Mother Country. The UNO Committee and all other critics might well miss the fact that there was no cabinet at all in Gibraltar, within the true meaning of that important word, for the door of the innermost council was blocked permanently ajar by the foot of the Governor and his officials.

But one only finds out such conditions by reading the small print of constitutions. On the face of it, and at the lowest estimate, there had been a very considerable step in the direction desired by Gibraltar and required by UNO. The delegates, strengthened both by the fulfilment of their undertakings and by their magniloquent new titles, must have looked forward with confidence to their next visit to UNO at New York.

The leaders of Gibraltar, with understandable pride, put the new constitutional advance at its highest valuation—coming of age, full responsibility for their own affairs, self-government. The British Government, knowing the United Nations firm insistence on de-colonization, did not seek to diminish its concession to the Colony. Thus, between them, they presented waiting and watching Spain with a ready-made basis of claim far stronger, far sounder, than any she had had before.

That incontrovertible basis is the final, pull-back string of the Treaty of Utrecht:

'And in case it shall hereafter seem meet to the Crown of Great Britain to grant, sell, or by any means to alienate therefrom the propriety of the said town of Gibraltar, it is hereby agreed and concluded, that the preference shall always be given to the Crown of Spain before any others.' It must revert to the landlord, and not to the lodgers.

The climate of international opinion was perfectly propitious, the machinery of UNO was waiting and willing, so, with more con-fidence and clarity than ever before, Spain went to New York and staked her claim. The Gibraltar Question became once again, one of the world's problems. This time, Spain declares and Britain knows, is the last. The Gibraltar Question must now be answered.

Here is an answer to the Gibraltar Question which was offered to me by a Spanish lawyer. It is a wildly improbable solution but, at the same time, a witty and cogent one. It contains the Spanish attitude and point of view.

'Let Britain keep Gibraltar,' says this jurist, 'on a new, cast-iron and permanent basis of cession, guaranteeing open frontiers and every privilege and facility.'

'Thank you,' I said to him, wondering what could be the pay-off for such an offer.

'On the map of England,' he went on, 'not too far from our northern ports, I have found a promontory called Portland Bill. It seems to be very like Gibraltar, about the same size and shape. Not a very useful place—unless it is properly exploited. Now in exchange for the perpetual sovereignty of Gibraltar and all the rights to do as you wish with it, let you offer to Spain exactly the same, by a copy of the new treaty, at your Portland Bill.

'There we would make a port and a naval base, and fortify the hill with guns and rockets, pointing—naturally—at the mainland, as they mostly do in Gibraltar. We would make it a free port, and we would bring in our good brandy, gin—(which we invented),—sherry, champagne and tobacco, and anything else, be it from Tokyo or Timbuktu, which we could dispose of profitably. All imports would be duty free. Some narcotics might find their way in, but in accordance with international agreements we would do what we could to inhibit that trade. Should Spain ever become a democratic republic again, and so, anti-clerical as is her nature, our nationals might import such prostitution and pornography as lay within our laws, which would probably be, as they once were, much more liberal in such matters than yours. Homosexuality would be tolerated, as it is under Spanish law. The ultimate penalty in our new colony would be death by garrotting, according to our law and custom. We would undoubtedly organize a bullfight every Sunday, for there are many *aficionados* in England now, and I do not doubt that they would flock to see it, as they do in Spain today. We would have a great gambling casino, too. I do not doubt that, with all our experience in these matters, we would develop a lucrative tourist trade, as well as a rich entrepôt trade, as you call it in Gibraltar, of fast import-export.

'We should, of course, have the right to admit people of all nations to our *Portlando Billo* to visit or reside at our discretion, and we would build up a Spanish-speaking population of all colours and creeds. We Catholics foster no colour bar, as you know. Anyone, regardless of his racial background or his social history, his funds or his purpose, anyone who felt he had good reason to live under the Spanish flag in a place so detached and so inconvenient, and who saw prospects of prospering there, we would make him welcome. We would even welcome immigrants from Gibraltar, which is more than you, in England, will do yourselves. We would demand that all our people could enter England as and when they wished, to travel or stay there, subject only to the usual time limit on tourists. English workers, entering our territory as commuters, would be paid Spanish wages and subject to the trade union laws of our country.

'We would also offer political asylum to anyone arriving at our gates or port, and sanctuary, pending extradition proceedings, to all alleged criminals. Exercising our full sovereignty over our *Portlando*

Billo, we would not expect to be asked to account for any of our subjects or visitors there, nor for their trade nor manner of living.

'Now in the event of war, whether England be neutral or, as seems more likely, engaged, *Portlando Billo* would, of course, remain Spanish, to be put to such use as our government might see fit. In the event of our colony being attacked by some enemy of Spain, and of Spain being unable to defend it, then England shall not violate our sovereignty by making this a pretext to enter it and defend it. Rather, England shall let it fall, in default of Spanish defence, to whomsoever attacks it.

'In the event of Spain tiring of the responsibility for her colony, or finding it unprofitable, or its citizens disaffected or troublesome, or should *Portlando Billo* become a cause of international contention or anti-colonial pressures, then the sovereignty of the place may be handed over by Spain to the local inhabitants, whomsoever they may then be, for them to take such political course and make such international associations and alliances as they may, from time to time, see fit. And they may hold the place for themselves as best they can, or sell it, or give it away to such nation as may seem propitious to them.'

'Very good,' I told him. 'But there is a catch in all this.'

'What is that?'

'That Great Britain, no more than Spain, would seriously consider setting up an awkward enclave like Gibraltar in this day and age, nor would the United Nations countenance it. But Gibraltar exists and has existed as a British possession for 260 years, and her people, wherever they came from and for whatsoever reason, have been British subjects for a long time, and that they do not wish to change.'

'No,' said the Spaniard. 'They do not wish to become Spanish and go to work. They want full freedom to run their own racketty community. They want close association with Britain, for free hand-outs and defence. They want friendship with Spain, for easy smuggling and tax-free recreation——'

'They want as much as they **can get**,' I said. 'Like all men—everywhere——'

'They have had too much for too long,' said the Spaniard, getting angry now. 'They cannot have it any longer. They will have to change their way of life to live with our great new Spain. Or, perhaps, go away to *Portlando Billo*, which I do not doubt your ever-

generous country would place at their full disposal, and start all over
again.'

That is the voice of Spain on the subject of Gibraltar, the voice
of implacable dislike and distrust, not to say hatred and contempt.
Should it arise from envy and malice, or from insult and injury, is
not material. It is the voice which was heard at length before the
UNO De-colonization Committee in 1964, and which continues to
speak in Spain's press and in her diplomatic correspondence. Whilst
Gibraltar remains British, that voice will never be silenced.

When Sir Joshua and Mr. Isola, re-elected and reappointed as I
have described, flew out to New York to meet the foe in September
1964, there, waiting for them, was Dr. Diaz Gonzalez, delegate from
Venezuela, in no better humour, we may take it, for the abuse which
his country had suffered in Gibraltar throughout the past year.
Beside him, his friends, the redoubtable Sr. Jaime de Pinies of Spain
and Sr. Velasquez of Uruguay. There too was Mme. Rousseau of
Mali, who hates all military bases, and the Arabs, mysteriously
sympathetic to their ancient enemy, Spain—the delegates from
Tunisia, Syria and Iraq.

And who are these grim-visaged, hispanic newcomers at the petitioners' table? No one we know. No one distinguished, surely, or we
would have seen them before. . . .

Then Sir Joshua Hassan, for twenty years mayor of Gibraltar,
recognized one of Spain's new petitioners. It was his neighbour, his
opposite number across the 'frontier'—Don Pedro Hidalgo Martin,
the mayor of San Roque.

There must have been a shuffling of maps on the committee
tables. Where on earth is San Roque? A big city, surely, or Spain
would not have sent its mayor to plead her case at this international
tribunal. . . . Here it is—down here at the bottom of Spain, a mere
dot on the map of mountains. It is, in fact, the little hillside town,
founded just out of gunshot by the Spanish refugees of 260 years ago,
the fugitives from the British conquest and rapine of Gibraltar in
1704.

No, San Roque is not a big city, but it looms big on the horizon,
and on the conscience, of Gibraltar. Its town hall holds the original
charter of the disputed municipality, and its arms carry the legend:
'The most loyal etc. city of San Roque, in which resides that of
Gibraltar.'

Don Pedro Hidalgo was the first of the petitioners to be heard by the Committee. He said that he wished the Gibraltarians well, and that he had no wish to evict them in their turn. He sought the integration of Gibraltar with the Campo area of neighbouring Spain, which he claimed to represent. Then they could all march forward to prosperity together as friends and neighbours. He did not make it clear what Gibraltar was to live on if she ceased to be a military and naval base and a 'free port', and if her tourist attractions were to be placed in straight competition with those of Torremolinos and Marbella.

He went on to say that if, by unilateral decision, Great Britain gave Gibraltar full local government in contravention of the Treaty, then Spain would feel free of all obligations towards the place and would proceed to isolate it. The people of the Campo would suffer for a little while, until re-employed in Spain; the Gibraltarians would suffer permanently. As though by way of apology for his threats—which he categorized as 'warnings'— Don Pedro complained that he had been attacked in the Gibraltar press, had received threats of physical violence, and had had to close his offices in La Línea.

The second speaker was a Spanish professor, Don Camilio Barcia Trelles, an expert on international law—and on Gibraltar. His main point, reached with vast and learned prolixity, was that the Gibraltar Question cannot be answered by permitting the people self-determination, since under the Treaty the people do not exist, and even if they did exist they would be under Spanish jurisdiction.

Sir Joshua Hassan rose to the defence next day, and excelled himself. He dismissed Hidalgo as 'a public official', drawing attention to the fact that he was not democratically elected and, hence, not representative of true public opinion. He said that the founding of San Roque was only a hoary legend, that Spain was 'dragging this historical corpse across the trail which this Committee is called upon to follow'. He pointed out that Spain could not say, on the one hand, that the original Gibraltarians had been driven into exile, and on the other, that they were still in Gibraltar under the oppression of a foreign colonizer. Spain had sought to mislead the Committee by introducing this human factor, but the strongest human factor lay with the 20,000 decent people who had sent him here.

What did Sr. Hidalgo seek? Not that the people of San Roque should return to Gibraltar, but that the process of de-colonization should be halted in Gibraltar and the place returned to Spain. But how 'returned'? The people had not come from Spain, were not Spanish, never had belonged to Spain, and did not wish to belong to Spain. Where would be the justice in 'returning' them?

Sir Joshua went on to explain who his people were, and to show that, in spite of mixed ancestry—a condition neither rare nor bad—they were now an ethnic entity. He concluded by appealing to the delegates. He had come to them, last year, to seek their support for the constitutional advancement of his community; it would be bitter irony if they now stood to lose from the Committee's consideration. 'I feel confident that you will uphold the very spirit and letter of the United Nations Charter and support our claim to the right of self-determination.'

Mr. Peter Isola agreed with all that Sir Joshua Hassan had said and seemed to show that the people of Gibraltar were unanimous on the main issue. No one pointed out to him that although there was no disagreement then, there might well be in the future. He devoted much time to replying to Spanish press attacks on the Gibraltarian community, and rightly said that his people could not relish joining a country where they appeared to be so hated and despised. This Committee's mandate was to study, and to further, the wishes of the people in each colonial territory it considered, not merely to hand communities from one colonial power to another.

Don Jaime de Pinies, Spain's delegate, put his faith in the Treaty of Utrecht, and sprang the constitutional trap. He said that Great Britain, compelled to countenance de-colonization in general, sought to remain in Gibraltar by invoking the principle of self-determination. But there cannot be self-determination, obviously, until there is self-government. To grant self-government to the Gibraltarians would be a clear breach of Article X of the Treaty upon which Great Britain took her stand and which was her only claim to be in Gibraltar.

The manœuvre began in 1950, said Sr. de Pinies, when Britain inaugurated a Legislative Council in Gibraltar. Spain, never asked nor told, protested soon afterwards, and Lord Salisbury, for Great Britain, had rejected their protest in 1953. Later, General Franco had offered bi-lateral talks on the whole question of Gibraltar and its future. Great Britain had replied that the talks were not necessary, since there was no intention of proceeding any further towards self-government in Gibraltar. All of these exchanges, he said, had been kept secret from the public both in the United Kingdom and in Gibraltar. Constitutional advancement proceeded, at intervals, in spite of assurances that it would cease.

Here I interrupt to recall that the main constitutional advance during the period under discussion was forced on the British Government by the Gibraltarian politicians when they revolted against certain proposed taxes and resigned from the Legislature. Lord Salisbury, who could not have foreseen such behaviour, may well have spoken in perfectly good faith. But what of Mr. Nigel Fisher? On the 30th April 1963, Sr. de Pinies asserted, when Mr. Fisher was a responsible Minister, he assured the House of Commons that no constitutional changes were under consideration for Gibraltar. This statement had the effect of misleading Spain and was very soon followed by constitutional changes.

And but a few months ago, said Sr. de Pinies, the British Government had denied that the Treaty of Utrecht constituted even limited rights for Spain in 'a part of its own territory'. And two days ago, Britain had stated to this Committee that she 'fully accepted that the people of Gibraltar should choose the form of their association with Britain'. Thereby Britain reduced her *raison d'être* in Gibraltar from the basis of a contractual agreement with Spain to that of the wishes of a population created by Britain. That was the end of the Treaty of Utrecht.

'If self-determination were granted to Gibraltar, Spain would regretfully make it a condition of normal relations that the United Kingdom should withdraw completely from The Rock. Unless this occurred Spain would sever all links with Gibraltar and declare its inhabitants *persona non grata* in Spain.' The only acceptable and reasonable solution to the Gibraltar Question, ended Sr. de Pinies, would be the return of Gibraltar to Spanish sovereignty.

Mr. Cecil King, the United Kingdom's permanent delegate, told the Committee that the constitutional changes in Gibraltar would in no way damage the interests of Spain. But later in the debate Spain told him that only she could judge that. Certainly, Britain was in no position to guarantee it. Once granted self-government, to which they seemed so close, or self-determination empowering a choice, say, of full independence, the Gibraltarian government might do as it pleased. It might, conceivably, be overpowered by its own people and The Rock might become a communist republic. That would be unlikely, as things are now, but other courses harmful to Spain are less so. With a majority of the Ministers directly or indirectly interested in the 'entrepôt trade', what could be more likely than that it would be encouraged, facilitated and extended? It would be perfectly legitimate for them to reduce the import duty on tobacco, or on whatever happened to be highly taxed across their frontier—and most damaging to the interests of Spain.

Mr. King stated clearly, with the Treaty of Utrecht lying open before him: 'For over 250 years my Government have exercised sovereignty over Gibraltar, a sovereignty established and reaffirmed by Treaty.' Had I been the Spanish delegate opposite I think I would have had these words from the Treaty printed on a placard and suspended from my neck—'without any territorial jurisdiction'. But diplomatic negotiations proceed less emphatically.

Mr. King also stated: 'My Government do not accept that there is any commitment under the Treaty of Utrecht binding us to refrain from applying the principle of self-determination to the people of Gibraltar.' The Spanish placard in this case would have read: 'In case it shall seem meet to . . . by any means alienate the propriety of the said town . . . it is hereby agreed that the preference . . . shall always be given to . . . Spain before any others.'

The main speeches on the Gibraltar Question, for and against, claims and disclaimers, were all good, but none of them was good enough to convince, to carry the day. The Question was too old and too wide, too fraught with side issues, to be solved, or even simplified. Some days of questioning followed the presentation. Sir Joshua Hassan made it clear to the Committee that the Gibraltarians had never claimed independence. They wanted free association with Britain, and envisaged no change in sovereignty. The question of conflict with the Treaty would not therefore arise, in his opinion, and it was for that reason only that he had not mentioned the Treaty in his original statement.

That statement of his was, of course, very far from being reassuring or satisfactory to Spain, or to the Committee. 'Free association', by the fact of being free, could be abrogated at any time by the Gibraltarians of the future. Like most Latin peoples, they are demonstrably volatile and excitable in their politics. Hassan had, it is true, exercised a very long and stable hegemony in Gibraltar, but that may have been because he had, as everyone could see, long and delicate negotiations with Great Britain in hand, and no one wished to interrupt the course of constitutional advancement. His word 'envisaged', in his statement, would be suspect, too. It implies that the Gibraltarians do not intend, at the moment, to drop their allegiance to Britain, that they do not seek to do so 'so far as he could see'. But with the best will in the world, Sir Joshua could not see ten years ahead—nor even five. He knew it, and so, in honesty, he chose the cautious word. The Spaniards and the Committee knew it, too. The fact is that the political climate of Gibraltar has changed greatly in the two years since those words were spoken, with the growth of a large new party demanding Integration.

Later in the week the delegate from Uruguay caught out Mr. Cecil King by quoting a recent British document which stated, in another connection, that self-determination was not a right, as it had been claimed for Gibraltar, but merely a principle.

At about this stage in the argument Mr. King decided to throw down his ace. They were all agreed, he said, even Spain, that Gibraltar was a colony. The sole business of this Committee was de-colonization. But Spain's dispute with Britain, based on a claim to this British territory, was not a colonial question at all. It was something greater. This Committee, therefore, was not competent to discuss the matter.

After nine days of discussions, this would seem disappointing, to say the least of it. But the Committee, tired, perhaps, of Gibraltar, seemed to be very glad to wash their hands of it. They thanked the petitioners and dismissed them to await the verdict.

It was advice, rather than a verdict, which reached the petitioners some two weeks later:

'The Special Committee has in addition noted the existence of a disagreement or even dispute between the United Kingdom and Spain over the status and situation of the territory of Gibraltar.

'In these circumstances the Special Committee invites the United Kingdom and Spain to undertake without delay conversations in order to find a negotiated solution in keeping with the charter of the United Nations.'

Mr. King, for Great Britain, immediately objected to the words 'status and situation'. His Government, he said, would not feel bound by the terms of any recommendation by the Committee touching on sovereignty or territorial claims. The Spaniards, on the other hand, would not wish to discuss anything else. The Committee had washed its hands, and knocked their heads together, and told them to reason together. But mere reason, sad to say, will never solve the Gibraltar Question.

As before, Gibraltar's representatives received a triumphant welcome home, with the whole population out in the streets. But Sir Joshua was cautious.

'This is not an occasion for defeatism,' he told the people, 'nor is it one for celebration so far as the future is concerned.' As it immediately transpired, there was no future. That day was the end of happy, carefree, profitable life for the people of Gibraltar. But they had been warned, again and again, and now Sir Joshua warned them yet once more. He asked them, in five different ways, to behave themselves, and they all knew what he meant for in only one respect was the behaviour of Gibraltar open to criticism. 'I tell you', he said, 'that we have to be a little introspect (sic; circumspect?), to think a lot, to make sure that our conduct is the very best possible, that we are . . . an honest community.'*

That day, quietly and without announcement, Spain recommenced the frontier delays which had proved so effective ten years before. A few days later the Spanish Customs officers apprehended a Gibraltarian motorist and charged him with smuggling transistor radios. From then until, months later, the traffic stopped, from risk and fear, the Spanish coastguards systematically seized the smuggling launches based on Gibraltar. In February 1966 they stationed a patrol boat right in the mouth of Gibraltar's harbour. When the Gibraltar police launch asked them to move out the Spanish captain retorted that his business was not civil but military.

When asked if this sudden severity of contraband control is designed to penalize Gibraltar for her defiance at UNO, or to drag Great Britain to the bargaining table under duress, Spain makes one simple reply. 'Smuggling from Gibraltar had been on the increase for some years back, and we have a right and duty to discourage it.' At all times, they have strictly observed the terms of the Treaty

* *Gibraltar Chronicle*, 12th October 1964.

by permitting provisions to be imported into the Fortress by land from Spain. They may still legally, stop that import.

The Gibraltarians reimposed their unofficial boycott on Spain. Since they could not drive there in their cars—except with long delay—they refused to walk. As a matter of principle, they say, and of pride, they have made themselves voluntary prisoners, and The Rock has been, for two long years, and more, 'a beehive without a garden'.

*   *   *   *

Joan and I, now retired from the Service, spent the years 1964 and 1965 on the Costa del Sol. At first, we came to Gibraltar frequently, to visit friends, exchange books, and buy the few goods unobtainable in Spain. We used to leave our car in La Línea and walk through the 'frontier', a cumbersome approach, but tolerable on occasion. On our return the Spaniards would charge us twenty-five per cent duty on everything we had bought. 'On stationery?' I complained. 'On bacon and cheese? Show me the tariff of imposts. Take me to the Chief Officer.'

'There is no tariff here,' the Chief of Customs told me. 'It does not apply at La Línea. This is not, and never has been an official Spanish frontier. It is not a normal entry point. It is a police post.'

'It looks very like a frontier to me——'

'And I may look very like an Irishman,' he said. 'But I am not one. And now, friend, I have to warn you about that car of yours. It is in Spain on temporary importation, is it not?'

'Yes. I am still a visitor. I have not needed—yet—to take out a residence permit.'

'Exactly. So the car has not paid taxes?'

'No. Not yet.'

'Then I would point out to you that you may not leave it in Spain. The privilege of an untaxed car is personal, and you must personally remain in possession of the vehicle. Spain entrusts it to you. If you abandon it, then it will be my duty to confiscate it. I could have done so today.'

Joan and I bowed ourselves backwards from his presence and so, in the spring of 1965, Gibraltar lost her last overland customers.

Gibraltar's shops became empty of people, low of stocks. Even the bars suffered loss of trade. The people were losing money, or hoarding such money as they possessed. They are, by temperament, a spending rather than a saving people, and very few of them would have much in the sock. The streets became choked with idle cars— cars bought dirt cheap, duty-free, second and third hand, by every family on The Rock, for week-end excursions on the mainland. There was no joy in Gibraltar now, and no escape. There was endless debate, debate at all levels, informed and uninformed. But mostly uninformed, for the Government, such is the traditional style of the British Raj, gave the people little or no information as to their plight, present or future, nor as to their efforts, if any, to relieve it. As a result, hearsay took over and rumour ran rife. Suspicion, alarm and despondency spread. The columns of *Vox* were given over to strident complaint and vainglorious, futile defiance.

The debate continues still. Tourist traffic has declined by about fifty per cent—the erstwhile overlanders. The British bound for the Costa del Sol resorts found themselves forced to avoid Gibraltar and fly to Málaga instead. BEA, with a foot in both camps, reduced its Gibraltar flights. The decline in trade generally is estimated at be- tween forty and seventy per cent—depending on whether you are trotting the horse for buying or for selling. The rich Gibraltarians, living on their fat, take their leisure in Tangier or farther afield. The poor—poorer now, as prices rise daily, and cut off from the cheap markets in Spain—the poor sweat it out on The Rock.

Every few weeks, Spain tightens the screw a little, as Great Britain is doing to Rhodesia. Eight hundred Gibraltarians, resident in La Línea by custom and tolerance, but without formal permission, were sent back to Gibraltar. Passports signed by the chief official of the new and 'unrecognized' Government of Gibraltar were refused Spanish recognition, just as Britain is refusing those of Rhodesian Smith.

Certain citizens of Gibraltar have been declared *persona non grata* in Spain, and forbidden to enter. They are the members of the Legislative and City Councils, some officials and journalists, and men known to be implicated in the contraband trade. One of Gibraltar's reprisals was to publish figures proving that among the main buyers of smuggled whisky were the chiefs of the La Línea Customs, a disclosure which injured two Spaniards directly and 20,000 Gibraltarians less so.

No one knows, nor can guess, what Spain may do to Gibraltar

tomorrow, or next week. Recently, consequent on the American nuclear bomb accident at Almeria, NATO aircraft from Gibraltar were warned not to fly over Spanish territory. It seems a reasonable request, but such is The Rock's little airstrip that aircraft cannot use it without crossing parts of Spain. In February 1966 the Spaniards prohibited the importation of all and any goods at La Línea, declaration and payment of duty notwithstanding. Their 'police post', they say, is not manned to deal with merchandise. If you struggle into Gibraltar overland, from now on, you must leave it empty-handed.

What next? Object, some say, to the newly resident Moors, shipped into Gibraltar to make up the declining Spanish labour force? Moors are specifically forbidden in the Treaty. No one doubts that the first day it suits her Spain will slam the rusting gates of La Línea completely and for ever, leaving Gibraltar 'without any open communication with the country round about', in the manner agreed and intended.

After two years of this two-way blockade and boycott, Gibraltar is faced with becoming an island. More isolated, in fact, than most islands, for it is an island off an inhospitable coast, its islanders forbidden to trade and prevented from travelling there. Since there is no solution in sight, what should they do? What courses are open to the Gibraltarians today, to preserve their way of life, their tenure of their tiny homeland?

The most, perhaps the only constructive proposal, has come from Mr. Solomon Seruya, Hassan's chief rival in the Legislative Council. He suggested, and fully blue-printed, a policy of friendly co-opera-tion with Spain, a joint development of the Campo area to the benefit of both sides. He would, like every other Gibraltarian, remain British, in close association with Britain, but in even closer associa-tion, commercially and economically, with the next-door neighbour. The London *Times* published and commended this view, but Sir Joshua Hassan and his AACR waxed furious. Seruya was de-nounced, in his absence from The Rock, as something approaching a traitor, but he succeeded in reinstating himself on return by point-ing out that he had consistently proposed such a common-sense *entente* for many years. Furthermore, he could truly say, had his wise advice been taken in 1954, the present disastrous situation need never have arisen.

After some weeks of stalemate, bickering and frustration, Sir Joshua Hassan was compelled to form a coalition Government, and Mr. Seruya was given a ministerial post which, on the face of it, empowered him to proceed with his policy. Alas, it is, of course, too late for that, or for any other constructive policy. The effect of forming a coalition and making every member of the Legislature a 'Minister', was to silence all criticism and curiosity. The pattern of Legco meetings has now become: 'Nothing done, and no questions asked.' The Council has another three years to run before it need seek re-election. What will happen to it then is mere academic speculation, for it cannot see three days ahead.

It would take a greater Solomon than Mr. Seruya to find a solution for Gibraltar's problems. Spain has the whip hand, and she knows it. No sop will satisfy her, she is frankly and openly set on sovereignty. But the pressing and immediate problem is economic— how to develop a self-sufficient, island economy in Gibraltar at once.

The great garrison, six thousand men at one time, and a chief source of the town's income right up to 1960, has been run down to a token force. Now the R.A.F. is to be withdrawn. Liberal opinion in Parliament and press would reduce Britain's overseas commitments still further. There is a dockyard, but where is the navy? Turn over to civil ship repairs? Not with the shipyards of the United Kingdom closing down—and repairs in Gibraltar, in any case, have the reputation of being both slow and expensive. Smuggling—call it import-export, entrepôt, or what you wish—is forcibly prevented. The tourist trade, the great hope of Gibraltar wherein, just prior to the disaster, she was putting her money and her trust, has been halved and still declines. Every travel agent in the world has to tell his clients to avoid The Rock. Shall we raise taxes, then, to refurbish the place as a self-contained holiday paradise? But how do you tax men who are losing money? And, in any case, freedom from taxes has always been Gibraltar's chief offer and attraction to her visitors.

Let us, then, consider attracting new capital from outside. But how do you attract new capital to a concern in the hands of the Receiver? To a resort full of new, half-empty hotels, short of useful labour, and of most uncertain destiny and destination? No wise investor, British or foreign, will risk a pound on Gibraltar until her future is clarified. The press of the place has declared this fact and the big money of Gibraltar's own citizens is known to be safely stowed elsewhere.

Such, then, are the economic choices, and they are poor enough. The political choices are even less promising. Some, tired of their catspaw position between Britain and Spain, are crying 'Independence'. But that would be clearly illegal, and would invite Spain to immediate and easy invasion, on the precedent of Goa. The United Nations might heave a sigh of relief. Some are saying 'Self Determination' leading to 'Free Association with Great Britain'. That is the Government's choice, and it seems moderate and reasonable but, as we have seen at UNO, it is not acceptable to Spain. It would have the effect of elevating the Gibraltarians to full management and control, and that would be against the Treaty and, it is claimed, inimical to Spanish interests.

Now a strong group, almost a political party, has arisen to campaign for the only other choice—the only other approved, in general, by UNO. It is 'Integration with Great Britain'. Spain, claiming that all her little colonies are integrated 'provinces' of the Fatherland, could not object to this. The Group has made a sound study of the constitutions of the Channel Islands, the Isle of Man, and other quaint and archaic survivals. But it has omitted to ask the essential, basic question. Would the Mother of Parliaments, currently and consciously embarrassed by eleven built-in backwoodsmen from the only integrated territory, Northern Ireland, welcome other candidates for integration? Would Westminster welcome a couple of Gibraltarians now, elected as they are by a few hundred votes, to entertain it with complaints about Spanish insults and declarations of dignity, or to campaign for further contributions from the British tax-payer? It is better not to ask.

The endless debate continues. Now a new spectre arises and begins to prey on the common man in Gibraltar—the spectre of unemployment. There is plenty of manual work, so much that Moors have to be imported to do it. But the few Gibraltarians who were willing and able for manual work have been in employment long ago and remain so. The unemployment is growing among the white-collar workers. One cannot set a clerk to cobbling, nor ask a car salesman to cut people's hair.

So, in desperation, for they love their sunny Rock, the Gibraltarians have sought permission to emigrate to Britain. May they have a special immigrant quota, in view of their plight? To this plea the British Government, with its new Immigration Act, has had to give a regretful refusal. It would look like colour discrimination, they say. Besides, it would not be in the best interests of Gibraltar. No, there was nothing for it but to wait.

Spain kept on pressing for talks, in accordance with the instructions of the Special Committee, saying that the subject of sovereignty must be included. Britain refused to discuss sovereignty, or to discuss anything until the 'frontier' returned to normal.

Mr. Wilson, who had been Prime Minister of Britain since the Gibraltar Question became acute, was in no position, with his precarious majority, to seek a showdown with Spain. His erstwhile opposition to Spain, in matters such as the supply of frigates and the joint army manœuvres, brought him nothing but abuse and criticism. Gibraltar's leading friend in Parliament, Major Patrick Wall, seemed far from being the most influential man in the House. The more redoubtable Mr. St. John Stevas was sympathetic, but was insulted by the Gibraltar press for having a swim during his visit, and seemed disinclined to pursue the fight.

In October 1965, on the expiry of the prescribed year, the parties reported to the UNO Committee. They said that they could not agree on a basis for the requested talks on Gibraltar. The Committee reported this disagreement to the General Assembly. On 16th December 1965 the General Assembly of the United Nations Organization knocked together the heads of Britain and Spain, and told them to hold the talks without further delay.

Still busy with other matters, with nothing to be gained in the matter of Gibraltar and much to be lost, Mr. Wilson stuck to his two conditions. Spain refused to accept either of them. Then, in February 1966, he made up his mind to dissolve Parliament and hold a General Election in March. If he increased his majority he would have both the power and the time to deal with Gibraltar. If he decreased his majority he would lose power, and enjoy watching the Tories handling the Gibraltar gelignite. With these alternatives in mind, then, the Labour Government removed both the conditions, and agreed to talk on Spain's own terms.

We have already investigated UNO's three recommended courses for emergent colonies. These talks will bring them out into the open,

for public examination. They will discover that none of the three
can answer The Gibraltar Question, thus:

1　*Independence* Britain throws Gibraltar overboard, in full
breach of the Treaty of Utrecht. Spain would be justified in
rendering The Rock untenable, or in seizing it at once. This
is a very unlikely course, and one which Britain has fore-
sworn.

2　*Integration* This course, sought by many Gibraltarians, implies the full political incorporation of Gibraltar with the
United Kingdom. It would not suit Britain; it would infuriate
Spain; many Gibraltarians would have strong objections. For
Britain, it would be a liability, an embarrassment, and a
nuisance. For Spain it would be an acerbation of the territorial
insult. For the rich leaders of Gibraltar it would mean a head-
long flight, with their funds, from the threat of British taxation.
All present problems, political and economic, would become
more serious. The only gainers would be those Gibraltarians
who feel a pressing need for a welfare state; it would be better
and cheaper to allow such unfortunates entry to the United
Kingdom. Integration is a most unlikely outcome, against all
common sense, internationally troublesome and dangerous,
and subject to the censure of UNO and the world.

3　*Self-determination* This, leading to immediate declaration of
Close Association with Great Britain, is the timidly voiced
official choice. But both Britain and Gibraltar have been fear-
ful in furthering it, for it would be in breach of the Treaty.
Self-determination pre-requires Self-Government, for you
must be free to choose before you choose. Self-Government
cannot be granted, for The Rock can be handed to no one but
Spain. Once freed, Spain could argue, if only for ten minutes,
the Gibraltarians might choose Close Association with China.
Britain has no right to free them. Spain need never agree to
this course of action, and will never agree to it, and to promote
it unilaterally would be to ask for trouble. It is not to be
considered as a possible solution.

With those three standard formulas discarded, the talks must
proceed to seek agreement or, at least, compromise. I can

see three possible outcomes, and three only. They are as follows:

(a) Deadlock on the basic question of Sovereignty. Neither side prepared to face the risk of final arbitration on the key words of the Treaty—'without territorial jurisdiction' and 'propriety'. The talks may be abandoned. The frontier will then be further restricted, or closed completely, and all Gibraltarians banned from Spain. The community would then have to be fully subsidized by Britain, a hand-out of some £3 million per annum, indefinitely, or pending assisted emigration of the population to Australia or such other Commonwealth country as will welcome it.

(b) Britain offers Spain a limited form of cession—e.g. with some degree of autonomy or devolution for the Gibraltarian community within the Spanish state. But Spain, having fought a bitter war to rescind the devolution of the Basques and Catalans, and having Unity as one of the three main planks in her platform, must reject the offer. She will go on citing the Treaty, which prescribes the return of Gibraltar without any strings. One of her declared objects is to end the privileges of the Gibraltarians and hence, she says, the abuse of her hospitality.

Spain might cunningly accept some such compromise, however, and then seize Gibraltar later, on some pretext which the Gibraltarians might be expected to provide.

(c) Britain cedes Gibraltar to Spain, fully and freely. Spain promises to be kind to the Gibraltarians. Gibraltarians are offered the choice of retaining British citizenship and emigrating, or accepting Spanish citizenship and remaining on The Rock. The result of such a plebiscite, in my view, and in disregard of local statements to the contrary, would be a fifty-fifty split in the population. Many hundreds of Gibraltarians had opted for residence in Spain in my time there, so that there was a community of eight hundred of them in La Línea alone. To retire to a castle in Spain is even more a Gibraltarian dream than it is an English one. To do business and make money in Spain, under Spanish law, is another matter.

Of these three possible outcomes of the talks, (a) and (b) which fail to reach agreement with Spain, are merely temporary. They would leave Gibraltar in a state of chronic siege, leading to ultimate desolation. Subsidizing a nation to help it get to its feet is an under-taking acceptable to the British people; subsidizing a nation with-out hope of betterment, as though to help it into its grave, that is another matter. Britain is in no position to underwrite funereal pomp.

Solution (c) emerges, sadly indicated as the only final and lasting choice, whatever others may be interpolated to delay it. It offers the Gibraltarian either democracy in exile or direction at home. It is a bitter choice, but all the circumstances point to it. Some of the people are aware of it already, and are facing it bravely, but a majority will complain most bitterly when the day comes.

For the Gibraltarians, and for me, for a while, with them, the way of life was too good to last. We had the best of both worlds and a foot in each camp. Untaxed and duty-free, we throve on Britain's security, generosity and justice, and drank in the sunshine and sus-tenance of Spain. In the end, the wheel of colonialism turned full circle at Gibraltar. The cry of the old American colonists was re-versed when Britain handed The Rock representation without taxa-tion, self-government and subsidy in a package deal, with freedom to call the tune and freedom from paying the piper. But such tax havens and human heavens are not viable, and the day of retribution had to come.

Now that one hundred million people, British and Spanish, may quarrel, may even come to blows, over the future of the 20,000 citizens of Gibraltar, may they come to see it as their duty to sub-mit quietly to arbitration, to make their hard choice without any further complaint. The fervent and vociferous loyalty of the Gibral-tarian, and his professed gratitude to his British benefactor, might now be proven by his calm acceptance of this first and final sacrifice.

I lived in Spain throughout 1965, on very limited funds, and I found no hardship of any kind. Were I a Gibraltarian on the day of reckoning I would accept Spanish citizenship and, I hope, go into Spain like St. James of old, armed with the knowledge of human worth and dignity and the vision of the good life. In Spain I would work, however slowly, towards democracy, towards freedom and justice. If the Gibraltarian, with his special experience, can help that beautiful and generous country to achieve government as good as Britain's, then his children, or their children, may come to live as he himself has lived, with the best of both worlds.

*   *   *   *

There could be no promotion for me in Gibraltar. I was second-in-command of the Works Department. The top job—Commissioner —had been Gibraltarianized before my arrival, and it was understood that it would always remain so, other things being equal or unequal. Mainly for this reason, I kept pressing for a transfer. I was approaching forty, and under-employed. Such was the shrinkage of our erstwhile Empire that it took the Colonial Office and its off-shoots five years to find me another post, although I was, I honestly believe, one of the most highly qualified men in the Service.

It came through in 1961 and I accepted transfer to the Gilbert & Ellice Islands Colony, where I became Commissioner of Works. When I waded ashore there the Resident Commissioner greeted me with tears in his eyes: 'Thank God you've come, at last! I've been screaming for a qualified man for five years!'

We left Gibraltar in full swing, full boom, taking no thought for the morrow. Were we glad to go, or sorry? Both, as usual. Glad, because it was becoming difficult, under devious political pressures, for a senior civil servant to do his duty 'without fear or favour', and to keep his mouth shut. Glad, because we needed a change. My journalism—I was critic for the *Gibraltar Chronicle* in Art, Drama, Cinema and the Bullfight—was growing stale. My daughter had just graduated from high school; my son was marking time in a local private school. As for Joan, it was difficult to judge; she always says she likes what I like, but in this case I think she did. We were of an age to be restless.

We were sorry to leave because we had a love-hate relationship with Gibraltar and its people. I have said too much already of the things I hated there. The folly, as I saw it, still see it, was the grit in my oyster. That grit was long suffered in silence by a civil servant, and is now spewed out in this book. The love remains with me, love for the gaiety, the wit, the honest roguery, tenderness and simplicity of the ordinary Gibraltarian.

The people of The Rock have a greeting which is not to be heard elsewhere. In the street they hail each other with 'Good-bye!' It is a straight translation of the word they used to use before they became self-consciously British, before they learnt English and cricket. That word was the Spanish '*Adios*', which men exchange in passing.

In 1964 we were back in Gibraltar, retired, at last without either trammels or powers. The people could take us or leave us now, for we had no official existence. They took us with such warmth that we could make no progress in the streets. I took refuge in the Government Offices and called on my first friend, old Mauricio Carvillo. He raised his eyes from his work, leapt up and rushed at me to give me an *abrazo*: 'John! My dearest! Good-bye!'

We began to exchange our news. I noticed that Mauricio was blushing slightly . . . he had reviewed that 'Good-bye', and he was vaguely aware that it was not English. When I rose to go he ran round his desk and clasped my hand again. '*Maravilloso! Maravilloso* on seeing you again, old chap!' And then, as I walked through the door, he called after me: 'Hello!'

BIBLIOGRAPHY

The author read and studied the following books and periodicals:

The History of the Herculean Straits by Thomas James, London, 1771.

History of Gibraltar by Ignacio Lopez de Ayala, Madrid, 1766, and in James Bell's translation, London, 1845.

Fr. Romero's account of the British Conquest of Gibraltar; MS in Garrison Library; 1706 or so.

A Siege Journal by Col. Guise; 1727; in Garrison Library.

A contemporary MS on the Siege of 1727; Anon; Garrison Library.

An Account of the Siege of Gibraltar, 1727; by W. Smith; MS in Garrison Library.

Reflections on the Situation of Gibraltar; Anon; 1731; in Garrison Library.

Siege Diaries, 1779–83, by Capt. John Spilsbury; Gibraltar; 1908.

Siege Diary, 1779–83, by Col. John Drinkwater; Gibraltar; 1790.

A French version of the Great Siege, by Chevalier d'Arcon, and one by Le Duc de Crillon. Garrison Library.

Siege Journal by Samuel Ancell; London; 1784.

Siege Journal by Catherine Upton; London; 1781.

A Description of Gibraltar; Anon; 1782; Garrison Library.

The Rock, a Collection of legends, songs etc., Major Hart, London, 1839.

The Traveller's Handbook for Gibraltar, London, 1844.

How to Capture and Govern Gibraltar, General Gardiner, London, 1856.

A History of Gibraltar, F. Sayer; London; 1865.

Gibraltar and its Sieges, J. H. Mann; London; 1870.

Reminiscences of Gibraltar, Anon; Gibraltar; 1880.

Gibraltar, Henry M. Field; London; 1889.

Antiquities and Curiosities, Dewing; London; 1901.

The Caves of Gibraltar, Duckworth; Gibraltar; 1910.

Gibraltar and Malta, Alister MacMillan; London; 1915.

323

Gibraltar under Moor, Spaniard and Briton, Kenyon, London, 1911.
The Jews of Gibraltar, Serfaty, Gibraltar, 1933.
Gibraltar and the Mediterranean, G. T. Garratt, London, 1939.
Gibraltar Directory and Guide Book, many editions, by Benedict R. Miles, published at intervals in Gibraltar.
Gibraltar in the 18th Century, Yale University Press, 1942.
The Story of Gibraltar and *The Gibraltarian*, by Dr. Howes, published in Gibraltar in 1946 and 1951, respectively.
A Paper on Gibraltar for the Institute of International Affairs, by C. E. Carrington, 1956.
Proud Fortress, by Allen Andrews, Evans Brothers, London, 1954.
Gibraltar, Colony and Fortress, R. A. Preston, Canadian Historical Review, 1946.
The Gibraltar Question, R. A. Preston, Queen's Quarterly, Canada, 1954.
The Journals of the Gibraltar Society, in the Garrison Library.
The Proceedings of the Archaeological Society of Gibraltar, 1956–57, containing *The Gibraltar Tunnels* by Col. D. M. Eley, *The Structure of the Rock of Gibraltar* by Lt. Comdr. G. D. J. Jones, and other interesting papers.
The Town Clerk of Canterbury, England, a garrison and cathedral city of comparable size to Gibraltar, sent me comparative data.
The Rock Paintings of Southern Andalusia, Breuil, 1924.
Notes on Gibraltar, Sir C. Munro, London, 1928.
Garrod's Paper on the Gibraltar Skull, published by the Royal Anthropological Institute.
Gibraltar's City Hall, by J. T. and D. M. Ellicott, Gibraltar, 1950, and several press articles by D. M. Ellicott.
The Birds of Southern Spain and Gibraltar, Lt. Col. A. J. S. Tuke, Gibraltar, 1954.
The private notes on ornithology of Robert W. Coelho, M.B.E., M.B.O.U. of Gibraltar.
English Government and Politics, F. A. Ogg, Macmillan, New York, 1944.
Constitutional History of England, G. B. Adams, Cape, London, 1944.
The Anatomy of Britain, Anthony Sampson, Hodder & Stoughton, London, 1963.
The Colonial Reckoning, Margery Perham, being the B.B.C. Reith Lectures for 1961, Collins, London.

The Files of the *Gibraltar Chronicle*, *El Calpense*, *Gibraltar Post*, and *Vox* were frequently consulted and are accredited by footnote in the text.

The Bibliography on Gibraltar compiled by Wilbur C. Abbott in 1934, was very useful.

Many Government Reports on all aspects of administration in Gibraltar have been studied and are quoted in the text.

The Author read most of the important Spanish works on the subject of Gibraltar. The classic history by Ignacio Lopez de Ayala has been a source for most subsequent histories, including this one. Montero's history, not yet translated into English, provides many interesting sidelights from the Spanish point of view. *Gibraltar, La Roca de Calpe*, by Ledesma Miranda, Madrid, 1957, gives the Spanish viewpoint completely and magnanimously. The work of Jose Pla Garceles gives the polemics of the Gibraltar Question prior to the current (1966) crisis.

During 1964 and 1965 the Author read the Spanish press for references to Gibraltar, and found the Madrid daily *ABC* and the Málaga daily *SUR* particularly useful. He had to bear in mind, however, that the press in Spain is officially controlled.

INDEX

ACCR, 209, 223 et seq., 295, 300, 314
Abrines, Richard, 131
Abyla, Mont, 21, 48, 87
Abyss, The, 34, 82
Abyssinia, 222
Aden, 199, 243
Admiralty, 148
Administration, 168, 212, 229
Administrators, xi, 193, 245
Aduana, 206, 284
Advisory Council, 230, 233
Africa, 24, 48, 49, 67, 78, 81, 144, 152, 154, 192, 194
Africa, North, 2, 180, 218
Agriculture, American Dept. of, 269
Alameda, 8
Alamoana, 265 et seq.
Alectoris barbara, 54
Alexandra, Queen, 168
Alfonso, King, 135, 136
Algeciras, 16, 17, 29, 43, 44, 59, 62, 135, 142, 200, 271, 276
Algeria, 24, 268
Almeria, 314
Amalia, 32, 33
America, 2, 68, 152
Americans, 197, 207, 227
American War, 101
Amery, Julian, 296
Ampleforth, 181
Andalusia, 14, 61, 78, 79
Anderson, Wm., 148
Andorra, xii
Anglican Bishop, 134, 180
Anglican Cathedral, 180
Anglican Religion, 67, 152, 169, 180, 212
Anglo-Spanish relations, ix, 141, 154, 155
Anne, Queen, 93, 118, 123, 130 et seq., 239
Ansell, Samuel, 103
Anti-Bull Club, 224
Apartheid, 207
Apes, Rock, 48 et seq., 238
'Appointments Overseas', 278
Arab Conquest, 117, 122
Arabia, 152
Arabs, 305

Aragon, 79
Architects, 221
Architecture, 157 et seq.
Arcos, Rock, 85
Arcon, Chevalier d', 102
Argel, 83
Armada, Invincible, 84
Army, British, 25, 99, 170
Arms of Gibraltar, 82
Armstrong, gunmakers, 217
Article X, 283 et seq., 307
Ashworth, Mr., 138
Asylum, Political, 198
Atlantic Ocean, 43, 82
Atlantic winds, 36, 144
Atlas Mountains, 20, 35, 87
Attorney-General, 130 et seq., 184, 231 et seq.
Augsburg, League of, 84
Australia, 154, 163, 319
Austria, Emperor of, 93
Axis Powers, 195, 228, 291
Azzopardi, Family, 198

Baffin Bay, 154
Baldorino, A. J., 225
Balearic Islands, 67, 72, 83, 100
Balenciaga, 167
Bali, 78
Banda, Dr., 178
Barbarossa, 83
Barbary, 57, 117
Barbary partridge, 57, 58, 60
Barbecula, 38
Barcelona, 89
Barton, Mr., 126 et seq., 138, 140
Basques, 319
Bay, The, 1, 24, 59, 97, 100, 140, 142, 162, 185, 219
Baynes, Col., 130
Bazan, Alvaro de, 83
B.B.C., 24, 268, 298
B.E.A., 313
Belfast, 3, 4, 65, 148, 194, 213
Belon, 38
Berbers, 76, 79
Bergel, Y., 131
Bilbao, 274
British Empire, 152, 154, 167, 279

327

British Government, 126, 136
British residents, 161
British Constitution, 181
Brothels, 212, 214
Building materials, 159
Bulam's fever, 121
Bullfights, vii, 7, 193
Burke, Edmund, 148
Byng, Admiral, 96, 97

Cabinet, The, 244, 247, 249
Cadiz, 2, 24, 39, 83 et seq., 89 et seq., 105, 128
Calabria, 14
Calpe, 19, 77
Calpense, El, 210
Calvi, J. Bautista, 83
Campamento, 134, 205, 276
Campo, 185, 200, 306
Canada, 154
Canary Islands, 73
Canterbury, 180
Cape Town, 24
Capture of Gibraltar, 90 et seq., 132
Carbonera, Sierra, 20, 205
Carlist cause, 85
Carnarvon, Earl of, 123, 129, 133
Carteia, 22, 37 et seq., 76, 94
Carthage, 38
Carthaginians, 2, 38, 39
Cartuja de Sevilla, 80
Carvillo, Mauricio, 5, 15, 48, 197, 322
Casablanca, 16, 32, 228
Caspian Sea, 180
Castiella, Sr. Fernando, 285
Castile, 79, 81
Castillo, Canovas del, 289
Castle, Moorish, 77, 159
Catalan Bay, 44
Catalans, 72, 319
Cathedral, of St. Mary the Crowned, 86, 91, 156, 180
Catholic Church, 134, 140, 179, 212
Catalonia, 89
Caveman, 23, 24
Caves, 20
Cemeteries, 170
Census, 115, 120 et seq., 172
Ceuta, 35, 78, 83, 94, 135, 271, 288
Chadwick, 166
Chamber of Commerce, 124, 130 et seq., 168 et seq., 199, 220 et seq., 270
Channel Fleet, 148
Channel Islands, 88, 136, 316
Charity, Public, 166 et seq.
Charles, of Austria, 85, 88
Charles II, 84
Charles III, King of Spain, 89, 91

Charles V Wall, 84
Charter of Spanish Destiny, 82
Charybdis, 21
Chellaram, 200
Chester, Mr., 126 et seq., 138, 140
Chiappe, Mary, 250
Chief Justice, 184
Chief Member, 258
Chief Minister, 246, 249
China, 152, 154
Cholera, 163, 172
Christian Bros., 8, 74, 181, 182
Churchill, Sir Winston, 46, 54, 291
Cicero, 39
City Council, 15, 25, 171 et seq., 220 et seq., 256
Civil engineering, 15, 32, 34
Civil liberty, 222
Civil rights, 162
Civil Service, 26, 63, 221, 241, 261
Class system, 201
Coalition, 315
Coalmen, 209 et seq.
Cockfighting, 107 et seq.
Coffee, 211, 272
Colonial complex, 69
Colonial Empire, 88
Colonial Government, 53, 229
Colonial Office, 137, 181, 321
Colonial Secretary, 126, 130, 132, 230, 232
Colonial Service, 25
Colonialism, 152
Colony, 139, 166, 211
Columbus, 2, 81, 82
Commerce, 121, 131
Commissioner of Lands & Works, 15
Committee of Twenty-four, 250, 253, 299
Commons, House of, 97, 308
Conn, 119
Constantinople, 83
Constituencies, 232
Consul at Cadiz, 123
Contagion, 121
Contraband, 122, 204, 207, 221, 235
Convent, The, 86, 156, 292
Convicts, 163
Cordoba, 77, 78, 80
Cordobes, El, 295
Cordon Sanitaire, 160
Cornhill, The, 18
Cornwall, 38
Coronation Tour, 291
Coronation Visit, 225 et seq.
Corruption, 120, 122
Cost of Living, 227
Costa del Sol, 280, 312, 313

Cotton goods, 130, 139, 161
Council of Gibraltar, 247, 248
Council of Ministers, 246
Cricket, 193
Crillon, Duc de, 102
Crime, 175
Crimea, 105
Cro-Magnon Man, 22
Cromwell, Oliver, 84
Crooks, J. A., 131
Crown, British, 195, 196
Curare, 113
Currents, 43, 82
Customs, 29, 133, 138, 140, 280, 284, 293
Cyprus, 181, 197, 243, 292

Daily Telegraph, The, 263
Darwin, Charles, 21
De-colonization Committee, 305 et seq.
Defence Security Officer, 292
Dept. of Education, 27
Democracy, xi
Depts., Heads of, 26, 221, 241
Destination Bond, 132, 133
Dialdas, 200
Diaz, Dr. Gonzalez, 301, 305
Diet, 42, 46
'Differences, with Spain, Recent', 283
Directory, The Gibraltar, 210
Dior, Christian, 167
Disease, 160
Docks, 260
Dockyard School, 181
Domestic service, 29
Downside, 181
Drake, Sir Francis, 84, 152
Dublin, 150, 174, 193, 206
Dugan, Patrick, 148
Düsseldorf, 21
Dutch, The, 104
Duties, 118, 123 et seq., 132, 139, 220, 239 et seq., 273 et seq.
Duty Signal, 150

East Africa, 199
Economy, 29
Eden, Sir Anthony (Earl of Avon), 291
Edinburgh, H.R.H. Duke of, 231
Education, 177 et seq., 238
Education, Board of, 174
Education Committee, 181
Education, Compulsory, 178
Education, Director of, 242
Education, Minister of, 225
Edward VII, 168, 195
Egypt, 152, 197, 215
Eisenhower, General, 12, 227

Elections, 250
Electoral procedure, 232
Electricity supply, 171, 174
Ellice Group, 178
Elliot, Col., 93
Ellicott, Mrs. D.,viii, 170
Eliott, Gen. G. A., 99 et seq.
Emergency Food Supply Co., 169, 211
Emerson, Ralph Waldo, 4
Employment, 134, 203
England, 135, 152
Englishmen, 2, 64, 91, 116, 196, 224
Epidemics, 121, 159, 170
Essex, Earl of, 84
Estate Duty, 222
Especiales, Los, 204
Estepona, 43, 135
Europa, 87, 140
Europe, 2, 20, 23, 24, 51, 53, 153, 155
Evacuation, The, 222, 224, 228
Exchange Committee, 128, 130, 131, 168, 220, 222
Executive Council, 219, 222, 232, 233, 239, 241, 246, 249
Expatriates, 220
Expenditure, Public, 221, 238
Exporters, 126, 127, 133, 273
Export trade, 138, 211

Fair Wages Clause, 209
Fat Rock, The, 205, 206, 285
Fernando Poo, 289, 296
Field, Dr. Henry M., 217
Figueroa, Juan Romero de, 91
Figuras, Las, 24
Fiji, 193, 199
Finance, 234, 235, 278 et seq.
Financial Secretary, 232, 239
Fish Migration, 43
Fisher, Nigel, 308
Fishing, 43, 44, 161
Fitzgerald, Capt. J., 51 et seq.
Flanders, 104
Flag Officer, 157
Flamenco, 213
Flemings, 98
Floating Batteries, 102
'Floating Republic, The', 148
Flying Bombs, 224, 228
Food Collectors, 50, 54
Foreign Office, 126, 267
Fortifications, 84, 103, 164
Fortress, The, 64, 84, 92, 139, 155, 166, 200, 217, 218, 223, 228
Fox, Brigadier, 96
France, 49, 105, 135, 143, 154, 268
Francia, Francis, 128, 130, 137, 139
Franciscans, 86, 123, 156

Franco, General, 195, 196, 198, 227, 286, 290 et seq., 307
Fratino, 84
Fraud, 133, 284
Freedom of the Port, 9, 93, 118, 123, 130 et seq.
Free Trade, 138
French, 72, 84, 153, 164, 197
French Navy, 89, 96, 145, 146 et seq.
Frontier, The, 118, 126, 139, 193, 204, 208, 293
Fry, Elizabeth, 166
Fulham, Bishop of, 180

Gaggero Family, 260
Galib, Abu-abdullah ben, 78
Galilee, 22
Game, English, 107
Gardiner, Gen. Sir Robert, 132, 164, 170
Garrison, The, 143, 159, 218, 315
Garrison Library, The, vii, 270
Garside, David, 147
Gasworks, 171
Gaulle, Gen. de, 105
Genoese, 67, 72, 81, 83, 100, 115, 116, 160, 164, 198
Geology, 19, 20, 49
George I, 98
Georgian architecture, 157
Germans, 22, 98, 105, 197, 290
Germany, 49, 195
Gandhi, 178
Gibraltar, throughout
Gibraltar, Bishop of. 134, 138
Gibraltar Chronicle, vii, viii, 64, 65, 129, 144, 210, 246, 269, 270, 321
Gibraltar Confederation of Labour, 224
Gibraltar Constitution, 246, 280, 301
Gibraltar, Dean of, 181
Gibraltar Man, 21
Gibraltar Post, 256, 271
Gibraltar Society, 21
Gibraltar Tradition, The, 97, 99, 106
Gibraltar Question, The, 282 et seq., 302, 306 et seq.
Gibr-al-Tarik, 77
Gilbert Islands, 278, 321
Glaciation, 24
Glasgow, 130, 136, 137, 206, 213
Glynn, Patrick, 148
Godley, Gen. Sir Alex, 54
Government, H.M., throughout
Government House, 156
Government, Spanish, 135
Governor, throughout
Governor of Algeciras, 203
Governor in Council, 246

Granada, 77, 80, 82
Grand Casemates Gates, 7
Grants-in-Aid, 173, 235
Greece, 21, 82, 195
Greeks, 19, 35, 36, 38, 107
Guadalupe, 105
Guadarranque, 31, 37, 76
Guns, 142, 217 et seq.

Hamilton, Lady, 148 et seq.
Hapsburg, 85, 90, 93
Harbour, 142, 219
Hardcastle, Mr., 137
Hashish, 271
Hassan, Sir Joshua A., 224 et seq., 232, 240, 250 et seq., 262, 264, 300, 305 et seq.
Hassan, King, 262
Hawkins, mutineer, 148
Hayek, Professor, 229
Heathfield, Lord, 105
Hermione, H.M.S., 148
Hesperia, 35, 87
Hesse-Darmstadt, Prince of, 85 et seq.
Hindus, 5, 154
Hitler, 219, 227, 290
H.M. Stationery Office, 272, 284
Holland, 49, 93, 99
Hong Kong, 154, 167, 169, 192, 194, 206, 214, 278
Honours List, 233, 234, 301
Housing, 15, 172, 173, 221, 228, 238, 262
Howes, Dr., 115
Hunter, Gen. Sir A., 124
Hypochondria, 160

Ibañez, Blasco, 61
Iberians, 38
Ice Ages, 23
Ifach, 19
Immigration Act, 317
Imossi, James L., 209, 260
Importados, 260
Imports, 272 et seq.
Income groups, 70
Income tax, 235 et seq.
India, 2, 68, 130, 152, 154, 181, 192, 197
Indians, 10, 72, 197, 198, 200
Indies, 83, 86, 98
Independence, 316, 318
Independents, 250 et seq.
Indonesia, 2
Interglacial, 49
Integration, 229, 230, 310, 316, 318
Inter-marriage, 179
International Law, 132, 133

Iraq, 305
Ireland, 4, 33, 37, 42, 65, 68, 85, 88, 92, 152, 174, 181, 192, 197, 230
Iribarne, Sr. Fraga, 268, 270, 271
Irish Brigade, 98
Irish clergy, 135
Irishmen, 67, 92, 104, 119, 150, 196, 215
Irish missions, 180 et seq.
Irish Nationalists, 230
Irish nuns, 184
Irish problem, 184
Irish Town, 8
Isabella, Queen, xii; 81, 82, 283
Islam, 77, 80, 177, 122, 144
Isle of Man, 316
Isola, Peter J., 225, 226, 251, 252, 253, 300, 307
Israelis, 197
Italians, 115, 160, 164, 197, 198
Italy, 97, 154, 195, 266, 268, 297

Jacobites, 98
Jaen, 77, 78
Jamaica, 16
James II, 85
James, Col., 78
James, Saint, 2, 22, 320
Janda, La, 77
Japan, 152, 154, 214, 297
Japanese, 72, 231, 269
Jehovah's Witnesses, 180
Jerez-de-la-Frontera, 80
Jews, 2, 67, 100, 115 et seq., 179, 198, 224, 225
Jews, Sephardic, 72, 79, 81, 160, 162, 179, 281
Johnson, Dr. Samuel, 147, 237
Joyce, James, 75
Joyce, Valentine, 148, 150
Jurassic Age, 20

Keightley, Gen. Sir Charles, 197
Kenya, 61, 65, 243, 292
Kenyatta, Jomo, 178
Key, Gibraltar, xii; 153
Kennedy, President, 184
Kimberley, Earl of, 124, 132
King, Cecil, 308, 309, 310, 311
Kipling, Rudyard, 154

Labour Exchange, 174, 208
Labour force, 275, 285
Labour Government, 166, 230, 317
Ladies' Needlework Guild, 167, 211
Lagunda de la Janda, 37
La Línea, 16, 29, 200 et seq., 271 et seq., 293, 294, 306, 312, 313

Lancaster, Osbert, 158
Lands & Works Dept., 221
Language barriers, 201
Language, English, 70, 72, 182, 183
Language, Spanish, 70, 73, 182, 183
Latins, 193
Lawlor, Denis, 148
Leghorn, 117, 118
Legislative Council, 172, 225, 231 et seq., 241, 246, 253, 254
Levanter, 1, 58 et seq., 170, 185
Levantines, 179
Levy, Judah, 131
Liberal Party, 138, 232
Libraries, 183
Licudi, Hector, xi
Lighthouse, 87
Line Wall, 217
Lisbon, 38, 85 et seq.
Liverpool, 130, 137, 206
Llanito, 70, 71
London, 16, 61, 62, 129, 149, 158, 159, 218, 224, 228, 234
Loreto Convent, 184
Loreto Order, 181
Lottery, 236, 237
Lourdes, 86
Low, Prof. Riet, 24

Macacus inuus, 54
Macaques, 49
Madeira, 16
Madrid, 89, 113, 125
Magna Carta, 240
Main Street, 8, 106, 159, 199, 200
Málaga, 61, 77, 92, 96, 125, 128, 175, 200, 206, 224, 280, 313
Malta, 67, 72, 163, 181, 198, 230, 234, 243
Malta fever, 45
Maltese, 104
Manchester, 130, 136, 138, 164, 166, 206
Marbella, 135, 306
Martin, Kingsley, xi
Martin, Pedro Hidalgo, 305
Martinique, 105
Mboya, T., 178
McCarthy, Charles, 148
Medina Sidonia, Duke of (*Marques de Gibraltar*), 81, 82
Mediterranean, throughout
Mediterranean Fleet, 143
Melbourne, 194
Melkarte, 37
Melilla, 128, 135, 289
Mellaria, 38
Memorial, The, 131 et seq., 222

Memorialists, 133
Merchants, 116, 119, 128, 131 et seq.,
    166, 211, 220 et seq., 235, 277
Merchant Shipping Act, 128
Messina, Straits of, 21
Methodist Church, 169, 180
Michael's Cave, St., 21
Micronesia, 178
Middle Hill, 54
Mifsud Family, 198
Miles, Benedict R., 156
Military history,   ix
Milk, 45
Millionaires, 200, 223, 225, 260
Minorca, 67
Minorcans, 160
Ministers, 140, 241
Ministry of Labour, 203
Miranda, Ledesma, 21, 86
Mission education, 178 et seq.
Mixed marriages, 73
Monopolies, 118
Montegriffo, A. P., 251
Montenegro, xii
Mons Calpe, 19
Moorish castle, 159
Moors, 1, 2, 49, 61, 76 et seq., 100, 115,
    164, 197, 210, 314
Morocco, 3, 18, 60, 76, 80, 117, 262,
    271, 283
Moriscos, 81
Mount, The, 157
Mundella, A. J., M.P., 139

Naples, 83, 104
Napier of Magdala, Lord, 123 et seq.,
    140
Napoleon, 67, 68, 145 et seq., 153
Nasser, President, 3
National Association for Prevention of
    Venereal Disease, 214
National Relief Fund, 211
NATO, 214, 297, 314
Naval Hospital, 143
Nazis, 195
Neanderthal Man, 21, 23, 24, 288
Nehru, 178
Nelson, Lord, 34, 103, 143 et seq.,
    153
Nelson's Pillar, 150
Newcastle, Duke of, 132
New Mole, The, 125
New Statesman, The, xi
New York, 158, 300, 301
New World, 82, 83
New Yorker, The, 18, 263
New Zealand, 154
Nightingale, Florence, 166

Nkrumah, K., 178
Nominated Members, 231
North Africa, 3, 227
North Mole, 219
North Sea Fleet, 148
Northern Ireland, 16, 68, 177, 179, 224,
    316
Nugent, Family, 96

Observer, The, 280
O'Connell Street, 150
Official members, 231
Official reports, 270, 272
Opposition, The, 233
Oran, 128, 130 et seq.
Order in Council, 131
Ordinances, 130, 133, 141
Ortega y Gasset, 51
Oryx, 49
Orwell, George, 70
Overseas Aid Scheme, 173
Overseas Civil Service,viii, 27, 193

P. & O. Line, 133
Pacific Ocean, 154, 208
Pacifico, Don, 195
Pakistanis, 72, 197, 198
Palmerston, Lord, 195
Palos, 2, 81, 83
Pancistas, 2
Parkinson's Law, 116
Paris, 77, 158, 214
Patriotism, 192 et seq.
Parliament, 105, 130, 139, 141, 148,
    230, 232, 296
Paul, Saint, 2, 40
Pax Britannica, 74, 243
Peel, Sir Robert, 174
Peninsular War, 154
People of Gibraltar, 64 et seq.
Peregrines, 53
Perham, Dame Margery, 245
Permanent Secretary, 184, 249
Persians, 131
Phillip V, 82, 90, 98, 119
Phoenicians, 2, 37, 38, 41
Piedra Gorda, La, 2, 205
Pigot, Capt., 148
Pillars of Hercules, 18, 21, 23
Pigeon, H.M. Gunboat, 125
Pinies, Sir Jaime de, 305, 307
Piropo, 14
Pirrie, Foote & Co., 137
Pirrie, Mr., 139
Pithecanthropus erectus, 24
Pitt, William, 1
Pizzarello, Alberto, 44
Plagues, 121, 160, 170 et seq.

Police, 109, 174, 215
Police, Commissioner of, 184
Polite society, 25
Political parties, 223
Polynesians, 193
Poor Fund, Jewish, 167
Poor Fund, Protestant, 167
Poor Law, 169, 211
Pope, H.H. the, 180, 230
Population, 160 et seq.
Portadown, 230
Port of call, 133
Port Captain, 125
Port Department, 128, 140
Port Development, 260
Port Mahon, 100
Portland Bill, 302 et seq.
Portugal, 14, 117
Portugal, King of, 85
Portuguese, 2, 67, 116, 160, 164, 197
Portus Albus, 38
Pottinger, Sir H., 88
Poverty, 46, 121, 159, 166 et seq., 211, 219, 228
Povedano, Family, 162
Presbyterians, 67, 180
Press, The, 3, 222, 233
Prince of Wales, 211
Privy Council, 247
Prostitutes, 174, 206, 212 et seq.
Proportional representation, 232
Protestants, 91, 178
Public health, 170
Public schools, 178
Punta Secreta, 37

Queen's Gate, 54
Queen, H.M. the, 243

Raffles, Sir Stamford, 88
Rainfall, 57
Raleigh, Sir Walter, 84
Ramos, General, 92
Ray, Cyril, 70
Reade, Mr., 123
Recano, J. H., 131
Reconquest of Spain, 79, 86
Red Cross, 167, 168
Red-legged Partridge, 56
Redman, Sir Harold, 239
Red Sands, 170
Reed, John, 269
Refugees, 16
Regent of France, 97
Reilly, Mutineer, 148
Repatriation, The, 16, 228
Representatives, Elected, 231

Republic, Spanish, 198
Revenue, 122, 131 et seq., 235, 277, 281
Revolution, Industrial, 207
Rhodes, Cecil, 88
Rhodesia, 313
Rif, 76, 183
Risso, A. J., 224
Riot Act, 209
Rock, The, throughout
Rock Gun, 217, 218
Roderick, King, 77
Roman Catholic Church, 67, 81, 162, 169, 198
Romans, 2, 19, 35, 36, 39, 49, 77, 103, 107, 166
Rome, 82
Rooke, Admiral Sir George, 84 et seq., 148
Rosia Harbour, 34, 125, 142 et seq., 157, 217
Rosia Road, 170
Rousseau, Mme, 305
Royal Air Force, 25, 183, 219, 315
Royal Engineers, 155
Royal Institute of British Architects, 159, 221
Royal Navy, 25, 91, 98, 100 et seq., 148, 170, 219, 265
Royal Regiment of Artillery, The, 53
Royal Society for Prevention of Cruelty to Animals, 7, 167, 212
Runway, The, 227
Russia, 152, 154, 290, 297
Russo, Sir Peter, 162, 251 et seq., 262
Ryan, Esmond F. E., vii

Sahara, 3, 20, 24, 76
Salamanca, Irish College of, 181
Salaries, 208, 221, 227
Salinas, Gen. Diego, 90, 91
Salisbury, Marquess of, 307, 308
Sandys, Mr. Duncan, 246
Sanguinetti, Mario, 159
Sanitary Commissioners, 168, 173
Sanitation, 170 et seq.
San Lúcar, 2, 83
San Roque, 41, 94, 115, 134, 305 et seq.
Santiago y Perminon, 124
Sapient Man, 22
Sardines, 43, 44
Sardinia, 56, 60
Savoy, 104
Scandella, Rt. Rev. Dr., 134, 136, 140
Scorpions, 64
Scotland, 192
Scots, 196
Scylla, 21
Searle, John, viii

Secretary of State, 26, 123, 129, 133, 136, 220, 240, 241, 246
Secretary, Civil, 130
Secretary of State for Foreign Affairs, 140, 141
Self-determination, 290, 316, 318
Self-government, 223, 229, 245, 318
Selwyn Report, The, 229
Sephardim, 117
Serfaty, A. W., 251
Seruya, S. A., 225, 251, 261, 314, 315
Servants, 28 et seq.
Seville, 2, 14, 15, 77, 80, 83, 86, 206
Sewerage, 171 et seq.
Shaftesbury, Earl of, 166
Sharks, 44
Shaw, Bernard, 214
Sherpas, 17
Shipowners, 130, 137, 260
Shipping, 127, 128, 275
Shopkeepers, 116, 130, 199
Sicilians, 72
Siege, The Great, 100, 105, 156, 283
Sieges, Spanish, 85
Sierpes, Calle, 14
Sierra Nevada, 20
Sindicato, 209
Singapore, 61, 194, 198
Slave-owners, 135
Slaves, 97, 147
Smith-Dorrien, Gen. Sir H. L., 211
Smugglers, 126, 129, 137, 139, 174
Smuggling, 29, 118, 122 et seq., 134, 139, 141, 161, 164, 208, 235, 261, 265, 267, 268 et seq., 275, 276, 280, 311
Social conditions, 166 et seq.
Social structure, 70, 278
Sortie, The, 101
South Africa, 207
South Barracks, 157
South District, 156, 157
South America, 154, 211
Sovereignty, 282 et seq., 317, 319
Spain, throughout
Spaniards, 2, 7, 29, 115, 116, 122, 132, 133, 160, 185 et seq., 198, 204
Spanish Civil War, 15, 16, 70, 173, 222
Spanish Government, 125, 132, 133, 138, 139, 243
Spanish Inquisition, 91
Spanish Police, 109, 213
Spithead, Mutiny at, 148
St. Andrew's, 225
Stagnetto, Family, 162, 251
Stalin, 219
Standard, Oil, 214
Stanhope, Earl, 97

Steamships, 162, 198
Stevas, St. John, 317
Stewart, Eve Graham, 5, 6, 177, 184
Stewart, Paul, 96, 298
Stewart, Joan Crawford, viii, xi, 5, 14, 28, 42, 184, 298, 321
Straits, The, 2, 18, 20, 36, 43, 48, 57, 76, 82, 84, 86, 122, 143, 144, 153, 162, 163, 217
Suez, 83, 197
Sultan of Morocco, 119
Suva, 194
Swiss, 197
Switzerland, 104
Syria, 305

Tangier, 17, 24, 84, 210, 224, 265, 268, 269, 271, 290, 313
Tarawa, Battle of, 104
Tarifa, 77, 78, 80, 81, 83, 86, 122
Tarik ben Zeyad, 76, 78, 105, 155
Taxation, 127, 167, 168, 173, 207, 220, 235, 261, 277, 278, 281, 315
Tax Haven, 236
Territorial waters, 267
Tetuan, 271
Thompson, Mr., 139, 260
Thornton, Henry, 131
Times, The, 231, 314
Tobacco trade, 29, 125 et seq., 161, 164, 211, 235, 261, 266 et seq., 275
Tolpuddle Martyrs, 163
Torremolinos, 306
Tory Party, 124, 169, 230
Toulon, 89, 145
Tourism, 226, 238, 239, 241, 315
Tower of Homage, 77
Town Plan, 229
Toynbee, Arnold, 69
Trade, 120, 127, 241, 273
Trade Restriction Ordinance, 197
Trade Tax, 236, 238
Trade Unions, 178
Trafalgar, 103, 142 et seq.
Trafalgar Cemetery, 143
Transport & General Workers' Union, 209, 212, 222, 224, 231
Treasury, 128
Trelles, Camilio Barcia, 306
Triay, Louis, 251
Tunisia, 39, 305
Tunny, 40, 144
Turks, 82, 83
Tyre, 82

Ulster, 68, 69, 184, 194, 228, 230
Unemployment, 174, 211
United Kingdom, xi, 166, 173, 201, 211

United Nations Charter, 307
United Irishmen, 148, 150
UNO, xi, 225, 243, 250, 251, 279, 299, 300 et seq.
Upper Rock, 20, 53, 58
Uruguay, 305, 310
U.S.A., 46, 154, 166, 214, 244, 254, 271, 279, 291, 299
U.S.S.R., 154, 279
Utrecht, Treaty of, x, 119, 164, 250, 267, 282, 283, 302

Vandals, 40
Valdesoto, Count of, 92, 96
Valencia, 78
Varela, Don Bartoleme, 94
Vasquez, 162
Vatican, The, 180
Vaughan, Nancy, 252
Vejer-de-la-Frontera, 144
Velasquez, 305
Venezuela, 300, 305
Venice, 37, 83
Venta animadora, 213
Vicar Apostolic, 134
Vichy French, 228
Victoria, Queen, 152, 165
Victorian Era, 154, 165, 192, 193
Victoriana, 11, 152 et seq.
Victory, H.M.S., 145
Villeneuve, Admiral, 145, 149
Vincent, Cape St., 84
Virginity, 201
Visigoths, 2, 40, 48, 76, 77, 288
Vox, xi, 258, 263, 265, 281, 313

Wages, 207 et seq., 227, 275
Wahnon, Family, 198
Wales, 192
Wales, Prince of, 195, 211
Wall, Major Patrick, 317
Walloons, 104
War Department, 219

Waterloo, 147, 153
Ward, Ned, 91
Waterport, 4
Water supply, 57, 170 et seq., 256
Webb, Sidney and Beatrice, 229
Welfare Department, 209
Welfare State, 166
Wellington, Duke of, 147, 174
Welsh, 196
Wesley, John and Charles, 169
West Africa, 39, 289
West Indies, 73
Westminster, 88, 124, 222, 230, 232, 316
Whigs, 124, 156
Whitehall, 94, 125, 136, 139, 193, 230, 277
Wilberforce, William, 166
Wild Geese, The, 98
William III, 85
William IV, 157
Wilson, Harold, 317
Windchargers, 62
Winds, 36, 58
Woolwich Academy, 99
Women of Gibraltar, 69
Workers, 207 et seq.
Works Department, 74, 209, 321
World Wars, 3, 16, 21, 54, 104, 142, 157, 166, 168, 173, 174, 178, 195, 222, 227, 290

Xenophobia, 65
Xerri, 198

Yellow Fever, 121, 160, 162, 172
York, H.R.H. Duke and Duchess of, (later King George VI), 168

Zammitt, Family, 198
Zebedee, 22
Zuner, F. E., 49, 50
Zulus, 154
Zurich, Gnomes of, 269